Models of Family Treatment

MODELS
OF
FAMILY TREATMENT

ELEANOR REARDON TOLSON
and
WILLIAM J. REID
Editors

New York COLUMBIA UNIVERSITY PRESS *1981*

Library of Congress Cataloging in Publication Data
Main entry under title:

Models of family treatment.

Papers originally prepared for the Charlotte Towle
Memorial Conference on Family Treatment, held at the
University of Chicago, Oct. 11–12, 1979, and sponsored
by the University of Chicago School of Social Service
Administration.
Includes bibliographies and index.
1. Family social work—United States—Congresses.
I. Tolson, Eleanor Reardon, 1942–   . II. Reid,
William J., 1928–   . III. Charlotte Towle
Memorial Conference on Family Treatment (1979: University
of Chicago) IV. University of Chicago.
School of Social Service Administration.
HV699.M57   362.8′2′0973   81-4341
ISBN 0-231-04950-1   AACR2

Columbia University Press
New York   Guildford, Surrey
Copyright © 1981 Columbia University Press
All rights reserved
Printed in the United States of America
Printed on permanent and durable acid-free paper.

Contents

To the memory of Charlotte Towle

Models of Family Treatment

Introduction

ELEANOR REARDON TOLSON

The divorce rate has sharply increased since 1968 although the trend was visible as early as 1962 (Rallings and Nye 1979:223). Azrin et al. provide a succinct summary of the problems associated with marital distress.

> Marital disharmony is a major social problem. Approximately one out of four married couples are unhappy with their marriage. . . . This unhappiness is not a transient state: the longer one is married, the greater is the probability of dissatisfaction. . . . Termination of unhappy marriages by divorce is increasing, as is also the number of children in the disrupted marriages. . . . Crime and delinquency is greater for children who are products of unhappy or broken homes. . . . About one-half of first admissions to state mental hospitals result from marital stresses as the single major precipitating condition. . . . Since 95 percent or more of the adult population has at least one marriage in a lifetime . . . marital disharmony is a pervasive social problem. (1973:365)

As the number of divorces has increased, new family forms have evolved. Among them are the single-parent family and various combinations of families that result from remarriage. Stable families, too, experience distress as they live through normal developmental conflicts, as they are impacted by crises like illness and unemployment, and as societal changes require new adjustments like the alteration in traditional roles which results from the necessity for two incomes.

In the last twenty years theories about families and models for working with them have proliferated. The number of books and articles

written about the topic has grown commensurately. Current riches
have created new problems for the practitioner. It is difficult to discern
the differences and similarities among the approaches and even more
difficult to select appropriate treatment strategies. The Charlotte Towle
Memorial Conference on Family Treatment, from which this book
evolved, was an effort to bring order to this complex literature.

The conference occurred on October 11 and 12, 1979. The participants were leaders in the various schools of thought about family treatment and each contributed a position paper, which is published herein.
The most difficult activity in planning the conference was identifying
the approaches. Our goals were to identify the "purest" or least eclectic approaches so as to minimize redundancy and include as many
of the major ones (those practiced by more than one charismatic individual) as possible. We tried on a number of categorizations before
deciding on the one encompassed here. Some strategies are missing.
One of the omissions is work with groups of families. Since those who
work in this manner use several different theoretical orientations, and
since money and space did not permit including all of them, the approach was omitted. This example is offered to illustrate the kind of
thinking that occurred in regard to making choices.

The next set of decisions concerned whom to invite to present the
approaches. The committee wanted to attract a group of contributors
who would reflect the interdisciplinary aspect of family treatment,
including some of the leading exponents of the approaches and social
workers. The scholarly quality of previous work was examined prior
to extending invitations. Representing the gurus are John Elderkin Bell
and John Spiegel, both of whom knew Charlotte Towle. They are the
major developers of the positions they present, which are, respectively,
the small group and an ecological approach.

Eileen Gambrill undertook the Herculean task of presenting the various behavioral approaches. Ann Hartman ably stands in for Murray
Bowen, as does Marianne Walters for Salvador Minuchin and the structural approach. Geraldine Spark presents an innovative technique
which is rooted in psychoanalytic thought. Lynn Segal describes an
approach developed at the Mental Research Institute at Palo Alto. We
think the contributors are thoughtful, articulate, creative, and wise.
We are grateful to them for their cooperation throughout.

Since our purpose was to present the approaches in a manner that
would facilitate contrasting them, we suggested an outline for the pa-

pers. The outline follows:

1. Underlying theory or empirical findings on which the approach is based
2. Assessment of the family constellation and of its presenting problems
3. Pretreatment considerations concerning when to do family treatment and whom to include in treatment
4. Considerations during the beginning phase of treatment, including engaging the client, setting goals, determining length and frequency of interviews, choosing a focus for treatment, and making a contract
5. Treatment strategy and techniques
6. Application to marital and other subtypes
7. Populations and problems for which the approach is more effective, least effective
8. Evaluation of the approach through single case studies, group designs, or other means
9. Application to families who are poor and disorganized, and to families who are reluctant to become involved in treatment
10. References

In addition to the seven papers describing models of family treatment, Sanford Sherman was asked to write an overview of the area, especially as it pertains to social work, and Richard Wells was asked to summarize research findings. Both competently fulfilled their assignments. Rae Meltzer prepared an article that contains excerpts of the conference dialogue. Meltzer also helped us to identify a number of specific questions to be addressed in the conference:

1. What is your definition of family treatment?
2. What is your criteria for treating or exploring the possibility of treating more than one person in a family? How do you decide whom to include, how often, and in what combinations?
3. When you engage in family treatment, what are your goals?
4. Over what period of time does treatment extend and how frequent are the interviews?
5. Do you make use of contracts and, if so, how?
6. What specific data and information has the highest priority for you in the assessment process? Do you rely more on self-report or on direct observation for gathering data?

7. How much importance do you place on the "presenting problem"? Does the "presenting problem" form the basis of your treatment contract?

8. What does the clinician (therapist-social worker) specifically contribute to the treatment process?

9. How much do you emphasize the "here and now" transactions in the family session in your treatment procedures?

10. What are the *most* powerful treatment procedures for effecting change in the family?

11. If available research evidence were used as the primary basis for constructing an approach to family treatment, what would the approach look like and for what purposes would it be used?

12. What outcome criteria should be used to evaluate the effectiveness of family treatment? Is it always necessary to obtain measures of change in the family's functioning as a system and, if so, what are the most promising strategies for obtaining such measures?

13. What should be regarded as a reasonable follow-up period for assessing the duration of gains achieved in family treatment?

The portions of dialogue that have been shared in Rae Meltzer's article pertain to the questions about assessment and treatment. Some of the most lively conversation was provoked by showing the contributors a brief film of a family discussing a problem. The contributors were asked to assess the problem and to indicate what they would do to alleviate it if they were treating the family. Meltzer has done an admirable job of capturing both the content and tone of the discussion that followed.

Finally, each of us has written a chapter in order to summarize the insights and demonstrate how they might be utilized. Reid illustrates how the approaches can be used with a task-centered framework. Tolson contrasts the approaches and develops an eclectic metamodel for choosing among them.

We are indebted to many people. Deans Harold Richman and Margaret Rosenheim consecutively supported this effort. The committee members—Rae Meltzer, Helen Harris Perlman, John Schuerman, and Bernece Simon—offered wise and patient counsel throughout the planning process. Meltzer graciously consented to chair one session of the conference and Simon undertook the awesome job of summarizing the discussion. Esther Wald generously contributed her time to serve as reporter. Sharon Goodman's competent secretarial skills were invaluable.

Finally, we are indebted to the friends of Charlotte Towle who have contributed so generously to the memorial fund over the years. We, like them, wish to honor Miss Towle and sincerely hope that our endeavor justifies their trust.

References

Azrin, Nathan, Barry Naster, and Robert Jones. 1973. "Reciprocity Counseling: A Rapid Learning-Based Procedure for Marital Counseling." *Behavior, Research, and Therapy,* 11:365–82.

Rallings, E. M. and F. Ivan Nye. 1979. "Wife-Mother Employment Family and Society." In Wesley R. Burr, Reuben Hill, F. Ivan Nye, and Ira L. Reiss, eds., *Contemporary Theories About the Family,* 1:203–23. New York: Free Press.

1

A Social Work Frame for Family Therapy

SANFORD N. SHERMAN

"Group Approach in Casework . . . Renewal of an Abandoned Practice"
—Charlotte Towle (1959)

Social work is distinctive among the helping professions for its historic concern with the family. In the "social diagnostic" period, early in the century, the family figured large in social work practice and in its literature, this prominence lasting into the early years of the Great Depression. With the growing influence on social work of the dynamic psychologies, especially on its clinical practices, and—no small factor—the deference given in schools and agencies to psychiatrists as consultants and teachers, in the 1930s and 1940s, the family, along with other social institutions, receded from center stage of social work. The focus was on the individual person.

Not ever exclusively, however. The social tradition was too deeply ingrained in social work—much more evident, of course, in social group work and in community organization of its specialties by virtue of their primary task being directed to multi-person units. The 1930s had seen the growing institutionalization of a three-specialty division of social work, in terms of "methods": casework, group work, and community organization. Some specialization was in the nature of a profession's growth and inevitable in the deepening professionalization of social work. The purpose in the division was to distinguish among the processes inherent in different levels of social organization: the individual person, the small group, and the community; and among the differentiated skills and methods of professional work on these levels, all of which are based upon common social work knowledge and values.

In the period that followed—through most of the 1950s—these three "preserves" were carefully cultivated, side-by-side, by their respective specialists, but with growing strictures against crossovers either of ideas or of practice. The very structure of specialties fed back to deepen their discreteness. There was certainly enough to learn and refine in each "preserve" to keep the profession busy, and, additionally, although in a general way the wholeness of people and their behavior was hypothesized, there was a paucity of middle- and lower-ordered concepts to link these levels of social organization in actual experience. Yet it was obvious, in the abstract, that these were not discrete levels of human experience or of professional practice. The literature of social work, its statements about its task, has always been studded with caveats against undue separations of the individual, family, group, and community.

This gap between abstract affirmation of the psychosocial unity of behavior and the inadequate means at hand for implementing it in practice—with specific living human beings—has been an enduring challenge to social work particularly, and perhaps more than it has been to other helping professions, just because social work's scope has always broadly included the individual and society. This major anomaly made for a tension and a hunger that translated, in the 1960s and 1970s, into eager receptivity to promising theories from the social and behavioral sciences, and to the promise of family therapy—among other practice innovations.

So there was a double-edged consequence to the social work tripartite "methods" division: deepening knowledge in each division but also a concomitant tendency toward getting fenced in, toward delimitations, each division with respect to the others. In social casework, one important impediment that "went with the territory" was the diminished attention to the "social"—institutional and interpersonal—that seemed for a time an inevitable accompaniment to the exciting explorations of the inner life of individuals, with an exclusively one-to-one modality. Flexible use of other modalities was inhibited because it would constitute adventuring into other social work fiefdoms and, conversely, the one-to-one structure of helping tilted the content of interviews away from social experience. To include appraisal of the "social" was affirmed as a general desideratum, but direct contact with the living interpersonal experience and its conceptualization—as for example, in small groups—were considered to "belong" to the fields of practice other than social casework. Since treating or helping with personal problems was generally accorded to be the province solely of casework, the net effect was that the individual modality was treated as immutable for almost all therapeutic effort in social work.

It is salutary that the present ferment in social work on the reclassification of specialties is resulting in a consensus on a clinical social work practice that gains its distinctness from purpose and task rather than from modality (individual, couple, family, or small group). It should also give us pause today about identifying family therapy as a specialty, or about equating family therapy with a family group modality. Seeing family members together is not sacrosanctly reserved for family therapists; seeing some family members together is not necessarily family therapy.

In the interest of continuity of identity, it is of use to emphasize that social casework (which accounts for so much of clinical social work), even during its extreme pendulum swing toward the psychological and psychiatric, kept some connection with its social heritage. The connection was evident in several ways. In its psychology, there were the cautions to caseworkers to confine treatment to ego functions, to support rather than attack defenses, to stay out of the darker realms of the unconscious, to clarify rather than interpret, to project goals of improved social functioning rather than of resolution of psychic conflict. Some of the initiative for this narrowing of the psychological base of social work may have been in the interest of preserving its difference in identity from the more frankly psychological disciplines but, more determinatively, the abiding purpose was to draw topographic boundaries of its psychology that would keep social work practice out of deep intrapersonal "fishing" and would keep it on the perimeter of the psyche, nearest to the interface of person and environment. In the areas of technique and scope, social casework practice theory persisted throughout its historical development in maintaining environmental "intervention" or "manipulation" (unfortunate choices of terms!) on its preferred list, as, more recently, it has done with "advocacy" and "eco-systems intervention." The social dimension also entered into the conception of casework as a "problem-solving" (as differentiated from person-treating) process (Perlman 1957); into notions of limited goals of equilibrium-restoration (Regensberg 1954); into all the marriage and family counseling forerunners of today's practices.

This culling of some representative ideas and practices from the casework of the past exemplifies its never fully abandoned striving to operationalize what were termed "psychosocial treatment" (Hollis

1964), "social treatment" (Austin 1948), "improvement of social functioning" (Scherz 1956), and so forth. In tandem with this *intraprofes-
sional* striving are the mission and function that have always been
ascribed by the outer society to social work; it is generally conceded
that helping the socially disadvantaged, rendering "bread and butter"
and welfare services, and working with social problems like delinquency or person-abuse are social work's special province. However
some social workers might want to have it, this public image of social
work itself keeps clinical practice from straying too far from the social
frontier.

But quite apart from extremes of social pathology, even with garden
variety family or personal problems that are not confined to any one
class or group, the prospective clients, referral sources, and social
agencies themselves combine to effect a triage in which people who
perceive their problems as largely centered on themselves tend to look
to psychiatrists and psychologists or their clinics for help; and those
who see their problems as caused largely by forces or people outside
themselves tend to turn to the social agency. Whether the self-per-
ceptions in either case are accurate or are part of personal defensive
strategems, the point is that is where they begin and where they turn
in the use of help. In addition, beyond the factors influencing selection
of a social agency, and whatever drew the client there, the "social"
of the social worker and social agency identities does naturally draw
the mutual probing of client and worker in their initial encounters
toward the interpersonal, the environmental, formulation of problem.

So, no matter how much and what form of top growth has enhanced
social work over the years, it has remained rooted in the "social"—
by virtue of the place given it by society's need of social work, by the
clients and their felt needs, by the continuous empirical testing by
social work of practice theories. In its history, social work forays into
the dynamic psychologies and psychiatry that seemed at the times to
be extreme, and to repudiate a social heritage and mission, in a historical perspective are seen as feelers stretching outward for enriching
contributions.

Evolving Practices in Family Work

It has been essential, in this paper on family therapy, to review the
vicissitudes of the social component in clinical ideology and practice

because, understandably, the family has been a prime expression of that component in concept and in practice and is so today. As suggested earlier, however differently family processes were understood and approached clinically over the full history of social work, the family was a central consideration in theory and in practice, except during the psychological–psychiatric ingestive decades, when the interest in the family qua family made way for the concentration on the individual and his psychology and psychopathology, with the family more peripherally in evidence only as the developmental matrix for the individual. From one social work era to another, different knowledge systems tended to dominate the thinking about the family and therefore the approach to it. These knowledge systems that succeeded each other were, successively, class-based; genetic; ethnic and racial; frankly religious, or religiously tinged; moral; sociologic and democratic; psychologic; and psychoanalytic. Techniques with the family changed with the knowledge contexts from coercion to inspiration to persuasion to modeling to education to collaboration, to exclusion from the treatment process, and so forth. The interventions were directed variously at one responsible family member alone; both parents; every individual family member; members of the kinship network; neighbors, tradesmen, church and school; the community of families itself, and so on. A review such as this inevitably brings one to respect the truly fabulous background of work with the family in social work. The conclusion is inescapable that family therapy is at home in social work. Siporin (1979) counters exclusivist claims by Johnny-Come-Latelies outside social work to work with families by detailed references from the social work literature of sixty years.

From era to era, and up to fairly recent years, whatever the knowledge base or context, and however much or little the family entered into practice, working with the family inevitably reduced itself to working with its individuals, usually one by one. The family was spoken and written of as a whole, but this remained largely an abstraction; and when the practitioner addressed a specific live family, in his mind and in his approach he assembled its members one by one.

It was not as though the profession was unaware of this contradiction between concept and practice. Though the practice tools were slow in coming, for years we have worried at holistic ideas. It was plausible that social institutions like marriage and the family had their own wholeness and identities and were more than mere congeries of their individual members. Plausible also, in more recent years, was the idea that marriage and the family were critical links if we were to move closer to psychosociality, since they are the very next steps beyond the individual in the continuum of social organization and are the locus for intimate biosocial union and basic need fulfillment (Gomberg and Levinson 1951). Moreover, difficult as it is to define the boundaries, grasp the dimensions, or identify the inner processes of any social institution, at least a family is usually in one place and has legal, economic, biologic, social, traditional bonds; it is of a size and relative discreteness that its individual parts and some kind of boundary are perceptible by its own members and by the "outsider" as therapist or observer. Larger social organizations or even those which are of similar size but which are less centripetal lend themselves less to interventions.

The problem with conceptualizing the family in a clinically useful way has always been that to move from individual member to the family entails an abrupt shift in level of abstraction, from the very organic unity of the individual to the comparatively differentiated bio-social severalness of a family group. By and large, the concepts and vocabulary of clinical social work have been individual-centered. On the other hand, social planners and social policymakers in social work use terms and a language for classes of families, not individual ones. The single family falls between. A no-man's-land has lain between these branches of social work. So the therapist, however moved in the abstract by the ideas of families qua families, in practice was inevitably controlled by clinical concepts and a patterned strategy of treatment that directed his thoughts, feelings, and moves toward the individual person—in a literal, physical, tete-a-tete sense and, as well, in the sense of his cognitive-emotional self-projection (Sherman 1961). In an effort not to remain locked in the individual client's phenomenologic field, the early family-oriented therapist might turn toward significant other members of the family. With his available tools still only indi-vidual related, however, the therapist could include within his ken other family members only by "looking outward" from the appointed center, the index client, or by temporarily abandoning him or putting him on the back burner of his awareness and relating to other family members, each in turn as individual.

We are describing a direction of appraisal and therapeutic interven-tion from the individual out toward others, a direction in which, for each individual, members of his family are "environment"; truly, "others." Even in the multi-person conjoint sessions, the pre-1960 therapist directed himself substantially at one client at a time although in the presence of (and monitored by) the others. Or the conjoint sessions were confined to taking history or to confirming the therapeutic contract, and in any case were usually considered supplemental to the one-to-one relationship where the "real" work could go on (Flesch 1948; Sacks 1949).

In a collateral development, a breaking up of the casework–group work dichotomy that confined casework and thus much of clinical social work to individual modalities resulted in the burgeoning in the late 1950s and 1960s of group forms of counseling and therapy (Sherman 1955; FSAA 1964). These group forms inevitably helped to loosen some of the bonds on ideas about interpersonal behavior, and thus, by extension, intrafamily behavior. They also helped the transposition of insights about group process to family process. They were important antecedents to conceptions of family therapy.

Conceptual frames of reference for families had been continually attempted, reaching for that which would capture the organismic wholeness of the family. Lacking the means, the clinical lexicon, there were various resorts to analogy and paradigm. Thus, we saw the references to "family group"; "family diagnosis"; the family "gestalt"; the family as "organism"; as "unit of treatment"; as a "whole"; to applied axioms like "the whole (family) is greater than the sum of its parts" and "the family (like a chemical compound) has qualities different from those of its elements." These terms represented ideas which, general and of different "logical type" though they were, kept stirring the porridge of imagination and ferment, and readiness for middle-level concepts that would bring us closer to clinical practicality. (Excellent summaries are to be found in Gomberg 1958 and Pollack 1958.)

A landmark development or major step taken in any humanist or scientific field is never a product of a "Eureka" discovery by one person but is preceded by a string of many ideas and fragments of ideas, and of people who thought them or tried to use them. They remain just that—strung out bits and pieces—until some catalytic combination of ideas and people and timing brings them into a systematic reconstruction. There results a qualitative breakthrough that brings with it a new vision.

Always, too, there are trends or events in the larger society that create a readiness, or neediness, or at least a hospitableness, for the innovation in the specific field; innovations are always a matter of interplay of many different-ordered systems. In contemporary society, the vast social changes, in sum those of physical dispersion and emotional fragmentation, threaten the stability of the family, and among the reparative measures "society" homeostatically "invites" may well be family therapy. In social work, from its past in which there was the recurrent tug of the psychosocial, and of so many organismic ideas about the family, we have moved into family therapy that is of a qualitatively different order, that brings with it a different framework for appraisal and professional interventions. This will become evident as we proceed to discuss some inspirations and ideas (not uncharacteristically borrowed from other fields) that helped make the difference: social role, cultural value, communication and general systems theories. These theories fit together and have enabled social work (hand-in-hand with psychiatry and psychology) to weld together the myriad ideas about the *social* and the *family* that had been buzzing around, and progressively more insistently, particularly in the collective consciousness of social work since its psychological "revolution" of the thirties. We will discuss each of these theories in turn, although they are all constructs of interpersonal and person-to-group relationships, and thus are interdependent. Their discussion will make evident why family therapy is such a major breakthrough in clinical practice: it has been germinated by, is inseparable from, and is continuously stimulating, a revisionist dynamic psychology of the individual.

Family Roles and Functions

It has not been a novel idea that people tend to follow familiar patterns in their behavior within the different positions they occupy in society, and that these patterns are shared in great measure with others in similar or the same positions. But, in fairly modern times, the studies of culture transformed what was simply taken for granted as customary and social obligatory behavior into what we now recognize as social role theory. Culture concepts added the understanding of cultural and subcultural templates that made role, *social* role (Biddle and Thomas 1966).

Social role theory has been elaborated by social scientists who are concerned with classes . . . species . . . of role behaviors. Although as clinical workers we bump into the barrier of logical types when we try to complete a synthesis of *social* role with *individual* psychology, try to fuse the cultural templates with personal adaptive patterns, at least in the attempt we have brought the social and psychological within "speaking distance" of each other. We leave the social science realm in the strict sense as we adapt social role theory to the clinical task and "psychologize" it (Boehm 1959; Perlman 1968). Then, the construct of role is brought down from a high level of abstraction to specific units of person-situation-person action that can be readily apprehended and "digested." It compacts interpersonal and person-to-task and person-in-context features. Ego psychology "breaks down" total, imponderable behaviors to analyzable, relatively perceptible components (for example, executive, observing, synthesizing functions; rationalization, projection as defenses); an "applied" social role concept does a similar thing for social behavior. When we, as the actor or the observer, try to imagine a person's relationship to a specific social institution, we can get lost in totalness and abstruseness; but in our mental imagery we *can* match a person and a role—attributes of personality and aspects of role behavior (Sherman 1961). A person is part of, or related to, an institution almost entirely via his role or roles in it.

In the family, role sets form a connective tissue between individual members and the family as entity. A formula that captures this circular relationship would be: family ↔ role organization ↔ individual behavior. An observer of family behavior can shuttle his perceptions almost instantly between specifics of a family *member's* role performance and the specifics of his personality; *family* role organization and patterns of role behavior, on the one hand, and family identity, on the other. A crisscross interdependence of perceptions of individual and family phenomena is self-evident.

To characterize a family in its *wholeness* is a difficult challenge. In making the attempt, one finds himself lapsing into describing it part by part. One big assist in apprehending relatively complex and not completely physically bounded entities (such as families) as wholes is provided by reference to their functions. To use family functions as framework, we must choose among several different parameters that all have their validity; the choice depends on the use to which the functional classification is to be put. In clinical social work, we are interested in the functions a family serves in maturation and socialization; it does not much matter whose formulated set of psychosocial functions we elect to use as an example. I became accustomed to a classification put forward by Nathan Ackerman (1958) with which the staff of the Jewish Family Service Mental Health Clinic experimented as a base for making a family "diagnosis." This classification listed six functions of a family:

1. Provision of basic maintenance (food, shelter, etc.)
2. Development of social togetherness and affectional bonds
3. Support for personal autonomy
4. Sexual differentiation
5. Mutual support among members and their acceptance of social responsibility
6. Encouragement of individual creativity

Admittedly, this is a limited inventory; for instance, the relation of the family to cognitive faculties of its members is inadequately represented. But the principal purpose of illustration can be served by it. Employing some such scheme is a necessary step of reduction to make possible an appraisal of the quality and degree of functional effectiveness of a family, and, thereby, its social and mental health. Having some means to look within at how it works helps us to take a specific whole family into our ken; otherwise, either we are stuck with imponderable sociologic classes of families, or we immediately must leapfrog family identity and turn to the individuals within it.

The relationship of family function to family role deployment to individual member behavior has its parallel in any well-conceived social institution having assigned functions to perform in a larger scheme of things. Comparison with other natural, or even synthetic, social organizations serves to sharpen consciousness of the part-whole functional relationships within families. In each family, we can discern the patterned deployment of roles among family members, where effective, where impaired, their supports and complementations, their conflicts and discontinuities. This *role organization is an instrumentation by the family of its functions* and it, in turn, helps to shape and modify member behavior and also set the compasses of allowable variations in it. Inversely, the web of interacting individual personalities of the family members affects the nature and effectiveness of role behavior, and through that intermediacy, the performance by the family of its functions.

Utilizing in clinical work with individual families a *social* concept, as social role, we have had to make several adaptations. We have already mentioned the "adding" of psychological to social determinants of role. What culture tells us about roles in families, classes and species of families serves as a frame or context, within which we perceive the congruences and incongruences (and their meaning) of the role organization and behavior of the idiosyncratic families and their members who are our clients (Spiegel 1957). Clinical responsiveness to an individual family requires that we both apprehend large units of role organization and behavior in it and break them down to the minutest perceptible components. That is a necessary level not only for perceptions but also for movement in therapy. For example, the family roles of parenting—or, specifically, fathering and mothering—are by themselves far too global to be worked with, but functional subprocesses like exercise of authority, leadership, or nurture are uniquely divided, shared, complemented, defaulted, even warred over, in each family and not confined only to those having the status of father and mother. These processes are the substance of role behavior. Roles define how these very processes are divided or shared among family members—*all* family members.

To illustrate our family "equation," suppose hypothetically a therapist perceives that in family A fulfillment of the function of support for members' autonomy is poor; the family is enmeshing and undifferentiating. Beyond seeking the cause in one or another of the parents, further insight into this family's distinctive character can accrue from examining the distribution among all family members of elements of role behavior and their functional or dysfunctional effect, like encouragement of self-interest, allowance for independence strivings, fulfillment of dependency needs, respect for others' and one's own privacy; and, as well, false privacies, intrusiveness, confusion over who thinks or feels what, and other potentially pathogenic skews in the role performances. Pertinent too are the elements of timing and context: for example, when do acts of intrusion occur, over what personal or family business, in conjunction with what other events, engendering whose support or what conflict, and so on. We see that every family member is implicated (or has some "role" to play) in processes of support (or subversion) of personal autonomy for self and others in the family. The family itself has developed directions and benchmarks for various processes involved in personal autonomy to which all members contribute, and by which all family members measure their own actual or desired autonomy (as in other aspects of identity), and they interact circularly with the values of each individual family member as, of course, they do and did with outside cultures.

Cultural and Family Values

Social workers, as others, found in cultural value concepts means, of at least middle-level specificity, for particularizing person-culture integration (Pumphrey 1959; LaBarre 1961:5–13; Feldman and Scherz 1967:250–64). Thinking in terms of value constructs lends some degree of organization to what otherwise appears like a boundless sea of detail. These concepts break down culture to component benchmarks for social behavior. They make possible a deepened understanding of the relativism of standards of behavior in ethnicities, classes, religions— in all human groupings. Relativism in social science and the humanities, a twentieth century "product," has provided some of the pedigree of family therapy, not only in having advanced cultural relativism, but, as we shall later discuss, in being one probable source for the concept of behavior as relational, which is a keystone in family therapy theory.

The obvious is freely acknowledged, that the family is the principal forum and medium for intergenerational transmission of values. Cultural value theorists have explored the sources and contexts for value systems in societies, their continuity, their conflicts, their relation to the shape of their particular societies (Kluckhohn 1958; Stein, 1958). A view of a family as a microcosm of society, as a small society in itself, adds to our conception of family values; each family is then envisioned not just as an intermediate channel in value transmission from culture to person, but as an entity having its own distinctive value system, symbolically organizing the role behavior and the very existential values of its members. Again, the family value system is not closed but is constantly reworking and integrating cultural value changes, reflecting family members' personal attributes, and interacting with parallel other systems (Perlman 1968).

Families, just as larger social organisms, develop "their own" value systems. In some families, these value systems are hardly touched by the changing conditions of their society or their own fortunes; in other families, they are more flexibly adaptive. As in larger social units, so in families, values do not change as readily as specific behaviors. Family myths (for example, love requires sacrifice; happiness is a life goal per se) persist though colored by changes within the family or in its socioeconomic or educational levels, occupations, residence, ecology, and so forth. A family's values combine into a distinctive system and are not just a collection of individual values.

Further, family values are interpretable at various levels of generality—just as broader social values (Kluckhohn 1958). We can infer value *orientations* in families; as specific values can be overt, orientations are more immanent, more related to meanings and to small group and individual dynamics. Value orientations in a family generalize clusters of specific values, and they can be inferred as governing the way in which the family fulfills each of its functions. Family B provides an example. In its exercise of the function of sexual differentiation, we detect a strong gender prejudice, putting males in the superior and females in a subservient position. This orientation is shared by both parents—though not without some conflict between them—with sources in a complex of psychological, ethnic, and class factors. A whole inventory of specific values of a related prejudicial kind makes up this orientation, from spending patterns (automobiles before household needs), and recreational and cultural preferences (spectator sports), to timing of any lovemaking (male readiness and initiative), to expectable sexual gratifications (not essential for wives), to education (college for sons, dispensable for daughters), and so on. The possible additions to the list are without limit. There are agreements and complements, but also cracks and conflicts, in this subsystem of sex values—especially, as one would expect, with the growing seepages into the family from outside culture change—but it has been a powerful energizing and directing force in this family's life.

Systems and Communication Theories

Systems and communication theories are in the great tradition of the quest for a unifying theory concerning the organization and dynamics of organisms. Obviously, theories that deal with "organismic features of life, behavior, society" (von Bertalanffy 1969:36), and with how people exchange behaviors and information, are directly relevant to all areas of social work (Hearn 1969; Polansky 1971). They have influenced family therapy wherever and however that therapy is practiced. They require full treatises to do them justice. I will mention just a few ideas, those that have made the deepest impressions on my views and practice of family therapy.

In everything I have written to this point, there is an underlying communications systems perspective, but not specifically named as such—although some systems and communications "purists" would dispute that one can be both systematist and psychodynamicist (Jackson 1969). I do believe it possible to have a perspective that combines the individual person and systems, subjective experience and expressive behavior, as Ruesch (1951), Grinker (1959), and other have demonstrated. This integrative assumption threads the discussion of all aspects of clinical work in this paper, and I believe it is shared by a large segment of clinical social work as a general value, although we also share incompleteness in its implementation (Mitchell 1961; Leader 1978; Sherman 1978).

At first encounter, the idea seems almost trite, but upon further thought, most profound: namely, the general principle of wholeness of physiological and social phenomena and the ordering of these "wholes" *in a hierarchy* (von Bertalanffy 1969:43–44). For example, we need to stretch our minds to encompass the notion of having a person's feelings about being a parent as being not only a *part* of his affective wholeness but as having properties of a *whole*, of a system; just as much a system as a family, kinship group, community, and so on. An individual's behavior in his family role(s), his cognitive or affective life, his entire personality are each conceptualizable as both a *part* of the individual person and as a *whole* with interdependent parts. When in family treatment we encompass aspects of the wholeness of the family and the wholeness of each of its members, we can descry hierarchies of role behavior, values, leadership, dependence, even defensive patterns, although as we verge toward frankly psychological entities in this listing, we invite more objections from systems "purists," who, with some validity, dispute the use of psychological symbols or metaphors for groups of people.

A perspective on systems hierarchies lends a useful relativity to choices among clinical approaches. The vantage point from which the clinician views the interlocking systems often decides the point of his therapeutic entry. The therapist who is oriented exclusively toward individual treatment focuses on the individual person and from that vantage point looks "down" to the individual's component behaviors and, one would hope, "up" toward the family. The family therapist focuses on the family patterns, looks "down" to the individual members' behavior and subjective experience and "up" to the kinship group, community, other subcultures. The individual therapist, naturally enough, has traditionally not thought in systems terms and, therefore, to the extent family enters his purview, he considers the client's relations with selected individual members, and similarly selectively fractionates larger social contexts. Systems-thinking clinicians have a means for admitting more of whole contexts up and down the social continuum. (But they too are open to error, that of bypassing idiosyncrasies.)

Given the interdependence of knowledge systems, it is not too far-fetched to consider relativism in social work theory as influenced by relativity in theoretical physics, nor are trends in biology too remote for comparisons with social work. In biology, there have been dramatic discoveries and a continuing search to explain, at the microscopic level, the mechanisms of genetic inheritance and programming exciting even to the lay mind. Media have popularized the romance even of hardware like the electronic microscope. Paralleling this analytic effort, there has been another equally fascinating development. Sociobiology and ethology (Frankel 1979) seem to have come into their own. Ethologists study, through *observation of natural states, whole* animals, their *whole* patterns of behavior and, necessarily, behavior of whole herds, because a single animal's behavior shows more sense of purpose in the context of its functional hierarchical relationships in the herd. Study of the biologic organism invites analysis *and* synthesis, micro *and* macro complementary approaches. The hierarchy of biologic systems, of gene and herd and micro and macro biology, has its easy parallel to that of the human affect or act and the family; of psychotherapy and family therapy.

Parenthetically, ethology and family therapy bear further comparison with respect to modality. It is in the nature of all clinical work that it plucks its subject from living situations and natural associations and brings it into an artificial setting, the therapeutic session. (I disregard, for my present purpose, that the synthetic situation has its own dynamic utility.) Family sessions have some of the artificiality of the manufactured situation *plus*, however, an importation of a piece of man-in-nature, in living context, that no other modality can provide. This fact makes it so compelling to have at least a few sessions with the entire family in family therapy—and as family therapy influence widens, in all therapies, whenever possible.

The principle governing the interdependence of systems is that all living systems are open, not closed (Rapoport 1968); the boundaries or "skins" that enclose healthy, growing organisms are not barriers that close them in *away* from other systems but are definitions of separateness, one very essential purpose of which is to *facilitate* interchange with other systems. Too much closure in systems is pathogenic. Complete closure is death. Mutual dependence and openness among the different levels of systems with the family—as between the family and outside cultures—take on new meanings. We take as given that lability is essential for the individuals or between them. At higher levels, marital unions, parent-child dyads or triads, sibling groups, and other natural subsystems become "splits" within the family when they close off. So do alliances within families that form naturally to serve as structure for mutual support when they close off to the detriment of those in and those outside the alliances (Wynne 1961). Social participation or isolation of a family, open- or close-mindedness to contemporary events, ideas, movements, neighborliness, and so on, are vital aspects of a family "diagnosis," the family's open exchanges with the outside having decisive interdependence with individual mental health.

Personality theories of whatever stripe point to the process of self-differentiation as a necessary, vital part of growth of an organism. This has been generalized as a systems concept, with a feature that von Bertalanffy terms "progressive mechanization" (1969:40–41), which has proven very relevant to communication in families. The burst of interest in games theories, family rules and communication codes, family myths, and the like, was probably evoked in part by this systems notion, which when applied to the family, premises that a necessary condition to the family's *progressive* differentiation is the mechanization—routinization, stereotyping, reduction to involuntarism—of successive levels of function, quite as though the consciousness of family members must be freed by routinization of behavior at earlier and lower stages in order for it to go on to higher stages of differentiated activities. This describes a process of natural growth in the life cycle of families, with mechanization being a decisive factor in that growth. As any condition or process of healthy growth, it also has its pathogenic counterpart: mechanization or hardening can occur in patterns of dysfunction, and they can then submerge out of awareness of family members, thus not freeing growth but preventing it. Much of the comment in the literature on "family rules" and the like are concerned with those pathogenic possibilities, and they point to a central task in family therapy—some would have it as its only task—which is to recognize and intrude upon the well-established, largely implicit rules and regulations governing the mutual behavior exchanges (i.e., communication patterns) in the family when and where they are dysfunctional for the family and individual members. Family therapists who work only on this level (Haley 1968) generally also limit therapy content and focus to the here and now, and they consider a diversion any investigation of antecedent events or developmental stages, whether of the individual person or of the family.

Systems theory also has altered the concept of homeostasis, which social work had adopted as a way to explain the integrity of social organisms. Terms like "steady state" or Menninger's "heterostasis" do better in implying qualities of a social or behavioral system—its porosity, creativity, generativity. Whatever we call it, it is a construct necessary to enable us to image the wholeness of a family and the probable trajectory of its behavior, yet leave room for unpredictableness.

We have seen that all family therapists, by definition, must be concerned with how the family fulfills its functions and with the systems of role behavior forming the family's innards. The terms "role behavior," "interaction," and "communication" are practically interchangeable. Communications specialists have demonstrated aptly that all behavior is communicative, or stated inversely, that communication is the social expression of behavior. So it is that Albert Scheflen can conclude that "communication deals not only with new information but also with the regulation of behavior—with maintaining equilibrium and with the completion of social tasks (1967:98).

Absorbing this conception into clinical practices has taken some doing on our part. We had to leave the one-dimensional hyphenation of communication with language, which in families we saw was often less eloquent or candid than other modes of communication, like vocal delivery, gestures, posture and all kinesics. Then we made yet another step forward with the awareness that an essential part of the "message" or the "messages" themselves in communication are the surrounding circumstances, accompanying behavior, contexts of setting, timing, conjunction with other events and actions: the "metacommunication." We could grasp better now what the early contributors to communication theory (Ruesch and Bateson 1951; Grinker 1959) had meant when they called our attention to the communication signals in all behavior, and to the straitjacket imposed on clinical thought by traditional, linear cause-effect approaches to behavior.

Simple cause-effect or stimulus-response models of behavior have been amplified (some say, replaced) by the communication and systems concepts which have found a particularly fertile ground in family therapy. If my own experience is typical, a large initial jolt is needed to penetrate a well-entrenched ideational system of thought that is largely dynamic psychological with social trimmings, before the mind really opens itself to radically different premises. Dynamic psychology, in over simple terms, premised individual behavior as primarily a function of the state of the person's emotional economy (a "deposit," in turn, of endowment and internalized developmental experience); individual maladaptation or dysfunction, by the same premise, being a function of impairments or conflicts in the person's emotional state. *Past* social influences are assumed to have gone through processes of internalization of, and to have become introjects of, patterns for behavior. Large chunks of social experience, particularly in the present tense, are left outside this system of explanations and remain inexplicable in behavioral and personality terms for even the best socially intentioned visionary.

The inversion of these psychological premises that communication theory poses, again put in oversimple terms, is that personal emotions are a function of behavior; with individual behavior, in turn, being a function of larger behavior systems—e.g., the family.

Actually, few family therapists in or out of social work take such an extreme theoretic position, but many do make it an operational premise in therapy focused exclusively on family communication (Montalvo 1967). Integrationally motivated therapists see in the concept of the "inverse" flow from system to behavior to inner personal emotion, attitude, etc., not a substitute but a complement for dynamic psychological premises, forming a complex of interdependent, different-ordered systems of explanation, linked hierarchically and laterally by means of two-way channels.

Our understanding of the interchanges within the family, whether of the minutest behaviors or of total selves, has been furthered by such concepts as feedback, which refers to a continuous process of a person's testing the accuracy, appropriateness, and functional merit of his acts and expressions by their perceived effect, enabling him to continually make corrections. It is an autonomic trial-and-error process that governs interpersonal conduct and intercourse and that is a basis for learning (Polansky 1971). An analogy of human feedback can be made to the cybernetic device in the machine, and it is often likened to the functioning of the thermostat. Boszormenyi-Nagy describes essentially the same principle, in a more elegant way, when he states the need for a psychology that would include the developmental dimension, but which would go beyond to a "reciprocally self-defining, self-other relational" system, which he would term a "dialectical psychology": "The self becomes a self only by virtue of its being a center of something else; moment by moment it is grounded in the existence of an

Other. This is not a new concept, but the real puzzle is this: what happens to the Other the moment I make him the ground of my existence?'' (1961:91).

Nagy knows part of the answer. The self at the same time is both "center" and "ground" for others' existence. This is the dimension of systems ideas that boggles the mind with its existential riddles. Nagy leaves off at the level of a two-person dialectic. Yet, in building family theory from the ground up, so to speak, at each step there is a geometric multiplication of the number of interactional channels. At the level of a *three-person* subsystem (two parents and child for example), each person is in reciprocal exchange with the systemic threesome, with the other twosome, as subsystem, as well as with each other individual, and so on to other subgroups in the family.

There is a difference introduced to clinical perceptions the more we conceptualize subsystems, like dyads and triads, and their interaction. For example, the practice is still common of examining relationships, only on a one-to-one basis, as child-mother, child-father, father-mother. We still see in that most prosaic of instruments, the dictation summary outline, a careful channeling of perceptions of the index client in one-by-one relation to others in the family. In contrast, if the clinical perceptions and appraisal are also systemic, we open awareness to the child's interaction with the marital and parental *union* itself, not only with the parents individually. The properties of that union, its complementarity and conflicts, supports, sexual differentiation, loving, etc., are properties of a system that is in continuous interchange with the child and that does not have the identical properties of the individual parent-child interaction. The nature of the union significantly influences the child in development of sexually differentiated identity although it is usually given little weight alongside the much more touted individual identification process with the parent of the same sex. With the parental pair, the child *identifies with the wholeness of heterosexuality*, itself a bio-psycho-social subsystem. This opens up delicious possibilities for further study of identification (as other) processes in individual growth in families, identification with systems up and down the ladder of complexity of systems.

An Integrative Family Therapy

To return to therapy, in the earlier discussion of the hierarchy of systems an underlying idea presented was that family therapy, in focusing on the family, has made a choice of a particular portal of entry into that hierarchy from individual to community. Also stated, in short, was a view of dysfunction as a *systems* disturbance. That individual developmental experience, internalized patterns and objects, should have a significant place in the family therapist's approach is disputed by a number of family therapists. One regret I have is that in social work some self-styled systems family therapists have prematurely in their careers settled exclusively in this groove without ever having investigated, or practiced within, any other framework. Avoiding psychodynamics simplifies the universe of variables one has to know and deal with, but it does leave many questions open.

Scheflen (1978), in an anecdotal article, makes the point that there are various points of view extant in explaining behavior in the family, all valid in their way, but maintained as opposing doctrines by different groups. His article relates that, during an observed interview, daughter Susan was seen to smile. For this bit of behavior there were numerous explanations from the observing clinical workers, each explanation belonging in a different framework. Scheflen classified the explanations as follows:

A. Explanations "within" Susan:
    1. As an expression of Susan's inner feeling of the moment (amusement? scorn? sarcasm?)
    2. As a S-Ro, a response stimulated (or caused) by her father's verbal approach
    3. As itself a stimulus or cue (provocation?) of mother's reprimand that followed the smile
B. Interactional explanations
    1. As part of a mutually cued and responded chain of behaviors in the group
    2. As part of a reiteration in the present of a learned pattern of approach, smile, response
    3. As a meta response (not a response in kind to father, but one implying a judgment, therefore having the value of a comment on the ongoing events) and part of a meta sequence in the group

Each of the several explanations has a sophisticated framework from which it stems. Each of the explanations and its framework, Scheflen pointed out, have their usefulness, but also are limited to a particular slice of the total reality. However the therapist deals with his particular perception, whether it is tucked away in his mind or expressed to the family, willy-nilly it will feed into the therapy with the family, influencing its direction and helping to shape a therapeutic system that has its own distinctive aspects, choice of modalities, and treatment goals for the family.

One can draw a direct line of relationship from the preferred explanation of behavior to the choice of modalities in the therapy, and to the goals of treatment. As earlier indicated, there are family therapists whose explanations of behavior are like those in A above, "within Susan," and who use primarily, even solely, individual modalities; and whose goals of treatment are stated in individual terms. At the other end of the range, there are the family therapists whose preferred explanation of behavior is "left-wing" interactional, who vary in choice of modalities but usually elect to use family group sessions, and whose goals are stated in terms of family system change. It is the old psychicsocial argument all over again but in modern dress: are psychodynamic and communication explanations of behavior compatible? Jay Haley (1969) a family therapist whose sense of humor blunts the sharpness of his extreme sallies on the side of communications-only therapy has said, "The current attempt to save psychoanalysis by broadening its concepts to include a family view has an effect in family therapy rather like the fate of a fresh breeze when it strikes the air pollution of a large city." Scheflen's point, on the other hand, is that all the explanations offered for Susan's behavior, from psychodynamic to family communicational, are each partial, and he makes out a case for eclecticism: different explanations in different connotations being relevant and employed to serve different purposes at different times in the therapy. To the flexible clinician this makes real sense and expresses what he flexibly tries to do. Short of the synthesis of frameworks, which may never happen, eclectic inclusiveness must be the answer for social work. The flak being experienced today in family therapy is reminiscent of the cannonading in the 1950s over group therapy and counseling, which about that time were beginning to appear in social agencies. Social work, then, mirrored the dispute between group dynamicists (who influenced social group work attitudes) and psychodynamicists (on whose side caseworkers were arrayed). The issue under dispute was whether the group or the individual in the group was the focus of treatment and the reference point of therapy goals (Scheidlinger 1956; Konopka 1949; Sherman 1955). Over time, this dichotomy has been considerably resolved and the two approaches are so close that one can appropriately characterize as eclectic the beliefs and practice of the very large body of practitioners in the center. Must we repeat this history step-by-step in family therapy?

There is something left unfinished in a flat affirmation of family system goals, leaving out the individual. It *does* have the virtue of neatly completing a syllogism: individual therapy aims at individual change, therefore family therapy aims at family change. However, in life, almost always, for therapist and client alike, therapy has as its ultimate goal and its effectiveness is measured by, change in individual persons—in their subjective discomfort and in their individual adaptation. In fact, reports from all sides on family therapy practices always connect them with forms of individual malaise or maladaptation, which seemed to be the reason why the families were in treatment in the first place. And always, in each reported case—not excepting the most exclusively communication-based—the measure of success in the therapy is stated as the relief or improvement in functioning of that person or sometimes an additional family member as well. Even more: the determination of what change is to be sought in the family structure, the selection of the part of communication patterns to focus on, is almost always a function of some appraisal of an index member—the "presented problem" member. The *content* of the therapy and the *object* of the *interventions* may be entirely in family terms, but inevitably on behalf of and with an *end purpose* of individual change, achieved indirectly by the route of change in the family system of which he is part.

This is consonant with the therapeutic alliance that is usually wrought with the client family. In the beginning, there is the presentation of the problem, almost always that of an individual member. When there is too facile a first presentation by the applicant of the family as problem: "we all need help," "we don't communicate," "there's no togetherness in the family," therapists have learned to beware. Often the family form given the complaint is a pathetic use of a cliché as cloak for an individual complaint, and it makes for an especially refractory defense. Then the family therapeutic task is to ferret out the underlying, felt complaint in order to be able to put it in its true family context, and to begin the work on its interactional expression.

For the family therapist to begin to move the context of his interchange with the family from individual person to family, he is aided no little by interviews with the family as a group. In the group session, the therapist exploits the natural pull in the conjoint presences by promoting the transplanting of subjective, intrapersonal thought and affect, and conflict, into interpersonal expression, into communicational modes. But if he doctrinairily avoids engaging with the intrapersonal, how then does he help the family members interact? Or begin to see the problem as a family problem? Culturally, socially, biologically, psychologically, even spiritually, dysfunction is accepted as a personal and individual phenomenon, *felt* as such, presented as such. Members of a family can develop, at best, a kind of duality of perception and motive for being helped. In interaction with the therapist they can take on an acceptance and some understanding, initially mostly on faith, that the individually experienced and perceived difficulties are also family troubles which need to be the focus of treatment. But usually, at bottom, they all also hang on to the premise that they "are coming" as a help to the index member.

Whatever our clinical orientation, we can encourage a whole family's participation in therapy beyond the initial compliance, not by ukase, or faith, but by having touched and retouched the presenting problem of the individual and linked it with specific processes or conflicts in the family group. The willingness of the family to "take on" the therapist, rather than pushing the index member before them, hangs on some acceptance that the member is expressing *their* trouble and on their beginning to feel that *they* are all in trouble, but the recasting is never total.

Connections need to be made between individual dysfunction and family dysfunction, not only for the family members to enter a family therapeutic alliance, but because these connections are indispensable in family treatment strategy. Our mind's eye shuttles constantly in our therapist role between evolving family interaction and the individual malady. We do not lose sight of the latter even as it becomes transformed into family interactional terms in the process of therapy, because even the path taken by the transformation expresses the nature of the deformity of the whole family.

As integrational family therapists see it, the goal of family therapy is better stated as the amelioration of individual distress and dysfunction *through* family change. The superordinate goal remains the well-being and improved functioning of person by person—"and nothing, not God, is greater to one than one's self is"—with our increasing skills in helping families to change becoming a most effective means to that end.

References

Ackerman, Nathan W. 1958. *The Psychodynamics of Family Life*. New York: Basic Books.

Austin, Lucille. 1948. "Trends in Differential Treatment." *Social Casework* 38(3):111–18.

Bertalanffy, Ludwig von. 1969. "General Systems Theory and Psychiatry: An Overview." In W. Gray et al., eds., *General Systems Theory and Psychiatry*. Boston: Little Brown.

Biddle, Bruce J. and Edwin Thomas. 1966. *Role Theory*. New York: John Wiley.

Boehm, Werner W. 1959. "The Social Work Curriculum Study and Its Implications for Family Casework." *Social Casework* 40(8):428–36.

Boszormenyi-Nagy, Ivan. 1961. "Communication versus Internal Programming of Relational Attitudes." In Nathan W. Ackerman, Frances L. Beatman and Sanford N. Sherman, eds., *Expanding Theory and Practice in Family Therapy*, p. 91. New York: Family Service Association of America.

FSAA. 1964. *Report of the Committee on Group Treatment in Family Service Agencies*. New York: Family Service Association of America.

Feldman, Frances L. and Frances H. Scherz. 1967. *Family Social Welfare*. New York: Atherton Press.

Flesch, Regina. 1948. "Treatment Goals and Techniques in Marital Discord." *Social Casework* 29(10).

Frankel, Charles. 1979. "Sociobiology and its Critics." *Commentary* 68(1):42.

Gomberg, Robert M. and Frances Levinson. 1951. *Diagnosis and Process in Family Counseling*. New York: Family Service Association of America.

——1958. "Family Diagnosis: Trends in Theory and Practice." *Social Casework* 39(2-3):73–83.

Grinker, Roy R., ed. 1959. *Toward a Unified Theory of Behavior*. New York: Basic Books.

Haley, Jay. 1968. "Ideas Which Handicap Therapists." In Milton M. Berger, ed., *Beyond the Double Bind*. pp. 67–82. New York: Brunner/Mazel.

——1969. "An Editor's Farewell." *Family Process* 8(2):156–64.

Heárn, Gordon, ed. 1969. *The General Systems Approach: Contributions Toward an Holistic Conception of Social Work*. New York: Council on Social Work Education.

Hollis, Florence. 1964. *Casework: A Psychosocial Therapy*. New York: Random House.

Jackson, Don. 1969. "The Individual and the Larger Contexts." In W. Gray et al., eds., *General Systems Theory and Psychiatry*, pp. 387–96. Boston: Little Brown.

Kluckhohn, Florence. 1958. "Variations in the Basic Values of Family Systems." *Social Casework* 39(2):63–72.

Konopka, Gisella. 1949. "Knowledge and Skill in the Group Therapist." *American Journal of Orthopsychiatry* 19(1):56–60.

LaBarre, Weston. 1961. "The Bisocial Unity of the Family." In Nathan W. Ackerman, Frances L. Beatman, and Sanford N. Sherman, eds., *Exploring the Base for Family Therapy*, pp. 5–14. New York: Family Service Association of America.

Leader, Arthur. 1978. "Intergenerational Separation Anxiety in Family Therapy." *Social Casework* 59(3):138–44.

Mitchell, Celia. 1961. "A Casework Approach to Disturbed Families." In Nathan W. Ackerman, Frances L. Beatman, and Sanford N. Sherman, eds., *Exploring the Base for Family Therapy*, pp. 68–82. New York: Family Service Association of America.

Montalvo, Braulio, Salvador Minuchin, Bernard G. Guerney Jr., Bernice L. Rosman, and Florence Schumer. 1967. *Families of the Slums*. New York: Basic Books.

Perlman, Helen H. 1957. *Social Casework: A Problem-Solving Process*. Chicago: University of Chicago Press.

——1968. *Persona: Social Role and Personality*. Chicago: University of Chicago Press.

Polansky, Norman A. 1971. *Ego Psychology and Communication*. New York: Atherton Press.

Pollak, Otto. 1960. "A Family Diagnosis Model." *Social Service Review* 34(1):19–28.

Pumphrey, Muriel W. 1959. *Teaching of Values and Ethics in Social Work Education*. Vol. 13 of *Project Report of the Curriculum Study*, Werner Boehm, ed. New York: Council on Social Work Education.

Rapoport, Anatole. 1968. Foreword to *Modern Systems Research for the Behavioral Scientist*, Walter Buckley, ed., pp. xiii–xxii. Chicago: Aldine.

Regensberg, Jeanette. 1954. "Application of Psychoanalytic Concepts to Casework Treatment of Marital Problems." *Social Casework* 35(10):424–32.

Ruesch, Jurgen and Gregory Bateson. 1951. *Communication: The Social Matrix of Psychiatry*. New York: Norton.

Sacks, Patricia. 1949. "Establishing the Diagnosis in Marital Problems." *Social Casework* 30(5):182–87.

Scheflen, Albert E. 1967. "Explaining Communicative Behavior." In Nathan W. Ackerman, Frances L. Beatman, and Sanford N. Sherman, eds., *Expanding Theory and Practice in Family Therapy*, pp. 93–98. New York: Family Service Association of America.

——1978. "Susan Smiled: On Explanation in Family Therapy." *Family Process* 17(1):59–68.

Scheidlinger, Saul. 1956. "Social Group Work and Group Psychotherapy." *Social Work* 1(3):36–42.

Scherz, Frances. 1956. "Treatment of Acting-Out Character Disorders." In Cora Kasius, ed., *Casework Papers 1956*. New York: Family Service Association of America.

Sherman, Sanford N. 1955. "Casework-Oriented Group Treatment." In Cora Kasius, ed., *Casework Papers 1955*. New York: Family Service Association of America.

——1961. "Concept of the Family in Casework Theory." In Nathan W. Ackerman, Frances L. Beatman, and Sanford N. Sherman, eds., *Exploring the Base for Family Therapy*, pp. 14–29. New York: Family Service Association of America.

——1979. "Family Therapy." In Francis J. Turner, ed., *Social Work Treatment*, pp. 449–78. New York: Free Press.

Siporin, Max. 1979. "Marriage and Family Therapy in Social Work." *Social Casework*.

Spiegel, John P. 1957. "The Resolution of Role Conflict within the Family." *Psychiatry* 20(1):1–16.

Stein, Herman D. 1958. "Social Science in Social Work Practice and Education." In Howard J. Parad, ed., *Ego Psychology and Dynamic Casework*, pp. 226–40. New York: Family Service Association of America.

Towle, Charlotte. 1959. "On the Contemporary Scene in Social Work." *Social Service Review* 32(3):272. As quoted by Helen H. Perlman in *Helping*. Chicago: University of Chicago Press, 1969.

Wynne, Lyman. 1961. "The Study of Intrafamilial Alignments and Splits in Exploratory Family Therapy." In Nathan W. Ackerman, Frances L. Beatman, and Sanford N. Sherman, eds., *Exploring the Base for Family Therapy*, pp. 95–116. New York: Family Service Association of America.

2

The Small Group Perspective: Family Group Therapy

JOHN ELDERKIN BELL

Family Group Therapy is a formal approach to family treatment constructed out of experience over a span of twenty-nine years. It developed within attempts to help troubled families and emerged from ongoing therapist experiences, thought, and organization of principles and methods. The therapy aims to achieve beneficial and rapid family progress toward attaining goals the family members set for themselves. The overall form of the therapy keeps evolving and developing as action and reflection lead me to new ideas and to the the discarding of some old ones. The basic principle behind the treatment method is that family functioning and organization are changed *within* controlled interaction and its predictable and unpredictable interpersonal and personal consequences. The interaction involves the group of the family and a therapist, and is structured to reach the standard that all family members will meet together with the therapist regularly and consistently as a group until the family attain their goals for the therapy, and then prefer to continue family life apart from direct contact with the therapist.

Sources of the Therapy

Psychoanalysis provided for me the primary intellectual and practice discipline out of which family group therapy came. My first conception of the therapy developed in the late summer of 1951, and began to be implemented in October of that year. At that time, I was a professor at Clark University in Massachusetts and the primary staff person in clinical psychology in the Department of Psychology. As specialties, I was engaged in research on child development and projective techniques, and functioned part-time as a child analyst. I was thirty-eight years old. I had been married ten years, had been a professor for nine years, and was a national figure in the field of personality measurement, having written the first book on projective techniques.

My career as a psychologist followed two earlier careers—first, as a chemist, aborted by the difficulties of finding a professional position at the time of graduation in 1933 in the depths of the depression; second, I spent six years as a clergyman, half the time in training and the rest in parishes.

I then decided to become a psychologist and, in 1939, went to New York from Western Canada, where I was born and lived for the first twenty-five years of my life. In the intellectually lively and socially advanced life at Columbia University and in New York, the scarcely more than infant field of clinical psychology was dominated by psychoanalysis. As I studied, I was excited by its theories and practices. Though money was tight, I undertook a personal analysis and training in child analysis. These experiences intensified and unified the developmental process, out of which my person and career as a clinical psychologist, teacher, and child analyst evolved.

After the second world war, I was additionally influenced by the development of group therapy, although I did not study or practice it, believing that its results could never achieve the depth of psychoanalysis. But my students were much stimulated by the new concepts and practices in group therapy and transferred them to me osmotically. Also, field theories were expanding rapidly and I was impressed in thought and action by the works of Kurt Lewin and his followers, especially Roger Barker, a colleague at Clark University and a close personal friend. My preference for the psychoanalytic point of view remained most centrally influenced by the writings of Susan Isaacs, Melanie Klein, and especially Anna Freud, whom I had the privilege of inviting to Clark University for her first visit to this country.

The theories of psychoanalysis were both individual- and family-centered, although practice was with individuals. The taboos against simultaneous treatment of adults and their children by the same therapist were loudly proclaimed and enforced. They did not inhibit my thinking about the whole family, though—even about the place of fathers. My own experiences, particularly in the ministry, had prepared me to think rather broadly of families and to expect and appreciate tremendous diversities among them. After visiting in the homes of four thousand parishioners during my period in the ministry, I could not help but retain a knowledge base from which I could affirm that effective family functioning takes many forms, and that disorders emerge from many sources and show themselves in a multiplicity of ways.

When a decision to experiment with a family approach entered my mind in 1951, the ground seemed ready, but I was affected by obvious risks. I expected intense protest by psychoanalytic therapists and a need to protect myself from possible professional and public censure for breaking from established practices. Nevertheless, I ventured to invite a family to meet with me to see if together we could work out the problems that had brought their thirteen-year-old to the brink of expulsion from school for violent behavior.

The model in my head was to replicate earlier experiments, when on several occasions I had invited a child's teachers and parents to observe analytic sessions with the child from behind a one-way mirror. This effort to educate parents and related adults was illuminating to them and functional in deepening their understanding of the children. I glimpsed the possibility that meeting together with the whole family would promote a still deeper understanding, because the barrier of the glass wall would be gone. I did not anticipate that the parents and other family members would want to get into the action. I thought of myself as a child analyst with a family audience.

The dynamics of the early family sessions were so potent, however, that almost immediately I learned that I could not expect family members to remain an audience, but would have to deal with them as individuals, a subgroup of the family, and as integrated into the total family. So I quickly made shifts toward a therapy program centering on the whole family. Success was easily apparent and I continued the practice.

For the first two years, I was essentially underground. My work was not announced to my students or colleagues. My wife, also a child psychologist, was my confidante. Twenty families and two years later, I went public at a professional meeting of the Eastern Psychological Association (Bell 1975).

What worked for me became my theory and directed my protocol for practice. As soon as my work became known, others began to try the methods, to contribute ideas to me, and to share their ideas with others. I found that development of family group therapy depended less and less on psychoanalytic theories, although some of my own practices were affected by group analysis after the British model.

To state the base on which my approach has been developed is not an easy task. I have found psychoanalysis, group analysis, social theory of both process- and task-oriented groups, general systems theory, and social ecology especially shaping my treatment practices and theory. Of all, it has been the direct experience of working with families that has most formed my ideas and the technical approaches and objectives that mean family therapy to me. Theories from the social sciences that might have seemed potential sources of illumination had but minimal impact on my early work. As with other therapies, the invention of practices was pragmatic and inductive. I tested my ideas in process activities and developed my methods by terminal reflections on treatment sessions themselves—or, at termination, by review of the treatment course.

Initiating Treatment

For me, treatment begins when a family as a whole, or through a representative, presents a specific problem or complex of problems that is beyond the coping capacities of the family. I invite the whole family to attend, according to their definition of who is included in their family. I make it plain that I will not see individuals or a part of the family separately. This is why I call the treatment Family *Group* Therapy. Early in my full-time university days I regarded family therapy as a research topic and the therapy, the content to study. I asserted some control by limiting intake to families where two parents and some children were living together and available for therapy. As my experience and knowledge expanded, I began to use *household* for the most common definition of whom to include in the family group. Even here I made exceptions where a family had opened space for a renter or a person functionally distant from the ongoing family life. I began also to see that the family did not need to have two parents to make it a family group; and in some instances, where geography separated the family, the therapy would have to be conducted in spite of the absence of a person. Later I worked with families extended beyond the nuclear group. Practically formed one criterion to define whom to include. Thus over the years I have become less structured with regard to whom the family may define as belonging to their family, but I have continued to follow the principle of family *group* inclusiveness.

I recommend Family Group Therapy particularly where a disturbed or distressed person's problems suggest some related family pressures or difficulties (often a part of the initial problem description). I do not pretend that I can always make a definitive judgment about family involvement, even though I assume that a person's behavior generally has its roots in a two-way process—from the individual and from the social environment, particularly the family.

Of course, I have no questions in my mind about introducing family group therapy when a family comes requesting help for a problem they define as a "family problem."

Content

Presenting problems are taken seriously. But I have learned over the years that these problems, sufficient for entering into relation with me, are commonly screen problems, masks for the deeper issues that will ultimately be faced in the treatment. Yet, I do not underestimate the serious concern of at least some family members about difficulties presented at the beginning.

The content usually hints at fundamental problems that are not yet explicit. The radically important and central issues are normally too dangerous to expose in an untested relation with a stranger, and often within the family itself. By inference, the therapist may get some hints about the nature, severity, and centrality of unexpressed or indirectly presented problems, but they cannot become content to discuss openly until the family members in therapy reach a required level of confidence in, and comfort with, the therapist and with one another.

For a family to begin treatment with a therapist who is not known, without being able to predict how all their members will function, confronts the family with new and anxiety-producing dangers. They must test where and how safety can be found. This requires that each family member gain experience of the therapist and the situation over time.

I assume that the difficulties the family talk about at first are real issues, though not generally crucial. Because of the screen nature of initial presenting problems, I do not focus my treatment on them. I would regard such treatment as constricting, and likely to be superficial in impact on the family. As the therapy unfolds, problems of greater complexity and significance for the whole family will be met and presented; or, layers covering the initial problems will be stripped away, so the family can get to their center.

Assessment and Contract

I do not engage in a defined period of assessment, nor do I make a specific judgment, on the basis of a referral, about a family's suitability for therapy. In the sessions, I begin to learn about them and their functioning. Such learning takes place as I observe: (1) who is present; (2) who speaks and who holds back; (3) the manner of their speaking; (4) to whom they speak (most often directly to me, as though I were the primary listener, but by the very nature of the group to each family member and to the family as a whole); (5) the content of what individuals say about themselves, other family members, people outside the family, and therapy and the therapist, their problems and those of others, and so on; and, (6) the facial expressions, postures and movements of each body, tones of voice, and the changes in them during the session and in relation to content.

I reserve for myself and for the family the right to arrive at a decision as to the appropriateness of my undertaking to help them. Mostly I begin with an assumption that I can and then test that assumption within the relations and knowledge about the family members that develop in early sessions with them. My openness about the tentativeness of a commitment to work with them involves a bond that I will arrive as soon as possible at a judgment as to whether or not I see a favorable prospect for our working together, and that I will expect them to make and tell me about similar judgments they make.

I suppose this entrance to therapy could be described as an assessment, but the central issue is not content about a stated problem, it is the quality of the relations that develop between the family and me, and within the family in my presence. If after two or three sessions the family seem not to have moved toward some open participation by each member, and if there is a failure by any member to make a commitment to take part in the therapy, I would stop to evaluate the sessions and arrive at my own recommendation about continuing the therapy. In this evaluation, I would examine first what I could do to control the dominant vocal members of the family and release the nonvocal, inhibited, or hostile persons. Toward these ends to some extent, I would use my knowledge of task-oriented group processes, especially from the National Training Laboratories studies, and of interpersonal, spatial, and environmental factors that affect groups to facilitate the participation of each family member. However, such efforts sometimes promote separation rather than building cohesion, and are sometimes ineffective because uncontrollable factors are dominant. These factors might include variables such as the age or physical features of a therapist, and nonfamily aspects of a family member's life, such as activities at school or work. I would refer the family to another family therapist, recommend some other mode of treatment, or propose other methods of problem solving.

I have learned over the years—and am comfortable with the fact—that I work well with many families, but not effectively or comfortably with some; for example, where one family member is defined as schizophrenic. This is linked not only to my own theoretical position about the bases of schizophrenia, in particular the organic components, but also to my own experiences, dating back to the late 1930s, in trying to learn to engage effectively with schizophrenics in hospitals. In fact, I would question the suitability of family therapy, as I practice it, when a family member is institutionalized, disoriented, mentally retarded, newly handicapped or critically ill, especially if the cause appears organic. The reasons for unsuitability would vary, of course, in such a variety of cases.

When I am not satisfied that I can help a particular family, I generally express that reservation to them, though not necessarily in such a firm manner as to force discontinuance. I try to assist them to tell me their reactions to the therapy and to me, so we may examine our relations together to help all of us assess the possibilities of therapeutic success. I expect some families to find it difficult, if not impossible, to work with me.

The contract, as far as it can be so called, deals with the conditions under which therapy may proceed: (1) all members of the family, as defined by them, will attend, with the exception that preschool children may be deemed unsuitable and may be left in someone else's care; (2) at the beginning there will be a trial period; and (3) a session will be postponed if a family member cannot attend.

I also specify that the particular content introduced by the family will come not from my probing but by their initiative, and that they must set up their own goals for the therapy.

Let me disabuse any who may think that this is a passive role for me. It is not. I am generally process-centered and I direct and mediate the development and continuity of the therapy group. In contrast, the family's preoccupations are oriented primarily to intrafamily or personal matters, secondarily to the therapy process, and even less to its conscious management.

Treatment Strategies and Techniques

More critical than the issue of presence or absence of individuals is the matter of the allowed content in reference to persons. I take the position that content must be restricted to aspects of the relations among those family members who are present. Thus, failure of a family member who has agreed to take part in the therapy to appear for a session is, for me, a contraindication to continuing the therapy at that time. I tell the family that we will not be able to work together that day because the person is absent. This sounds harsh and is so received by some families, but I have a sound basis in experience and thought for this position. Evidences of any preference in relating to some family members is a threat to the involvement and security of each person and particularly of anyone who may not be present.

One family member may block the treatment. If so, I do not see value in shifting to treat the remainder of the family unless the center is clearly to remain on relations among the residual group, and there is a clear understanding that content about the reluctant individual must be excluded from communications. Unless a family member is present, I do not engage in, or allow, discussion about him or her, although family members may test the strength of my commitment to this position. Talk about a person outside the group deflects attention to, and progress in, the interactions among those in the therapy. The effort to introduce such content about outsiders is a common device to escape from the interactional pressures within the group—pressures that promote the progress of the therapy and quicken its pace.

The family's *presence* as a group is a profound statement to each family member. It affirms that each person has centrality in the group, that the group is incomplete in the absence of any family members, and that I attach value and importance to the family group as a whole and thus to each person. Indirectly, it affirms also that each family member participates in some ways in generating and in resolving problems of _family_ concern.

Definition of _family_ concern is perhaps relevant at this point. During the whole course of family group therapy, except perhaps at the very end, problems are being presented, struggled with, defined or redefined, and shelved or solved. When all family members point to one person as having problems with his or her self or with the family as a whole, and that person concurs with the others, then it is appropriate to speak of family concern. Readiness to address the problem issues is usually present and therapy may proceed. There is no assurance that an individual referred to as a problem, or as having a problem, will accept that definition of his or her behavior. In fact, he or she may dismiss the idea that the behavior is a problem. Here we do not have a stated problem of _family_ concern; we have concern in a segment of the family.

I believe that dealing with the problem associated with the individual would show preference to a concerned segment of the family. That would align me with the concerned segment rather than with the family as a whole. So I define for myself that the family problem at that moment is a lack of concurrence, and I attend to that.

Throughout the treatment, the _family_ is at the center for me. The treatment starts by connecting the whole family with me. The therapy group, the whole family plus the therapist, is constructed. This is an instrumental group organized for the therapy process, by which it is time limited, not in the sense of a predetermined time but in my thinking, planning, and efforts to move the therapy toward the anticipated termination. Then the therapy group is dissolved.

Establishing the Therapy Group

The therapy group in Family Group Therapy has many of the characteristics of the group in group therapy. But the differences are also significant, and they relate to the continuity of the "patient" group. Unlike regular group therapy, the family begins therapy as a formed group and usually continues as such following the treatment. So, in some senses, the family in its group identity, dealt with as a single entity, may be equated with a single patient in individual therapy.

Nevertheless, in both group and family group therapy, establishing the therapy group (therapist plus patient group or therapist plus family) is an early stage, not to be overlooked in concern over the content of what patients or family members are saying and doing.

I engineer the formation of the therapy group by engaging each person, always in the presence of the whole family and in reference to the group as a whole. I visibly keep the total group in my view. No individual escapes my attention if I can help it, and attention does not dwell centrally on any individual. In posture and eye-scanning, I attend to each person as nearly simultaneously as possible. I sometimes speak of my attention as free-floating. It embraces the whole group of the family and links me to the group as a whole, by that to the relations among them, and thus inferentially to each individual.

Of course, there are times when I slip and become unduly preoccupied with an individual, sometimes myself. My preoccupation soon becomes evident to the family and commonly leads to some withdrawal by a family member. Restitutive attention to the whole group is then required, or else the therapy will slip backwards, break down, or even terminate.

Goals

Two sets of goals dominate family group therapy, those of the family and those of the therapist. For the family, the goals may be divided into intake goals versus outcome goals. Intake goals are for entrance into the therapy and involve such concerns as establishing the parameters of the therapy, exerting some control over the situation, facing anticipated hazards, gaining protection, assuring escape if necessary, testing relations with the therapist, anticipating the future in the treatment, testing how others will respond, and getting finished with the therapy. Outcome goals are anticipated at the beginning but are also emergent during the therapy and shift as intrafamily relations and family interpretations of those relations change. They concern treatment and family life objectives seen by any family member, self or other. Under optimal conditions, outcome goals concern solving problems, promoting family well-being, and thus the well-being of individuals.

My primary goal as therapist is to facilitate the process of therapy, and thereby to assist a family to reach their objectives, whether stated or not. My therapist objectives concern moving the therapy ahead toward the goal of ultimate termination. I do not prescribe solutions to family problems, since solutions must be grounded in the nature, functioning, perceptions, and values of each family. But, in general, I seek a beneficial outcome for the family on their own terms and according to their own values.

I know that for me there is a risk that I might inadvertently yield to family pressure on me to prescribe a family goal or a problem-solution. I avoid such prescriptions for they may not be truly adapted to all the seen and unseen contingencies that need to be taken into account, and thus will not be workable. So, I try to insist that the family state and restate their own goals in words and actions, gain family consensus on them, struggle to reach them, and master ways to adapt their individual and group living to attain them.

Process

My primary strategy is to achieve and maintain the active participation of each family member who is present in the therapy setting, and thus in relations with other family members, at all times during the therapy sessions. This has to be won. At the beginning, the most unusual aspect of the treatment for the family is my presence as a therapist. This is true in a general way but, as a person, I become known in the therapy situation only by what I do that makes me known to the family. As in any new relation, much sizing up of mysteries about a stranger is necessary before deep trust develops. No matter what family members may have learned about me prior to coming to the therapy, they have to arrive at their own sense of my reality as a person, but even more as a therapist. Thus, I am more interested in defining my role and their participation than in intensive exploration of the nature and history of the family. I want the relations in the treatment to develop, so that the family can face and reshape their problems during progress in therapy sessions, and in the interactions and reflections among the family when they are together at home.

I use the initial statement of difficulties as a center around which issues of strategy can be planned and handled. I refer especially to the orientation of the family to the treatment.

The first statements by a family about the problems they face and the solutions they see and recommend, if they propose any, are made characteristically by a single family member, or by a coalition group of those in the family who have been active in seeking help in working through problems as they see them. Their statements are directed to the therapist, for the most part, though at the same time they are heard, or possibly heard, by the other family members.

At this beginning point, particularly if one family member has been singled out as a scapegoat, a principal problem-bearer, the gaining of open participation by that individual in actions other than defending the self becomes a target for me. The well-practiced and routinized family attack-defense patterns have to be disrupted. Whether the scapegoat is a child, as is common, or an older family member, I seek to create the chance for that person to express himself or herself in the midst of the family in new ways, and particularly in the face of family hostility and efforts to constrain the person. The opportunity for the person is gained by my directing the group. It is reached by my providing and assuring the chance for each individual to speak and be heard. I model the listening act, intrude when a person is interrupted and attacked by another family member in what seems an unwelcome way, so that the perspective of each side may be presented and the emphasis on interaction rather than on verbal content can be maintained. I echo what persons say and thus help an inarticulate person to express more clearly what is said and expand on it. At the same time, I assure all family members that the chance to take part is open to them, ideally all the time.

Since the primary aim is to help the family to interact within their group, I do not encourage any family member to talk to me, as they tend to do at the beginning. Nor, in general, do I turn persons off abruptly. Rather, I make sure I have positioned myself so that I can interact easily with all family members right from the beginning—and I try to do so at all times by my body orientation, alertness, gaze, listening, and seeing. Then, by the movement of my body and my gaze, I try to keep all aware that I am including them. When I am addressed, I turn to the person who is speaking. In responding I speak to the whole group (especially through posture and movement), rather than singly to a person.

As nearly as possible, I try to keep alert to signs from each family member that at this moment he or she is withdrawing or taking part in a different way. Such signs are shown in both words and body action. If a family member seems to be changing participation toward withdrawal, I would intervene to refer to the interpersonal process going on. For example, I might say to a speaker: ''I notice that as you are talking, ———(name of other family member who has been observed) is looking out the window'' (or any other outwardly observable *action* of the family member). I contribute observations on what I see happening among them. Such observations relate only to the behavior of family members that is visible to me and potentially or actually to them. I do not speak of my impressions of a person's motives, thoughts, feelings, or other internal processes that can only be learned by inference. I do not elaborate my observations by tacking on interpretations about why the behavior occurred. I avoid such inferences and interpretations, since they are not outwardly interactional, are personal rather than family matters, and to mention them puts emphasis on the relations between the therapist and the individual family member about whom the inference has been made. I learned early that interpretations like the ones that became familiar to me in psychoanalysis seem to dry up the flow of a family's common efforts toward problem solving, disrupt continuity in family growth, and lead to interactional problems between the therapist and the *family*, or to the kinds of dependence on a therapist wherein new family problems are not tackled without the therapist's sanction and counsel.

If, however, a family member seems to be showing by speech, posture, body movement, or gesture, that he or she wants to get into the action in a different way, I might reduce somewhat my attention to an ongoing speaker and increase it toward the person who seems to be seeking to speak.

When the whole family interaction is lively and free, I do not interrupt for any purpose except to terminate a session.

Through this family-centered program, the family members begin to increase the modes by which, in the therapy, they relate to the therapy group as a whole (family plus therapist), the family as a separate whole, and themselves as individuals. Such differentiations increase the flexibility of their interactions and the integration of family members into more effective group action.

Open participation of the whole family with one another is thus finally achieved in the presence of the therapist. The effects of the participation do not extend to all family matters, nor do they lead of necessity to democratic consensus. But in relation to presented crises and problems, family participation becomes fully rounded. In this regard, the process is democratic; each person, being valued, becomes a contributor to the solution of problems. At the same time, one family member may seem to dominate by putting forward a proposal, demanding its acceptance, and winning the day. This could be adjudged to be dictatorial, but it is so only if the opportunity is denied to other family members to act out or speak their reservations, to propose other ideas (they do not necessarily do so), and to be seen and heard. The therapist is the dominant person to assure this participative opportunity. The solutions to particular problems may be carried out, as well, in an autocratic way, with one or more family members taking control, possibly because a family may value the continuation of roles and habitual patterns of family action. I do not aim to see the family remodel their whole functioning, though ripple-effects spread to some extent, and often extensively, throughout the family. Commonly such a rippling takes place in relation to a situation parallel to those which brought the family to the therapy.

Framework of the Techniques

The technical framework within which the therapy is promoted is developmental, as is manifest in stages common to many forms of family therapy. These are: (1) the therapy group (therapist and all family participants together) is established. The therapist orients the family, responding to their requests for clarification and elaboration of the orientation, and supports and encourages their participation. The family tests the dimensions of the therapy group and begins to learn about how the therapist will function. (2) The family begins to open in new ways their communications with one another and with the therapist. They struggle for power and domination of the group. Hostility by individual family members toward others emerges and shows itself, often intensely. (3) The family achieves a common level of participation for all their members. They reach consensus on primary family issues and goals for the therapy and their family. (4) The family group explores, experiments with, and tests ways to solve problems and to achieve family goals. They amend roles, develop new family priorities and affirm functional old ones, experiment with new family interactions and procedures to reach common family objectives and to solve their problems. They move toward implementing and improving their proposed procedures and attaining their family goals. They evaluate their progress and eventually affirm their readiness to function successfully as a family without the therapist. (5) The family and the therapist prepare for and achieve separation.

Problems are created in any family. None escape. They come both over a long time through the continual restructuring and development of the family, and in the immediate past in respect to crises, often those that bring a family to treatment. In general, major remaking of the family as structured over time is not sought, though restructuring in part occurs directly and in a spread of effect from the therapy. The immediate goal is to work through a current crisis, to help the family to experience success in problem solving and family development, and possibly to achieve new patterns for confronting future crises.

Major restructuring of families is a worthy goal, but therapy as I conduct it does not aim for such a radical outcome, though it may occur. As to definition, I reserve the term "therapy" for recognizing and treating a disease or disorder (in the classical meaning of these terms), rather than in reference to some problem identified within a formal professional classification scheme.

Forms of Family Treatment

I do not think that Family Group Therapy is a preferred mode of treatment for all problems that persons in a family can show or present to a therapist as a basis for seeking help. Every problem an individual brings in individual therapy may be seen by that individual, other family members, or the whole family group, as a family problem. But it need not be so seen. Many problems are more fundamentally those of a person, and have to be so accepted for treatment to be effective—if indeed it can be. In such cases, individual examination and, if necessary, individual treatment are indicated. So also, expanding the framework, other problems are indeed those of a social order and require social action beyond a family for resolution. Family group therapy may be instituted for alleviation of social distress, but that is most often palliative, not fundamental.

My work has included some efforts in the direction of methods other than family group therapy to reach family goals where family group therapy was not likely to be feasible or productive. Since projects and programs sought fundamental family changes and progress outside a therapy frame, they may be regarded as separate from the family group treatment I have been describing. A brief description of some of the alternative programs follows.

1. *Family context development.* Many of the basic and treatment-oriented institutions with which a family member becomes associated are organized around needs and programs of the institution, so that not

infrequently there is an absence of, or greatly limited, direct consideration for the families of the persons associated with the institution. This applies both to staff and to those whom the institution serves. Such lack of concern about families is logical but often needlessly harmful to the persons associated with the institution and to family relations. Consideration for families cannot come in without changing the institution's programs, policies, operations, and physical structures. I have been working for the past five years in two hospitals to modify their associated family relations. By placing primary attention on changing the hospitals, changes that can affect many families simultaneously can thus be—and have been—implemented (Bell 1978).

2. *Targeted family education and reeducation.* Education of families is common. I cite it here because I have been working on the development of some programs where the education is directed toward target groups that have not been reached extensively—particularly families associated with some obscure and infrequent illnesses; for example, Alzheimer's disease and amylateral sclerosis.

3. *Alternatives to the natural extended family.* Because families move frequently, extended family relations are often reduced and many single families become isolated. Community institutions—such as schools, religious institutions, and large corporations—can, and often do, promote interpersonal relations. It is uncommon, however, for these to be based on deliberate efforts to bring whole families together; children, for instance, are often not included nor welcomed. I proposed and have been excited to be a part of a church project to create small, time-limited multi-family groups to meet in the various homes of the group members to become acquainted or to strengthen ongoing interfamily relations. Each year, at a prescribed time, such multi-family groups are composed by random selection among families who wish to take part. The program that began ten years ago with one group of five families is now entrenched and involves nearly all the individuals and families associated with a moderate-sized urban church (Bell 1975).

4. *Family crisis support.* Families under crisis are especially vulnerable to many side effects that in the extreme may lead to family dissolution. If the problems were purely psychological, they could perhaps be mastered through the support of talking them through with a counselor. But often the problems become multiple and overwhelming, even to the point where a family dissolves. Support comes often from noninstitutionalized help through friends, neighbors, and members of the extended family. Deliberately organizing programs of support has a long history, especially in the field of social work. Still, however,

new programs need to be, and are being, developed to meet newly acknowledged crises. One such program, that also involved family training, was the Family Focus Program at the Stanford Medical Center (Bell 1975; Sasano et al. 1977). This program grew from my experiences in hospitals in Africa and Asia, where families provide the basic care for hospitalized patients (Bell 1970). Associates and I set up a home into which newly handicapped patients and their families could move, so they could be trained and could prepare together for posthospitalization. This, on occasion, made the difference between a family placing a patient in an extended care facility or taking the patient home. Derivative psychological and social benefits facilitated rehabilitation at a time when Family Group Therapy would be inappropriate.

5. *Created surrogate families.* Numbers of ill and disturbed persons become so isolated from their families that family centered therapies would be irrelevant for improving their conditions. Nevertheless, they could profit from being based in a family group setting. Since, with these isolates, it is extremely difficult to place them in settings where they experience themselves as on a peer level with others, or are given opportunities to use their individual and limited capacities for others, special programs become necessary. Such a program was developed in relation to patients for whom placement in the community had proven inappropriate, but who were willing, if not enthusiastic, to try community living. The difference between this and previous attempts to place them grew out of deliberately planned bases for their interdependence. The small group of five patients were chosen on the criterion that each had strengths to compensate for weaknesses in the others and in themselves. Together they could mobilize the necessary skills and resources for independent living, while mutual interdependence led to a substitute for their natural families. Planned interdependence made possible social living in a noninstitutional setting (Bell, McDonough, and Toepfer 1976; Bell 1977).

I have cited these projects as a form of evaluation. Their need would not have arisen had family group therapy proven to be a universal method for dealing with family problems. Early on, I was optimistic about the breadth of family therapy's applicability, since the alternatives were few and their suitability was suspect. The method has been widely applicable. Where it did not succeed for me, I assumed first that the problem was in my lack of skills, or secondly, in the method. Now I know that there are families where the treatment is not suitable and where other approaches are needed.

Within the above projects and others, I have been oriented to the family as a basic social unit, and have developed methods to apply therapeutic, social, ecological, and public health models to comprehending the problems and planning interventions on behalf of families. I have maintained a need to keep the metaphor of the *family as a unit* central in my pictorial representations of reality. My own analysis and other basic reflections on my development and functioning have revealed to me many of the sources and reasons for my preoccupation with the family. I also recognize my preference for dealing with complexities and attempting to analyze and organize them artistically.

These directions in my thought and work are shown in my calling the method family *group* therapy. For myself I restrict that title to the process where the therapist always meets and works with the family as a group. I differentiate this model from others where the therapist meets with individuals representing the family, part-families (for example, the parents, or a mother and child), families plus nonfamily individuals as in network therapy, or several families together. All might regard themselves as engaged in "family therapy." I would prefer that the titles for their methods had greater specificity (as some have) for clarity of thought, order in communication and teaching, planning of strategies, attaining of optimal treatment outcomes, and evaluation. However, I have no ground of quarrel more basic than a nominative one with those who use the term family therapy loosely, particularly because I endorse and respect their aims and their successes and want to continue in communication with them (Bell 1980).

References

Bell, John E. 1961. "Family Group Therapy." *Public Health Monograph 64*. Washington, D.C.: Government Printing Office.
——1970. *The Family in the Hospital: Lessons from Developing Countries*. Washington, D.C.: Government Printing Office.
——1975. *Family Therapy*. New York: Jason Aronson.
——1977. "Family in Medical and Psychiatric Treatment: Selected Clinical Approaches. *Journal of Operational Psychiatry* 8:57–65.
——1978. "Family Context Therapy: A Model for Family Change." *Journal of Marriage and Family Counseling* 4:111–26.
——1980. "Family Therapy." In Alfred M. Freedman, Harold I. Kaplan, Benjamin J. Sadock, eds., *Comprehensive Textbook of Psychiatry*, pp. 2217–25. Baltimore, Md.: Williams and Wilkins.

Bell, John E., Joseph M. McDonough and Hazel Toepfer. 1976. "Achieving Community Living by Preplanned Interdependence." *Psychosocial Rehabilitation Journal* 1:7–18.

Sasano, Emi M. et al. 1977. "The Family in Physical Therapy." *Physical Therapy* 57:153–59.

3

The Elements of Structure in Therapy

MARIANNE WALTERS

We tell ourselves stories in order to live. The princess is caged in the consulate. The woman on the ledge outside the window on the sixteenth floor is a victim of accidie, or the naked woman is an exhibitionist, and it would be "interesting" to know which. We tell ourselves that it makes some difference whether the naked woman is about to register a political protest or is about to be, the Aristophanic view, snatched back to the human condition by the fireman in priest's clothing just visible in the window behind her, the one smiling at the telephoto lens. We look for the sermon in the suicide, for the social or moral lesson in the murder of five. We interpret what we see, select the most workable of the multiple choices. We live entirely, especially if we are writers, by the imposition of a narrative line upon disparate images, by the "ideas" with which we have learned to freeze the shifting phantasmagoria which is our actual experience.

Joan Didion

Therapy, most particularly family therapy, is indeed the imposition of a narrative line, a construct (some call it diagnosis, psychosocial history, treatment plan) on a set of statements, problems, ideas, and behaviors that one—or a group of people—places in front of us. From the moment of meeting with people who come to us to help solve problems or to cure symptoms, we become involved with a thesis, or hypothesis, about what went wrong or what is going wrong. We trade ideas with our clients, we offer alternatives, we suggest solutions and encourage new perceptions of old data. We bring to this encounter our own values, belief systems, personal idiosyncrasies, life experience, and special style. We utilize knowledge from a wide range of sources: behavioral sciences, anthropology, the study of human development, psychopathology, medicine, and sociology. We accumulate clinical experience and apply it pragmatically or theoretically. And, as healers, we bring to our work a belief, or a set of beliefs, or, perhaps, for the more passionate among us, an ideology, about what creates change.

The art of creating change in and among the people who seek, or are referred to, our services is our special province. Our set of beliefs about change organizes, and in turn is organized by, a set of ideas about causality in human behavior and psychological events. Together, this provides us with a frame of reference which describes and defines our practice. As practitioners, we are *never* objective observers; we are *always* participants in a process . . . the end result of which may, or may not, be therapeutic for our clients. Whether we interpret a communication, provide a directive, elicit a response, or if we are but evolving a diagnostic picture, we are participating in the process of creating constructs, themes, narratives with which we can describe and explain—and, hopefully, use to change—the conditions and concerns which bring people into our purview. Szasz puts it well: "mental illnesses are metaphorical diseases that stand in the same sort of relation to bodily diseases as disliked or disapproved television programs stand to defective television receivers; . . . psychotherapeutic interventions are metaphorical treatments that stand in the same sort of relation to medical treatments as criticizing, editing, and rewriting television programs stand to repairing television receivers" (1974:vii).

Family therapy has provided a handy umbrella for the torrent of new approaches, ideas, practices, and interventions which have at their core the notion of the interrelatedness of things, of man and behaviors in context, of social units as determinants of psychological transactions. Systems thinking has flooded the marketplace of mental health and the family has become the locus of theory and practice that deals with human interaction. Clearly, under this theoretical umbrella lies a haven for many points of view about change. While we begin to understand that the whole is larger than its parts, it is uncomfortable for us still, to work with the "system" rather than its' component parts. In describing this discomfort, Lewis (1978:12), refers to ant societies: "They . . . seem to live two kinds of lives: they are individuals, going about the day's business without much evidence of thought for tomorrow, and they are at the same time component parts, cellular elements, in the huge, writhing, ruminating organism of the Hill. . . . We do not like the notion that there can be collective societies with the capacity to behave like organisms." We were weaned on the worker-client relationship, reared on the needs of the individual, and reached adulthood mindful of the unique and particular content in the growth and development of each human being. These are compelling imperatives and difficult to subsume within systems theory. In practice, these issues and discomforts are reflected by a polarity in the use the therapist makes of content, rather than process, in effecting change.

I believe family therapy to be a methodology for constructing change-producing interventions, rather than a methodology for working with families, and am beginning to wish I had a term other than family to put in front of my therapy. There are many reasons for this, which time and purpose do not permit me to elaborate here. Briefly, these reasons have to do with some of the oppressive and restrictive aspects of family life and traditional roles and functions associated with the family; social changes that are occurring, the implications of which many family therapists remain innocent in their practice; and the concern I have that the application of family therapy techniques (when taught under this rubric) are not reaching those not living in families.

Nonetheless, I do ply my trade under the aegis of family therapy and, particularly, that which has become known as systems or structural family therapy (see Minuchin 1976). But I am convinced, that within this "family" of ideas, beliefs, and techniques remains a schism, both operational and theoretical, between the use of process and content in creating change.

Process refers to the repeated patterns of transaction between the participants in a system. Process is the interaction among the members of a system that implicitly defines and structures the roles, rules, and functions of those members. Process is the behavior that elicits the response, and the response that confirms the behavior. When a person is sad there is usually someone who is helping to make her sad; but her sadness functions to maintain the pattern of behaviors between them. Process is a circle of interaction, a circuit of behavioral messages, which gather momentum and power in their repeated usage. Process is behavior defined in terms of more than one: if I am weak and you are strong, then your strength helps to keep me weak, my weakness helps to keep you strong, and, further, "his" participation in the multiple transactions that maintain this balance helps to keep you and me from conflict. Process defines and proscribes the rules and parameters of operations which maintain a particular pattern. Process is a *circular* continuum. It is always in motion. Process is the context of content.

Content is the narrative line, the story, of the client/family. It is their

natural métier (as for all of us who do not communicate through pictures
or dance or mime). Content is the family's description of behavior and
events; it is history and a catalogue of cause and effect. It is shared
experience and common cause. It is a ledger of good and bad, right
and wrong. And it is the individual, idiosyncratic perspective of the
roles, rules, functions, and behaviors of members of a system, by
members of a system. It is the truth in the eye of the beholder.

Content is the cloth woven by the threads of interaction, meshed
through shared experience and bound by implicit and explicit rules.
Content is a linear continuum, a sequencing of events. It describes and
orders experience, validates or disqualifies behaviors, explains issues,
defines problems, and relates the past to the present. But content,
within a psychological or therapy framework must, by definition, be
static. It describes conditions of being or having been, not of becoming.

The work of the therapist is to transform the process in such a way
as to alter the content. In structural therapy, process *is* the message;
content is the medium. Intervening in who says what to whom and
when, *is* the message; interpreting what is said, is the medium; restructuring a sequence of events among and between participants in
the event, *is* the message; reframing the event is the medium.

Let me give you a couple of examples. Recently I sat with two other
therapists behind the one-way mirror while a fourth was working with
a family. All four of us are family therapists and supervisors of therapy.
We all base our work on systems concepts. And each of us comes from
a different viewpoint about how to do family therapy. The family being
seen consisted of two parents; father, a man in his late fifties, is a
professor of European history; mother, a few years younger, is in
vocational rehabilitation. They have two children. The elder, a daughter, is successfully completing her last year of college. The younger,
a son, has dropped out of school, and has returned home, is despond-
ent, withdrawn, unable to work or manage any contacts outside of the
home, and recently in a state of despair, threatened to kill himself.

This was the third session with the family. All the members are
articulate and tend to be highly intellectualized about themselves and
their situation. The therapist has worked well to change the perspective
of the family from sick patient to a situation within which the interactions and structures are creating particular symptoms in a member
of the system. The therapist's thesis, or theme, was that the son's
behavior had the function of detouring conflict between the parents by

keeping mother tied to an already overloaded, protective, highly tuned-in pattern of interaction with her son, so the distance and estrangement between husband and wife would not surface.

In the therapy session, the boy and mother sat facing each other, with the daughter on the other side of her mother and the father somewhat outside of the "circle," but attentive to what was being said. The family understood the ideas concerning the function of the son's behavior, and there was considerable discussion both elaborating on, and diffusing, the line of reasoning suggested by the therapist. Particular events were analyzed, disputed, evaluated. And each time the son spoke of his problems, and expressed his concerns for himself and his parents, his mother "helped out" with explanations, interpretations, admonitions, or support. When the therapist challenged the son's willingness to be the patient and thus increased the level of discomfort, his mother distracted both the therapist and her son with new information and irrelevant history. The father remained apart, occasionally voicing agreement or disagreement on some point. The sister was benign and helpful to whomever, in turn, seemed uncomfortable.

This process continued for about a half hour. Then the therapist came out to talk with the observers. We all agreed with his assessment of the system. And each of us had a different schema for the therapy. One observer suggested that there should be separate sessions with the couple to work through issues in the marriage. The other observer agreed with this but added that the father needed to do some work around his unresolved relationship with his own father, which had, early on, interfered with his connection with his son. Both these observers agreed that there should be a task outside of the session putting father in closer proximity to his son, such as placing him in charge of son's plans for leaving home. The therapist felt that further work was needed to alter the parental perception of the son as the vulnerable member of the family, and conversely to alter the perception of the son that he was needed to save the marriage.

I suggested that the therapist should continue the session with the family, asking the father to sit by his wife and interrupt her every time she began to explain why their son was so sad and dysfunctional.

Now, we each had the same goal; that is, to put a boundary between the parental and child subsystems and to disengage the son by strengthening the spouse subsystem. But our therapy took different routes—a function of different theoretical frameworks for how to create change. I cannot speak for the others, and anyway my purpose here is only to define and prescribe my own concepts. My suggested intervention was designed to interrupt a pattern of interaction, manifested *in* the session, which exemplified the underlying schema of the system. The purpose of the intervention was to activate father in a way which would both put him in closer proximity to his wife, and highlight the need to disengage mother and son. It would dramatize the dilemma, and allow the therapist to become *engaged* in the process—throwing his weight to the father, supporting the parental subsystem, and restraining the son from entering into their transactions.

Surely, the marriage would need to come into the focus of the therapy, as wife feels abandoned by her husband, and he estranged by her closeness with their son. But this piece will have already been set in motion by challenging and beginning to restructure the family's usual way of doing business with each other.

Let me cite another example of the differential use of process and content within a family systems framework. One of my students was working with a young mother, a single parent and her only child, a daughter, while I sat behind the mirror with the other trainees. The mother had been referred to us by the school where her seven-year-old child was failing, despite good intelligence. Her teacher complained of inattentiveness, disrupting the class, and temper tantrums when corrected or disciplined. Mother described her relationship with her daughter as totally out of control. The child would not mind, was clinging and intrusive in every aspect of mother's life. Mother was afraid to go out of the house with her daughter because of the scenes that would ensue. The child was also enuretic.

In the session, the little girl was disruptive and distracting, despite efforts by both the therapist and her mother to settle her down or engage her in the session. The mother became increasingly disorganized. She spoke of a variety of people in her life—her mother (who lives next door), her boyfriend, the teacher, the welfare worker, her sister—who were telling her what to do, how to do it, and who made her feel incompetent as a mother. She was defensive when the therapist attempted to direct her behaviors in the session. When the therapist offered support, the volume and pressure of her words, concerns, associations, and stories increased.

The therapist came out to talk with me and the group of observers. We all agreed with his assessment of the system: to the degree that mother felt incompetent with her daughter, she became more dependent on significant others in her family and social network; to the degree that she was dependent, the other members of the system became more enmeshed; and to the degree that these interactions became a "condition," a state of being, the child's power, her disobediance and intrusiveness, functioned to maintain the homeostasis. Or beginning at a different point in the circle: to the degree that the child was more powerful than her mother, mother behaved in more incompetent ways sustaining her enmeshed conflict with other members of the system.

How to intervene in this circular process? Several members of the group suggested that the therapist have separate sessions with the mother to help her explore her feelings and relationships, define her strengths, and support her in autonomous behaviors. All agreed that the grandmother should be asked to attend some sessions, and some suggested a school conference. Others suggested that the therapist assign a task putting mother clearly in charge of one event in the daily round of transactions between her and her daughter.

I suggested the therapist tell the mother she had too many voices in her head and so was unable to find her own voice; and, that he then ask her, in the session, to begin to learn to speak with her own voice by using shorter sentences, giving brief, explicit instructions to her child about what she expected. The therapist was to expand this theme by explaining to the mother that to the degree that she spoke in long, disconnected sentences, her daughter could not "hear" her. Mother was to begin *now* by directing her daughter to sit down with her and listen to some rules about bedtime. The therapist would monitor this transaction with suggestions, directions, interruptions, examples, support. He would need to reinforce mother's competency in this particular instance until both mother and child experienced it.

This theme, a metaphor for the system, would need to be repeated in many different ways. The therapist would need to "stroke" the child, while diminishing her power. Surely, the grandmother would need to be included in the therapy, but only after a typical pattern of interaction between mother and child had been challenged and restructured. The child, as well as her mother, will need to acquire alternative behaviors for negotiation, attention, communication, and power. The grandmother, the teacher, the boyfriend would all be functional in this process.

Therapy must challenge the reality of the client/family. The challenge must counter the usual and familiar perceptions and actions of the family. It must divide before it can multiply; disrupt before it can regroup; short circuit existing circuits before new impulses can be wired. Change requires new pathways for energizing a homeostatic condition.

In change, there is always disruption, a sense of dislocation, which sets up a counterreaction of adherence to familiar ways. Therapists talk of this as "resistance." This "resistance" is sometimes thought of as negative, or as posing a barrier to the progress of therapy. In fact, it is this very pulling back that alerts the therapist to having made a successful foray into dysfunctional processes. This push and pull, like Dr. Doolittle's "push me-pull you" two-headed animal, provides the polarity, the opposition, the creative tension which is needed to energize people for change.

Thomas Kuhn, in describing the process of scientific discovery, writes, "Novelty emerges only with difficulty, manifested by resistance, against a background provided by expectation. Initially, only the anticipated and usual are experienced even under circumstances where anomaly is later to be observed . . . . Awareness (and I would add, experience) of anomaly opens a period in which conceptual categories are adjusted until the initially anomalous has become the anticipated. At this point the discovery has been completed" (1962:64).

Change does not occur in a continuum. It is characterized by the altering of a series of sometimes disparate or disconnected events, which, at a certain point of accretion, are transformed into a new synthesis. Thus, it is necessary for the therapist to *select* the significant events or sequences, and to reframe or employ them in ways which connect to the underlying process. In order to provide continuity, in a situation which is dislocating, the therapist needs a theme, a thesis, which formulates a perspective and suggests a plan. This can be shared with the client/family in whole or in part. It can be direct, or a metaphor, whichever is the most impactful for a particular family.

The therapist who engages in structuring and organizing process needs to selectively direct her own affect and actions in effecting change. Ideas, reasons, and interpretations can be transmitted as effectively through demonstration as through declaration. Above all, a therapist must believe in the essential competence of her clients. The family whose son is truanting school today went to the school picnic together last spring. Robert Jay Lifton, in describing the concept of "Protean Man," writes: "I believe we must call into question a number of conventional concepts. I have in mind those concepts which stress a precise demarcation, the kind of fixity and permanence of the self that is usually implied by such terms as 'character' and 'personality.' I think we require, in fact, a radical departure from this point of view in order to grasp the ever more significant elements of change and flux which characterize not only our external environment but our inner experience. . . . Protean Man [is] named, of course, after that intriguing figure of Greek mythology [Proteus] renowned for his shape-shifting'' (1969:37).

Shape-shifting is a handy metaphor for therapy.

To describe the elements of structure in therapy, given the imperatives regarding change which have been discussed, I find it useful to pursue the analogy of literary composition. Do you remember the "little" book that guided you through high school English, freshman composition, or Ph.D. thesis? A book that revels in brevity, precision, method, focus, but always good naturedly. I am, of course, referring to Strunk and White, *The Elements of Style*. In chapter 2 of this wonderfully helpful book are a series of instructions for writing under the title, "Elementary Principles of Composition." These instructions seem entirely compatible with some basic principles for structuring therapy. What follows are the instructions of Strunk and White for writers, with suggested application for therapists.

I. Choose a suitable design and hold to it. (p. 10)

A structural design provides the basis for every kind of writing. The writer may adhere to it in varying degrees, adapt it to his particular needs, but a theme or procedure is essential.

Therapy is a construct, and the therapist the writer of a narrative based on the content presented by her clients, but always linking and binding this content to the manifest (and not so manifest) patterns of behavior and interaction—the process—*within* the session. The therapist constructs a therapeutic theme and uses process to elaborate, reframe, persuade, and provide alternatives. The theme is an abstraction of process that is both observed and elicited by the therapist in the therapy hour. Process is employed by the therapist to prove or disprove, add to or subtract from, exemplify, highlight, or diffuse the therapeutic theme. The theme is always an extrapolation of the system, presenting a proposition that both describes and prescribes. The theme is a thesis or hypothesis about how the system or a part of it operates, as demonstrated by the behaviors, communications, rules, roles, and functions which emerge during the session. The theme can be a metaphor which extrapolates from a volume of data, from a range of impression, and from a thousand associations, a view—a vantage point from which the client(s) and therapist can construct a new perspective of the dilemma.

The therapeutic theme provides the therapist with a reference point, a frame with which to process the multiple inputs within a therapy session. It helps the therapist to maintain focus, while enlarging the picture; and conversely, a place to attach and incapsulate the multiple images that may blur the larger picture.

II. Make the paragraph the unit of construction. (p. 11)

Paragraphs may vary in length; they function as an aid to the reader, signaling new steps in the development of the subject.

The therapist constructs sequences which order and highlight the mass of information, images, and impressions which accumulate during any session. The progression of sequences which the therapist develops over time establishes an order of priority and hierarchy for the family. It provides a form and a structure for change-producing interventions.

The therapist creates boundaries and sets parameters by indicating when a topic or an action is a "paragraph," a unit. Process and content can be organized by the therapist by holding to a given paragraph (sequence), returning to a previous one, or providing a relevant transition to a next sequence. A sequence in therapy, like rhetoric, serves to make a detail prominent, underscores an action, directs attention to a moment, emphasizes an idea, enlarges an interaction.

A sequence is also used by the therapist to partialize. People in stress—people with anxiety about problems in their lives—tend to globalize their experiences and their descriptions of events. Things become either-or, bigger than life, and thus immobilizing. Sequences help to break this process up into its component parts and to delineate beginnings and ends.

III. Use the active voice. (p. 13)

The active voice is more direct, vigorous, and emphatic than the passive. Brevity can be a by-product of this vigor; the stronger sentence usually becomes shorter.

If therapy, as Jerome Frank suggests, is the art of persuasion, then the therapist must engage in behaviors and speak in ways which are impactful. Change requires energy. "Actions speak louder than words" is one of those homilies that make a lot of sense. Declarative statements, opinions, and the direct reactions of the therapist provide a counterpoint to communication between family members, and with the therapist. The active voice employs many verbs and so can aid in shifting discourse to action, description to behavior, statement to negotiation, cognition to experience. The therapist requires a large repertoire of techniques to engage a family in change. The one-liner, the pithy comment, the use of repetition, and exaggeration, are all ways of focusing attention and dramatizing an event.

IV. Put statements in positive form. (p. 14)

Definite assertions are always preferable to noncommital statements. This extends even to the negative, which should be used for the purposes of denial or contrast, but never for evasion. The reader wishes to be told what is, and will be dissatisfied with being told what is not.

People tend to describe their situation with qualifiers that assert and diffuse simultaneously. Therapy needs always to affirm competencies—even negative ones. Thus it is better to say, he is disobedient, rather than he does not always obey; she is dissatisfied, rather than she is not usually satisfied; the two of you communicate badly, rather than the two of you do not always communicate well; she is distracting you, rather than she does not pay attention to you. These at least are definite actions rather than responses, and thus infer an expection that the opposite can also be produced.

V. Use definite, specific, concrete language. (p. 12)

Prose is always made more vivid when the specific is preferred to the general, the definite to the vague, the concrete to the abstract. The particular should be used to exemplify even the most general principle.

This hardly needs further exposition to be applied to therapy.

The therapist needs to create a therapeutic "field" that is workable, a reality that is manageable. Therapy needs to be grounded, to have a center. The only observable data we have is what goes on in the therapy session, whether this be in the office, home, or schoolroom. All else is either reportage, memory, or guesswork. Theories, interpretations, ideas and abstractions are a significant part of therapy, but they must be demonstrated through concrete examples, and specific experiences which can be verified as having or not having a salutary impact on the family.

VI. In summaries, keep to one tense. In summarizing the action of a drama, the writer should use the present tense. (p. 25)

In therapy, the present is the most secure place for change. History is manifest in the present and yesterday's experience will condition today's behavior.

If content is the expertise of the client/family, process must be the expertise of the therapist. In order to create a different experience, a new perspective for our clients, we must organize a context within which we provide the direction and the structure. In order to create change, we must be able to challenge the reality of the family within an arena (process) that is not their familiar terrain (content).

To challenge to create change, is to join, to be engaged, to be direct, and to be gentle.

References

Didion, Joan. 1979. *The White Album*. New York: Simon and Schuster.

Kuhn, Thomas S. 1962. *The Structure of Scientific Revolution*. International Encyclopedia of United Science, 2d ed. enlarged. Chicago: University of Chicago Press.

Lewis, Thomas. 1978. *The Lives of a Cell*. New York: Penguin Books.

Lifton, Robert Jay. 1969. *Boundaries: Psychological Man in Revolution*. New York: Random House.

Minuchin, Salvador. 1976. *Families and Family Therapy*. Cambridge: Harvard University Press.

Strunk, William Jr. and E. B. White. 1972. *The Elements of Style*. 2d ed. New York: Macmillan.

Szasz, Thomas S. 1974. *The Ethics of Psychoanalyses*. New York: Basic Books.

4

A Behavioral Perspective of Families

Eileen D. Gambrill

Behavior modification, or behavior therapy (these terms are used interchangeably here), has expanded greatly over the past two decades, and a significant part of this growth consists of the application of behavioral principles within family settings (Bandura 1969; Leitenberg 1976; Gambrill 1977). The first book-length history of behavior modification has now appeared (Kazdin 1978). This history reflects the variety of endeavors that are now encompassed under the term "behavior modification"/"behavior therapy." One framework within behavior modification is applied behavior analysis, the application of the experimental analysis of behavior to problems of clinical and social importance (Baer, Wolf, and Risely 1968). Here, there is a focus upon overt behavior in natural settings employing intervention methods derived from operant conditioning.[1] There is an interest in the intensive

---

[1] The term conditioning refers to a change in the frequency or form of a behavior as a result of environmental influences. In *operant conditioning* the frequency of the behavior is altered by its consequences, whereas in *respondent conditioning* an originally neutral stimulus comes to elicit a response as a result of being paired with an unconditioned stimulus (an event that elicits a response without any prior learning history) or with a conditioned stimulus. Operant behavior refers to performances that are increased in frequency by operant reinforcement. For example, in *negative reinforcement* an aversive event is removed, contingent upon a behavior, and there is an increase in the future probability of the behavior. Antecedent events acquire influence over operant behavior as a result of the associations between behaviors and their consequences. The associations between behavior and environmental events are known as *contingencies* of behavior.

Schedules of reinforcement may be *continuous*, in which every behavior is followed by a reinforcer; or *intermittent*, in which some behaviors are not reinforced. There are different types of intermittent schedules, each of which has a specific pattern of effects

study of individual subjects within single case study designs. Social learning theory represents another conceptual framework within behavior therapy (Bandura 1969, 1977; Staats 1975). Within this framework, it is assumed that there is a reciprocal influence between the individual and the environment. Respondent conditioning, external reinforcement, and cognitive mediational processes are all considered important in understanding behavior. A parallel response view is accepted in which it is assumed that behavioral, cognitive, and physiological responses may, or may not, covary in relation to a particular situation.[2] Mediational variables, such as anticipated consequences, are given a central role in modulating the influence of external variables upon behavior. Much of the research related to the influence of model presentation upon behavior has arisen within this framework, as has the initial emphasis upon self-management and self-reinforcement.

Yet another area emphasizes the application of the principles of respondent conditioning and counterconditioning (Wolpe 1969). The constructs of fear and anxiety are considered key ones. In all three frameworks, there is an insistence that observable constructs be anchored to observable referents. Cognitive behavior therapy has been proposed as a fourth framework (Mahoney 1974; Meichenbaum 1977). Emphasis is placed upon the role of cognitive processes as mediators of change. The importance of perceptions and interpretations of events, rather than external events, is stressed. The influence of various types of covert statements has received special attention to date. A spirited debate has arisen as to whether cognitive behavior modification is a new framework, and whether it is behavioral (e.g., Bandura 1978).

Behavior therapy is not a set of techniques. The importance of the variety of clinical and research activities referred to by this label lies

---

upon behavior. *counterconditioning* is a procedure in which a conditioned stimulus (some neutral event that has been paired with an unconditioned reinforcer) is presented unaccompanied by the usual reinforcement and another response is evoked in the presence of the conditioned stimulus. For example, in the procedure of systematic desensitization based on relaxation, a response of relaxation is evoked in the presence of the event which previously elicited an anxiety reaction. *Response cost* is a procedure in which some positive event or opportunity is removed contingent on a behavior, resulting in a decrease in the future probability of that behavior.

[2] It is assumed that there are different response repertoires which may or may not be related (see Bandura 1969). For example, we may experience an emotional reaction but not be able to verbally describe the factors related to this reaction, and, we may or may not demonstrate overt behavior that matches the emotional reaction. Our thoughts may be influenced by variables different from those that influence overt behavior.

in the methodology of approaching the assessment and alteration of behavior. There is an emphasis on evaluation of outcome, on careful description of procedures, on changing overt behavior rather than inferred entities, and a concern with applying principles derived from research—especially from the areas of psychology and social psychology. Other characteristics of a behavioral approach which are reflected in work with families include a focus upon current controlling events related to observable behaviors, and a rejection of special causative factors related to most problematic behaviors.

Underlying Theory and Empirical Findings

Behavioral intervention in family contexts is based upon the extensive empirical literature within psychology and social psychology that describes the relationships that exist between behavior and environmental factors (Bandura 1969). This literature provides compelling evidence that behavior is influenced by its current antecedents and consequences. Social responses have been shown to be one of the most important sources of influence. Rewarding and punishing events represent the two broad classes of consequences that affect behavior. Some environmental events serve as positive reinforcers; that is, they increase the future probability of behavior they follow. Other events function as punishing events; they decrease the future probability of behavior they follow. Events are relative in terms of their effects upon behavior. What may serve as a reinforcing event for one person may not for another. For example, parental attention does not function as a positive consequence for all children. Or, an event may only function as a reinforcer for an individual in certain situations. Whether an event will decrease or increase behavior which it follows can only be determined by arranging a contingency between a behavior and the consequence and examining the subsequent rate of the behavior. The concept of "an operant" is an important one within a behavioral framework. This is defined as a class of behaviors, all of which have a similar effect upon the environment. A child, for example, may gain attention from his mother while on shopping trips in a variety of ways, such as tugging at her skirt, yelling, or threatening to push down displays. If the parent attends to these behaviors, and if her attention functions as a positive reinforcer, these behaviors will be more probable in this setting in the future. If they are all members of the same operant, a program designed to alter one will also affect the rate of the others. Collateral effects of behavior change may also be found in which a change in one behavior induces unexpected changes in other behaviors that are not obviously related.

Family members may shape very unpleasant behaviors by withholding attention until particularly annoying behavior occurs. For example, children can easily shape aggressive behavior in their parents (Patterson 1973). Shaping, in which successive approximations to a desired outcome are reinforced, provides a valuable means to develop appropriate repertoires of behavior. Distinct differences in reinforcement practices have been found between parents who generate aggressive children and those who do not. The former type of parent is less likely to track minor incidents that lead to behaviors such as fighting between children. They are more likely to use ineffective measures such as yelling or nagging. They tend to ignore prosocial behaviors or punish them, and they frequently provide reinforcement for inappropriate behaviors (Patterson, Cobb, and Ray 1973; Taplin 1974). They also make ineffective use of commands (Delfini, Bernal, and Rosen 1976). Mothers of deviant children are less predictable compared to mothers of "normal children" (Patterson, Littman, and Lorber 1979). There is thus greater "uncertainty" as to how mothers will respond.

Research within psychology describes the effects on behavior of various parameters of reinforcement, such as temporal factors (the delay between behavior and its consequence), the scheduling of consequences (for example, continuous or intermittent schedules of reinforcements), the frequency of reinforcement, and the amount of reinforcement. For example, ratio schedules of reinforcement, in which consequences are dependent upon response output, generate higher rates of behavior than interval schedules, in which reinforcement depends upon the passage of time. The empirical literature within social learning theory also describes the influence of punishing events upon behavior. Here, too, the schedule on which the contingency occurs, as well as other factors such as the intensity of the aversive event and the consistency with which it is applied, affects behavior. A variety of events, such as deprivation or fatigue, may moderate the effects of all these contingencies. For example, under conditions of high deprivation, lower quality reinforcers will be tolerated, higher levels of unpleasant events will be endured to attain a reinforcer associated with the state of deprivation, and additional effort will be expended (Millenson 1967).

The various effects of model presentation upon behavior have received considerable attention, and the influence of the observation of models forms an important aspect of a behavioral view of how coercive behaviors, such as yelling, demanding, and hitting, are learned by children (Patterson 1976). The effects of operant extinction, in which a behavior is no longer followed by its usual consequences, have also been studied extensively and various factors explored that influence resistance to extinction. Events that occur prior to behavior acquire influence over behavior by virtue of their association with reinforcing contingencies. Antecedents which are associated with the reinforcement of specific behaviors will increase the probability of such behaviors when they are presented. For example, if a child's demanding behavior is typically reinforced by a parent right before mealtime, her presence at this time will function as a cue for such behavior. Conversely, antecedent events which are associated with punishment of specific behaviors will decrease the probability of these behaviors when they are presented. Since reinforcement contingencies differ in different situations, behavior varies accordingly. There is a great deal of evidence supporting the situational specificity of behavior (Mischel 1968). The rearrangement of antecedent factors offers one way to alter behavior. Antecedents are a critical part of chains of behavior in which a reinforcer for a prior response also serves as a cue for the next response in the chain. Disruptive behaviors of children tend to occur in clusters or chains of behavior (Patterson 1976).

The literature within social learning theory supports the influence of symbolic processes upon behavior (Bandura 1969, 1977),[3] and recent years have witnessed a sharp increase in interest in cognitive variables within some behavioral frameworks (e.g., Mahoney 1974; Bandura 1977). There is still an insistence upon the examination of performance variables when measuring effects. The empirical literature related to respondent conditioning and counter-conditioning represents yet another area that is employed in the application of behavioral principles to applied concerns. This literature is drawn upon to describe ways in which neutral events acquire reinforcing properties—for example, how

[3] These include organization of stimulus events and acquisition of mediating hypotheses or rules through feedback. Rules are assumed to influence response selection.

parental attention may become a reinforcer—and in the design of programs to develop more adaptive emotional reactions.

It is important to keep in mind that the material discussed above represents bodies of empirical data concerning the ways in which behavior is developed, maintained, and altered. Various theories have been advanced to account for these data. For example, there are a number of different theories that attempt to account for the effects of model presentation upon behavior. Whenever possible, applied efforts are based upon the empirical data, rather than upon the theories that attempt to account for observed effects. In fact, an applied behavior analysis framework eschews theory altogether. Extensions must often be made in practice when data concerning specific behaviors and factors that influence these are not available.

Originally, a behavioral view of the family focused upon dyadic interactions in which there was an interest in describing patterns of behavior within dyads in a family, such as between a mother and a child. The concept of reciprocity was borrowed from social psychology (Patterson and Reid 1970). It is assumed that family members influence each other and that the type of events offered by a family member, positive or negative, will tend to be reciprocated by other family members. This assumption has received some support. For example, Reid (1967) found an average correlation of +.65 among family members in their exchanges of unpleasant events. Family members who offer high rates of positive events to other family members also tend to receive more positive events. It should be noted that such data does not provide support for a definition of reciprocity that assumes a temporal relationship between the behavior of one person and the immediate consequence provided by another (Gottman, Notarius, Markman, Bank, and Yoppi 1976). There is, for example, no evidence that temporal reciprocity discriminates between distressed and nondistressed couples. Parity achieved over time through rule-based exchanges may be critical, rather than reciprocity on a moment to moment basis (Weiss 1978). Some have proposed a "bank account" model as being descriptive of satisfying and stable marriages in which positive deposits exceed negative withdrawals (Gottman et al. 1976). Pleasurable and unpleasurable events are independent, that is, a change in one may not result in a change in the other. Marital satisfaction seems to be influenced more by unpleasant than by pleasant events, in that a modest change in the former may lead to a large change in satisfaction (Wills, Weiss, and Patterson 1974).

Within a social learning approach to family interaction, it is assumed that whenever people live together, the desire will arise to alter behaviors of other family members, and that, often, the skills to achieve change in a positive fashion—for example, by offering positive reinforcement for appropriate behaviors or by negotiating changes—are not present. Such family members do not possess effective communication and reinforcement skills. Instead, they use aversive means to try to alter behavior, such as demanding change. Demands for change are unpleasant, and the recipient may, in turn, increase her use of aversive events, resulting in an escalation of unpleasant interaction. Or, the other person may finally comply with the demand, so reinforcing demanding behavior. Interaction patterns that are characterized by repeated encounters in which one person "coerces" positive events from another by presenting unpleasant events such as nagging, that are terminated by compliance of the "victim," have been called coercive interaction patterns (Patterson and Reid 1970). The behavior of the "victim" is maintained by negative reinforcement. Such patterns are distinguished from a reciprocal interaction pattern in which there is a fairly equitable exchange of positive events.

An interactional view of development is accepted, in which it is assumed that children influence their parents and parents influence their children. Observational studies of families indicate a high rate of coercive behaviors even in nonproblem families, offering ample opportunities for children to learn such behavior through watching others. Observations in the homes of "normal" children revealed that coercive behaviors that attempt to influence others through providing pain (such as hitting) were found to occur between .02 and .5 times per minute (Patterson 1976). High rates of aversive behaviors have been found in other settings, such as nursery schools (Patterson, Littman, and Bricker 1967). The positive consequences resulting from aversive actions are noted by children. Victims of coercive actions may learn that the possibilities of further attacks can be decreased by becoming aggressive themselves. Experience is also gained from being victims of siblings. Children may first learn to effectively counter the coercive behavior of their sisters or brothers and then learn to imitate them. If attempts to influence the reactions of peers and siblings are effective, the probability of their occurrence will increase. In one study, it was found that 80 percent of aggressive incidents observed in a preschool class were reinforced by victim reactions of giving up objects, crying, or running away (Patterson, Littman, and Bricker 1967). Learning of aggressive behaviors may hinder development of prosocial skills.

Failure of family members to employ appropriate skills for altering the behavior of those with whom they live is assumed to lead to higher rates of aversive events exchanged among family members, which will, in turn, have a number of other negative effects on the family (Patterson 1976). Family members will tend to start to avoid each other; there will be more behaviors each would like to change in the other; they will engage in fewer recreational activities together; their attempts to negotiate behavior changes will quickly break down as the other person responds to aversive events which sidetrack the discussion away from the problem; family members will develop negative self-evaluations, and marital distress will become more prominent.

Recent studies have shown the importance of considering all family members in trying to understand how behaviors are developed and maintained in family settings (Patterson 1976). It has been found that all members of families with aggressive children, except fathers, have high rates of coercive behavior compared to family members in non-distressed families (Patterson 1976). These studies highlight the important influence of antecedent events upon behavior. For example, aggressive behavior on the part of an identified problem child may largely be in reaction to an attack by another family member. The attack is an antecedent which increases the probability of such aggressive behavior.

Parents of clinic-referred children often issue too many commands; use vague commands or ones given in a threatening, angry, humiliating or nagging manner; give commands that cannot be fulfilled; and interrupt the child before he or she has time to comply with the command (Delfini, Bernal, and Rosen 1976; Green, Forehand, and McMahon 1979). Thus, the type of commands as well as the rate of commands, employed by parents appears to be an important antecedent influence upon child deviant behavior. The important influence of antecedents upon such behavior is further shown by the lack of effectiveness of parental punishment on child deviant behavior when this behavior involves a counterattack, rather than an attack upon some family member (Patterson 1976; Snyder 1977). When parents "punished" such coercive behavior,[4] children labeled as problematic were more likely to continue deviant behavior. Coercive children are often not as responsive to "normal" social reinforcers, such as parental attention (Wahler 1969). Thus, problem families can be differentiated from non-

---

[4] Use of the term "punished" here refers only to the form of the consequence, not to its effect on behavior.

problem families by their responsivity to consequences, as well as in the schedules of consequences for different types of behavior. The influence of antecedent variables would help to account for the modest correlation found between child deviant behavior and the positive consequences for this behavior (Patterson 1976).

Recently, more attention has been devoted to the way in which family members perceive themselves and other family members. Mothers of aggressive children perceive themselves negatively. The relationship between the application of a deviant label to a child by the parents, parental attitude and negativity toward the child, and the actual rates of deviant behavior have been explored within a behavioral framework. Children who are so labeled do not necessarily have higher rates of deviant behavior than their siblings or peers who are not labeled as deviant (Lobitz and Johnson 1974; Arnold, Levine, and Patterson 1975). However, parents of referred children have a more negative attitude toward the labeled child and offer him more commands and negative feedback. They also punish prosocial behavior more than parents of nondeviant children. Thus, parental attitude is a better predictor of referral of these children than the child's behavior. Such findings highlight the importance of assessing and altering parental attitude toward a referred child.

A number of factors may account for the discrepancy between parental attitude and observed rates of child deviance, such as marital distress, parental tolerance levels for deviance, parental expectations, a decreased tolerance for stress due to external variables such as loss of income or illness or parental psychopathology (Lobitz and Johnson 1974). Certainly the interaction between the unique characteristics of the particular child and those of the parent offer a potential source of explanation. A parent may not like a child as much as her other children and so become finely tuned to negative behaviors. An ongoing cycle in which prosocial behavior was not reinforced as frequently, and in which negative behaviors received undue attention, might result. Other family members may be involved, such as a younger sister who is skilled in setting up her brother to engage in behavior that the mother dislikes. Or, perhaps, the parent finds that additional attention is given by a spouse when she reacts negatively to one particular child. Perhaps one child just happens to be around more during a time when a parent is under a great deal of stress and, perhaps, he "accepts" a deviant label from his parent. As in any other situation, there would be no assumption of one single explanatory factor within a behavioral perspective. Rather, the particular factors that might be important in each case would have to be determined through a careful assessment.

A number of studies have found a direct association between the degree of marital discord and the degree of child deviancy. Parents who have higher levels of marital discord are more negative toward their children and have more deviant children (Johnson and Lobitz 1974). The relationship between parental negativity, attitude toward a referred child, and marital distress is supported by a recent study which found that the addition of marital intervention to parent-training resulted in decreased negativity toward the labeled child by parents, especially for wives, as well as a reduction in the perception of child deviance (Rabin 1979). To date, there is little information as to what comes first, marital discord or problematic parent-child interaction, or whether ineffective reinforcement and communication skills lead to both.

It is assumed that feelings and attitudes about family members are dependent largely upon the contingencies of reinforcement experienced in their presence and that the most effective way to alter negative feelings and attitudes is to rearrange the contingencies shared by family members. The overall frequency of pleasant events exchanged between a couple, or between a parent and child, may change in a negative or positive direction over time, which will, in turn, alter the feelings and attitudes of family members toward each other. Changes in the rates of positive and negative events may also be related to satiation (loss of reinforcer effectiveness) and scheduling effects that have not begun to be explored in the context of family life (Glisson 1976). Problematic exchanges between family members may be corrected if they have effective communication and problem-solving skills, and if they support positive changes via effective reinforcement practices. However, family members may either not possess effective skills, or may possess such skills but fail to employ these with one another. For example, although members of a distressed marriage may possess problem-solving skills, as shown by their ability to employ these when interacting with opposite-sex strangers, they do not employ these skills with their mates (Birchler, Weiss, and Vincent 1975). An improvement in communication and problem-solving skills, where these are lacking, is seen as a means toward the end of increasing the exchange of positive events between two or more family members.

Events outside of the family may influence family interaction in a negative or positive fashion. Some families experience constant crises and do not have the problem-solving skills to handle these. Such crises can disrupt child management skills that may be available (Patterson, Littman, and Lorber 1979). Many authors have pointed to the growing isolation of the family from traditional support systems. Isolation decreases opportunities for new parents to develop appropriate parenting skills by observation of models and limits support available in times of stress such as unemployment or illness (Risley, Clark, and Cataldo, 1976). The mothers of deviant children have far fewer social contacts in their community compared to mothers of normal children (Wahler, Leske, and Rogers 1979; Patterson, Littman, and Lorber 1979). Thus, in a behavioral view of the family, one must look not only within the family to identify events related to behaviors of concern, but also outside of the family to identify factors that may facilitate or limit the possibilities of change.

Assessment

Assessment is a planned enterprise in a behavioral approach. Information is collected and organized in accord with factors shown to be important concerning relationships between behavior and environmental events. There is a focus upon identification of specific desired outcomes, and a focus on client assets, and the discovery of environmental resources in contrast to a focus upon pathology. Direct samples of behaviors and related antecedents and consequences are obtained whenever feasible. Assessment is not a static endeavor, but rather an ongoing effort as evaluation of progress reveals the extent to which initial assessment offered an accurate account.

The following tasks must be accomplished during initial contacts with clients: obtain a clear description of problems of concern and the contexts in which these occur; obtain a base line concerning the frequency, duration, or magnitude of behaviors of concern; determine the maintaining conditions related to problematic behaviors, as well as factors that may mitigate or aggravate such behaviors; locate personal and environmental resources that can be used in change efforts, including events that will function as reinforcers for significant others (those who influence problem-related behaviors); identify specific objectives; and identify factors that may facilitate or hinder accomplishment of desired outcomes. This information will be used to select plans for achieving desired outcomes, for monitoring progress, and for maintaining changes.

The empirical literature on which behavior modification is based draws attention to the importance of a molecular analysis of behavior and surrounding events in order to understand the relationships that exist between the events and the behaviors. A distinction is made between a topographic description of behavior, in which the form of behavior is carefully described; and a functional analysis of behavior, in which the relationships between antecedent and consequent events and specific behaviors are identified. Both types of information are important. Without a topographic description, it will be difficult, if not impossible, to locate maintaining factors related to a behavior. If a parent describes her child as "uncontrollable," or a teenager describes his mother as "impossible," the behavioral referents for these terms must be identified, as well as the situations in which these behaviors occur. Exactly what does the child do when he is said to be "uncontrollable"? When and where do such behaviors occur and who is present? Who is typically not present? How long does the behavior last and how intense is the behavior? There is an effort to describe "behaviors-in-situations." In a functional analysis of behavior, the events that influence the probability of behaviors are identified. Given the extensive documentation that family members cue and reinforce behaviors about which they complain, it is likely that the complaining party maintains the annoying behavior. It is also likely that he or she fails to reinforce desirable behaviors. If the frequency of the annoying behaviors increases and decreases in accord with the consequence of attention, a functional relationship between such attention and these behaviors has been shown. In practice, such relationships are typically assumed rather than demonstrated.

Collection of base line data, describing the frequency, magnitude, or duration of behavior prior to intervention, offers additional definitional precision and provides a basis upon which to assess the effectiveness of intervention programs. Since clients may overestimate or underestimate the frequency of specific behaviors, this provides useful corrective data. Gathering base line data is an important part of assessment within a behavioral approach.

Another important task to be accomplished during assessment is identification of the objectives to be achieved. Specific objectives must be identified for each area of focus, as well as intermediate objectives that may be required to attain them. A specific objective describes what is to be done, by whom, when and where the behavior is to occur, and with what frequency, duration, or magnitude. It is also important to identify intermediate objectives. Criteria that will be used in judging performance should be included in the description of objectives. The objectives selected should, of course, be related to the problems the clients seek to resolve and should be achievable. Some desired outcomes can be identified at an early point of contact with family members. Others can only be selected after additional assessment information has been gathered.

Yet another important task of assessment consists of finding out how to achieve desired outcomes. This requires additional information such as identification of desirable alternative behaviors and descriptions of the use of reinforcers, punishing events, and antecedents, such as rules and instructions by family members. Family members often apply reinforcement contingencies in an ineffective manner and make ineffective use of antecedents. For example, requests for behavior change by parents may be made in an unassertive manner and rules are often unclear. Focusing on desirable behaviors encourages family members to attend more closely to positive characteristics of one another. This focus helps to enhance self-esteem. The parents' view of their capability as parents may improve after identifying various prosocial behaviors on the part of their child (McAuley and McAuley 1977).

Personal and environmental resources that can be used in change programs must also be discovered. Information must be gathered concerning available reinforcers and the significant others who may offer these reinforcers. Special skills of family members that could be of value should be identified. Perhaps a parent has good record-keeping skills that can be helpful in tracking progress. Perhaps a parent knows what to say to praise a child. A child may be able to ask for things in appropriate ways, or may possess social skills for interacting with his peers. A concern for locating available skills helps to distinguish problems related to behavior deficits from those related to motivational deficits. In addition to a careful search for personal resources on the part of family members, it is also important to identify environmental resources. There may be a local recreational center that a child may attend, giving parents more time to themselves. Perhaps a couple in an unhappy marriage live in an area where many outdoor activities are available that they would both enjoy, even though they do not sample these reinforcers at present. This emphasis on discovering personal and environmental resources is in keeping with a constructional approach to change in which one builds upon client assets. This emphasis is a hallmark of a behavioral approach (Schwartz and Goldiamond 1975).

Another important consideration during assessment is the identification of physical, cognitive, emotional, cultural, or ethnic factors that may facilitate, or limit, the achievement of desired outcomes. For example, the maturational level of a child or the intellectual level of a parent must be considered. Cultural norms and role prescriptions within a family may influence objectives and plans. The beliefs of family members may present a limiting factor, such as the belief by parents that severe punishment is the only way to discipline a child. The client may have a conceptualization of his problem that may hinder the achievement of desired outcomes. Client accounts of their problems are thus important to determine. Parents may have inappropriate expectations of their children that require alteration rather than the behavior of a child. Perhaps a parent intensely dislikes a child and, even though the child's behavior improves considerably, will continue to dislike him. Parents may have a very demanding work schedule, be depressed, or be heavy drinkers, which will limit their capability and willingness to participate in change programs. Gains or losses that each family member may experience if desired outcomes are achieved should be determined. Intervention plans should be designed to avoid losses if possible. Given the relationship between marital distress and child deviancy, the possibility that a distressed marriage might be related to deviancy should be explored. This is raised as a possibility, not taken as a given in all families. The converse might also be true—that difficult child behavior results in a distressed marriage. Although within a behavioral framework attention is focused on current concerns and maintaining factors, collection of some historical information may also be important—such as the duration of a problem and the circumstances surrounding the beginning of the problem. Past circumstances may, or may not, reflect current maintaining factors.

A variety of different types of information must thus be collected during assessment. The filter through which the usefulness of information is viewed is always in relation to these questions: How helpful will this be in making critical decisions, such as deciding what problems are of concern? Is intervention warranted? What specific objectives should be pursued? How should they be pursued? How is progress to be monitored, and how will positive changes be maintained? A number of different sources of assessment information are employed, including behavioral interviews, observation in the natural environment, analogue measures and client-gathered data. Other sources which are used when appropriate include archival records, reports from other professionals, and questionnaires. Multiple sources of assessment information are employed, with a special concern for gathering samples of relevant behaviors and their maintaining conditions. Emphasis upon the use of multiple measures stems from the incorrect picture often presented by one source alone. For example, parental reports concerning their children's behavior may be quite inaccurate (see Evans and Nelson 1977). When possible, a direct sample of the behaviors of concern and maintaining factors is gathered. This often involves entering natural environments such as the home, school, or playground, or setting up role play situations in the office. Thus, behavioral practitioners must be skilled in the use of observation, as well as in gathering information within behavioral interviews, and in facilitating self-monitoring by clients in the natural environment. They should also be familiar with well-validated self-report instruments that may be of help in assessment and evaluation.

The Behavioral Interview

Reports provided in the behavioral interview offer one important source of information, although, within a behavioral approach, they should not be used as the sole source of assessment information. The behaviorally trained social worker must be skilled in asking questions that have a high probability of prompting useful information. Knowledge of the empirical literature related to given problem areas increases the possibility of asking pertinent questions about related factors. Behavioral interviews focus on questions about "what," "when," "where," and "who," rather than "why" questions. The interviewer must be skilled in arranging facilitating conditions within the interview, not only to increase the likelihood that the client will offer helpful information, but also to make the client as comfortable as possible and to encourage positive expectations. Blame is avoided, support is offered when useful information is shared, and the topical focus of the interview is guided toward useful areas. The interviewer should be familiar with possible biasing factors in self-report data such as the "hello–goodbye" effect (the tendency to present problems as worse than they are during initial contacts and better than they are following intervention), and, the fallibility of retrospective reports. Observation of the interaction among family members during interviews may also offer helpful information.

Observation in the Natural Environment

Whenever possible, a sample of relevant behaviors and maintaining events is gathered in the natural environment. Since clients are often unable to offer accurate descriptions of relevant contingencies, collection of observational data is an important part of assessment. The behaviorally trained social worker must be skilled in providing non-inferential accounts of interaction, and in arranging observational settings, so that a relatively accurate sample of interaction is available. Initial observation periods focus on identifying specific behaviors of concern and related antecedents and consequences. Later ones serve the purpose of collecting more precise information, such as frequency counts of specific behaviors or maintaining consequences. Data may be recorded in a variety of ways, dependent upon resources available and characteristics of the behavior. Frequency counts, interval or time samples, or sequential notation of behaviors and their cues may be made (Gelfand and Hartmann 1975). Information concerning family interaction in the home may be gathered by means of an audiotape recorder that is placed in the home and activated at preselected or random times either by the parents or by the professional (Christensen 1979).

Analogue Measures

Direct observation in the natural environment may not be possible for a variety of reasons, and in its place an artificial situation may be arranged that simulates conditions in the natural environment. Observational data are collected within this situation. For example, children and their parents may be asked to interact together in the office where their behavior can be observed. Clients may be instructed to interact in specific ways in order to sample selected behavioral repertoires. For example, a parent may be requested to ask her child to follow a series of instructions. Analogue measures are frequently used to assess communication problems between family members. Interaction during these periods can be tape-recorded for later review. Like any other source of assessment information, this method has its advantages and disadvantages (Nay 1977). It should be noted that behavior in the office does not necessarily reflect behavior at home (Hughes and Haynes 1978).

Client-Gathered Data

Clients, including children, often help to gather assessment information about themselves or about significant others. Parents may be asked to keep track of how often they praise their child for appropriate behaviors. Or a parent may be requested to keep track of the frequency of selected behaviors of her child for certain periods during the day. Clients may keep track of what happens before and after behaviors of concern occur, as well as of the frequency of the behaviors. Appropriate recording forms or mechanical devices such as wrist counters are made available to make recording less burdensome. In behavioral programs designed to increase marital satisfaction, partners may be asked to note the number of ''pleases'' and the number of ''displeases'' received from their partner on a daily basis (Weiss, Hops, and Patterson 1973). Here too, as with other sources of assessment information, the behaviorally trained social worker should be aware of possible reactive effects (changes in behavior due to awareness of being observed) (Ciminero, Nelson, and Lipinski 1977). Client involvement in collection of assessment information in natural settings serves a training function, in that the client receives experience in defining problems in a more helpful way and in gathering data that may be used in pursuit of desired outcomes.

Other Sources of Assessment Information

Useful information may sometimes be provided by self-report inventories. The value of such instruments is related to their demonstrated validity and reliability, and to the availability of normative data. For example, changes in ratings of marital satisfaction on the Locke-Wallace Marriage Relationship Inventory (Kimmel and VanderVeen 1974) may be employed as one measure of progress. Ratings on this scale help to describe a couple in relation to normative data available for other couples. Precounseling inventories provide a range of information that can be reviewed prior to the first interview with family members (Stuart and Stuart 1972). Physical examinations and assessment of the cognitive abilities of children by reliable and valid tests may be important, as well as archival material such as school grades or arrest records.

Who Will be Involved?

The data collected during assessment will indicate what family members should be directly involved in an intervention program. Assessment information should indicate who is responsible for maintaining behaviors of concern, and whose behavior, if changed, could help to achieve desired outcomes. Family members included in intervention efforts have gradually broadened within behavioral approaches. Early clinical studies in which a referred child was involved usually focused on the mother-child dyad. Later studies have made special efforts to include fathers as well as siblings. For example, in some programs, fathers are given the first choice of problems to focus upon and siblings are included in later meetings (Patterson et al. 1975). The routine inclusion of all family members is a good policy, since family members are less likely to feel excluded and will be in a more informed position to facilitate change efforts, and interaction among family members can be observed.

The child and the parents may be seen together for the first part of the initial interview and then interviewed separately (Patterson et al. 1975). This provides an opportunity for the parents and the child to share information they may not feel free to talk about in front of each other. Parents and the referred child may then participate together in later interviews. An interview with the child offers an opportunity to find out how he views his own behavior, and that of his parents, and to make a general assessment of his physical state and developmental progress. Also, since children are often actively involved in planning and carrying out intervention programs, especially those who are seven years of age or older, initial interviews provide an opportunity to start to engage the child or youth in a working relationship (McAuley and McAuley 1977). When very young children are involved, behavioral programs focus more exclusively on the parent(s) in initial interviews, although here, too, both parent(s) and the referred child are involved during observation in the home.

There is no assumption that all family members should always be involved in an intervention program, or that all family members will change if one changes. In each case, an individual assessment must be conducted. The results of this assessment will indicate who should be involved. Other family members such as grandparents, who may or may not live with the family, may help to maintain problematic behaviors and, if so, should participate. Siblings or peers should be integrally involved in intervention if their current behavior relates to the achievement of desired outcomes. Their behavior may not be related to problematic behavior, but they may be able to help to achieve desired outcomes, as when the brothers and sisters of handicapped children learn to help their siblings (Cash and Evans 1975). Both partners should take part in programs designed to increase marital satisfaction. This is in accord with data showing that we help to maintain the behaviors of significant others, and that conjoint counseling is more effective than working with only one spouse (Gurman and Kniskern 1978). In the case of a referred child, especially children seven years of age or older, both the parents and the child should participate in interviews.

What should be done if family members who are involved in the maintenance of a problem, or in the possible creation of a later one, refuse to participate in an intervention program? Do we just forget about these families or should we examine what can be done within the less desirable format of working with one member of a family even though other family member(s) are involved? Given that desired outcomes could be achieved in work with only one family member, it seems that we are ethically bound to offer such opportunities to the client.

Initial Contacts

Components of initial contacts include determining the clients' expectations concerning counseling, and their conception of problems experienced; finding out what has been tried in order to alleviate problems and with what success; offering the client clear explanations for procedures suggested; offering a more helpful conceptualization of the client's problems; informing clients about what will be expected of them, and what they can expect from the intervention process; and creating positive expectancies. Initial interviews offer a beginning opportunity to collect information concerning the client's potential for altering the way in which he or she interacts with other family members. Intervention within a behavioral approach has a more educative emphasis compared to many other forms of family intervention, in that procedures employed and the rationales for these are clearly described. It is hoped that such information will help clients to learn useful skills that may be employed in relation to other problems later on.

Within these common components of initial contacts, variations occur in terms of how they are operationalized. For example, in some behavioral procedures, a problem profile is collected during initial contacts. Information collected is written down, including the label for each concern, who labels each a problem, whom it is a problem for, the date, examples, and the situation in which it occurs (Gambrill, Thomas, and Carter 1971; Stein, Gambrill, and Wiltse 1978). Clients are requested to provide information about current desired changes. Problem areas may be noted by the social worker that are not mentioned by the clients and that may be added to the list after discussion with the clients. Each family member who is interviewed is requested to identify problems or desired outcomes and to indicate their preferences concerning which areas they would like to address first. A problem profile may indicate problems that are interrelated. When a referred child is involved, changes the child would like to see in the family should also be determined. The child can be asked to write down items that occur to him during the week (Patterson et al. 1975).

Criteria of importance in problem selection include the annoyance value, interference in the client's life, centrality of the concern selected in a complex of problems, possible cost of intervention, accessibility of the problem, and resources available. Whenever feasible and ethical, the desired outcomes the clients would like to achieve, are focused upon. A behavioral analysis may reveal that some desired outcomes may be unattainable, since there is no access to them or to the controlling conditions. Desired outcomes that seem inequitable to the social worker could not be accepted. For example, parents may have unrealistic expectations of a child. Developmental norms offer criteria concerning what is realistic. They may indicate that some concerns do not warrant intervention efforts and that they will probably naturally disappear.

Following selection of concerns to focus upon, the task of problem definition and collection of information concerning maintaining conditions and ways to achieve desired outcomes is addressed. Clients, including children, are typically actively involved during this stage of assessment in helping to gather information in the natural environment. For example, a mother may be asked to keep a record of how often problem behavior occurs, how often it is punished, how often good behavior occurs, and how often it is rewarded. A child may note activities he enjoys. A parent may keep track of alcoholic beverages consumed, as well as the contexts in which he drinks. Such homework assignments are an important part of initial contacts with clients and the commitment of clients to carry them out is actively solicited during the initial stages of contact. Persistent refusal to carry out these initial tasks is often an early indication that intervention efforts will fail (McAuley and McAuley 1977). It is the social worker's responsibility to select assignments that the client can complete successfully.

Involvement in gathering information, as well as discussions during interviews, aids in establishing a more useful vocabulary in discussing desired outcomes and possible ways to achieve them. Clients tend to locate problems in the behavior of significant others. For example, couples in unhappy marriages often blame their partner for failure to resolve problems. The client's own involvement in maintaining unwanted behaviors is often revealed to him (her) through information collected at home.

Another variation among behavioral procedures employed with families is whether a written counselor-client contract is formed. In that objectives to be pursued are clearly defined and intervention procedures clearly described in all behavioral approaches, including client and social worker responsibilities in carrying these out, contractual agreements are clearly drawn in all behavioral approaches. Use of a written contract helps to insure that agreements are clear. A written counselor-client contract contains the following information: objectives to be achieved; interventions, including the responsibilities of all involved parties; criteria to be employed for evaluating progress and identification of a time for such evaluation; privileges gained or costs incurred dependent upon fulfillment of responsibilities; a clear method of evaluating whether responsibilities are carried out and privileges are awarded; time limits of the contract and the names, in signature form, of all involved parties. Time limits will be suggested by an estimate of the length of time that may be required to achieve desired outcomes. In some cases, the court may force acceptance of certain time limits.

Separate time limits may be established for achievement of an overall goal (such as return of a child from foster care to his natural parents) and individual objectives that have to be achieved to attain this goal, such as a decrease in parental drinking.

A written contract encourages clients and counselors to clearly identify the objectives of services and their mutual responsibilities. Contracts help to prevent unfair or hidden agendas that a social worker or client may have. Responsibilities of the social worker include provision of competent service, in which selection of assessment and intervention methods is based upon the empirical literature; offering clear descriptions of the nature of and rationale for procedures that are employed, as well as prospects for success, and any possible disadvantages; informing clients about protections that will be assured to them, such as confidentiality; and arranging for evaluation of progress. Responsibilities of the client include providing needed information; carrying out agreed-on assignments; and keeping appointments except when emergencies arise.

Contracts may be formed at different points during assessment. A contract formed at an early stage can describe expectations relevant to contracts with all clients. Early contracts may clarify agreements to start work on certain problems and specify conditions that will permit collection of assessment information regarding additional desired outcomes (Schwartz and Goldiamond 1975; Stein, Gambrill, and Wiltse 1978). Intermediate objectives, as well as desired outcomes, should be included in a contract as soon as available. Contracts may be formed after assessment is completed and intervention plans are made. Such contracts include detailed descriptions of the responsibilities of all involved parties and notation of specific criteria to be used for measuring success.

Contact Patterns

Contact patterns with clients within a behavioral approach are likely to be more variable compared to those in other intervention frameworks in terms of place, participants, and duration. This is especially true with intervention programs involving young children and their parents. The stress upon collection of a sample of behavior and maintaining conditions in natural settings encourages meeting in the home, in the school, or in other natural contexts. For example, in one behavioral program involving parents and children, about three to four hours of observational data are gathered prior to intervention (McAuley and McAuley 1977). Brief telephone contacts with clients are frequently used to collect client-gathered data, to check on progress, and to offer support to clients for carrying out homework assignments. In some programs, daily, brief telephone calls are made to collect data (Patterson et al. 1975). These calls last about five minutes. If clients do not have a telephone, they can be requested to forward data they collect on postcards provided by the social worker. Office meetings may occur more frequently at first and last longer than one hour. In some behavioral intervention programs involving young children and their parents, training sessions are held on a daily basis in the home. Over the course of intervention, meetings may occur less often and be briefer in duration, perhaps one half hour. Intervention in the home precludes the concern for generalization of effects from the office to the home setting.

Engaging Clients

Focusing on current problems of concern to the client enhances engagement in the counseling process, as does the creation and maintenance of positive expectancies, and the provision of explanations as to what will be involved, what will be expected of the client, the length of time that will be required, and the responsibilities of the social worker. It is important to determine the client's expectations of intervention and to clarify the degree to which these are realistic. For example, a parent may expect the social worker to alter the behavior of her child by seeing him alone. She may see no relation between her own behavior and the behavior of her child. Special incentives may be necessary to engage clients and to keep them involved in change programs, especially when maintaining consequences in the natural environment are unlikely. In one program, a mother received points that she saved toward a driving lesson for offering reinforcement to her children. The children were also trained how to offer positive statements to their mother (Patterson and Reid 1970). Promise to work on a problem of concern in another setting, such as school, may be made contingent on progress in altering parent-child interaction at home (Patterson et al. 1975). Parenting salaries have been found to reduce attrition, especially with low-income single-parent families

(Fleischman 1979). Higher attendance and greater assignment completion by parents resulted from payment of a deposit equal to the total program fee at the very beginning of intervention (Eyberg and Johnson 1974). Portions of the fee were refunded contingent upon attendance and assignment completion. Some clients may be more inclined to continue their participation if intervention takes place in a group context, such as a parent-training group. Training spouses to support each other in the use of new skills may also facilitate continuing engagement in programs (Kelley, Embry, and Baer 1979). Perhaps the greatest incentive to continue to engage in programs is experiencing positive effects. Careful measurement of possible changes, a hallmark of behavioral programs, heightens the possibility of providing such feedback on an ongoing basis.

Intervention Strategies

There is a close relationship between assessment and selection of intervention strategies within a behavioral approach. The information gathered during assessment should directly inform the selection of intervention plans, as well as reveal instances in which intervention is not feasible. Assessment should indicate how contingencies of reinforcement have to be rearranged, what reinforcers can be used, and what significant others are available to offer these in order to achieve desired outcomes. Assessment will also indicate the role of other factors such as inappropriate expectations of family members, dysfunctional conceptions of problems, negative attitudes that are not correlated with actual rates of behavior, and external factors that place a strain on family life—for example, inadequate housing, unemployment, few social contacts, illness, or unsympathetic school or court authorities. In addition, assessment will indicate when significant others will not participate, requiring selection of some other intervention format, such as training a child in selected skills (Craighead, Craighead, and Myers 1978), or working with only one spouse. Parents must often be instructed concerning the norms for appropriate child behavior.

The main format employed in relation to parent-child problems, especially with young children, entails an emphasis on the role of the parents as social change agents, and on retraining the parents in more effective reinforcement practices. It is assumed that they can learn more effective skills, and that they will employ these with their children. Siblings may also be involved as change agents (e.g., Cash and Evans 1975). Behavioral programs thus focus on the involvement of the child's natural caretakers. If problems are present that limit the possibility that these caretakers will become involved in parent training programs—problems such as depression, marital distress, or alcohol abuse—these will have to be addressed. The older the child, the more likely his active involvement in the program will be required to achieve positive results, since increasingly his sources of reinforcement will lie outside of the family.

The time and effort devoted to a given family will depend upon a number of factors, including available skills of the client, agency policies concerning contact with clients, the duration of problems, and the nature of the desired outcomes and related factors. For example, parents may only have problems with one child and possess effective child management skills. A high rate of success with such families in a short period of time (one to two weeks of intensive intervention) has been reported by some authors (McAuley and McAuley 1977). Additional time will be required when problems are experienced with more than one child, and when parents have a deficiency in parenting skills. Still more time may be needed when parents disagree over child-rearing practices which may be indicative of wider marital problems (Patterson, 1973, 1976; McAuley and McAuley 1977). Averages of thirty hours (Patterson 1973) and twelve hours (Eyberg and Johnson 1974) have been reported in working with families with a referred child, where a range of complexity in terms of assessment considerations was present. Behavioral programs designed to increase marital satisfaction are often carried out within eight to twelve sessions and tend to follow a more traditional contact pattern of weekly meetings. Training is usually conducted in the office with both partners present. Weekly homework assignments comprise an important part of intervention efforts.

If desired outcomes are achieved, contacts with clients are gradually reduced in frequency and duration, with special attention devoted to trying to facilitate maintenance of positive changes. Ideally, follow-up contacts would always occur.

Training Parents in More Effective Reinforcement Practices

A wide range of childhood problems have been altered by training parents in more effective reinforcement practices—among these prob-

lems are aggression, noncompliance, tantrums, destructiveness, stealing, truanting, anxiety, inappropriate toileting behaviors, stuttering,
asthma attacks, seizures, food fads, childhood obesity, moderate to
severe behavior deficits and surfeits associated with various types of
handicaps, and behaviors of children labeled autistic. A number of
parent training manuals have been written (Bernal and North 1978).

Methods of training parents differ along several dimensions, including the location of training (clinic or home); the means of instruction
(assigned readings, programmed material, lectures, group discussions,
films, direct training including model presentation, coaching, rehearsal
and feedback); the participants who are present (e.g., the parent(s)
alone; child and parent(s); parents, child, and siblings; or a group of
parents); the requirements made of the parents in terms of sophistication of learning behavioral principles; and the duration of intervention (Graziano 1977). A variety of training devices have been used,
including video- and audiotape; hand, sound, and light signals; and
communication via wireless transmitters. The extent to which parent(s)
and children are seen together during intervention varies considerably
within different training formats. Factors influencing format selection
include the age of the child labeled as deviant, the perceived potential
of the parent to learn new methods of child management via didactic
instruction or training in the office, and the resources available to the
trainer. To date, the focus of training has been on altering the behavior
of mothers, although more recent efforts involve the father and siblings
(Patterson et al. 1975; McAuley and McAuley 1977; Kelley, Embry,
and Baer 1979). Tasks to be carried out at home are an integral ingredient of all programs. The parents may receive training without the
child in the office and then be requested to employ their skills in relation
to carefully pinpointed child behaviors at home. Other training formats
include the child as well as the parent(s). For example, a parent may
learn how to rearrange contingencies of reinforcement while interacting
with her child in the office and then be asked to employ these skills
at home. Yet a third format consists of training the parent in the natural
environment. For example, the parent can be cued at home when to
employ different procedures such as positive reinforcement, time-out,
and operant extinction. Training at home may be carried out only after
instruction in the office has failed to achieve positive results (Patterson
et al. 1975). All programs involve an incremental format in which new
skills are discussed and developed only after more elementary skills
have been acquired. Close contact is maintained with the parents at

home, usually by telephone, to check how the program is progressing, to offer help with problems that arise, and to offer support to family members.

Parents are often trained in a set of procedures and the principles upon which these are based, in contrast to being helped to alter the frequency of one or two specific behaviors. It is hoped that training in the general principles of behavior will help family members to use these effectively with other problems in the same or different situations. Training in some of the important components of effective reinforcement practices begins during the initial assessment stage when clients learn how to pinpoint specific behaviors they would like to change, and learn to record the frequency of behaviors and to identify related antecedents and consequences. Ideally, they learn to use observation as their first reaction to a problem, that is, to collect information. During intervention, parents first learn how to use positive reinforcement to develop and maintain appropriate behaviors. It cannot be assumed that significant others possess effective reinforcers. Such a repertoire may have to be established. Parents then learn how to use time-out and extinction to decrease inappropriate behaviors. Training in the effective use of time-out is important, since differential reinforcement (positive reinforcement of appropriate behavior combined with ignoring of undesirable behaviors) often fails to result in a change in deviant child behaviors (Wahler 1969; Herbert et al. 1973). Use of time-out is combined with the positive reinforcement of appropriate behaviors. Learning how to shape new behaviors is an especially important skill for parents to learn if their children have extensive behavior deficits. Instructions, model presentation, rehearsal, coaching, and feedback are employed to help parents learn new skills. Audiotaped presentations of specific problems that may arise, for example, during the use of time-out, may be used to give parents practice in responding correctly in such situations (Nay 1975). Parents are instructed to use new procedures only with behaviors that have been carefully pinpointed during assessment. After successfully using new skills to alter these behaviors, other behaviors can be selected for change. Parents also receive training in more effective use of antecedents such as instructions and rules.

Training may be preceded by asking the parents to read material explaining the principles of reinforcement. Programs vary in terms of duration and intensity of intervention, ranging from short-term intensive intervention (daily training programs in the home over a one- or

two-week period [McAuley and McAuley 1977]), short-term noninten-
sive intervention (six weekly meetings), to programs that may last
fifteen weeks and include weekly individual and group meetings. Over
one hundred hours of intervention have been devoted to some families
(Patterson 1974). Paraprofessionals are often employed in the training
of parents. For example, Tharp and Wetzel (1969) trained paraprofessionals who served as trainers of natural mediators, such as parents
and teachers, who in turn implemented new contingencies of reinforcement with their children. A wide variety of target behaviors have been
addressed by paraprofessionals. These individuals are often college
students who have taken courses in behavior modification and who
have received practicum training.

Establishing Point Programs

Token or point programs may be required as a motivational system
to encourage appropriate behaviors on the part of family members.
They may be needed when appropriate reinforcers are not naturally
available within the family context, when it is unlikely that social
reinforcers will be used consistently in an unambiguous form, when
it is difficult to arrange immediate presentation of reinforcers; or when
there is a need to remind significant others to reinforce behavior (Ayllon and Azrin 1968). Whenever such systems are used, arrangements
should be made for fading these out so that changes will be maintained
under naturally occurring conditions.

Communication Training, Problem-Solving Training and Contracting

Communication training and problem-solving training and contracting are frequently employed both with older children and their parents
and with couples in distressed marriages. Family members learn how
to identify specific changes they would like, how to identify specific
positive events they could offer to other family members, how to share
information and feelings with other family members in a constructive
fashion, how to offer positive feedback, how to problem solve in a
positive manner, and how to negotiate and contract for behavior exchanges. Clients learn to discriminate between helpful and nonhelpful

verbal and nonverbal behaviors when talking to each other. The specific behaviors selected to focus upon should be indicated by assessment of the communication patterns that exist among family members. Kifer et al. (1974) trained parents and their children to handle conflict situations in a more constructive fashion, using instructions, practice, and feedback to increase complete communications, identification of issues, and suggestion of options. The aim was to increase specific behaviors that encourage conflict resolution and to decrease behaviors that heighten conflict.

Clients learn to identify appropriate and inappropriate problem-solving behaviors. Appropriate behaviors include pinpointing specific behaviors that would please family members, proposals for compromise, supportive statements that facilitate problem solving, requests for information, and asking other family members how they like certain options. Family members learn to employ cues (antecedents such as rules) for positive relationship behaviors and learn how to reinforce constructive relationship behaviors. An important part of training consists in helping family members acquire more effective methods of communicating about interaction possibilities. Weiss (1978) has identified four areas of relationship accomplishment: (1) objectification (family members need to make reliable discriminations among benefits received, situations that influence behavior, and communication options); (2) support/understanding (here, accomplishments refer to skills which provide comforting and understanding behaviors, such as reflecting skills and the use of paraphrases); (3) problem solving in which the accomplishment is the producing of products and meeting objectives; and (4) behavior change. The achievement of behavior change in a constructive fashion requires skills in the first three areas. Negotiation training is a form of guided problem-solving training in which family members learn to negotiate behavior exchanges. A game format is sometimes used to rearrange antecedents so that more positive problem-solving behaviors will occur among parents and their children (Blechman and Olson 1976).

Contracts are written agreements among family members that describe specific relationships between behaviors and consequences. The specific exchanges that are to occur between family members are described and expectations of all participants are made explicit. Contracts help to clarify roles and behaviors and discourage vague expectations of significant others. All involved parties take part in formation of the contract and entries are made on contracts only with the agreement of all participants, and only when clients are capable of carrying out the specified responsibilities. Written contracts have been used to alter a range of behaviors including "delinquent" behavior (e.g., Stuart 1971; Tharp and Wetzel 1969). Contracts are a tool for helping clients learn to negotiate changes and to use positive reinforcement and response cost effectively. When skill levels are very low and natural reinforcers are not very effective, they provide a way to increase desired behaviors in a positive fashion. As clients' skills increase, the use of written contracts can be faded out.

Applications to Marital Relationships

The emphasis within a behavioral approach to marital problems is on helping partners learn more positive means for bringing about desired behavior changes in one another. Effective conflict resolution and containment skills are considered essential for maintaining marital satisfaction (Patterson, Weiss, and Hops 1976; Stuart 1980). They affect the quality and quantity of positive and negative events exchanged between a couple. A variety of intervention procedures may be used to increase skills, dependent upon what is found during assessment. Procedures employed include communication skill training, problem solving, and marital agreements or contracting (Weiss 1978). Couples learn to identify desired changes, to generate alternative ways of achieving changes, and learn to predict and evaluate the consequences of different agreements. Modeling, rehearsal, structured exercises, instructions and feedback are used to help partners acquire more constructive skills (Jacobson and Margolin 1979; Thomas 1977). Homework assignments are an important part of behavioral intervention programs. Many couples have effective communication skills but do not use them in discussions with their partners. This indicates that performance deficits seen in distressed couples may be due to the disruptive stimulus effect partners have on one another, rather than to a deficit in appropriate problem-solving behaviors (Weiss 1978). Communication training is often sufficient to achieve desired outcomes; that is, often it is not necessary to draw up written contracts between partners.

Relationships have been found between the rate of positive events exchanged between couples and their marital satisfaction, as well as between the adequacy of communication and marital satisfaction. For example, distressed couples share fewer recreational activities (Weiss, Hops, and Patterson 1973) and exchange more negative messages and fewer positive ones compared to nondistressed couples (Birchler, Weiss, and Vincent 1975). The relative independence between the exchange of negative and positive events highlights the importance of attending to both during intervention.

As in any situation, a careful assessment is necessary to identify possible problem areas, interrelationships among these, factors that relate to problems, and intervention programs that might increase marital satisfaction. Within a social exchange perspective of marriage, it is important to consider alternative sources of reinforcement that may exist. For example, a decrease in the exchange of positive events may result from an alternative relationship, perhaps a vicarious one. Here too, as with parent-child concerns, one should not look just within the dyad but also at the individual lives of the partners and the relationships with other family members, and possible external stresses that might be related to marital distress. This assessment will indicate who else and what else should be involved in change efforts.

When assessment reveals a low rate of exchange of positive events and a high rate of exchange of negative events, intervention programs are designed to try to reverse this picture. The exact means employed to achieve this will depend upon the available skills of the couple. For example, if communication skills are lacking for conflict resolution or decision making, and they often are, training in more effective skills will be offered. It is important that both partners participate in the programs. Conflicting expectations may also lead to marital distress. Intervention efforts can help to identify partners who are unwilling to compromise, or who hold expectations that are impossible to fulfill.

There is a rapidly growing literature within behavior modification describing the use of behavioral methods with couples who present various types of sexual dysfunctions (e.g., LoPiccolo and LoPiccolo 1978). This work has drawn upon the research of Masters and Johnson (1970). As always, the specific intervention methods selected will depend upon what is found during assessment. Anon (1974) has offered a helpful series of steps in terms of the extensiveness of intervention that may be required, ranging from giving permission, offering limited information, brief intervention, and more extensive intervention that may be required when sexual dysfunction is complicated by other factors, such as marital discord, a drug or alcohol problem, or depression. Both partners should participate in assessment and intervention.

Attention is also devoted to the marital dyad when sexual problems are related to other presenting problems, such as excessive alcohol consumption and depression (Azrin 1976; McLean 1976).

How Effective Are Behavioral Methods with Families?

An important characteristic of a behavioral approach is an emphasis upon careful evaluation of outcome. A variety of research formats have been used to evaluate outcome, including single case studies, analogue studies, and various types of comparative studies, in which two or more different types or quantities of intervention are evaluated. Debates can be found in the behavioral literature concerning the relative utility of different research designs. Some, for example, disparage the value of analogue studies in which intervention is evaluated in situations that are similar to those in the natural environment. Others argue for their value in assessing the utility of methods in relation to given outcomes. Many have argued against placing emphasis upon global comparative studies in which ill-defined intervention packages are compared (e.g., Kazdin and Wilson 1978). The important question in relation to effectiveness is what intervention works best with what problems with what clients? The question should thus be raised in relation to a given problem area, given clients, and selected intervention methods. The topic of effectiveness of behavioral methods with families is so broad that only an overview can be offered here. Reviews of the literature in relation to selected problem areas should be consulted for detailed examination of outcomes achieved.

There are a number of pragmatic concerns in evaluation, including the cost and time involved in bringing about change. Additional concerns include the possible presence of positive or negative side effects, and the extent to which positive changes are maintained over time and generalize to other behaviors or settings. The importance of the unique contingencies of reinforcement in different settings highlights the need to plan for the generalization and maintenance of effects, rather than simply to "train and hope" for such effects (Stokes and Baer 1977).

A focus on altering the naturally maintaining conditions has been one method of trying to increase the likelihood of persistence of effects. Family members who influence each other are involved in change efforts. Whether the new behaviors of family members will persist over time will depend upon whether these behaviors are reinforced. Other methods employed to try to increase the possibility that positive change will persist include removal of any artificial program components, so that behavior will be maintained under naturally-occurring conditions; the development of self-management skills of family members; and training family members in a set of skills that can be used in a range of situations.

There is no doubt that many problem behaviors of children have been improved through parent training (O'Dell 1974; Graziano 1977). Some studies indicate that changes in the behavior of family members persist and that positive changes occur in relation to family members who were not involved in the training program (Arnold, Levine, and Patterson 1975). However, the utility of parent training is far from proven (Patterson and Fleischman 1979; O'Donnell 1976). Altering a parent's behavior in relation to selected behaviors of one child does not necessarily enable the parent to use new contingencies for other behaviors of the same child in the same, or different, settings or with other children. Positive changes do not always persist. The appraisal of results achieved partially depends on how long one expects positive effects to be maintained without any additional intervention. For example, many studies report positive effects in terms of a reduction in various measures of delinquency during the program but note that these effects have vanished at follow-up (O'Donnell 1976). Changes created in one setting, such as the home, are unlikely to result in changes in other settings, such as the school. Given the different contingencies of reinforcement that typically exist in different settings, this is really not surprising. Studies comparing a behavioral approach with other approaches in terms of altering family interaction have often shown a behavioral approach to be more effective. For example, a behaviorally oriented short-term family systems approach was found to be more effective in decreasing recidivism of delinquent youth than client-centered and eclectic-dynamic approaches (Klein, Alexander, and Parsons 1977). The development of behavioral programs to address troubled marriages is not as extensive as work with parents and their children. Recent reviews of the literature conclude that behavioral intervention with couples appears promising (e.g., Wells 1980; Jacobson 1978). Often, design limitations such as inadequate controls and measurement limit the conclusions that can be drawn from a study. Follow-up data may be lacking and training programs are sometimes vaguely described.

Many behavioral programs designed to alter the presenting problems of children and adolescents have included families from the lower socioeconomic classes and many single-parent families, whereas studies focusing on improving marital satisfaction have involved mainly middle-class families. The possibility, within a behavioral approach, of employing a variety of intervention roles offers a great deal of flexibility in selecting intervention methods that will be appropriate for a range of clients (Kanfer and Phillips 1969). For example, if discussion within the interview and homework assignments are not effective, training may be carried out directly in the home environment or role playing can be used to develop new skills. Behavioral methods can thus be employed with clients who vary widely in their verbal skills.

There are a number of factors that appear to be related to the degree of success that is achieved in modifying the behavior of family members. An obvious one, but one which is often overlooked, is the amount of effort expended in trying to achieve desired outcomes. In some studies, the intervention has been minimal, for example, offering three training sessions to try to alter the interaction patterns between "delinquent" youth and their parents (Weathers and Liberman 1975). The care with which plans are made for the generalization and maintenance of change is another factor that will influence the persistence of change. A critical factor is the extent to which all relevant areas related to desired outcomes are considered. For example, if a marital problem is related to a parent-child problem but is ignored, little change in the latter problem may occur or changes seen may not persist. Yet another factor is the extent to which subsequent events may occur, such as illness, unemployment, separation, divorce, or depression. Continued disruptions characterize many of the families included in evaluative studies of behavioral programs. Some believe that a sustained impact on such high-risk families is not possible (Wahler, Leske, and Rogers 1976). These families have recently been described as "insular" families to reflect the more limited and more stereotyped communication network both within these families and between the family and other people such as neighbors (Wahler, Leske, and Rogers 1979). Programs seem to be more successful with families in which the origin of a problem with a child lies in some feature peculiar to the individual child (McAuley and McAuley 1977). Programs are more likely to fail in families with widespread interactional difficulties among family members.

These findings point to the need to continue to search for variations of methods that might help family members achieve and maintain desired outcomes. For example, provision of booster sessions following training helps family members to maintain positive changes (Patterson 1974). Offering training in a group setting may be especially important for parents and children who tend to be isolated from other people in their community. Payment may have to be offered to engage family members in change efforts. Increased attention is being devoted to the discovery of naturally reinforcing communities in which desirable behaviors will be supported (Stokes, Fowler, and Baer 1978), and to the development of self-management skills that can be employed by one family member when other family members will not participate in a program. Attention is also being devoted to the development of preventative strategies (Risley, Clark, and Cataldo 1976). The factors that influence family life are so varied, including individual, family, community and societal factors, that it is unlikely that any method can succeed in altering interaction within some families. The point should also be considered that family troubles are partially related to undue encroachment by the gradual removal of more and more areas of expertise from the family (Lasch 1977).

There is no doubt that the attention given to evaluation of outcome within a behavioral approach has increased the sophistication of research methods and the awareness of biasing factors within given designs that has benefited the entire area of interpersonal helping. The emphasis within a behavioral approach upon identification of desired outcomes in observable terms offers opportunities to social workers not only to carefully track progress for case-management purposes, but also to add to the knowledge base of the field.

References

Anon, Jack S. 1974. *The Behavioral Treatment of Sexual Problems, Vol. 1: Brief Therapy* Honolulu: Enabling Systems.

Arnold, J. E., A. G. Levine, and G. R. Patterson. 1975. "Changes in Sibling Behavior Following Family Intervention." *Journal of Consulting and Clinical Psychology* 43:683–88.

Ayllon, Teodore and Nathan H. Azrin. 1968. *The Token Economy*. New York: Appleton-Century-Crofts.

Azrin, Nathan H. 1976. "Improvements in the Community-Reinforcement Approach to Alcoholism." *Behaviour Research and Therapy* 5:339–48.

Baer, Donald M., Montrose M. Wolf, and Todd R. Risley. 1968. "Some Current Dimensions of Applied Behavior Analysis." *Journal of Applied Behavior Analysis* 1:91–97.

Bandura, Albert. 1969. *Principles of Behavior Modification*. New York: Holt, Rinehart, and Winston.

——1977. *Social Learning Theory*. Englewood Cliffs, N.J.: Prentice-Hall.

——1978. "On Paradigms and Recycled Ideologies." *Cognitive Therapy and Research* 2:79–103.

Bernal, Martha E. and Juel A. North. 1978. "A Survey of Parent Training Manuals." *Journal of Applied Behavior Analysis* 11:533–44.

Birchler, Gary R., Robert L. Weiss, and John P. Vincent. 1975. "Multimethod Analysis of Social Reinforcement Exchange Between Maritally Distressed and Nondistressed Spouse and Stranger Dyads." *Journal of Personality and Social Psychology* 31:351–60.

Blechman, Elaine A. and D. H. L. Olson. 1976. "Family Contract Game: Description and Effectiveness." In D. H. L. Olson, ed., *Treating Relationships*, pp. 133–49. Lake Hills, Iowa: Graphic Publishing.

Cash, Wanda M. and Ian M. Evans. 1975. "Training Pre-school Children to Modify Their Retarded Siblings Behavior." *Journal of Behavior Therapy and Experimental Psychiatry* 6:13–16.

Christensen, Andrew, 1979. "Naturalistic Observation of Families: A System for Random Recording in the Home." *Behavior Therapy* 10:418–22.

Ciminero, Anthony R., Rosemary O. Nelson, and David P. Lipinski. 1977. "Self-Monitoring Procedures." In Anthony R. Ciminero, Karen S. Calhoun, and Henry E. Adams, eds., *Handbook of Behavioral Assessment*, pp. 195–232. New York: Wiley.

Craighead, W. Edward., Linda Wilcoxen Craighead, and Andrew W. Meyers. 1978. "New Directions in Behavior Modification with Children." In Michel Hersen, Richard M. Eisler, and Peter M. Miller, eds., *Progress in Behavior Modification* 6:159–201. New York: Academic Press.

Delfini, L. F., M. E. Bernal, and P. M. Rosen. 1976. "Comparison of Deviant and Normal Boys in Home Settings." In Eric J. Mash, Leo A. Hamerlynck, and Lee C. Handy, eds., *Behavior Modification and Families*, pp. 228–48. New York: Brunner/Mazel.

Evans, Ian M. and Rosemary O. Nelson. 1977. "Assessment of Child Behavior Problems." In Anthony R. Ciminero, Karen S. Calhoun, and Henry E. Adams, eds., *Handbook of Behavioral Assessment*, pp. 603–81. New York: Wiley.

Eyberg, Sheila M. and Stephen M. Johnson. 1974. "Multiple Assessment of Behavior Modification with Families: The Effect of Contingency Contracting and Order of Treated Problems." *Journal of Consulting and Clinical Psychology* 42:594–606.

Fleischman, Matthew J. 1979. "Using Parenting Salaries to Control Attrition and Cooperation in Therapy." *Behavior Therapy* 10:111–16.

Gambrill, Eileen D. 1977. *Behavior Modification: Handbook of Assessment, Intervention and Evaluation*. San Francisco: Jossey-Bass.

Gambrill, Eileen D., Edwin J. Thomas, and Robert D. Carter. 1971. "Procedure for Socio-behavioral Practice in Open Settings." *Social Work* 16:51–62.

Gelfand, Donna M. and Donald P. Hartmann. 1975. *Child Behavior Analysis and Therapy*. New York: Pergamon.

Glisson, Diane H. 1976. "A Review of Behavioral Marital Counseling: Has Practice Tuned Out Theory?" *Psychological Record* 26:95–104.

Gottman, John, Cliff Notarius, Howard Markman, Steve Bank, and Bruce Yoppi. 1976. "Behavior Exchange Theory and Marital Decision Making." *Journal of Personality and Social Psychology* 34:14–23.

Graziano, Anthony M. 1977. "Parents as Behavior Therapists." In Michel Hersen, Richard M. Eisler, and Peter M. Miller, eds., *Progress in Behavior Modification* 4:251–98.

Green, Kenneth D., Rex Forehand, and Robert J. McMahon. 1979. "Parental Manipulation of Compliance and Noncompliance in Normal and Deviant Children." *Behavior Modification* 3:245–66.

Gurman, Alan S. and David P. Kniskern. 1978. "Research on Marital and Family Therapy: Progress, Perspective and Prospect." In Sol L. Garfield and Allen E. Bergin, eds., *Handbook of Psychotherapy and Behavior Change: An Empirical Analysis*. New York: Wiley.

Herbert, Emily W. Elsie M. Pinkston, M. Loeman Hayden, Thomas E. Sajwaj, Susan Pinkston, Glenn Cordua, and Carolyn Jackson. 1973. "Adverse Effects of Differential Parental Attention." *Journal of Applied Behavior Analysis* 6:15–30.

Honig, Werner K. and Staddon, J. E. R. Eds. 1977. *Handbook of Operant Behavior*. Englewood Cliffs: Prentice-Hall.

Hughes, Honore M. and Stephen N. Haynes. 1978. "Structured Laboratory Observation in the Behavioral Assessment of Parent-Child Interaction: A Methodological Critique." *Behavior Therapy* 9:428–47.

Jacobson, Neil S. 1978. "A Review of Research on the Effectiveness of Marital Therapy." In Thomas J. Paolino, Jr. and Barbara S. McGrady, eds., *Marriage and Marital Therapy: Psychoanalytic, Behavioral and Systems Theory Perspectives*, pp. 395–444. New York: Brunner/Mazel.

Jacobson, Neil S. and Gayla Margolin. 1979. *Marital Therapy: Strategies Based on Social Learning and Behavior Exchange Principles*. New York: Brunner/Mazel.

Johnson, Stephen M. and Gretchen K. Lobitz. 1974. "The Personal and Marital Adjustment of Parents as Related to Observed Child Deviance and Parenting Behaviors." *Journal of Abnormal Child Psychology* 2:193–207.

Kanfer, Frederick and Jeanne S. Phillips. 1969. "A Survey of Current Behavior Therapies and A Proposal for Classification." In Cyril M. Franks, ed. *Behavior Therapy: Appraisal and Status*, pp. 445–75. New York: McGraw-Hill.

Kazdin, Alan E. 1978. *History of Behavior Modification: Experimental Foundation of Contemporary Research*. Baltimore, Md.: University Park Press.

Kazdin, Alan E. and G. Terence Wilson. 1978. *Evaluation of Behavior Therapy*. Cambridge, Mass.: Ballinger.

Kelley, Mary Lou, Lynne H. Embry, and Donald M. Baer. 1979. "Skills for Child Management and Family Support." *Behavior Modification* 3:373–96.

Kifer, Robert E., Martha A. Lewis, Donald R. Green, and Elery L. Phillips. 1974. "Training Predelinquent Youths and Their Parents to Negotiate Conflict Situations." *Journal of Applied Behavior Analysis* 7:357–64.

Kimmel, Douglas and Ferdinand VanderVeen. 1974. "Factors of Marital Adjustment in Locke's Marital Adjustment Test." *Journal of Marriage and the Family* 36:57–63.

Klein, Nanci C., James F. Alexander, and Bruce V. Parsons. 1977. "Impact of Family Systems Intervention on Recidivism and Sibling Delinquency: A Model of Primary Prevention and Program Evaluation." *Journal of Consulting and Clinical Psychology* 45:469–74.

Kozloff, Martin A. 1979. *A Program for Families of Children with Learning and Behavior Problems*. New York: Wiley.

Lasch, Christopher. 1977. *Haven in a Heartless World: The Family Besieged*. New York: Basic Books.

Leitenberg, Harold, ed. 1976. *Handbook of Behavior Modification and Behavior Therapy*. Englewood Cliffs, N.J.: Prentice-Hall.

Lobitz, Gretchen K. and Stephen M. Johnson. 1974. "Normal vs Deviant Children: A Multimethod Comparison." Paper presented at the Western Psychological Association Convention, San Francisco.

LoPiccolo, Joseph and Leslie LoPiccolo. 1978. *Handbook of Sexual Therapy*. New York: Plenum.

McAuley, Roger and Patricia McAuley. 1977. *Child Behavior Problems: An Empirical Approach to Management*. New York: Macmillan.

McLean, Peter. 1976. Therapeutic Decision Making in the Behavioral Treatment of Depression. In Park O. Davidson, ed., *The Behavioral Management of Anxiety Depression and Pain*, pp. 54–90. New York: Brunner/Mazel.

Mahoney, Michael J. 1974. *Cognition and Behavior Modification*. Cambridge, Mass.: Ballinger.

Masters, William H. and Virginia E. Johnson. 1970. *Human Sexual Inadequacy*. Boston: Little Brown.

Meichenbaum, Donald. 1977. *Cognitive Behavior Modification: An Integrative Approach*. New York: Plenum.

Millenson, J. E. R. 1967. *Principles of Behavioral Analysis*. New York: Macmillan.

Mischel, Walter. 1968. *Personality and Assessment*. New York: Wiley.

Nay, W. Robert. 1975. "A Systematic Comparison of Instructional Techniques for Parents." *Behavior Therapy* 6:14–21.

——1977. Analogue Measures. In Anthony R. Ciminero, Karen S. Calhoun, and Henry E. Adams, eds., *Handbook of Behavioral Assessment*, pp. 233–77. New York: Wiley.

O'Dell, Stan L. 1974. "Training Parents in Behavior Modification: A Review." *Psychological Bulletin* 81:418–33.

O'Donnell, Clifford R. 1976. "Behavior Modification in Community Settings." In Michel Hersen, Richard M. Eisler, and Peter M. Miller, eds., *Progress in Behavior Modification* 4:71–113. New York: Academic Press.

Patterson, Gerald R. 1973. "Changes in Status of Family Members as Controlling Stimuli: A Basis for Describing Treatment Process. In Leo A. Hemerlynck, Lee C. Handy, and Eric J. Mash, eds., *Behavior Change: Methodology, Concepts and Practice*, pp. 169–91. Champaign, Ill.: Research Press.

——1974. "Intervention for Boys with Conduct Problems: Multiple Settings, Treatment and Criteria." *Journal of Consulting and Clinical Psychology* 42:471–81.

——1976. "The Aggressive Child: Victim and Architect of a Coercive System." In Eric J. Mash, Leo A. Hamerlynck, and Lee C. Handy, eds., *Behavior Modification and Families*, pp. 267–316. New York: Brunner/Mazel.

Patterson, G. R., J. A. Cobb, and Roberta S. Ray. 1973. "A Social Engineering Technology for Retraining the Families of Aggressive Boys." In Henry E. Adams and Irving P. Unikel, eds., *Issues and Trends in Behavior Therapy*, pp. 139–210. Springfield, Ill.: Charles C Thomas.

Patterson, G. R. and M. J. Fleischman. 1979. "Maintenance of Treatment Effects: Some Considerations Concerning Family Systems and Follow-Up Data." *Behavior Therapy* 10:168–85.

Patterson, Gerald R., Richard A. Littman, and William Bricker. 1967. "Assertive Behavior in Children: A Step toward a Theory of Aggression." *Monographs of the Society for Research in Child Development*. 32(5):Serial No. 113.

Patterson, Gerald R., Richard Littman, and Rudy Lorber. 1979. "A Microsocial Analysis of Family Roles in Coercive Families: The Role of the Parents." Paper presented at the Annual Conference of the Association for Advancement of Behavior Therapy, San Francisco.

Patterson, Gerald R. and John B. Reid. 1970. "Reciprocity and Coercion: Two Facets of Social Systems. In Charles Neuringer and Jack L. Michael, eds., *Behavior Modification and Clinical Psychology*, pp. 133–77. New York: Appleton-Century-Crofts.

Patterson, G. R., J. B. Reid, R. R. Jones, and R. E. Conger. 1975. *A Social Learning Approach to Family Intervention, 1: Families with Aggressive Children*. Eugene, Ore.: Castalia Press.

Patterson, G. R., R. L. Weiss, and Hyman Hops. 1976. Training of Marital Skills: "Some Problems and Concepts." In Harold Leitenberg, ed., *Handbook of Behavior Modification and Behavior Therapy*, pp. 242–54. Englewood Cliffs, N.J.: Prentice-Hall.

Rabin, Claire. 1979. "The Effects of Adding Marital Training to Parent Training on Family Interaction." Doctoral dissertation, University of California, Berkeley.

Reid, John B. 1967. "Reciprocity in Family Interaction." Doctoral dissertation, University of Oregon.

Risley, Todd, Hewitt B. Clark, and Michael F. Cataldo. 1976. "Behavioral Technology for Normal Middle-Class Families." In Eric J. Mash, Leo A. Hamerlynck, and Lee C. Handy, eds., *Behavior Modification and Families*, pp. 34–60. New York: Brunner/Mazel.

Schwartz, Arthur and Israel Goldiamond. 1975. *Social Casework: A Behavioral Approach*. New York: Columbia University Press.

Snyder, James J. 1977. "A Reinforcement Analysis of Interaction in Problem and Nonproblem Families. *Journal of Abnormal Psychology* 86:528–35.

Staats, Arthur. 1975. *Social Behaviorism*. Homewood, Ill.: Dorsey Press.

Stein, Theodore J., Eileen D. Gambrill, and Kermit T. Wiltse. 1978. *Children in Out-of-Home Placement: Achieving Continuity of Care*. New York: Praeger Special Studies.

Stokes, Trevor F. and Donald M. Baer. 1977. "An Implicit Technology of Generalization." *Journal of Applied Behavior Analysis* 10:349–67.

Stokes, Trevor F., Susan A. Fowler, and Donald M. Baer. 1978. "Training Preschool Children to Recruit Natural Communities of Reinforcement." *Journal of Applied Behavior Analysis* 11:285–303.

Stuart, Richard B. 1971. "Behavioral Contracting with Families of Delinquents." *Journal of Behavior Therapy and Experimental Psychiatry* 2:1–11.

——1980. *Helping Couples Change: A Social Learning Approach to Marital Therapy*. New York: Guilford Press.

Stuart, Richard B. and Freida M. Stuart. 1972. *Marriage Pre-counseling Inventory and Guide*. Champaign, Ill.: Research Press.

Taplin, Paul S. 1974. "Changes in Parental Consequation as a Function of Intervention." Doctoral dissertation, University of Wisconsin.

Tharp, Roland G. and Ralph J. Wetzel. 1969. *Behavior Modification in the Natural Environment*. New York: Academic Press.

Thomas, Edwin J. 1977. *Marital Communication and Decision Making*. New York: Free Press.

Wahler, Robert G. 1969. "Oppositional Children: A Quest for Parental Reinforcement Control." *Journal of Applied Behavior Analysis* 2:159–70.

Wahler, Robert G., George Leske, and Edwin S. Rogers. 1979. "The Insular Family: A Deviance Support System for Oppositional Children." In C. A. Hamerlynck, ed., *Behavioral Systems for the Developmentally Disabled, 1: School and Family Environments*, pp. 102–27. New York: Brunner/Mazel.

Weathers, Lawrence and Robert P. Liberman. 1975. "Contingency Contracting with Families of Delinquent Adolescents." *Behavior Therapy* 6:356–66.

Weiss, Robert L. 1978. "The Conceptualization of Marriage from a Behavioral Perspective." In Thomas J. Paolino Jr. and Barbara S. McCrady, eds., *Marriage and Marital Therapy: Psychoanalytic, Behavioral and Systems Theory Perspectives*, pp. 165–239. New York: Brunner/Mazel.

Weiss, Robert L., Hyman Hops, and Gerald R. Patterson. 1973. "A Framework for Conceptualizing Marital Conflict, a Technology for Altering It, Some Data for Evaluating It." In Leo A. Hamerlynck, Lee C. Handy, and Eric J. Mash, eds., *Behavior Change: Methodology, Concepts and Practice*, pp. 309–42. Champaign, Ill.: Research Press.

Wills, Thomas A., Robert L. Weiss, and Gerald R. Patterson. 1974. A Behavioral Analysis of the Determinants of Marital Satisfaction." *Journal of Consulting and Clinical Psychology* 42:802–11.

Wolpe, Joseph. 1969. *The Practice of Behavior Therapy*. New York: Pergamon.

5

Intergenerational Therapy and the Marriage Contract

Geraldine M. Spark

The treatment method that will be described in this article is inter-generational therapy. In discussing its theoretical and clinical aspects, I shall focus mainly on the interlocking dynamics between the young and middle-aged parent and the continuing effect these dynamics have on the marital and parental relationships.

Focusing on overt communications and behavior may produce symptomatic relief in the marital relationship. However, basic structural changes will not occur unless the interlocking individual and couple dynamics and intergenerational family loyalty ties are examined and modified. In this connection I have postulated (1974) that a separation from the family of origin, even if caused by marriage, does restimulate the mourning process, reactivated from earlier losses. Facing these feelings and concurrently changing one's behavior to shift the primary loyalties to the new spouse are demanding tasks.

One could endlessly debate whether ties with maternal and paternal grandparents are sources of conflict and competition or resources of positive support and constructive influence on the nuclear family. Whether they fall into one or both categories, these relationships do exist and cannot be ignored (Spark and Brody 1970).

Theoretical Framework

Indebtedness to the contributions made by Freud and his followers regarding individual psychodynamics and the unconscious must be acknowledged. How these dynamics are interlocked with multi-generational transmission forces will be explored.

Ackerman (1961) stated that family function and structure do not occur accidentally but evolve out of an ongoing developmental process through relationships of individuals. The nature and structure of these relationships depend upon the individual family member's capacity to relate to others as separate and important beings; that is, on one's capacity for object constancy. According to Mahler (1975), the development of this ability to form healthy relationships begins with the early resolution of the separation-individuation process. Without successful completion of this early process, the capacity for utilization of relationships for mastery of later growth processes is dramatically limited. For example, insufficient resolution of the oedipal conflict hinders formation of a healthy marital relationship and family unit.

The infant begins its efforts to relate by moving physically and psychologically between the poles of symbiotic union with a nurturing person and independent self-definition and self-functioning. Within different contexts, and at different levels, this experiential ranging continues throughout life. It is clearly seen in the further struggle to refine self-other during adolescence. Blanck and Blanck (1968) have seen this again in the courtship and early marital relationship of couples as they struggle with separating from their families of origin and establishing primary relationships with one another. The couple's ability to utilize the marital relationship as a basis for further growth, their tolerance for experimental exploration with each other, will strongly influence the range of tolerance for merging and individuation established in the relationships between parent and child and between siblings. As Spark (1968) says, "Adults who unconsciously feel that their dependency needs have not been met or who have not resolved their separation problems with their families of origin, unconsciously tend to look to and cling to their spouse or children as hoped for sources of gratification. Whether or not their parents in reality gratified their needs, their introjected objects are felt as bad, depriving, non-nurturing persons. These infantile feelings may be transferred and reprojected onto a marital partner or children."

Fairbairn (1954) and Dicks (1967) helped extend object relations theories of transpersonal psychology. The essential contribution of Dicks is the theory that there is an unconscious and collusive process regarding shared, internalized objects between husbands and wives. One partner often carries psychic functions for the other. In other words, the partners in a disturbed marriage mutually use scapegoating, projection, and representation of the opposite self in their unconscious attempts to force the spouse to fit or repudiate the split-off internal objects, even when the real partner's personality drastically contradicts the projection. He believes that warring couples have a deep unconscious commitment to each other and need to protect their investment in the spouse. An example of this process is the husband who marries a woman because of her warmth and directness in expressing her feelings. His family style was one of being reserved, inarticulate, and passive, using silence as a main mechanism when his wife got upset. What had originally been attractive to him, he now experiences as being intrusive, demanding, and unacceptable.

The early family therapists, such as Ackerman, Wynne, Lidz, and Jackson, extended and integrated their knowledge of the individual to include the nuclear family dynamics. While they were aware of generational implications, families of origin were not routinely included in the treatment situation.

Bowen (1966) focuses on a differentiation of self in the marital, parental, and extended-family relationships. To help persons get out of the amorphous "we-ness" of the intense undifferentiated family ego-mass, he coaches them about their visits or "voyages" to their families of origin and other important family members. (See also "Toward Differentiation of a Self in One's Own Family" 1972.)

Boszormenyi-Nagy hypothesized that "on an unconscious level, behind the facade of the visible parent-child relationship may lurk the hunger of the infantile core of the parents' personalities, each seeking a parent-like object. In family therapy, the most important transference attitude and distortions operate between family members and not between patients and therapists. The current close relatives are the most important reincarnation of the internalized, significant object of one's infantile past." (1966:416)

Boszormenyi-Nagy and Spark (1973) introduce a dialectical perspective on marital and family theory around the concepts of invisible loyalty, filial indebtedness, justice, and the balance of merits. These concepts include, but go beyond, the individual and his unmet dependency needs. In marriage, it is not just two individuals who join together but two quite different family systems. If one does not intuitively perceive this, one marries with the fantasy that the partner will be an improved re-creation of one's own family of origin. Each mate may then struggle to coerce the other to be accountable for his or her

felt injustices which come from his or her family of origin. By improving
and rebalancing loyalty ties, verbal understanding, or material exchanges, and by urging constructive repayment of indebtedness to
one's parents, the family therapist can help the married couple improve
their relationship to each other and to their children. Instead of denying
or avoiding each one's family of origin, they join each other, in a
teamlike way, in being realistically responsible to the older generation.
The hoped for goal is more reciprocal adult to adult relationships with
the older parents and adult siblings.

In some marriages the spouses become disappointed when all their
needs are not being met. In some instances they then turn to a child
in order to have these needs gratified. This is a "parentified-child"
who tries to be parentlike to his parent, thereby sacrificing his/her
unmet dependency needs of a child. Or there may be overgiving, both
emotionally and physically, in the hope that the child will not experience the deprivation that the parent did. The couple may overgive
to their children at their own expense, while also neglecting the older
parents. Children may make themselves available as scapegoats, becoming the target of "badness" in order that parents not experience
their own aggression and despair. Then the underlying anger, resentment, and guilt feelings toward their families of origin may remain
untouched. Yet, these experiences of exploitation and injustice may
be important long-term motivational determinants.

When a child feels that sides have to be taken, he may experience
a split in his loyalty to both parents. If the marital relationship is
permitted to be split as a result of such alliances, there is less possibility
of reconciliation between the adults.

Behind many conflicted and disappointed marital relationships lies
the search for better parents and families which is part of "The Invisible
Marriage Contract." As Leader describes it, "For many individuals
who are enmeshed in conflict with their parents, marriage sometimes
seems to hold out the promise of finding new family experiences and
correcting old ones. It holds the attraction of apparent opportunities
for physical and emotional separation, a new home, and most important, a new family with a new set of ready-made parents. However,
most of these marriages are doomed to failure because the neurotic use
of in-laws can seldom resolve old conflicts" (1975:488).

The therapist begins to help each person in the marriage or family
to face these invisible loyalty ties and obligations, so that a rebalancing
of time, effort, interest, or concrete services can begin to take place.

The therapist helps to dispel feelings of disappointment, anger, and fear of trusting. If constructive action ensues, guilt feelings can be relieved and the functioning of all family members may be improved.

Assessment and Pretreatment Considerations

The usual overt conflicts presented by couples center on finances, children, housekeeping chores, church attendance, and socializing. Detailed information about the sexual relationship is more frequently withheld until a more trusting relationship with the therapist has been established. This intimate area of marriage is frequently the least openly discussed between the partners, since it often stirs up intense feelings of shame, inadequacy, and failure. Although other issues also require mutual reciprocity and consideration, the sexual partnership requires the utmost in consideration as well as comfort in obtaining gratification of one's own needs.

Some improvement does occur as a result of focusing on clarity of communication, increasing the capacity for listening, heightening the awareness of the other person's feelings, stimulating assertiveness, and encouraging more "I" positions. Yet, despite the symptomatic changes that may ensue, the couple may still remain locked in their irreconcilable differences. They may continue to feel that their needs are not met in the way they expected and may even continue to talk about separation or divorce.

A major task of marriage and family life is a synthesis of both families of origin. One goal is an integration and unity, which is workable for both adults and children, i.e., a defining of constructive values, patterns of relationships which encourage and permit growth and individuation, role definitions and clarifications, generational and sexual identities, support of creative potentials. This connects directly with the quality of relationships between the nuclear and extended families.

As the older persons are going through the aging stages, redefinitions of roles, relationships, and reciprocity are necessary in order to maintain the synthesis between the nuclear family and the families of origin and, simultaneously, to be constructively available to the aging family members. The eighth and final stage of life as described by Erik Erikson (1963) is filled with great stress: failing health; loss of spouse, relatives, and lifetime friends; living arrangements may not be suitable; income may be greatly lessened. Denial of loyalty ties often results in guilt-laden feelings in spouses and children. They may become chronically depressed, drink excessively, suffer from psychosomatic disorders, or even engage in abusive behavior.

Boszormenyi-Nagy and Spark state there is in some instances "the wish to be adopted by one's in-laws" (1973:224). This phenomenon may introduce such ramifications as unconsciously placing an excessive demand on the aged in-law and rivalry with one's mate for the attention of his parents. It can also be used as a defense for not working through, or facing, one's commitments and responsibility to one's own family of origin. A double blow may be experienced by the marital pair when "the 'adoption myth' is exploded by the non-adoption of the in-laws." The hope is that the new family will provide the needed order, connectedness, rootedness, and security.

In conclusion, not every adult family member is able, or willing, to do reconstructive work. For some, the losses and pain from the past, and even continuing in the present, make such reconstructive efforts feel as if a Pandora's box might be opened. No amount of reassurance of the constructive potentials of such a process seems enough. In the face of such intolerable anxiety and lack of trust of self, of family of origin, and finally of the therapist, termination may ensue. For many families, short-term, crisis intervention may help in the removal of one's child's symptom, and the family may then choose to discontinue.

Treatment

A first phase of the intergenerational approach is helping each spouse be aware of the invisible marriage contract, namely, the nature and quality of the bonds to the family of origin. There are deep positive and/or negative loyalty ties to families of origin, or feelings of resentment over past or even present injustics, unpaid indebtedness or overpayment, too often resulting in guilt-laden feelings.

If resistance remains so strong that neither spouse can begin to consider bringing in their parents to the sessions, or even to discuss this possibility with them and extend an invitation, but the couple still can be helpful to each other, then the therapist must accept their decision. Another approach is the one Bowen uses: that they make personalized visits (and not "social"), while trying to become less reactive to those important persons. This eventually will help the older persons to begin to experience the emerging maturity of a son or daughter. The growth process can occur regardless of whether the older generation participates directly in the sessions.

Sessions with Members of the Family of Origin

Prior to the older parents' participation in the sessions, much preliminary work must take place. Even when the parents do not live in the same geographic locale, phone calls, letters, home visits, begin to facilitate the "reworking process." The young adults and aged adults are encouraged to share historical data with each other. It is essential to focus on the emotional characteristics, style, patterns, and values of past and present generations. Were their families tightly enmeshed or disengaged types of families? What can they begin to learn about their multi-generational transmission process on each parent's side of the family? This kind of preparation smoothes and facilitates the way for the invitation to attend in person.

Adults may resist including their parents and find the idea anxiety producing. Protective loyalty to one's family of origin can often lie behind the resistance. Whether the older parents are directly included in sessions or not, they are important and fundamental persons in treatment. Having them participate in vivo and with the therapist's help can facilitate the treatment process.

However, as I have suggested (1974), the family therapist must help the husband and wife convey to their respective parents and siblings that the purpose is not to use either generation as a destructive target for the other's hurt, disappointed, and angry feelings. Fears must be dispelled regarding verbal or physical loss of control of the adult's underlying angry feelings about past injustices committed by their parents. The tentative aims are steadily clarified: more adult-to-adult understanding and improved overall relationships. This can only develop as old feelings and accounts are faced and reworked.

And, as Framo states it, "The client, by having sessions with his or her own family of origin, takes the problems back to where they began, thereby making available a direct route to etiological factors. Dealing with real, external parental figures is designed to loosen the grip of the internal representatives of these figures and expose them to reality consideration and their live derivatives. Having gone backward in time, the individual can then move forward in dealing with the spouse and children in a more appropriate fashion, since their transference meaning has changed. This view of the relationship between the intrapsychic and transactional spheres constitutes the core of this theoretical orientation'' (1976:194).

The therapist tries to facilitate the dialogue between family members in order to help them clarify what issues from the past have remained unresolved in the present relationship. For example, are they still enmeshed with each other or overly distanced with each other? How is their current relationship affecting each other—and the other important people in their lives? Is it negative and destructive—or positive and supportive in this phase of their lives? Do they define it as being more adult-to-adult or has it remained fixed in the roles of parent and small child.

The therapist helps each one tolerate the painful aspects with which each one confronts the other. The goals, however, are to mend and improve the communications and understanding between them; they need to find new ways of meeting each other's current needs. Understanding in itself does not automatically produce constructive action. Mutual efforts need to be made in order that behavior changes occur. The therapist is an active participant in helping them in this difficult process.

Even after the therapist has been able to convey the potential value and meaning grandparental sessions might have, they require the support of each partner. The option of who goes first is left up to the couple. It is equally necessary to clarify why a son or daughter-in-law (and grandchildren) should not be included. It helps remove any shame or humiliation regarding secrets or history that older persons may not be comfortable discussing in front of an in-law and/or children. This way, accusatory or scapegoating tactics may be minimized or discouraged. One mother-in-law was furious at the therapist, claiming she had no problem with her son, that all their difficulties were due to her daughter-in-law and her family. This effort to ''scapegoat'' the daughter-in-law was her way of trying to resist and avoid the issues between her son and herself.

The clinical material will help reveal the nature of the current communications and relationships. The early identification and separation process is described as well as unresolved conflicts between the older parent and her son. Reference is also made regarding relationships between the previous generations.

Clinical Illustration

The young couple in their early thirties presented themselves as considering separation or divorce. Their disagreements centered on how and when money was to be spent (the wife being the main breadwinner), housekeeping chores, sexual incompatibility, and social activities. Their relationship could be characterized as more like a parent-child rather than as husband and wife. Both of them were highly educated, intelligent, and less openly conflictual than many other young couples. Each one had lost a father via divorce at a young age. The wife's mother had remarried but the husband's mother had not. It became readily evident that the wife remained currently involved as the parentified daughter, i.e., the caretaker of her own mother. A session was held with her maternal grandmother, aunt, and mother, which was stormy and chaotic because of a continuing family feud among all of them. The husband's session with his mother, who lived out of the state, is being presented. He was more guilt-ridden and immature than his wife. He was more dissatisfied with his overdependent functioning.

Joe's (the designated patient's) mother had not visited her son's home for over a year. There was veiled hostility between the daughter-in-law and mother-in-law and this visit was dreaded. Letters and phone calls had prepared the way. Joe had also reconnected with, and started to visit, his remarried father, whom he had not seen for two years.

Ther: What do you each know about the other's current lives?

Joe I hardly write but I know my brother and sister do not write and I feel guilty about this.

Mo: You do what you can and need not feel guilt.

Joe: It depends on how you feel about me not writing. If I'm not writing and hurting you then I feel guilty; or, if not writing hurts you then it is something to feel guilty about.

Mo: I wrote every week to my parents—whether I had anything to say or not—my brother never writes to me or to my parents.

Ther: Do you and Joe still need something from each other?

(They begin to describe and weave in the historical past relationships with the existing one.)

Joe: I was given a lot of independence when I was a kid—I don't know why—but I felt a lot of responsibility all my life—I carried it pretty well. Of all three children I never violated your trust, created no problems.

I was such a responsible kid—and never dated in high school. I love you, enjoy you. Other parents and children are really bitter. We never fought, like others. My younger brother Bill fights more. He can criticize you—there is more interchange. Me, I'm more of a reserved person, not necessarily bad.

Mo: I tried to help each of them to be independent, especially the last one, who may stay home and feel sorry for the mother. Other women do not even have children. Whatever I get, I feel lucky.

Ther: (*to mother*) There seems to be a special closeness between you. Joe had to be so good, not to add onto your burdens. Would he feel too guilty if he were to assert himself more?

Mo: He is like I am, willing to wait and not voice it; wait till I can get what I want. If it is really unpleasant enough, I will fight for it.

Ther: (*to mother*) Has Joe had to distance himself too much because of the special closeness, having to be super-careful and thoughtful?

Joe: Realistically, she handled my brother's and sisters' reactions. I suffered in silence instead—and wanted help. It would have been the last straw—for me to do this. Mother, I was scared to bring it up to you. I have a hard time asking for things. It's not always good.

Mo: I'm the same.

Ther: What's your reaction to your mother's pattern of waiting rather than have an open confrontation, or asserting herself?

Joe: I do that in some relationships, but not in my marriage—that's good but other relationships are hurting—and it also puts too much burden on my marriage, and too much importance. The difficulty people have with me is that they just don't know what I want; if they care they don't know how to show it or do anything for me—because everything is always all right with me. People find me a nice person, but I don't have many close friends. I'm like you are—
(The therapist thinks it would be helpful to focus also on the divorced husband and father who continues to play a significant part in their lives.)

Ther: What about Joe's father?

Mo: They haven't been with him—

Ther: What was your ex-husband like?

Mo: Aggressive—competitive, very insecure, and he'll do anything to win; threatens; and talks—he gives a good line.

Joe: Now I see my father differently. I'm more assertive and direct than he, which surprises me.

Mo: More honest.

Joe: And more secure—Bill [younger brother] and my father can be hurt easily. In the past I was afraid because he could hurt me. Now it is different, as compared to the past. It's a scary position to be in, since I avoid saying things that might hurt him even though you know they are true. It doesn't put me in a good light because I want to be more direct. I see dad as insecure, tooting his own horn. Misguided things. He tells me I'm my grandparents' favorite grandson. I don't believe it; they never said it to me—to make me feel good. Or how much he loves me—saying I did something in college which I hadn't done.

Ther: Is he trying to make amends for his past hurtful behavior?

Mo: He still feels very guilty—I just received two letters about himself, his work, his parents—

Ther: Are you over the hurt about him?

Mo: I think so (*laughs*); harder on the children.

Ther: Yet you never replaced him.

Mo: Oh, I still have this feeling for my father—my husband (*slip*), there's a love there of course.

Ther: What about the forgiveness of what he did to you, or the children?

Mo: I'll never forgive him for the children. But as far as I'm concerned, when the divorce came it was psychologically easier to cope with life.

Ther: (*to Joe*) What about your hurt?

Joe: The hurt part is not clear, but I was really scared of him—centered about his violence; upset and shocked when I heard you got a divorce. I was away from the city.

Ther: Does Joe blame you too?

Mo: Yes, because I didn't keep his father there—as if I broke it up and then they didn't have a father.

Joe: As a child, I did not blame you—the thing that would bother me though—you just described dad as aggressive. What it teaches me is that being assertive is bad, as if that's how you use women, how you destroy people.

Mo: You said it twice, you assume that he's bad?

Joe: He did wrong things, bad things, he abandoned his kids and wife—he also abandoned his parents.
(Despite the mother's legal divorce, the marriage commitment and involvement still center around the aging paternal grandparents, even more than her children. Joe continues to struggle with his divided loyalty with his parents.)

Ther: We got off the blame subject.

Mo: I don't consider Joe's father as bad as opposed to good.

Joe: That's the feeling I got—and it made it feel difficult, as if being assertive was not okay; especially bad if you are a man.

Mo: I tried not to give to the children a wrong impression—especially when you are hurting. The kids feel it.

Joe: I understood that.

Ther: What I think is good today is that you both can talk about it, since it did cost you both something. Joe, what brings the tears to your eyes?

Joe: As you said—we are talking about things that matter—I just said something that hurt your feelings, about dad and how it made it rough on me, and right away you felt bad—and I think I hurt you—and so you had to explain yourself.
(Spontaneously, the mother then began to connect these feelings with her family of origin, namely how she, like Joe, also has split loyalty ties as far as parents are concerned. They both are guilt-ridden and thus bound to each other.)

Ther: There's another part of this that may directly connect with Joe. If Joe's father has hurt you so badly, its almost as if Joe has to bend over backwards to be super-kind and nice and adult with you. As compared with the usual son's exchanges, who might be able to express resentment or anger. It's as if Joe has to make up for what his father did to you.

Mo: And he can't be natural with me or do the things you really feel inside because of this other thing that happened—

Ther: (*to Joe*) Does this make sense to you?

Joe: I was very aware—of how dad hurt you and therefore have to avoid doing the same thing and that gets into the assertive thing. But to think about hurting you, gets into—I remember how you worked when we were kids, taught school, cooked, washed dishes, marked papers, cleaned . . .
(The overprotectiveness and overgiving of the mother still continue to bind Joe to her as a result of her martyrlike behavior.)

Afterwards, the couple reported that a discussion with the mother-in-law continued well into the night. Before going to bed, the mother-in-law embraced her daughter-in-law for the first time and thanked them for the heart-to-heart talk. She had never revealed herself in such a personal and close way before.

Discussion

Such sessions are only a beginning of the relational reworking process. They provide an opportunity for each one to learn new and more detailed information regarding the parent's earlier life experiences. There is an initial attempt to clarify the effects on and possible costs that have been paid by family members. They abreact the painful feelings that are connected with multi-generational injustices and unpaid indebtedness. But finally, and most essentially, they focus on what can be changed and rebalanced in the here and now in order to meet the existing needs in each one's current phase of life.

On an individual level, for the first time, Joe was able to confront his mother with why he had been so overprotective with her and the effect it has now had on other close relationships. They both could see that he had merely transferred his dependency from his mother to his wife. For him to be assertive or aggressive was equated with being like his father, who was considered a bad and disloyal person. Inability to state his needs and secure their gratification had been an overwhelming obstacle in his capacity for marital intimacy and closeness with friends and colleagues.

Joe's mother seemed to have remained locked in a negative and split loyalty tie to her own parents. In adopting her in-laws as substitute parents and family, she has bypassed her parents, even though she has continued to dutifully write letters and visit them once a year. She has even permitted her ex-husband to hand over to her the total responsibility for his parents' welfare—at a price to herself.

Essentially she is the martyred, self-sacrificing person who unconsciously attempts to make others feel guilty in her excessive overgiving and overavailability. In reality, her dedication and supreme loyalty to her in-laws cover her own emptiness and loneliness and provide justification for her existence. Beneath the facade, there is vulnerability and an inability to obtain self-gratification; nor does she permit anyone to give to her.

Joe and his siblings were thus bound, albeit in different ways, in an excessively guilt-laden family system. As a result, they have great difficulty in extricating themselves in a comfortable and maturely independent way, especially as they were aware that their mother had so little gratification in her personal life.

As Joe and his wife continued to work in therapy, they became a supportive team in dealing with the obligations and responsibilities for each one's family of origin. Instead of using each other as objects on whom to project all their old despair, rage, and guilt feelings, they began to be supportive of the efforts each one was making on his or her "unfinished business" with his family of origin.

In having each one face his multi-generational transmission process, including his "assigned and assumed roles," they were able to more effectively differentiate between what was objective reality and what were essentially "transference" feelings.

As they moved toward "mature dependence" between them, the relationship was more peerlike, in contrast to the earlier one, which presented an imbalanced parent-child level.

Conclusions

Traditional marriage therapy, which focuses on overt issues in the relationship, can effect symptomatic changes. However, for structural changes to occur, the unconscious and collusive aspect of the marital relationship and the transgenerational transmission process should be faced and dealt with.

The inclusion in the therapy process of one or both sets of parents can facilitate fundamental and constructive change. This requires new forms of involvement such as time, interest, concern, or even concrete services, especially if the older persons are in any way incapacitated.

The intergenerational approach in marriage or family therapy requires modification in existing attitudes and understanding on the part of professionals as well as those couples and families who are requesting help.

This approach is applicable to all classes of society, depending on a person's capacity to trust, and a willingness to engage in, such a process. Every person, regardless of education and cultural background is in need of a family support system. While most of the poor and disorganized families look to social and legal organizations for such support, it is our responsibility also to reexplore with them the possibilities of reconnecting with those adults who shared in their lives, i.e., even with foster-parents whom they may have not seen for a number of years.

All the services offered in the community, and government benefits such as social security and medicare, are not substitutes for the human involvement, commitment, and sense of responsibility that may exist between family members.

References

Ackerman, N. A. 1961. "Dynamic Frame for the Clinical Approach to Family Conflict." In N. Ackerman, F. Beatman, and S. Sherman, eds., *Exploring the Base for Family Conflict,* pp. 52–67. New York: Family Service Association of America.

Blanck, G. and R. Blanck. 1968. *Marriage and Personal Development.* New York: Columbia University Press.

Bowen, M. 1966. "The Use of Family Theory in Clinical Practice." *Comprehensive Psychiatry.* 7(5):345–47.

Boszormenyi-Nagy, I. 1966. "From Family Therapy to a Psychology of Relationship: Fictions of the Individual and Fictions of the Family." *Comprehensive Psychiatry.* 7(5):408–423.

Boszormenyi-Nagy, I. and Spark, G. 1973. *Invisible Loyalties: Reciprocity in Intergenerational Family Therapy.* New York: Harper and Row.

Dicks, H. V. 1967. *Marital Tensions.* New York: Basic Books.

Erikson, Erik H. 1963. *Childhood and Society.* New York: Norton.

Fairbairn, W. R. D. 1954. *An Object-Relations Theory of the Personality.* New York: Basic Books.

Framo, J. L. 1976. "Family of Origins as a Therapeutic Resource for Adults in Marital and Family Therapy: You Can and Should Go Home Again." *Family Process* 15(2):193–210.

Leader, A. L. 1975. "The Place of In-Laws in Marital Relationships." *Social Casework* 5,6,8:488.

Mahler, M., F. Pine, and A. Bergman. 1975. *The Psychological Birth of the Human Infant-Symbiosis and Individuation*. New York: Basic Books.

Spark, G. M. "Parental Involvement in Family Therapy." *Journal of Marriage and the Family* 30(1):111–18.

——1974. "Grandparents and Intergenerational Family Therapy." *Family Process* 13(2):

Spark, G. M. and E. Brody. 1970. "The Aged are Family Members." *Family Process* 9:195–210.

"Toward the Differentiation of a Self in One's Own Family." In J. Framo, ed., *Family Interaction*. pp. 111–66. New York: Springer.

6

An Ecological Model with an Emphasis on Ethnic Families

JOHN P. SPIEGEL, M.D.

Since I am to write about an ecological approach to ethnic families, it is important at the outset to provide the reader with a map of the field of family therapy within which to place this approach. Therefore I believe it will be useful to sketch an outline of these similarities and differences into which one may plug the ecological—or, in my terminology—the *transactional field* approach. Remember that a map is not an exhaustive or an in-depth analysis. It is just a quick survey of the landscape.

Commonalities

Let us begin with the similarities. All family therapies hold in common certain ideological assumptions. Therapies may differ in the degree to which the assumptions are articulated or held at the center of attention, but the assumptions can be located at either the explicit or implicit level in the approach to theory, diagnosis, and treatment. These assumptions can be grouped under three organizing themes: systems perspective; structuralism; interdisciplinary orientation.

1. Systems Perspective

If a practitioner is a family therapist in any meaningful sense, he will pay as much attention to the family, whether nuclear or extended, as a system of interaction processes as he will to the individual who happens to be the identified patient or client. He will assume that if he is going to be able to help the identified patient, he will have to help the family change some of the habitual—or ritual—ways in which they interact, and which produce an insoluble problem for the patient. He will expect, as in any human problem, to encounter *resistance* to change and he will probably ascribe the resistance to a *homeostatic* mechanism which has become well established within the family system. Any variation or deviation from the basic routines of family interaction will be countered by a reaction among the members which restores the previous balance, no matter how pathological its effects for a given family member. In addition, the therapist's interest in the way the identified patient gets trapped in dysfunctional interactions will reduce his concern with the particular psychopathological label that others may have attached to the patient. For particular purposes of research or epidemiology, he may focus on diagnostic terminology; but when he is seeing a family, his attention goes to process rather than diagnostic outcome or any necessarily fixed internal state of the individual. It is the internal state of the family that is of concern.

2. Structuralism

In general, family therapists are structuralists in the sense of Lévi-Strauss and the Chomskian linguists—a point of view backed up by the long tradition of psychoanalysis. The observed behavior of family members is a surface phenomenon, generated by deeper and unobservable layers of structure which must be inferred. The various schools of family theorists infer the deeper structures under varying conceptualizations, but all of them look for hidden patterns, distorted or disguised interactions, disqualifications, metamessages operating at a level opposite to the message conveyed, unappreciated ego-masses, undiscovered coalitions, triads, rubber boundaries, pseudo-mutualities, schisms and skews, cultural value systems, or whatever. The task of the therapist, then, is to bring these deeper layers to the surface, so that family members can look at them and do something about them.

3. Interdisciplinary Orientation

As a rule, family therapists bring their professional or disciplinary training into their understanding of family process not as a rigid set of guidelines but as their contribution to the pooled effort involved in the treatment process. Each profession has something to give and to learn from the others. Cotherapists, for example, are often from different disciplines. Despite the tendencies of psychiatrists to consider themselves *primus inter pares*, theoretical and pragmatic contributions to the therapeutic process have frequently, as in the case of Jay Haley (1976) and Gregory Bateson (1972), emanated from outside of the helping professions. Sociologists, social psychologists, and psychiatric nurses have played a role in advancing the field. This openness to outside influences is more characteristic of family therapy than of any other treatment technology.

Divergences

The differences between the models emerge from two sets of dichotomies: (1) theoretical concepts borrowed from one field and then applied to family therapy versus a theoretical approach growing out of the direct experience with family therapy; and (2) narrowness of focus on just the family versus a breadth of vistas to include wider institutional contexts.

With respect to the first point, some family therapists have based their work on psychoanalytic or psychodynamic theory arising out of work with individuals and have simply broadened the theory to include the way the therapist interacts with the different family members. This approach grew out of child psychiatry, where the therapist always looked at mother-child interactions and sometimes saw one or another parent as a part of the therapeutic process, as exemplified in the early work of Nathan Ackerman (1958), James Framo (1965), and Ivan Boszormenyi-Nagy (1962). The theory of small group psychotherapy, as in the work of John E. Bell, has also been transferred and modified for application to the family as a group. Similarly, learning theory, or behavior modification techniques (Mash, Hamerlynck, and Handy, 1975), frequently with the addition of cognitive theoretical components, have been applied in family therapy. Some borrowing of theory and technique is inevitable, since we all stand on the shoulders of our predecessors. What is significant here is that the borrowed technique, for example in the case of the behavioral approaches, is made a central issue.

This borrowing stands in some contrast to the theory and techniques that have grown out of direct experience. Examples of this sort of innovative and creative coping with the direct experience encountered in working with families are Bowen's (1978) model, the structural approach developed by Salvador Minuchin and his coworkers at the Philadelphia Child Guidance Clinic, and methods of focused problem resolution currently used at the Mental Research Institute in Palo Alto, California. These theoretical and technical innovations are presented elsewhere in this book (articles 3, 7, and 8) and need no detailed comment here. My referring to these models is for the sake of placing them on my "map," since the belief is sometimes expressed that the models being presented in this volume are really all equivalent to each other. My view, on the other hand, is that we are faced with fundamental differences, so basic that the different approaches cannot be seen as equivalent to each other.

For example, the innovative aspects of the structural and problem-solving approaches are often so at odds with both common sense and with traditional psychodynamic theory as to require a 180-degree switch in the mind-set of the therapist. They both require, often from the first interview, a direct and sometimes dramatic intervention by the therapist, which bypasses the surface phenomenon to get to the deeper structures activating the family interactions. This is some contrast to the "wait-and-see," minimal interpretive techniques of the psychodynamically oriented therapists. Where the issue is "common sense," the intervention is more complex, since it frequently features a paradoxical form of communication which is alien both to the logic of ordinary communications and to the interpretive procedures of the psychodynamic approach. Similarly, both the structural and problem-solving models tend to focus on the "here and now" of dysfunctional family transactions, while waiting for the appearance of the developmental childhood experiences of family members insofar as this past history influences current behavior. Within the general context of extremely active interventions made for the purpose of surfacing hidden interaction patterns, other techniques, such as "family sculpting," or "guided fantasy," borrowed from gestalt techniques, often play a role.

The point I wish to make here, with respect to the geography of the "map," is that one could not have predicted the emergence of these innovative approaches from a knowledge of the prior history of the field of social work. By the same token, one cannot, at this stage, predict their relevance to the future of social work. Like all other human endeavors, the field of social service changes only very slowly. Although it is necessary to keep an open mind, it is not yet apparent, for example, how the technique of paradoxical communication can be useful to the human services generally.

Specialization versus Breadth of Institutional Contexts

The models discussed so far have been concerned almost exclusively with the family as a system in its own right. The relations between the family and wider institutional contexts stay in the background or emerge only with respect to symptomatic behavior—such as a child with a school problem or a couple involved in a court battle because of divorce proceedings. In such instances, attention may be focused for a time on the characteristics of the school or the behavior of the lawyers. With respect to the latter case, it is worth noting that a new branch of practice, a new subspecialty called Divorce Therapy—has recently been emerging. This is a beautiful example of the salience of *specialization* within the overall field of the family. We have Marriage Counselors, we have Couples Therapists, we have all the different schools of Family Therapists, we have Gay Therapists, and now we have Divorce Therapists! This narrowing of focus tends to fragment the field by creating an ever-lengthening list of subspecialties. Where will it stop? Soon we can expect the appearance of Alternative Life Style Therapists.

There are three interrelated approaches, however, that take a different, more varied and more flexible position with respect to family systems or subsystems, and that make an effort to deal with the interface between the family and the wider social system. The first is the ecological approach proposed by Edgar Auerswald (1968; 1972). Based on a sweeping indictment of Western ideology and cognitive styles compared with an equally penetrating analysis of Eastern belief systems, the ecological program attributes the fragmentation and specialization of our service delivery institutions to the hierarchical, linear thinking about space and time in which we have all been educated.[1] In its place, this program proposes a more complex and flexible thought structure that examines the relations of any system to its surrounding environment, or ecological niche. Where service delivery is concerned, this means transcending the firm boundaries and the associated "intake" policies of professional agencies (the "turf" problem) to make the connections that individuals and families need in order to modify the dysfunctional ways in which they are maintaining (or failing to maintain) themselves in their environmental situation. The epistemological stance adopted by this approach is considered necessary in

---

[1] The basic concepts of the ecological approach have been employed in a number of fashions, some not always specifically named. Labeled, for example, is the Health Ecology Project, under the direction of Dr. James N. Sussex, Dept. of Psychiatry, University of Miami School of Medicine (Sussex and Weidman 1975). Not specifically labeled as such, for example, is the epistemological and ecological approach adopted by Jay Haley (1976) in his "problem-solving" approach.

order to neutralize the resistance which any such "radical" restructuring of service delivery habits will inevitably encounter. For example, we all know of, and complain about, the inefficiencies and blockages to adequate care associated with the organizational structure and work habits of the usual service agencies. But most attempts at innovative solutions of this problem get washed away, after a period of time, by withdrawal of funding or burn-out of leadership through frustration or harrassment. The attention to the implicit Western thought-ways backing up such inefficient fragmentation and specialization may provide a more enduring thrust to attempts at innovative correction.

The second of these broader approaches is network therapy as proposed by Ross Speck and Carolyn Attneave (1972, 1973), and by Mansell Pattison (1976), among others. While still entailing an ecological principle, network therapy is more pragmatic, less ideological. The model assumes that any dysfunctional stalemate in the nuclear family may well be reinforced by the extended family, or by friends or significant others in the neighborhood or community, or even by relatives living at a distance. In therapy, attempts are made to assemble components from the wider systems, to reveal whatever pathological structures are being maintained by means of the network, to identify key persons involved in the reinforcing process, and to bring others into the network who may be able to provide a more benevolent, supportive function. Attention is paid to possible support systems wherever they may be located. Attention is also paid to the cultural and ethnic issues inherent in any environmental niche occupied by the family. Since those plugged into the network by the therapists, with the help of the family, may be drawn from any agency or institution, organizational boundaries may be breached, not because of *policy* considerations but because the representative of the neighborhood, the agency, or the institution gets so heavily involved in the dynamics of the network process.

The third of these broader models, the transactional field approach, is associated with my own work (Spiegel 1971a). It is more conceptual and at a wider level of generality than the other models. It is more complex and therefore difficult to compress into an abbreviated time/ space package. And, because it is designed for a broad span of families located, in our pluralistic society, in various ethnic and socioeconomic class positions, it is difficult to describe its applications to family therapy in any simple manner. Nevertheless, since this is my assignment for this volume, I shall attempt to do so.

Transactional Field Theory

The word *transactions* is now coming into increasingly popular usage in our professional literature, most of the time without the author or the reader realizing from what source it is derived. In my own work, I have traced it to a number of sources but have mainly emphasized the work of the philosopher, John Dewey, and the political scientist, Arthur Bentley, in their book, *Knowing and the Known* (1950). Like Auerswald, Dewey and Bentley were concerned with epistemology: how we know (or think we know!) what we know. Looking at the broad sweep of Western intellectual history, and especially at the topic in philosophy known as *metaphysics*, they identified two principal explanatory thoughtways, and then proposed a third to make up for the deficiencies of the first two. Keep in mind that metaphysics is concerned with the nature of *Being*, or *Reality*, though Dewey and Bentley were interested mostly in the nature of *Action*, as a way of getting at *Reality*. The first of the two ancient and honorable modes of explanation they called Self-Action. The explanation is based on the idea that an entity—a "thing"—is operating under its own internal powers or dispositions, like a clock all wound up and set to go. For example, Aristotle's explanation of gravity—that a stone falls to the earth because it is disposed to go back to its natural resting place—is a prototypical Self-Action concept. This explanation now sound selfish and naive, but self-actional thinking still operates in many avenues of our contemporary thoughtways. "Anatomy is Destiny," said Freud, referring of course, to the anatomical difference between the sexes. Genetic equipment is also destiny, even though the genes are being reassembled in terms of the DNA structures. Child development studies are increasingly concerned with the inborn, innate qualities of the human organism, bound to unfold in accordance with prepackaged programs. Personality traits are *there*, waiting to be measured and used as explanations of observed behavior. Object relations are *there*, things to be internalized or projected in accordance with current versions of ego psychology. National character is *there*, a thing that is representative of another thing, the Nation. The thing may be complexly patterned but nevertheless it is *there*, within the entity, waiting to be expressed in action, in accordance with its dispositional tendencies.

The second, less ancient but equally honorable mode of explanation is "Inter-Action," which involves thing acting upon thing acting upon thing. The origin of interactional explanation is traced to Newton's theory of gravity as the force of attraction exerted by objects upon each other over a distance of space. Concretely, the explanatory model is like a ping-pong game or a tennis match. A acts and then B reacts, though C may also get into the act, creating a triad. All sorts of contemporary observations of behavior, like "interpersonal relations," are based on this model. The Meyerian concept of mental illness as a series of "reaction states," which was used as diagnostic terminology in DSM I (American Psychiatric Association 1952), is a product of the interaction model. In psychotherapy, one takes note of the behavior and associations of the patient, then the therapist makes his interpretation, and then he watches for the patient's response. All stimulus-response observations and therapeutic procedures, such as behavior modification, grow out of interactional thinking.

The point here is not that self-actional or interactional thinking are wrong. They are merely ways of organizing observations in order to explain the behavior observed that have been developed in the course of the intellectual and scientific history of Western thought. Still, they are limiting. They are linear, unidirectional, proceeding in a straight line in time or space, as is the case generally for Aristotelian thought, from first to final causes. And they direct attention to things or entities or factors, arranged hierarchically, in dependent-independent relationships. They direct attention away from systems or processes where one cannot locate a "thing," a *ding an sich*, or any one direction in which the process is moving, back or forth, up or down, or sideways. And, furthermore, as Auerswald (1974) has pointed out, they create "blame systems" or perjorative labels. If B's behavior is a reaction to A, then A is to blame; and thus we get "schizophrenogenic mothers," passive or immature fathers, perverts, delinquents, and mental retardates, all acting or reacting in their roles as victims or victimizers, in linear (or "developmental") time.

To get away from such limitations, Dewey and Bentley proposed the term "trans-action." The word denotes system in process with system, where no entity can be located as first or final cause. In diabetes the processes associated with normal blood sugar levels are destabilized. But the "cause" does not reside so much in the islet cells of the pancreas, or their insulin production, or in the deposition of glycogen in or its release from the liver, or in the genes, or in the dietary habits of the individual, or in the food resources available to him in his ecological niche, or in his personality, as it does in all of them together—or "untogether." The ups and downs of the blood sugar, and its associated effects on other body systems, can be described as the product of the transactions of many systems, all working upon and with each other.

Similarly, in the case of an identified patient, whatever behavior is displayed is taken out of role assignments passing back and forth between nuclear family members; up to and down from an older generation; exchanged laterally with relatives, neighbors, and friends; interdigitated with schools, churches, workplaces and recreational opportunities; and enmeshed with the culture of the ethnic group, the region and the nation, the climate and the terrain—with all these systems chasing each other around by the tail, in or out of sync with each other.

It is obvious that we are talking the language of systems theory. But, the trouble with systems theory is that it is generally so difficult to describe the various systems, to locate them in time or space, and to specify their relations with each other, that the term is used loosely to describe a point of view. In engineering and in the "hard" sciences, the properties of specified systems can be identified and even translated into quantitative terms. This rarely happens in the social sciences and, where family therapy is concerned, systems theory is more an article of faith or ideology than a precise tracking of what is going on between the family and its wider social contexts. It is for this reason that I proposed the concept of a *transactional field*.

It should be clear by now that I like maps, especially when dealing with *terra incognita*. The arrangements pictured in figure 6.1 (Spiegel 1971a:42) are based on the notion that we have a great deal of knowledge about how systems work with each other, but that what is needed is an *image* of how foci in the field are related to each other. The word *focus* is used because knowledge is accumulated (the epistemological theme) on the basis of our looking at, inquiring into, and labeling

Figure 6.1
Organization of the Transactional Field

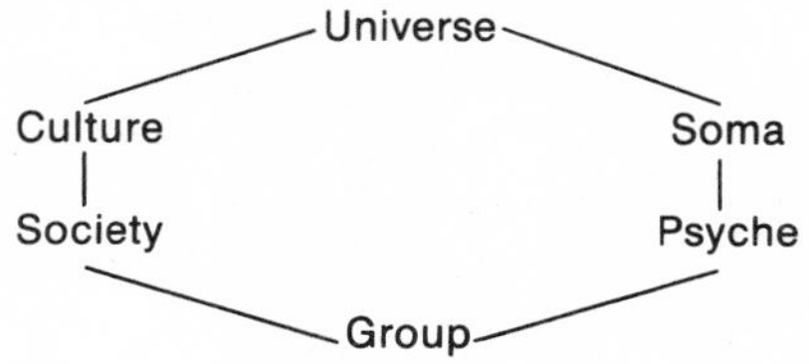

(naming) the processes of behavior. Whether this image is adequately related to "reality" is beside the point, since from the human standpoint reality consists of what we think it is. More relevant is: is this a useful way of organizing present knowledge? Does it supply a transactional answer to the unidirectional, action-reaction assumptions of the interactional model? Does it provide a way for the untidy collection of disciplines, specialties and subspecialties to enter into useful dialogue with each other?

Let us begin with the top focus, *Universe*, and travel around the field in a clockwise direction. Universe is concerned with knowledge about the "hardware" aspects of behavior, the subject matter of physics, astronomy, chemistry, geography and the nonliving world generally, all the way from the cosmos to the atomic nucleus. Universe includes the house or dwelling in which families live, the land on which it is built and the surrounding terrain, urban or rural, as well as the air they breathe, its temperature, humidity, purity, and the winds (or hurricanes) that carry it. For our purposes, it also includes the food resources they can consume, thus adding essential components to the ecological niche they occupy.

Processes included in Universe are in transaction with processes in *Soma*, and thus are life supporting. Soma includes the anatomical structures and physiological processes within the human organism. Destabilization of homeostatic processes within Soma can be associated with illness or death. Destabilization of transactions between Soma and Universe can be associated with accident, injury, or death, including current concerns about the contamination of the environment and the depletion of supplies of liquid fuel. What goes on in the somatic focus becomes the object of inquiry for biologists, biophysicists, physiologists, the medical professions, and health researchers generally.

Moving along to the next adjacent focus, *Psyche*, we include here all knowledge about energy transformations from Soma that are involved in complex processes of adaptation. Psychological processes concerned with cognition, perception, problem solving, conflict elaboration and reduction, emotional arousal, habit formation and communication are in transaction with each other within this focus. Also included are behaviors specific to situational contexts, whether at the family dinner table or in the bedroom. Thus the fiction we label as "personality" results from the integration of processes within Psyche and from transactions, on the one side, with Soma, and on the other, with the focus called *Group*.

Reference to situational contexts is a natural introduction to the Group focus. Here we encounter transactions taking place in ordinary, face-to-face small groups. It is in groups that behavior receives situational definitions and role attributions, as most human affairs take place in such settings rather than in solitary or mass situations. Included in this focus is all knowledge of the organized behavior of group members. Group problem-solving and decision-making, ways of communicating (or not communicating!) within and between groups, allocations of power and responsibility, divisions of labor and task assignments, group cohesion, leadership and morale—all such processes are under inquiry within this focus. For purposes related to family research and therapy, we would obviously begin our involvements as researchers or therapists within this focus, as the family is a prime example of a face-to-face group.

Small groups, however, do not exist in isolation from each other. They receive their forms, functions, and interrelations in accordance with their place in the larger network of social systems which we here label *Society*. In complex societies, this focus includes our knowledge of the major institutions, such as religious, educational, economic, legal, governmental, recreational and voluntary institutions, and the professions generally. Racial, national origin, social class, and ethnic systems are included, as is the family, as an institution characterized by discernible patterns, such as marriage and divorce rates, adoption, and alternative family life-styles. Social change and social control are topics within this focus, especially the rates and directions of social change. For our purposes here, we will be concerned mainly with ethnic family systems, in their relations to other social institutions within their ecological niche.

Insofar as our knowledge of social institutions is concerned with the *meaning* of social behavior, we have moved to the focus identified as *Culture*. By anchoring social institutions in a set of beliefs and values about the nature of the world and of human existence, Culture contributes to the survival of a society in its ecological niche. Cultural anthropologists have added to our knowledge base information about the extreme variation and diversity of different cultures scattered over the face of the globe. American society is itself an example of subcultural diversity, having never become the "melting pot" it was assumed to be at the time of the large-scale mass immigrations. Because of our current task assignment, we will here be concerned in a major way with the variation in the cultural standards, beliefs and values of different ethnic families. And, to close off this discussion and complete the circling of the transactional field, it is necessary to add that whatever we think about the nature of the Universe—whether it is born from an egg on the back of a turtle, created by God in seven days, or evolving from a big bang over billions of years—it is the knowledge assembled within the Cultural focus that forms the basis of our belief system.

Value Orientation Theory and its Applications: The American Case

The virtue of the transactional field concept with its arrangement of foci is that it helps us keep track of the process of imbalance, conflict, or destabilization from wherever it may arise within the field. It is destabilization which creates the need for therapeutic interventions. We usually conceive of our interventions as directed at the process of conflict, of anxiety and associated defense systems, within the individual, the family, or preferably, both. The ecological approach would have no objection to this traditional rationale for interventions, provided that we keep in mind that imbalance and conflict may arise from any focus in the field. It may begin with the Society focus during times of economic depression, war, or rapid social change. It may start from Universe, as in the case of hurricanes or other natural disasters. We would also note that illness, including mental illness, is only one aspect of destabilization—an aspect that gets overemphasized in the "medical model," with its tendency to control turf and to "pathologize" any destabilization it gets possession of. To make a "pathology" out of imbalances and role conflicts within the family is not very helpful and may be harmful. Its sources lie partly in the economic competition over who gets paid for what service, partly in our traditional interactional thoughtways that any problem requiring intervention in the name of "health" must be due to some "pathology" within that "thing" or "entity" that needs attention because it is to "blame" for the problem.

To make pathologies out of value conflicts and cultural misunderstanding within ethnic or minority families living in urban or ghetto working-class settings is even more harmful. For service providers in traditional, middle-class agencies, outpatient clinics, or even community mental health centers, it leads to the "last to be served—first to be dropped" syndrome associated with "no insight—bad patient" or "multi-problem family" images. The ecological approach, therefore, would suggest that the focus in the transactional field within which to begin the inquiry in families undergoing "acculturation" (and who isn't!) is Culture, because we are dealing with a clash of cultural understandings and norms. We also need to look at the strengths within ethnic families—those cultural values which have facilitated survival within the ecological niche.

But, again, for this purpose, we need a map. We especially need a map that will provide us with a way of contrasting the standards and beliefs of middle-class therapists acculturated to mainstream American values and the values of members of different white ethnic groups, and of the minorities. If the map "demands" specification of white ethnic values it can correct the usual overlooking of white ethnicity, as exemplified by the fact that clinical records rarely take note of the ethnic or national background of Caucasians. By the same token, if the map specifies a complex pattern of values for the minorities, it can correct the cliches and stereotypes to which "people of color" are often exposed.

The map we have been using is the theory of variation in cultural value orientations proposed by my colleague, Florence Kluckhohn (Kluckhohn and Strodtbeck 1961). In this theory, orientations are distinguished from concrete values, like the importance placed on honor, courage, or sexual purity, by their level of generality, in accordance with the following definition: *A value orientation is a generalized and organized conception, influencing behavior, of time, of nature, of man's place in it, of man's relation to man, and of the desirable and nondesirable aspects of man-environment and interhuman transactions.* In addition, the theory assumes that value orientations facilitate three functions within the Psyche focus of the transactional field: 1) Value orientations provide a program for selecting between more or less favored choices of alternative behaviors. This is their evaluative or *directional* function. 2) Value orientations provide a view of the nature of the world and of human affairs. This is their existential or *cognitive* function. 3) Value orientations are never taken lightly—people are ready to bleed and die for them. This is their emotional or *affective* function. It is also the main reason why people and organizations become so resistant to change, easily described as "It's a matter of principle!" accompanied by appropriate (or inappropriate) indignation. When involved with therapeutic interventions related to value change or conflict in the process of acculturation, we have to be attentive to all three of these functions.

The classification of value orientation modalities, or categories, set forth in figure 6.2 (Spiegel 1971b), is based on another set of assumptions: 1) there is a limited number of common human problems for which all peoples in all places must find some solution; 2) although there is variability in the solutions of the problems, this variability is neither limitless nor random, but occurs within a range of possible solutions; and, 3) all variants (all alternatives) of all solutions are in varying degrees present in the total cultural structure of every society. In other words, every society will be characterized not only by a dominant profile of first-order value choices, but also by substitute second- and third-order choices. Thus, in the process of sociocultural change, second-order choices may be moved into the first order and vice versa. It will be important for us to keep track of such shifts, not only for whole ethnic groups, such as Asians and Hispanics, undergoing the stress of acculturation, but for understanding generational problems between parents and children—and even between husbands and wives, where one marital partner is moving faster than the other, or they are in a cross-cultural (mixed) marriage.

So far, five common human problems have been identified as forming the substance of the different value orientation categories. They are: *Time*, which is the temporal focus of human life; *Activity*, the preferred pattern of action in interpersonal relations; the *Relational* orientation, which is the preferred way of relating in groups; the *Man-Nature* orientation, which is concerned with the way man relates to the natural or the supernatural environment; and, the *Basic Nature of Man*, concerned with conceptions of innate good and evil in human behavior.

The theory assumes three possible solutions for each of these common human problems; and the variation between and within cultures is based on the rank-ordering (pattern of preferences) of these solutions in a dominant-substitute profile of values. To save space and try to reach several goals at once, I shall define the solutions for each value orientation category in terms of figure 2, where the patterning of preferences for mainstream American life-styles (American middle class) is compared with profiles characteristic of rural Southern Italian and rural Southern Irish families drawn from our work with these migrant groups. However, in this section, we shall deal only with American values.[2]

---

[2] What follows is drawn from a larger study of ethnic families and mental health, supported by the National Institute of Mental Health, and reported in Papajohn and Spiegel (1975).

Figure 6.2
Value Orientation Profiles of Three Middle Classes

	American	Italian	Irish
Time	Future > Present > Past	Present > Past > Future	Present > Past > Future
Activity	Doing > Being > Being-in-Becoming	Being > Being-in-Becoming > Doing	Being > Being-in-Becoming > Doing
Relational	Individual > Collateral > Lineal	Collateral > Lineal > Individual	Lineal > Collateral > Individual
Man-Nature	Dominant Over > Subjugated > Harmony	Subjugated > Harmony > Dominant Over	Subjugated > Harmony > Dominant Over
Basic nature of man	Neutral > Evil > Good	Mixed > Evil > Good	Evil > Mixed > Good

In fleshing out the definitions of the value patterns, it is necessary to draw on information from the Society and Group (family) foci to specify how the individual family member may be involved.[3] Let us begin by running through the rank-ordered patterns for the American middle class, since they exert the pull toward which ethnic groups move. The three possible solutions to the dimension of *Time* in human affairs are, as might be expected, Past, Present, and Future. It is also no great surprise that the American middle class prefers the "Future" orientation in the first-order position. Americans spend a great deal of time planning for a far-flung future. They plan for the spacing of their children, they plan way ahead for their educational and occupational careers, and they plan for their retirement and old age. The sign in the executive's office says, "Think Ahead!" They cut up their days and weeks into small time segments which they keep track of in little black appointment books, and woe to the misguided who arrive late for an appointment or, shamefacedly, leave a meeting early, probably because they have to try to keep another appointment.

The emphasis on the future has certain other implications. It places importance on novelty and transience. Anything new is better than anything old—a new car, a new idea, or a new style. Youthfulness is highly regarded as the representative of the future. The elderly try to look younger, but with so little future left to them they tend to take a back seat or else are neglected. No one wants to be old-fashioned, left behind, or outmoded in the inexorable push for change of styles— in music, literature, clothes, and material culture generally.

When not compulsively devoted to the Future, mainstream Americans can take time out to live in the Present, their second-order choice. A "Present Time" orientation occurs in recreational settings, where people are supposed to have fun and forget about the Future. Even here, they are aware of taking time out and are apt to start looking at their watches, thinking, "I have to go home because I have to get up early tomorrow." Alcohol and psychedelic substances may be used to wipe out the claims of the future—but not for long without one's running the risk of being called an addict.

---

[3] Let us keep in mind that an individual is a composite of transactions around the field in his ecological niche. There would be no mountaineers without their mountains; no Polynesians without their islands, ocean, and boats; no giants, dwarfs, or athletes without their Soma; no geniuses without their Psyche; no bank presidents without the banking economy; no Catholics without their belief in Original Sin, Virgin Birth, and the possible evils of sex. A detailed and systematic account of this concept of "ethnic niche" in polyethnic societies is provided by Barth (1969).

In a weak third-order position, the "Past Time" orientation is usually given short shrift. Independence Day, Thanksgiving, and other past-time oriented holidays are used for Present Time enjoyment, not for serious reenactment of a highly valued past. American history is not recalled in detail, or with pleasure, and people have trouble remembering their family trees and other aspects of their origins, despite a small emergence of interest in rediscovering one's "roots." That they need to be rediscovered tells us in what low esteem the Past has been held. We are *pro* progress and *anti* tradition, nostalgia kicks to the contrary not withstanding. If anyone says, "That's the way we've always done it," someone else is likely to say, "Then it must be time for a change."

Since I am presenting a theory of *variation* in values designed to avoid stereotyping—for example, "All middle-class Americans are such and such. . . ."—it is important to note that some middle-class Americans refuse to wear watches or worry about the Future, while others connect with the Past by reading historical novels or biographies, listening to Renaissance music, collecting antiques, or by keeping track of their ancestors in the family Bible. These people do not conform to the dominant pattern. Nor do the ethnic families moving toward or into the middle class. But more of that later.

In the *Activity* dimension, the American rank-order choices are again a specification of the obvious. The "Doing" orientation is the achievement motive in American life-styles. The first questions asked of a stranger are, "What do you do? What have you done? What are you going to do?" meaning, of course, where and how well have you been "making it." Success, accomplishment in the eyes of "the other," such externally made value judgments are eagerly sought for and fought for, because self-esteem depends as much, if not more, on the outside world's view as on internal standards. The competitiveness of American life, the striving for upward mobility in jobs and social contacts are associated with "Doing." Parents ask themselves how well they are doing with their children, and how well their children are doing in school. Are they making enough friends? Are husbands competent breadwinners? Are wives up to snuff in housekeeping and other domestic affairs, including sexual competence? Young people, unless they rebel, resist, or drop out, are locked into climbing the steep educational ladder.

The "Being" alternative refers to the spontaneous expression of the inner feelings in given situations. Whereas "Doing" often involves controlling one's feelings to get the job done properly and thus gain recognition, the "Being" orientation implies that one cannot gain recognition without "being oneself." It does not imply pure impulse gratification, since all social roles are controlled by situational norms. However, there is more encouragement to be happy or sad, angry or loving, in accordance with one's current mood than is the case for "Doing." Particularly in a family gathering, but also in other situations, there is the assumption that one person cannot determine how to relate to another unless that inner "isness' is allowed open expression. The second-order position of "Being" in the American pattern is the consequence of its being restricted to a limited number of contexts, such as family and recreational situations. So pervasive is the social reinforcement for "Doing" that even in recreational situations, having a drink helps one to "be oneself."

The "Being-in-Becoming" orientation shares with "Being" a concern with what the human being is rather than what he can accomplish, but here the similarity ends. The development of different aspects of the person in a rounded and integrated fashion is paramount, and distinguishes it from the nose-to-the-grindstone feature of "Doing." One recalls Leonardo da Vinci who might start an engineering project, switch to a painting, and then, without having finished the work, turn to anatomical dissection. Developing different sides of his interests was more important than getting the job completed within a time frame. While it resembles Maslow's notion of "self-actualization," there are not many mainstream Americans who find the orientation appealing unless it can be confined to a hobby. A parent who finds a teenage boy so disposed is likely to worry that his son will become a dilettante and never get anywhere.

In the *Relational* dimension, the first choice of the "Individual" orientation reflects the preference for individual responsibility and autonomy versus responsibility to any collectivity in mainstream values. Children are trained from infancy to be independent and to articulate their own needs and opinions as separate human beings. The separation-individuation process not only begins early but is continuously reinforced as the children "sleep over" at the homes of friends (perhaps not even well known to the parents), go off to summer camps and away to college. Adults pursue their self-interests, stand on their own two feet and, if a group decision is required, each individual indicates where he stands by voting his own opinion. If a better job opportunity beckons elsewhere, a family member may just take off with a minimum of good-bye ceremony.

Every society, however, requires some responsibility to a collectivity, to the desires and feelings of the group membership. But there are two ways in which the group influence can be organized. One is in terms of the horizontal, or lateral, "all-in-the-same-boat" structuring of the group, and the other is in terms of the vertical, hierarchical, lineal structure of the group. The second-order choice of the laterally extended structure—the "Collateral" orientation—in mainstream American values reflects the democratic ethos on which the nation was founded and which it has struggled to implement despite many lapses. Everyone is on the same level, and power is to be equally shared in collaterally organized structures symbolized by the *United* States. This is the ideal way in which power is distributed and it holds for the family and in other contexts. Fathers would prefer not to be strong authority figures but to have decisions arrived at through a family consensus. It is difficult for people to admit openly that they enjoy being "the boss" and authority roles are often taken with an air of apologetic informality, as if to neutralize the inevitable hostility.

However, even though the "Lineal" orientation should ideally be in a weak, third-order position, there are many ways in which it strongly intrudes itself, contaminating and undermining the preferred Collaterality, and casting the shadow of hypocrisy upon our democratic principle. This is particularly the case with our minorities. "Racism," the product of superordinate-subordinate relational structures and of superiority-inferiority patterns of thought (the cognitive function of value orientations) is the prime example of the bias and prejudice[4] fostered by the "Lineal" orientation. There are other examples of the subversive operations of "Lineality." Large-scale bureaucratic institutions, with their tables of organization and their modes of communication and decision-making from the top down (but not vice versa) such as are found in government and industry, are set up on a "Lineal" basis.[5]

[4] Racism is biased and prejudiced, of course, only when viewed from the standpoint of individual and collateral orientations. The "Lineal" would regard it as natural and inevitable.

[5] Two conditions within the ecological niche require and justify the operations of the "Lineal" orientation: (1) under conditions of material scarcity, when a strong authority is required to control aggression and competition for the scarce resources, and to prevent the "war of all against all;" and (2) in emergency situations characterized by great danger when time pressures require the leader to count on instant and unquestioned obedience. In the history of the world these two conditions have been combined and mutually reinforcing, most of the time. Western "civilized" empires and Oceanic "primitive" tribes have fought each other for the control of scarce resources. Democracy, a relative newcomer, has made its appearance only when technology, transportation, and the sharing of raw materials has reduced the scarcity, increased the availability of material goods and possessions.

Like people, no culture is perfect, and I shall have occasion to comment on the goodness-of-fit, balance-imbalance question a little further along. If there are problems in the *Relational* dimension, there is also a problem in the *Man-Nature* category for mainstream patterns. The first-order choice, the ''Mastery-Over-Nature'' orientation, is based on the assumption that there are few if any problems occurring between man and nature that cannot be solved with the help of technology and the expenditure of vast sums of money. We have conquered infectious diseases, we have gone to the moon, and we have split the atom. We still have not mastered chronic illness, especially cancer and long-term mental illness, but there is hope. A few imbalances on our major ecological environment, spaceship earth, like war and weather, are more elusive but not impossible to control. We have only to run our fingers through the pages of the Yellow Book to find the expert who will solve our problem. Problem-solving, as some family therapists keep telling us, is where it's at. If parents have problems with children and children have problems with parents, then let's get to work. No need to suffer.

The problem is that some problems won't go away, at least not at the wave of the human hand, no matter how many instruments it may hold. In that case, we switch to our second-order, ''Subjugated-to-Nature'' orientation. This is particularly true for personal problems where the experts and specialists have been unable to help. Then an appeal is likely to be made to the Deity. God is powerful, man is weak, and when in trouble, pray. There are no atheists in foxholes! Or else the trouble simply has to be endured until it goes away, due to the benevolence of God or natural forces. The orientations within the *Man-Nature* category tend to be incommensurate with each other. The ''Mastery-Over-Nature'' and the ''Subjugated-to-Nature'' orientations are especially dichotomous, so that a switch is also a strain that has to be compartmentalized.

The ''Harmony-with-Nature'' orientation is not quite so far removed from the ''Subjugated-to-Nature'' position. It assumes that there is no necessary clash between man and nature. There are many forces and influences in the heavens, the earth, and beneath the earth, many gods, demons, angels, saints, spirits, ghosts, wee folk, or what not. Human problems arise when one has not attended appropriately to their influences and powers, or when one has not kept one's life in harmony or balance with all these sources of influence. Whether the Hopi way or the Indian Karma, the village saint or the native American's guardian spirit, the malevolent sorcerer or the benevolent shaman—all these figures must be attended to and supplicated or compensated. If it doesn't rain, the rain god may be angry, and a rain dance may help.

"Harmony-with-Nature" is in a weak, third-order position for mainstream Americans, likely to be put down as superstition or magical thinking, even though, secretly, many people may believe in some aspects of this orientation. It is likely to be popular with a few sects such as Zen Buddhists, former hippies or their descendants, and young people in rural communes living close to nature. But, however much it may be unacknowledged in the presence of middle-class professionals, many minority peoples and Southern European white ethnics strongly adhere to it.

The final category, *Basic Nature of Man,* has undergone change in the course of the short history of the United States of America. The original position of our Puritan ancestors was that man was born Evil-but-Perfectable. They were hypercathected to sin, the seductions of Satan, and the prevalence of witches. But, following the lead of nineteenth-century humanism, the growth of secular colleges and universities, and the popularization of psychology and the social sciences during the twentieth century, the concept of Original Sin has been displaced in favor of a more environmentalist view. The current, first-order "Neutral" orientation assumes that man is born neither good nor evil, but is more like a *tabula rasa*—a blank slate on which the environment, the parents, and the neighborhood and the school leave their imprint in the course of growth and development. This places a tremendous burden upon the parents in case the child should turn out badly—delinquent, neurotic, or worse—because of the operations of the "blame systems" previously referred to. However, there are always the experts activated by the "Mastery-over-Nature" orientation from whom help may be sought. The "Neutral" position also generates a pragmatic sense of morality, as punishment is no longer expected from God because of sin. Moral pragmatism suggests that, if possible, one should avoid hurting others, but there are no absolute prescriptions other than those legislated into law or responsive to an inner sense of decency, both subject to change.

"Innate Evil," in the second-order position, is, however, a continuous possibility. Fundamentalist sects have always promoted it, Born Again Christians and Jesus Freaks are attempting to resurrect it. When in deep trouble, it is comforting to be "saved," even if only in the next world. In this world, the "Savior" is a reassuring presence, whether in the form of clergymen trying to get their channels to God straightened out or therapists fighting off their rescue fantasies when faced with desperate clients. Meanwhile, large segments of the population may experience a heightened awareness of evil in periods of national stress. Under the stress of post–World War II recovery, McCarthyism was able to generate a Communist witch hunt, with anti-American radicals hiding under (or sleeping in) the beds of government employees, infiltrating Hollywood, and contaminating the media. Currently, under the stress of rising inflation and energy problems, we are being inflamed with fear of a handful of Russian soldiers in Cuba. The Red Menace rides again.

In the third-order position we find the "Good-but-Corruptible" orientation. Man is born good but wicked civilization corrupts, as Rousseau believed when contemplating the noble savage described in the reports of early South Seas voyagers. This orientation, however, is weak when faced with the "Neutral" orientation of environmentalist corrective programs—such as the Model Cities or Head Start—most of which fail to achieve their objectives. It is subscribed to only by a few "counterculture" adherents, such as the hippie women who, during the riots of the sixties, would approach a National Guardsman, put a flower in his rifle, and give him a kiss to bring out his innate goodness. The flower children have disappeared into rural settings where they can cultivate innate goodness far from wicked civilization.

This completes the account of middle-class American value orientation patterns. As was stated above, no culture is perfect. It is worthwhile to pause for a moment to look at some of the strengths and weaknesses in these patterns as they affect stress and strain and the forces of change.

It is evident that the first-order, or *dominant* American choices in each dimension fit together nicely—perhaps too well. If the personal achievement implied by "Doing" is to be facilitated, then it is good to be able to plan for the "Future," as an "Individual" not too constrained by family or group ties, with the optimism supplied by the "Mastery-over-Nature" orientation, and the pragmatic morality with which self-interest is justified afforded by the "Neutral" view of the Basic Nature of Man.

With respect to stress, this is a lockstep pattern, something of a pressure cooker, full-steam-ahead with little opportunity for relaxation without guilt or lowered self-esteem. It fosters a narcissistic self-involvement, about which there have been recent complaints. In addition, there is no room for tragedy. If an airplane crashes killing hundreds of people, somebody "goofed" or the technology is to blame, and loved ones are compensated with money. If a patient dies on the operating table, the surgeon has difficulty facing the family, since he has flunked the "Mastery-over-Nature" imperative, and may be seen as an inept "Doer." Grieving ceremonies are weak or absent and those who have suffered a loss may need the help of a therapist to undergo the separation process.

Furthermore, the dominant choices have, at least in the past, applied only to males. Women have been socialized for "inferior" second-order alternatives—taking care of day-to-day affairs ("Present"), dealing with children's and husband's feelings ("Being"), attending to relatives and keeping in touch with friends ("Collateral"). The efforts of the feminist movement to correct this split in the norms of the sex roles have been partially successful, resulting in some shifting, or at least sharing of values in the family.

Finally, there has been some resistance to the compulsive demands of Future time planning, with the result—especially for younger people—that a "Present Time" orientation is being given more prominence. Permissiveness for premarital and extramarital sex and the increased acceptance of homosexuality are responsive to this change, supported by moral pragmatism. If teenagers do not have to plan ahead to remain virginal in order to get married and have children, then why wait? If premarital teenage pregnancies become a problem, they are no more (or less) of a problem than the alternative arrangements for coupling, including gay marriages, associated with newer life-styles.

There is some danger of this essay turning into a sociological treatise. The intent, however, is to highlight one aspect of the problem faced by ethnic families undergoing acculturation. While such families are attempting to understand, and to learn to implement, the dominant value orientation patterns, those patterns are themselves undergoing change. The resulting confusion increases the stress of the acculturation process. This makes it very important for the family therapist to keep track of three acculturation issues: (1) the value patterns characteristic of the family's culture of origin; (2) the place they are occupying in the acculturation process—that is, what values have been or are being changed at the time of intervention; and (3) the family's understanding or misunderstanding of mainstream American values. In the case of cross-cultural marriages, there is, of course, a fourth issue: what conflicts have occurred or what accommodations (compromises) are being made to compensate for the differences between two native value patterns. This requires that the therapist be reasonably well acquainted with the value orientations of the culture of origin—the subject to which we shall now turn our attention.

The Value Orientations of Italians and Irish

In the *Time* dimension, Italians and Irish are similar, placing Present Time in the first-order position, with Past second and the Future last. This is a characteristic profile for most rural peoples engaged in farming, fishing, or a subsistence economy. Time goes around in large cycles of anniversaries and holidays, seasons for sowing or for reaping. The day is marked by the position of the sun or the bell in the church steeple and there is little need for a watch or a daily calendar. The "Present Time" orientation extends its perspective back into the past and forward into the future, so there is no expectation of, or preparation for, change. Things will happen the way they always have happened. However, if there is a hitch or an unusual problem, then there will be an appeal to the Past, usually by consulting the memories and getting the advice of the elder generation. The emphasis placed on the here and now of daily life makes for a relaxed family atmosphere.

One might wonder how, with so little training in planning for the future and for change, such people could undertake the gigantic step of emigrating to the United States, and to other countries. The answer is that the rural economies of Southern Italy and Southern Ireland were very depressed, eking out a living was difficult, and America was seen as a place where, because of the greater economic opportunities, one might live out similar life-styles with greater ease. One could join relatives already in the United States, who would help with getting started. Therefore, people from same villages tended to go to the same cities in this country, forming "Little Italys" and Irish neighborhoods where, except for the shift from rural to urban settings, there was no need to undergo rapid sociocultural change.

In the *Activity* dimension, we again find similar profiles between the two ethnic groups, one that is shared by many other national-origin groups. The "Being" orientation comes first, followed by "Being-in-Becoming" and then "Doing." The expressive emotionality of the Italians is well known. For the Irish, "Being" implies a somewhat more restrained behavior in the presence of strangers but family life is loaded with feelings, often conveyed more by subtle cues or by teasing than by words or direct confrontation. "Being-in-Becoming" for Italians has an aesthetic quality, an appreciation for sensory or physical differences in developmental paths. For example, an Italian mother told us that her children were doing very well in school. We asked her why, thinking, from our "Doing" perspective, that they must be getting good grades. She replied, "Because they have such beautiful eyes. All the teachers love them." For the Irish, the "Being-in-Becoming" orientation is more likely to find expression in appreciation for idiosyncracies of character, which form the basis for humorous stories. Almost every person in an Irish family is a "character" of one sort or another.

The fact that "Doing" occupies a last position for both Italians and Irish does not mean that there is any disposition to avoid hard work. Fathers often take multiple jobs to increase the family income. However, when they come home, they talk very little about their work unless they have a complaint or something exciting or dramatic has happened on the job. The family has little interest in how they are "doing," but a lot of interest in anything scandalous that will make food for gossip with the neighbors. Gossip is the principal form of social control in rural communities or neighborhood enclaves where everyone knows everyone else.

In the *Relational* category, there is a difference between the two groups. Italians prefer the "Collateral" while Irish prefer the "Lineal" orientation. Lateral relations are very important to Italians, and loyalty to the extended family system is demanded, as is closeness, physical and emotional. There is anguish over separation, which is to be avoided if at all possible. If someone has an accident and is taken to the emergency room of a hospital, the whole extended family is likely to show up to demonstrate their feelings, with much uproar and drama over the possible tragedy. Despite images of "the Godfather," Italian husbands and fathers take the second-order "Lineal" authority position only if there is strong disagreement within the family. Actually, because of the absence of a strong, superordinate authority, family (or neighborhood) arguments are apt to provoke collateral fission, a split which leads to protracted feuding. The "Individual" orientation is not encouraged. If a child becomes too independent, he is scolded for being "willful" or for "having a big head." If he persists he may be physically punished, slapped, or spanked. But, the next minute, acting out of the "Being" orientation, the parent is apt to pick up the child and hug him and kiss him. Large families are desired and few children have the feeling of not being wanted.

Among the Irish, the first-order position of the "Lineal" orientation is a problem. Husbands and fathers are supposed to be "the boss," but in rural Ireland, mainly for economic reasons, the socialization of the young males did not provide adequate reinforcement for this role. The farms had been cut up into such small pieces that the property could not be distributed to all the male children. Also, there was no system of primogeniture. It was up to the father to decide which of his sons—the favorites—would inherit the land and he was in no hurry to make this decision, as it would require his retiring to the "West Room." Young males, with no source of stable income, were kept on pocket money and were unable to marry. The restless sons moved to the city or emigrated. Ireland had the oldest age of marriage of any European country. At the same time, the virginity of unmarried females had to be vigorously guarded, lest they "fall by the wayside," damaging their chances of marriage. Unable to marry, with no sexual outlets except for prostitutes, the young males congregated in the pub, forgetting their woes with the help of drink and tall stories. Thus drinking became "a good man's weakness," a forgivable and understandable indiscretion, while taking responsibility for domestic affairs was delayed for too long. Under these peculiarities of the ecological niche, when marriage finally occurred, the wife was likely to be the stronger person, ruling the family from behind the throne in order not to publicly expose the weakness of the male head of the family. The men tended to overcompensate for this weakness through impulsive pugnacity. Sons were closer to their mothers than to their fathers, thus perpetuating the strain in the male role.

In the *Man-Nature* category, since the Roman Catholic Church is the official religion for both groups, the "Subjugated-to-Nature" orientation holds first-order position. Suffering is expected as a part of man's fate in this world. When we asked Italians how they were thinking of handling their problems, we frequently elicited a characteristic shrug of the shoulders with the response, "What can you do?" Where the Italians are pessimistic or dolefully accepting, the Irish tend to be stoical and tough-minded. Their characteristic response to trouble is, "It could be worse." The history of Ireland's suffering at the hands of the English indicates a certain reality in this view, though it is difficult to see how the current "troubles" in Northern Ireland could get any worse.

For Italians, the influence of the second-order "Harmony-with-Nature" orientation is still very strong. Partly it has been assimilated into the church through the powers attributed to the local saint, who is often appealed to on behalf of a sick family member or other personal difficulty. There is also a fear of evil spirits, particularly of the power of the "Evil Eye." The "Mal Occhio" is possessed only by certain people and one must be very careful not to arouse their envy, especially where children are concerned. Even second- and third-generation Italian-Americans may continue to fear the Evil Eye, seeing it as the cause of family problems, despite preliminary protests that they no longer subscribe to such "superstitutions."

Among the Irish, "Harmony-with-Nature" is manifested more by fanciful or mystical views of the powers in nature—elves, bog creatures, wee folk, etc. It contributes to a dreamy, Gaelic quality in Irish life-styles, a predilection for fantasy which is often so strong as to interfere with the ability to distinguish fantasy from reality. Fantasy formation has also been attributed to Ireland's misty climate. For both Italians and Irish, the "Mastery-over-Nature" orientation is taken seriously only by a few people. Even after exposure to American technology and problem-solving following immigration, the optimism and hope associated with this view takes a long time to sink in.

In the *Basic Nature of Man* dimension, Italians hold a "Mixed" orientation in first place, while the Irish subscribe to an innately evil position. Italians consider people to be born with the capacity to do good or evil, though some have more of one, some more of the other. In a family of large numbers of children, some may turn out to be priests (or even saints!), others may end up as gangsters, but most are somewhere in between. However the child turns out, it is not the fault of the parent but of "fate." Some parents are lucky, some are not. Nevertheless, one must beware of the potential for evil, particularly where male sexuality is concerned. Unmarried girls are not allowed to date, not allowed in the company of males without a chaperone, who is often an older brother or a married sister. The family's honor is at stake, and honor is something to be jealously guarded where human nature is mixed. Anything can happen and one must be prepared for the worst, which is, of course, a tragedy calling for retribution, perhaps in the form of "crimes of passion," as was the case for Romeo and Juliet. Still, the "Mixed" orientation is also associated with a relaxed sense of morality. People will steal if given the opportunity, as guilt is not internalized. It is shameful to be caught but not shameful if one can get away with it. Therefore, keep your bicycles locked—the moral of the Italian film *The Bicycle Thief*. A shame culture accents visible and public disgrace, not private morality.

For the Irish, the "Evil" orientation features a sharp awareness of sin and of the possibilities of yielding to temptation, which are always around the corner. Parents lose no opportunity to suspect their children of sinning and to correct them with angry denunciations designed to extract a confession. The child may respond with an equally angry and indignant denial. Whether confessing or denying, the child is learning the lesson the parent wants to teach: that sin is here to stay and one must always be on guard to restrain it or to repent for a transgression. This internalization of guilt is responsive to the harsher morality of the Irish Catholic Church as compared to the Italian. Italian Catholics celebrate Feast Days, while the Irish fast and repent. The Irish are also very reluctant to complain about pain or illness. This is associated not only with the tough-minded stoicism mentioned above, but also with the notion that pain and illness may be God's punishment for sinful thinking or behavior. Better, then, to pretend it is not happening to oneself and, certainly, to avoid public acknowledgment of illness if at all possible. For both Italians and Irish, mental illness in the family is particularly stigmatized and painful to acknowledge, but for different reasons. For Italians it is shameful and a sign of "bad blood lines," a blot on the family shield of honor. Or, it may be a sign of witchcraft. For the Irish, it is another, and worse, sign of punishment for sin. Both groups tend to somatize their emotional problems, wherever possible, thus seeming to lack insight. Insight into family relations, however, is present. It is a question of how to surface it.

In concluding this section, it may be helpful to point out the great cultural gap that Italians and Irish must traverse in accommodating to mainstream value patterns. Inspection of figure 2 reveals that first-order choices of the American middle class are in the last place for these two groups. If accommodation is to be performed without too much strain, it must be done slowly, in small steps, over several generations. The same thing tends to be true for other minority groups, such as Hispanics and Asians, although there is so much variation within these groups that all generalizations of this sort are suspect. With Hispanics, one must be careful to distinguish Cubans from Puerto Ricans, and both from Chicanos. Within the Asian group, Chinese and Japanese have very different values from Indians and Filipinos, to say nothing of Koreans, Vietnamese, and the Pacific Islanders. In each case, ethnographic information about the ecological niche is important to an understanding of family life-styles and to the conduct of family therapy.

Another conclusion is a caution directed at middle-class therapists, who, no matter what their ethnic origins, have been socialized in terms of mainstream values. This is especially pertinent to the value profiles of the helping professional. The therapist will be "Future Time" oriented, expecting people to keep appointments and to arrive on time if they are appropriately "motivated." He will expect families to be willing to work on therapeutic tasks over reasonable periods of time ("Doing" and "Future Time"), with the prospect of change before them ("Future Time" and "Mastery-over-Nature), while taking a pragmatic view of moral issues ("Neutral")—or, at least, he will expect to help them to distance themselves from an overweening moral burden, or an intense sense of shame. And he will want to help each individual become aware of his individuality, to separate himself from enmeshment in the family structure, and develop increased autonomy ("Individual"). He will tend to assume that these goals are universally applicable and therapeutically helpful. In the following section the question will arise: To what degree can these assumptions hold in working with ethnic families? If they are open to question, then it will be very important for the therapist to be aware of the difference between his or her values and those of ethnic family members and to work out a way of resolving the difference.

Implications for Therapy

The principal therapeutic technique employed in our ecological approach[6] is the activity of what we are calling the "Culture Broker." This is a concept borrowed from Hazel Weidman (1973, 1975), with some modifications. It also resembles the "Coach" concept proposed by Murray Bowen (see Hartman's essay in this volume), though it is used in a somewhat different fashion. It is based on the notion, familiar

[6] The current Training Program in Ethnicity and Mental Health, supported by a grant from the National Institute of Mental Health, is directed at teaching nonindigenous, "mainstream" mental health personnel (psychiatric residents, clinical psychology interns, and psychiatric social work students) the skills to provide alternative, culturally appropriate mental health services to specific subcultural groups, such as working-class Portuguese, Puerto Ricans, Italians, and Haitians in the greater Boston area.

to family therapists, that many problems in the family that have been traditionally viewed as personality problems arising from intrapsychic conflicts are as much, if not more, the product of role conflicts and distortions which have become entrenched within the nuclear and extended family system. However, to this structural view, we have added the idea that the role conflicts and distortions, the triangulations, cutoffs and scapegoatings, are related to conflicts and confusions in cultural values. This conforms, of course, to our theoretical position with respect to the transactions of the culture focus within the transactional field, arising from problems within the ecological niche. We believe that value contradictions occur even within fairly homogeneous cultures, due to the inevitable variations that take place. But they are particularly salient in a pluralistic society, such as ours, made up of a mosaic or patchwork of cultural groups. And it is unavoidable in dealing with newly arrived, emigrant or refugee families.

The function of the Culture Broker is to intervene with respect to value conflicts and confusions after determining what they are, and to help the family to resolve them, while leaving the direction of movement in the course of acculturation in the hands of the family—that is, not imposing his or her own values on the family. This requires a real effort on the part of the therapist to identify with the values of the family, to start "where they are at," and to respect and validate their value positions.[7] It is in this respect that prior knowledge of the ethnography and dominant value profiles of the ethnicity in question is almost indispensable.

It is convenient to look at therapeutic procedures from three aspects: (1) assessment; (2) the therapeutic contract and therapeutic goals; and (3) therapeutic maneuvers. Actually, all three aspects are intertwined from the first contact on, so that separation is somewhat artificial. This holds for all forms of therapy and especially for family therapy. However, in our case, interdigitations take a special twist. We work in community mental health centers where families are not referred to us. Our first contact is usually with an individual, ethnic patient referred from the emergency service, an inpatient setting, an outpatient clinic,

---

[7] It is undoubtedly evident that these procedures are being adopted out of the dominant, "mainstream," American value profile; give them *time* ("Future") to *work* on the value problems ("Doing" and "Mastery-over-Nature"), let them *choose* their own path ("Individual") in a *nonjudgmental* atmosphere ("Neutral"). What is perhaps different is that the therapist is required to be very self-conscious about keeping his/her own values on one side, and accepting and working within the values of the family, on the other.

or a neighborhood health team. It is up to our culturally trained team to bring the family into the picture.

Assessment is first directed at two points: evaluating the clinical situation of the identified patient; and determining his ethnic background, the backgrounds of family members, and the characteristics of his ecological niche—meaning the neighborhoods he is presently living in or has recently lived in. We do not take the view, subscribed to by some family therapists, that diagnosis is irrelevant. We are interested in the operations of the transactional field and are therefore obliged to investigate the intrapsychic processes of the identified patient—later of other family members. Furthermore, we are obliged to remain in liaison with other services within the hospital and community mental health centers, for whom diagnosis and prognosis is an important issue. In addition, we may be dealing with a culturally conditioned syndrome, such as the Puerto Rican *ataque*, or with a culturally sanctioned behavior, such as "pseudohallucination" which is not considered psychopathological in the eyes of the ethnic community. On the other hand, it may be so considered. An investigation is therefore in order.

For example, we were referred a young, female, Portuguese patient who had made a suicide attempt. Her story contained the following elements. Her mother had died a year ago. She had been depressed following the loss, and had frequent visual and auditory hallucinations of her mother appearing and speaking to her. The family had lived in East Cambridge, Massachusetts, for five years. The patient lived alone on the first floor of an apartment building. On this occasion, her dead mother had appeared during a spell of warm weather when the window was open on the street outside the apartment. The mother had called out to the patient from the street, asking her to come outside because she wanted to talk to her. The patient then jumped out of the window, which fortunately was low so that her injuries were not overly severe.

We knew that among the Portuguese recently arrived from the Azores, such visual and auditory hallucinations were considered normal after the death of a loved one. The spirit of the deceased is considered to be active, hovering around, and interested in the affairs of family members. In fact, failure to encounter the spirit is often considered to be characteristic of an unfeeling or unloving child. But is jumping out of a window considered reasonable in this context? As we did not know, we decided to use a "native informant" technique. We asked the family and the neighbors about it. There was general agreement that jumping out of a window was beyond the expected behavior, especially after the lapse of a year from the time of death. This confirmed the clinical assessment we had arrived at on other grounds, but we had to be sure.

Determining the cultural and ethnic background varies from simple to complex, depending upon the recency of emigration, the number of generations in this country, and the amount of intermarriage that may have occurred. This information should be included as routine in all family therapy, though it hardly ever appears in clinical records. Even at this conference, I would predict that there will be little if any note taken of ethnicity in cases discussed. In families thoroughly acculturated into the middle class or descended from a WASP background, it may not be considered necessary. Yet I consider that its routine absence is a part of our cultural blindness—an insensitivity based partly on our false "melting pot" ideology, partly on the denial and ignoring of the therapist's own ethnicity. In this country everyone is an ethnic, including WASPs, who may soon find themselves a "minority," at least in large metropolitan communities. Once one asks for ethnic or national background information, it is surprising how relevant it becomes, especially in the development of a genogram.

We use the genogram (Guerin and Fogarty 1972) as a part of our assessment techniques but, as has been reported from other programs, it takes a long time to gather all the necessary information. Families not oriented to the Past have forgotten, or have never known, the facts about their laterally or vertically extended relatives. Future-oriented people are too busy looking ahead or are cut off from information by emotional blockades. The Present Time–oriented minorities with whom we deal are too involved in their current difficulties to want to spend much time talking about their ancestors, especially as they do not see its relevance. They want their problems fixed up *right now,* or as soon as possible. As Present Time people often forget to keep appointments, it helps to make a home visit, and we see families in their homes as soon as we can gain an entrée for many reasons. There are apt to be some family portraits, which helps with the genogram. It is easier to determine how roles are assigned in the family by watching behavior in the natural ecological niche rather than in the artificial setting of an office. Furthermore, the therapist is likely to meet some family members who resist coming to the medical setting, or who are suspicious of the intentions of the family therapists. Such people are likely to find a reason to be absent on the first few visits but tend to get drawn in as family tensions begin to decrease.

Finally, the assessment procedure is associated with the forming of the therapeutic relationship or "contract." So many of our ethnic and minority patients "somatosize" their problems that we frequently are required to provide symptomatic medical diagnosis and treatment. Most of the headaches, backaches, chest pains, dizzy spells, etc., have already been worked up in medical clinics and found to be "functional," which is why the identified patient is referred. Most of the time the patient is resentful about the referral to a psychiatric setting, feeling that the doctors have let him or her down. Since this is the way the patient perceives his problem, we take the position that the complaints are "real" and require appropriate medical treatment, which we will provide or see that it is provided. We do not expect or ask the patient to have or develop insight into the psychological aspect of his psychosomatic problem. We usually find that as we ask about the *situation* in which the symptoms appear or get worse, the information about family conflicts will gradually surface. After a while, we will hear more about the family and less about the complaint, until we get to the point of being able to see the family. On the other hand, there are some families that can be seen sooner because of their concern about the identified patient.

Another way in which the assessment procedure is associated with forming the therapeutic relationship occurs with patients strongly oriented to "Harmony-with-Nature," who believe that their symptoms or problems derive from an evil spirit, a family curse, the evil eye, or the ingestion of a magical substance (usually white powder surreptitously placed in food or wine); and who have been cut off from the appropriate help by the medical establishment, or who simply do not know where to find a "native healer." We will then make an attempt to locate such a person and to bring him or her into the treatment situation. Or if a patient, say a Puerto Rican, is already seeing a "spiritist," we will attempt to establish contact with this person and to work out some form of collaboration. Since native healers, "root workers," spiritists, curanderos, and shamans generally are quite concerned with family relationships, it may be possible to work out an innovative if unorthodox form of collaborative family therapy. This kind of experimentation with "alternative therapies" has not happened too often in our work as many of the "alternative therapists" do not trust anyone connected with the medical establishment. For example, we are currently working with Haitian families, some of whom are deeply involved in voodoo beliefs and ceremonies. So far, because they avoid us, we have been unable to contact any voodoo priests, but we have not given up hope.

As is usually the case in most therapies, the therapeutic contract develops out of the assessment procedure. Here we take a somewhat different tack—or so I believe—from most other family therapies. Because we are dealing with families based on "Lineal" or "Collateral" orientations, it is important to line ourselves up with the head of the family, usually a father—but, in his absence, it could be a mother or grandmother. Since the head of the family holds culturally sanctioned power, we would not be able to gain entrée into the family without sincerely respecting that power, and the objectives he or she has in mind for family goals. Thus we would not be able to get very far if we indicated that one of our goals was to obtain autonomy or "individuation" for a wife or daughter. However, we may be able to free up some space for a wife or daughter to move toward greater freedom and self-assertion by indicating to the power holder that there probably is a better method of maintaining control of the family than that now being employed. In fact, we may also include a warning that current overcontrolling tactics are obviously generating rebellion and resistance, and that the daughter may end up by running away. In this fashion, we can identify with the values and goals of the head of the family while offering a better way of implementing them. This usually leads to solidifying a therapeutic relationship without alienating other family members by seeming to side too much with the power holder.

Once the therapeutic contract and goals are lined up with each other, the "Culture Broker" activity can be brought into play. This is principally a cognitive approach directed at unsnarling value conflicts and confusions by first defining them and then suggesting pathways for accommodation. For example, let us say that the father just mentioned is a Puerto Rican who has recently moved into a mixed neighborhood, and who is terribly worried about his fifteen-year-old daughter's virginity. He has insisted that the mother drive the daughter to and from school, will not let her leave the house unaccompanied by a family member, and will not let her date or go to school dances or other social affairs. His view is that no woman can protect herself in the unsupervised presence of an attractive or seductive boy who wants to have sex with her. He sees American sexual permissiveness and free dating as a disgusting and dangerous life style. Meanwhile the daughter, though bright, has been doing poorly in school and has complained of severe headaches—the reasons for the referral. The daughter explains her poor school performance on the basis of her headaches and inability to concentrate. In an individual interview she appears depressed and acknowledges anger toward her father. She is afraid to confront him for fear of his violent anger at any sign of disobedience. The mother agrees with the daughter, thinks the father is "crazy," but is also afraid to confront him openly.

We consider all the usual intrapsychic dynamics seemingly at work: the possible incestuous attachment of the father to the daughter; his hysterical personality formation; the daughter's repressed rage and sexual attachment to the father; the mother's envy of the daughter and her use of the daughter, implicitly, to retaliate against the father (triangulation). The therapist intervenes through an individual interview with the father, so as not to expose him to any loss of respect in front of the family—respect for the male role being of prime importance in Puerto Rican families. In the interview, the therapist agrees with his views about the importance of maintaining control and of preserving his daughter's virginity. He agrees that American dating patterns are quite permissive and that sexual intercourse under these circumstances is always a possibility. He validates the father's fears. But he points out that American girls have usually had a lot of unsupervised experience with boys throughout their school and neighborhood lives, and that they have been trained not only how to protect themselves, if they wish to, but also how to control their own feelings and behavior. Then the therapist explains the position of the daughter. She has been "grounded" prior to any misconduct. This is like a punishment in advance of the crime. Undeserved punishment is likely to bring out the very behavior it is designed to prevent. Wouldn't it be better to allow her some experience in order that she can discover for herself what is likely to happen, come home and talk to him about it? Can he be both the policeman and the judge at the same time? Perhaps he could talk this over with his wife, relatives or friends and find some way.

To condense this account quite a bit, the father finally permits the daughter to go to a church dance with her girl friends. Nothing untoward happens but she does give him a vivid account of the affair and he gives her some advice. Gradually the father gains confidence in her good judgment, and gives her a little more freedom. The daughter's depression lifts and her school work improves. At this point, with the father's increased confidence in his ability to solve problems, the therapy turns to the conflict between the husband and wife.

Undoubtedly, this outcome could be explained in terms of various theories of family therapy, to which we would have no objection. For us, what is important is that the family has taken a small step toward accommodation to mainstream American values. This small step validates the process of acculturation to peer group values working upon the daughter without undermining the Puerto Rican values important to the father's sense of self-worth and dignity. Such small steps can lead to a considerable reduction in tension between conflicting value systems, and—by reverberating around the transactional field—interpersonal and intrapersonal tension.

The question could be asked, have we not imposed our own American values on this family? We would say no. We have cognitively increased the range of choice by supplying information and suggesting possibilities which, admittedly, are in the American direction. But the family adopted the direction, after giving it a trial, because it worked. There was positive reinforcement, supplied by the external situation, not from the therapist.

As this account of the therapeutic implications of the ecological approach has been so brief, many other questions could be raised. Designing family therapy for ethnic and minority families is, in any event, in a very early stage. There is a paucity of literature on the topic. (Giordano and Giordano 1977). There is, as yet, little agreement among minority professionals on how to conduct therapy, much less on how to formulate theory to explain what should be done. However, with the steady increase in minority and ethnic mental health outreach services and research centers, supplemented by single- or multi-ethnic workshops and conferences, we have reason to hope that the ecological/family approach to such subcultural systems will undergo vigorous growth in the near future.

References

Ackerman, Nathan. 1958. *The Psychodynamics of Family Life*. New York: Basic Books.
American Psychiatric Association. 1952. *Diagnostic and Statistical Manual:*

Mental Disorders (*DSM I*). Prepared by the Committee on Nomenclature and Statistics. Washington, D.C.

Auerswald, Edgar. 1968. "Interdisciplinary versus Ecological Approach." *Family Process* 7:202–15.

—— 1972. "Families, Change, and the Ecological Perspective." In Andrew Farber, Marilyn Mendelsohn, and Augustus Napier, eds., *The Book of Family Therapy*, pp. 685–705. New York: Science House.

—— 1974. "Thinking About Health and Mental Health." In Silvano Arieti, ed., *American Handbook of Psychiatry*, pp. 316–38. 2d ed. New York: Basic Books.

Barth, Frederik. 1969. Introduction to Frederik Barth, ed., *Ethnic Groups and Boundaries: The Social Organization of Cultural Differences*. Boston: Little Brown.

Bateson, Gregory. 1972. *Steps to an Ecology of Mind*. New York: Ballentine.

Bell, John E. 1961. *Family Group Therapy*. Public Health Monograph No. 64. Washington, D.C.: Dept. of Health, Education and Welfare.

Boszormenyi-Nagy, Ivan. 1962. "The Concept of Schizophrenia from the Perspective of Family Treatment." *Family Process* 1:103–113.

Bowen, Murray. 1978. *Family Therapy in Clinical Practice*. New York: Aronson.

Dewey, John and Arthur F. Bentley. 1950. *Knowing and the Known*. Boston: Beacon Press.

Framo, James L. 1965. "Rationale and Techniques of Intensive Family Therapy." In Ivan Boszormenyi-Nagy and James L. Framo, eds., *Intensive Family Therapy*, pp. 143–212. New York: Harper & Row.

Giordano, Joseph and Grace P. Giordano. 1977. *The Ethno-Cultural Factor in Mental Health: A Literature Review and Bibliography*. New York: Committee on Pluralism and Group Identity, American Jewish Committee.

Guerin, Philip J. and Thomas F. Fogarty. 1972. "Study Your Own Family." In Andrew Farber, Marilyn Mendelsohn, and Augustus Napier, eds., *The Book of Family Therapy*, pp. 445–67. New York: Science House.

Haley, Jay. 1976. *Problem-Solving Therapy: New Strategies for Effective Family Therapy*. San Francisco: Jossey Bass.

Kluckhohn, Florence R. and Fred L. Strodtbeck. 1961. *Variations in Value Orientations*. Evanston, Ill.: Row, Peterson.

Mash, F. S., L. A. Hamerlynck, and L. C. Handy, eds. 1975. *Behavior Modification in Families*. New York: Brunner/Mazel.

Minuchin, Salvadore. 1974. *Families and Family Therapy*. Cambridge: Harvard University Press.

Papajohn, John and John P. Spiegel. 1975. *Transactions in Families: A Modern Approach for Resolving Cultural and Generational Conflict*. San Francisco: Jossey Bass.

Pattison, E. Mansell. 1976. "A Theoretical Empirical Base for Social Systems Therapy." Paper presented at the 23rd Annual Conference of the American Group Psychotherapy Association, Boston.

Speck, Ross V. and Carolyn Attneave. 1972. "Network Therapy." In Andrew Farber, Marilyn Mendelsohn, and Augustus Napier, eds., *The Book of Family Therapy*, pp. 637–65. New York: Science House.

——1973. *Family Networks*. New York: Vintage Books.

Spiegel, John. 1971a. "Transactional Inquiry: Description of Systems." In John Papajohn, eds., *Transactions: The Interplay Between Individual, Family and Society*, pp. 37–84. New York: Science House.

——1971b. "Cultural Strain, Family Role Patterns, and Intrapsychic Conflict." In John G. Howells, ed., *Theory and Practice of Family Psychiatry*, pp. 367–89. New York: Brunner/Mazel.

Sussex, James N. and Hazel H. Weidman. "Toward Responsiveness in Mental Health Care." In James N. Sussex, ed., *Psychiatry and the Social Sciences. Psychiatric Annals* (special Miami edition) 5(8):9–16.

Weidman, Hazel H. 1973. "Implications of the Culture Broker Concept for the Delivery of Health Care." Paper presented at the Annual Meeting of the Southern Anthropological Society, Wrightsville Beach, N.C.

——1975. "Concepts as Strategies for Change." In James N. Sussex, ed., *Psychiatry and the Social Sciences. Psychiatric Annals* (special Miami edition) 5(8):17–19.

7

Bowen Family Systems: Theory and Practice

ANN HARTMAN

Murray Bowen, director of the Family Center, at the Georgetown University School of Medicine, is one of the small group of creative and innovative researcher-clinicians who began to study the family in the late forties and early fifties. Out of the study and the effort to translate a growing understanding of the family into new ways of helping, the family therapy movement was launched. The growing interest and activity in the family field may be termed a movement—an intellectual, social, and political movement—because the family approach is not simply a set of techniques or strategies to be added on to traditional individually oriented practice. A family orientation involves a new and different way of thinking about the nature of people and their relations with each other and their world—a way of thinking that revolutionizes one's approach to clients and to practice.

This essay will attempt to describe Murray Bowen's theoretical contribution to the family movement, and will present some of the ways that theory has been translated into family treatment. Further, ways in which Bowen's theories might be extended in providing help to social work clients in a range of social work settings will also be suggested. Finally, the major significance of Bowen's work for the teaching and training of family oriented practitioners will be presented.

It is with considerable uneasiness that I approach the task of presenting materials based on Bowen's work, even though he apparently gives permission and even encourages his students to do so. He is quoted by Guerin as saying to families and to students. "These are my ideas, if you find them useful and pick them up, then they are no longer

my ideas, but yours'' (Guerin and Guerin 1976:9). I will attempt to
describe Bowen's ideas with as little distortion as I can manage but
hope that the description will encourage readers to go to Bowen's own
work, which has recently become readily available through the publication of his collected writings (Bowen 1978). I will also draw on the
writings of Bowen's colleagues and students who have reported their
experiences in translating the Bowen model into practice. Finally, as
a social work practitioner and a social work educator, I will describe
how I have picked up some of Bowen's ideas and found them useful
in social work settings, where they have enriched social work practice
and given direction to social work policy development in some very
interesting ways.

Bowen Family Systems Theory

The cornerstone of Bowen's approach is the concept of the family
as a system and the importance of that system in the development and
the life of all human beings. The emphasis on the family as a system
originally led Bowen's work to be characterized as a family systems
approach. Recently, because of the popularization and multiple and
confused meanings of the word *system*, Bowen has elected to specify
his contribution as Bowen Theory. Perhaps the most accurate label
might be Bowen Family Systems Theory, which retains the central
notion of the family system but specifies it and differentiates it from,
for example, Parsonian theory about the family as a system.

Bowen's approach was born, as was much of the family movement,
in the clinical study of schizophrenia. At the Menninger Clinic in the
late forties and early fifties, Bowen became impressed, as were other
family researchers (Wynne et al. 1958; Lidz et al. 1957; and Jackson
1957), with the "emotional stuck togetherness" and the intensely transactional nature of the nuclear family system (Bowen 1978:207). His
first studies focused on mother-child symbiosis. In 1951, continuing
this study, he designed a clinical research program in which mothers
lived in the hospital with their impaired children, sharing responsibility
for their care. Later, at the National Institute for Mental Health
(NIMH), the entire family was included in the research.

During this early period at Menninger, Bowen was deeply interested
in psychoanalysis. He embarked upon his family research in hopes that
it might eventually contribute to psychoanalytic theory. The impact

of these studies, however, and of his later family studies at NIMH, was to move Bowen away from a psychoanalytic orientation and from the use of disease and the medical model as a means of understanding and helping people with emotional dysfunction.

In an interview with Berenson, Bowen describes this time:

> I had no idea the research would take the direction it did. The big changes began soon after the research began. The early family researches of the 1954–1956 period were describing a completely new order of observations never previously described in the literature. I think it was related to the ability to finally shift thinking from an individual to a family frame of reference. . . . In my research, the change came as a sudden insight shortly after schizophrenic patients and their entire families were living together on the research ward.
>
> Then it was possible to really see the family phenomenon for the first time. After it was possible to see this phenomenon in schizophrenia, it was then automatic to see varying degrees of the same thing in all people. (1978:394)

Bowen writes with considerable passion about the importance of theory and its power in selecting from and structuring experience. This process, which tends to substantiate the originally held theory, frequently is out of the practitioner's awareness, yet dictates the direction of his or her work. Early in his research, in order to counteract "theoretical blindness" (Bowen 1978:394), Bowen insisted that all psychiatric and psychoanalytic terminology be replaced by descriptive words and phrases in order to free his research team to begin to think of alternative ways of selecting, coding, and understanding their perceptions (1978:355). Such "delabeling" tends to break down habits of thought and unconscious theoretical biases. This laid the groundwork for the slow shift to the family focus and the recognition of the family phenomenon. The concern about accurate communication and the baggage of meanings that can be carried by words led Bowen to select an alternative and very descriptive vocabulary in naming his new and developing concepts.

Bowen Family Systems Theory grew out of clinical research, including thousands of hours of observing families in action. As Bowen and his researchers began to perceive the new order of data which resulted from their shift to a family focus, Bowen sought a different framework or theoretical context. He felt that psychiatrists had used discrepant models in organizing their perception—for example, models taken not only from medicine, but also from literature (for example, the Oedipus Complex). His conviction was that human beings and the human family were a part of the natural world, and thus it was to the study of biology, ethology, phylogenesis, and other natural sciences that Bowen turned for models and for explanatory hypotheses in his theory-building effort. It was his hope that through this route, the study and treatment of both the family and of emotional problems could share the language of the sciences, one day becoming a science in a relationship of complementarity with the other sciences. (N.B: Ethology and sociobiology are particularly congruent areas for study in enhancing our understanding of the emotional processes within the human family. E. O. Wilson's work [1975], Dawkin's, *The Selfish Gene* [1976], and Goodall's study of chimpanzees [1971] are cases in point.)

It may be useful to clarify one final background issue before describing the theoretical framework, namely the relationship between Bowen's work and General Systems Theory (GST). The congruence between Bowen Family Systems Theory and General Systems Theory has been noted and has led people to assume that Bowen's thinking grew out of an exposure to GST. Bowen states he had little or no knowledge of General Systems Theory as he worked on his family theory. Systems thinking is an approach whose time has come and it is likely that the development of Bowen's systemic approach is yet another example of the parallel emergence of systems thinking in many fields.

Concerns about the sociology of knowledge notwithstanding, Bowen's family theory is quite congruent in language and in conceptualization with GST, partly, perhaps, because both approaches are deeply rooted in observation of biological processes. Further, Bowen's interest in linking the understanding of families with analogues in other systems, for example in cell biology, immunology, virology, and with various societal processes, is similar to the General Systems Theory goal of unifying science through the discovery of analogies or, in systems language, isomorphisms, among different orders of systems. This connection between Bowen's work and systems theory has relevance for social workers who have sought in the systems conceptualization a way of ordering the vast arena of our professional interest and concern. For those who think about social work in this way, Bowen's concept of the family and the individual in relation to the family is a useful and highly congruent contribution.

Bowen has perhaps pursued theory development more diligently than other of the pioneers in the family movement. His theory has grown and changed over time and each stage of its development has been reported in a series of papers by Bowen, which have now been gathered, ordered, and reprinted. I am reluctant to outline Bowen's major concepts as they are available in Bowen's own words. However, without presenting the theoretical underpinnings, the materials on assessment, intervention, and training would be hardly intelligible to those readers unfamiliar with Bowen's work. Perhaps this brief discussion will stimulate such readers to examine the original sources.

Differentiation of Self

Of prime importance in Bowen's Theory is the concept of differentiation of self. As the theory has developed, this key concept has also developed and, to some extent, changed. This becomes evident as one reads Bowen's theoretical papers chronologically. It is a complex concept and, according to Bowen, has often been misunderstood. My impression is that the confusion may grow from the fact that this major concept refers at once to intrapersonal, interpersonal, and family systems processes. When Bowen writes about it, he moves back and forth with ease in discussing intrapersonal and intrafamilial differentiation and fusion. This may create confusion but also it is the key both to the theory and to the practice as the concept not only conceptualizes parallel intrapersonal, interpersonal, and intrafamilial processes, but also provides the linkage between the levels. For clarity's sake, I will discuss the levels separately and then point to the linkages.

In intrapersonal terms, differentiation of self and its opposite—fusion—refer to the relationship between the intellect and the emotions in the control of a human being's life. If intellect and emotions are relatively differentiated, a person retains thoughtful, planful, and adaptive behavior even under considerable stress, whereas if intellect and emotions are fused, the individual is dominated by automatic emotional reactions. Such people "are less flexible, less adaptable, and more emotionally dependent upon those about them. They are easily stressed into dysfunction . . . they inherit a high percentage of all human problems" (Bowen 1978:362). A poorly differentiated person is "trapped in a feeling world." On the other hand, more differentiated persons are those whose intellectual functioning can retain relative autonomy in periods of stress, who are more flexible, more adaptable, and more independent of the emotionality around them. They cope better with life's stresses, their life courses are more orderly and successful, and they are remarkably free of human problems (Bowen 1978:362). When Bowen originally presented this concept, he did so in terms of a differentiation of self scale which describes profiles of the characteristics of those located at various points on the scale. This effort was to emphasize the notion of a continuum which included all people and which demonstrated that function and dysfunction were not a matter of qualitative difference but of degree.

Differentiation of self and fusion also relate to interpersonal processes. A highly fused person is dependent upon the relationship system. A large portion of the self is negotiable in that system. That is, behavior is directed toward pleasing or manipulating others rather than being directed by the self. A poorly differentiated person tends to fuse in intimate relationships. This fusion, which threatens what little sense of self there is, creates extreme stress and a variety of actions are called into play to deal with the anxiety which accompanies fusion. This will be described later. A well differentiated person maintains a solid self in the most intimate relationships and is able to take what Bowen calls "I" positions in the interpersonal system.

Differentiation of the self in the intrapersonal sphere and the interpersonal world are both rooted in differentiation within the family system. Bowen encountered extreme fusion in the families he observed in his researches on the families of schizophrenics. He originally referred to this "stuck togetherness" as the "undifferentiated family ego mass," a highly descriptive phrase but one he no longer uses. This term referred to the shared emotional process within the nuclear family—a process which followed definite patterns of emotional responsiveness. All families share, at least, to some extent, an "undifferentiated family ego mass" but it is most obvious in its extreme, such as in symbiotic relationships and in families where the "emotional closeness is so intense that family members know each other's feelings, thoughts, fantasies, and dreams" (Bowen 1978:160.) A fused family cannot tolerate an individuals attempts to differentiate. A less fused family, however, can allow its members to grow, to change, to individuate. These are familiar issues discussed in different terms by ego psychologists and by family theorists. In fact, the importance of the differentiation-fusion concept in Bowen Theory is reminiscent of Rank's emphasis on separation and individuation.

In Bowen theory, intrapersonal, interpersonal, intrafamilial differentiation and fusion are linked in several ways. First, an individual is consistent across the different systems levels. If a person is poorly differentiated from his or her family of origin, it is likely that she or he is also poorly differentiated in the nuclear family system and within all interpersonal relationships. Further, such a person is also poorly differentiated in the sense that the emotions dominate the intellect.

Further, there is a causal link between growing up in a poorly differentiated family, being a poorly differentiated person, and creating as an adult a new "undifferentiated family ego mass" which is patterned after the family of origin system. In dealing with the variables that determine level of differentiation, Bowen has said:

> It would be accurate to say your differentiation level is determined by the differentiation level in your parents at the time you were born, your sex and how that fitted into the family plan, your sibling position, the normality or lack of it in your genetic composition, the emotional climate in each of your parents and in their marriage before and after your birth, the quality of the relationship each of your parents had with their parental families, the number of reality problems in your parents' lives in the period before your birth and the years after your birth, your parents ability to cope with the emotional and reality problems of their time, and other details that belong to the broad configuration. In addition, the level of differentiation in each of your parents was determined by the very same order of factors in the situation into which they were born and grew up, and the levels of differentiation in each grandparent was determined by the same factors in their families of origin, and on back through the generations. (1978:409)

This view has powerful implications not only for assessment, but for the development of interventive strategies as well.

Triangles

The second key concept upon which the theory and the practice is based is the concept of the triangle or three-person system, which Bowen considers to be the building block of all emotional systems in and outside of the family. Very briefly, the two person system is basically unstable, and such a system deals with tension or with the drift toward uncomfortable fusion by bringing in a third person. In periods of calm, a triangle consists of a comfortable twosome and an outsider.

The outsider, however, attempts to develop a twosome with one of the original pair, thus shifting another person to the outside position.

The concepts of triangles and triangulation describe the structure and the process in all family systems and also elucidate social processes occurring in friendship and work systems. For example, if a colleague comes into your office, pulls a chair close to your desk, and begins to talk negatively about another colleague in a confidential tone, you are being triangled. That is, the visitor is attempting to gain closeness with you through a sharing of negatives about the third person, thus expelling that colleague. Triangles are universal in all families but become particularly dysfunctional when they are rigid and unmoving. Scapegoating is an example of a dysfunctional triangle. The parents deal with their problematic relationship by sharing critical and negative feelings about a child, thus finding some togetherness while keeping the child "stuck" in the outside position. Triangulating can serve to minimize intimacy and to avoid "person to person" relationships since two people, rather than talking about intimate or difficult and potentially painful issues between them, can always talk about other people or things. The concept of the triangle gives direction to treatment, since the modification of the central triangle in a family can allow the whole system to move and change. (For an interesting discussion and extension of the triangle, see Thomas Fogarty 1979).

Family Emotional System

Other concepts in Bowen's theory define and describe processes operating within the nuclear family and/or through the generations. The "nuclear emotional system" refers to the patterns of emotional functioning within the nuclear family system. Of particular interest to family therapists are those processes which are set in motion primarily to deal with, or accommodate to, the lack of differentiation in the marital pair. Lack of differentiation in a relationship creates extreme anxiety, as the couple is chronically threatened by loss of the self through fusion. Most couples, Bowen thinks handle the potential threat that intimacy entails by distancing one another. Chronic marital conflict can also serve this function. In such a marriage, the couple may have some periods of intense closeness but these times are quickly ended by a fight between the pair. Marital conflict thus serves to monitor and control the drift toward fusion. Some pairs fuse, becoming a single self. This requires that one member give up his or her self to the other. The outward result is a pair including a dominant overfunctioning mate and a dysfunctional adaptive mate. The other major mechanism undifferentiated couples may use in dealing with fusion is the triangulating of a child, as was discussed above. This method is a part of the "family projection process," in which parents project their anxieties and difficulties onto their children, and is the means by which the parents' lack of differentiation can be duplicated in the impaired child. When the family projection process occurs across the generations, it is called the "multi-generational transmission process." Bowen and his colleagues have studied families back for several generations in an effort to understand and track patterns of intergenerational transmission.

Emotional Cutoff

The last concept to be included in this brief summary of Bowen Family Systems Theory is the concept of the "emotional cut-off." Bowen describes this as follows:

> The degree of unresolved emotional attachment to the parents is equivalent to the degree of undifferentiation that must somehow be handled in the person's own life and in future generations. The unresolved attachment is handled by the intrapsychic processes of denial and isolation of self while living close to the parents; or by physically running away; or by a combination of emotional isolation and physical distance. The more intense the cutoff with the past, the more likely the individual to have an exaggerated version of his parental family problem in his own marriage, and the more likely his own children to do a more intense cut-off with him in the next generation. (1978:382)

As will become clearer in the following pages, the effort in therapy with a person or family which makes use of the emotional cutoff is to convert that cutoff into an orderly differentiation of a self in the extended family.

In summary, these major concepts of Bowen Family Systems Theory can be further demonstrated or operationalized by examining what a reasonably well-differentiated person might look like. People who are sufficiently differentiated can be close to their families without becoming lost in the emotional system and can be away from their families without cutting themselves off. They can be different from their families and risk taking "I" positions without being rejecting or fearing rejection. They can be *like* their families without losing a sense of self. They can love without fusing and can maintain a person-to-person relationship with each member of their family system without triangulating or seeking closeness with one at the expense of another.

If a person has achieved this level of differentiation from his or her family of origin, he or she will maintain similarly differentiated relationships in the nuclear family system and with others in the work and friendship systems. Such a person manages his or her life through planful, intellectual decision-making and has energy and interest available for productive, goal-directed activity.

Helping a client achieve a higher level of differentiation is the aim of therapy. Writes Bowen:

> The over-all goal is to help individual family members to rise up out of the emotional togetherness that binds us all. The instinctual force toward differentiation is built into the organism, just as are the emotional forces that oppose it. The goal is to help the motivated family member to take a microscopic step toward a better level of differentiation, in spite of the togetherness forces that oppose. When one family member can finally master this, then other family members automatically take similar steps. (1978:371)

The Differentiation of Self as a Therapeutic Model

Bowen has moved from seeing family members together, to seeing marital pairs, to currently doing much of his work with individuals. There are some who would say that he is no longer a family therapist. However, by his own definition, he is a family therapist, as he writes, "From my orientation, a theoretical system that 'thinks' in terms of family and works toward improving the family system is family psychotherapy" (Bowen 1978:157). In the development of his therapeutic approach, Bowen has moved back up the intergenerational family system in selecting the focus and arena for work. This change grew in part from increased knowledge about the power of intergenerational transmission and in part occurred serendipitously.

During Bowen's early years, he worked with the total family or with the parents and symptomatic child. In time he became convinced that although family group therapy restored emotional harmony in nuclear family emotional systems, it did so primarily through distributing the difficulties more evenly throughout the family. He considered it an effective short-term method of symptom relief but felt that it did not contribute to a higher level of differentiation of self in the family members.

After several years of working with family groups, Bowen began to ask parents to attend sessions without the children on the premise that if the parental relationship changed, the entire family system would change. His effort was to move the triangled child out of the marital system and to deal with the issues between the parents. In 1966 he wrote that the optimum avenue toward a higher level of differentiation of self

> is differentiation of a self from one's spouse, as a cooperative effort, in the presence of a potential "triangle" (therapist) who can remain emotionally detached. In such a therapeutic model, the pair must be sufficiently involved with each other to stand the stress of "differentiation" and sufficiently uncomfortable to motivate the effort. One, and then the other, moves forward in several steps, until motivation stops. (Bowen 1978:175)

Referred to as "Family Systems Therapy with Two People," this became the main approach of those working in the Bowen framework and continues to be frequently used.

In this model of marital work, there is emphasis on encouraging the marital couple to tell each other what they think and begin to take "I" positions which oppose the fused marital "twosomeness." When a member of the pair takes an "I" position, he or she will attempt to triangulate the therapist for support. The therapist must resist this, maintaining his or her own independent position. The other member of the marital pair will then attempt to use every emotional weapon available, including triangulating the therapist, to get the spouse to abandon the "I" position and to return to the fused position. However, as one wife reported after she was unable to manipulate her husband to forsake his independent stance, "One part of me approved of what you were doing, but somehow I had to do what I did. Even when I was excited and angry, I was hoping you would not let me change you. I'm so glad you did not give in" (Bowen 1978:222).

Before long, in this situation, the wife was ready to take a self-determining step and it was the husband's turn to become petulant and angry, attempting to block his wife's move. This seesaw process will continue until the couple reaches a level of comfort and satisfaction which tends to obviate motivation to continue this demanding work.

Concurrent with his clinical research and practice, Bowen, for many years, has been systematically studying his own family system, working to gain objective understanding of the system, to detriangulate himself from the major family triangles, to form person-to-person relationships with as many members as possible of his family of origin, and in the long run, to increase his own level of differentiation. In March 1967 he presented the work with his own family at a major conference of family therapists and researchers. One can imagine how electrifying this presentation must have been! Not only was the material compelling, as can be experienced by reading this fascinating paper, but his personal sharing was very moving and also revolutionary as it violated long-held cherished professional norms about self-disclosure. This presentation had many outcomes, one of which was the discovery of a new method of training and of treatment.

Following the presentation, the trainees in Bowen's program spontaneously began to attempt to make use of Bowen's theory of triangles and of returning to their families of origin in altering their own positions. I have noticed that same kind of contagion in my students as they are introduced to Bowen's work. Bowen's trainees reported on their visits with family members and their efforts were discussed in meetings with the group. Within the next months, Bowen became aware that this particular group of residents were not only doing superior work with their clients but they seemed to be improving their relationship with spouses and children. As Bowen later reported, "This surprise development was a turning point in my professional life" (1978:532). This discovery was followed by several years of testing out the use of the family of origin as the focus and resource for change in training and in therapy. The results of these efforts confirmed the initial experience of the power of this model in bringing about change and began to revolutionize family therapy as practiced at Georgetown (Bowen 1978:534).

This new therapeutic model was termed "defining a self in the extended family." It is a process through which the trainee or client becomes a student of his or her own family. It requires knowledge about the functioning of emotional systems and the motivation to do a research study on one's own family. The study process requires that the researcher begin to gain control over his emotional reactivity to his family and that he develop the ability to become a more objective observer. As the system becomes more "open" and he can begin to see the triangles and the parts he plays in the family reaction patterns, he can begin the more complex process toward differentiating himself from the previously unrecognized myths, images, distortions, and triangles (Bowen 1978:540). The role of the "therapist" in this model of help is as coach, teacher, and expert in family systems. It is interesting to note that when Bowen shifted to focus on work with the extended family, he began to put "quotes" around the word *therapy*, probably as an expression of his increasing distance from a medical model. Wrote Bowen in 1976, "The therapy based on differentiation is no longer therapy in the usual sense. The therapy is as different from conventional therapy as the theory is different from conventional theory" (1978:371).

My own understanding of this model of change is expressed in a story, which I have published elsewhere (Hartman 1979a) told by a member of a seminar I was conducting on family assessment. Responding to my discussion of defining the self in the family of origin, a woman in the group related the following:

"For thirty years I've always ironed in the dining room. My mother always did and I always did, and I never thought anything about it. A month ago, I loaned my ironing board to my married daughter who had just moved into a new apartment. I went up to the attic and brought down my mother's old ironing board. I set the board up in my dining room and as I used my mother's ironing board, I felt so close to her, so in touch with her again! I remembered her ironing and got to wondering why she had always ironed in the dining room. The answer was simple. We lived on a farm with no electricity. My mother used to have to heat the irons on the wood stove in the kitchen. She didn't iron in the kitchen because it was too hot with the stove going and thus she ironed in the dining room which was the closest room.

And suddenly it struck me—I didn't have to iron in the dining room! I had an electric iron—and could iron in any room in the house. Since then, I sometimes iron in the dining room but I also iron in the living room in front of the television or in the kitchen. I really became free to iron anywhere I wanted to!

Reviewing his experience with this model in 1974, Bowen wrote, "The overall conclusion is that families in which the focus is on the differentiation of self in the families of origin automatically make as much or more progress in working out the relationship system with spouses and children as families seen in formal family therapy in which there is a principle focus on the interdependence in the marriage'' (1978:545).

In considering the use of this model of help, there is uncertainty as to whether there should be a disciplined avoidance of focus on the nuclear family emotional system or whether the two approaches, each of which has been found to be helpful, should be combined. There has been some thought that work with the marital pair tends to undermine motivation for embarking upon defining a self with the family of origin. A review of available literature of people identified with the Bowen Family Systems approach would indicate that defining the self in the family of origin as a therapeutic model is used alone in some situations and in combination with other forms of family therapy, either family group or marital. My own practice experience has followed this pattern with a tendency to move back and forth between focus on here-and-now relationship issues and extended family work. In general, however, I would say that the here-and-now relationship work tends to restore calm and to lower the level of anxiety, thus freeing energy for extended family work, and that the major breakthroughs occur in the relationships between clients and the members of their families of origin. These breakthroughs then reverberate back into the nuclear family as there is enhanced functioning within that system.

As we now turn to a more detailed explication of the planned use of the extended family as the resource for and instrument of change, I will rely increasingly on my own efforts to translate the model into daily practice and on the work of some of those who have been influenced by the Bowen conception, such as Fernando Colon (1973), Elizabeth Carter and Monica Orfanidis (1976), Philip Guerin (1976), and several anonymous writers who have published their work with their own families. (See anonymous articles in the Georgetown Family Symposium, Volumes 2 and 3.) Bowen has provided the theoretical base, outlined the model in broad strokes, presented in detail his work with his own family, and pointed out the direction for change. The ''how to's'' of the daily application to practice tend to be worked out by the individual practitioner.

The Assessment Process

Assessment (or should we call it research?) is the cornerstone of the Bowen Family Systems approach and is a major part of the actual change process. In this model, however, assessment is not an activity carried on solely by the professional. The client takes major responsibility for assessment, for conducting the research into the family system. The professional, or coach, gives guidance and makes suggestions, but the client does the work and makes the discoveries.

The assessment process has two interlocking dimensions. One is the study of the intergenerational family system through time, an assessment which may cover from four to six or more generations. The other dimension concerns the nature of the current family emotion system.

The Intergenerational Family History

A major task—and at the same time an opportunity for learning and change—in the process toward increased differentiation is the obtaining, organizing, and understanding of the family history. Bowen, in discussing the contribution of intergenerational family history writes, "In only 150 or 200 years an individual is the descendant of 65 to 128 families of origin, each of which has contributed something to one's self. With all the myths and pretense and emotionally biased reports and opinions, it is difficult to really know 'self' or to know family members in the present or recent past. As one reconstructs facts a century ago, it is easier to get beyond myths and be factual" (1978:492). Such a study of even four or five generations begins not only to present and organize the facts, clarify distortions, demystify mysteries, and clear up confusions, but it also surfaces major or nodal events in the life of the family that have sent reverberating shock waves through the family system. The family history also makes clear recurrent family issues and themes that continue to impact the current generation. As Elizabeth Carter explains, "Unresolved issues in past relationships are carried into new relationships and new generations until they develop into on-going family themes around which family members polarize." Examples of such issues include attitudes toward money, sex, parenting, divorce, religion, achievement, and handling illness and death. To the extent that these have been emotionally charged issues in past family relationships, a kind of "party line" or set of family teachings, slogans, and prohibitions are developed and passed down through the generations. The usual reaction of family members is either to go along with the family policy or rebel and do the exact opposite, under the mistaken notion that doing or thinking the opposite of what the parents did or thought is freedom (Carter and Orfanidis 1976:196–98).

My own conviction is that the best way to gather and to organize intergenerational family history is through the use of the genogram, which organizes and presents for visual examination a vast amount of material about the family. An orderly visual presentation leads to a process of objectification, which allows one to stand outside and look at the family; and to begin to recognize themes, nodal events and their impact, and other characteristics of the family that make it as individual as a handprint.

Instructions for Drawing a Genogram[1]

A genogram is simply a family tree which includes more social data. It is a map of four or more generations of a family, which records genealogical relationships, major family events, achievements, occupations, illnesses, losses, family migrations and dispersal, sibling position characteristics, identifications and role assignments, and information about alignments and emotional and communication patterns.

The skeleton of the genogram tends to follow the conventions of genetic and genealogical charts. A male is indicated by a □, a female by a ○, and a person whose sex is unknown, by a △. The latter symbol tends to be used, for example, when the client says, "I think there were seven children in my grandfather's family but I have no idea whether they were males or females," or "My mother lost a full-term child five years before I was born, but I don't know what sex it was".

A marital pair is indicated by □———○, and it is useful to add the marital date, □—M. 6/2/54—○. Offspring are shown as follows:

A divorce is generally portrayed by two lines across the connecting line between the pair, and again, it is useful to include dates:

□—M. 6/63 ‖ ○
Div. 1970

[1] Portions of this material were published elsewhere (see Hartman 1978).

An ongoing relationship of a pair who are not married is indicated by a dotted line. A family member no longer living is generally shown by ⊠ d. 1967. Ages are noted within the circles and squares. Thus, a complex, but not untypical reconstituted family may be drawn as in figure 7.1.

Figure 7.1

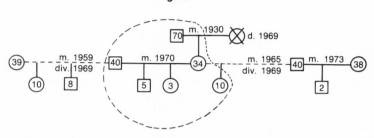

It is useful to draw a dotted line around the family members who compose the household. Incidentally, such a family chart enables the coach to quickly grasp "who's who" in complicated reconstituted families.

With these basic building blocks, expanded horizontally to depict the contemporary generation of siblings and cousins, and vertically to chart the generations through time, it is possible to chart any family, given sufficient paper, patience, and information. As one charts the skeleton structure of the family, it is also important to flesh this out with the rich and varied data which portray the saga of the particular family being studied. The following kinds of information may be gathered: given names, first and middle names, indicate naming patterns and surface identifications; dates of birth and dates of death record when members joined the family, longevity, and family losses. Birth dates indicate the age of family members when important events occurred. They indicate how early or late in a marriage a child came and the age of the parents at its birth. In a sense, birth, marriage, and death dates mark the movement of the family through time.

Birth dates also identify each individual's place in the sibship. This surfaces such potential roles as "older responsible," "firstborn son," or "baby." Place of birth and current place of residence mark the movement of the family through space. This information charts the family's patterns of dispersal, surfacing major immigrations or migrations, and brings attention to periods of loss, change, and upheaval.

Picturing the family's movement through space may communicate a good deal about family boundaries and norms concerning mobility. Is this a family that "holds on" or "lets go"? Further, the impact of world history on families often becomes evident as responses to war, persecution, westward migration, depression, industrialization, and even climatic or ecological changes, are often seen in relocations.

Occupations of family members acquaint one with the interests and talents, the successes and failures, and the varied socioeconomic statuses that are found in most families. Occupational patterns may also point to identifications and can often portray family proscriptions and expectations.

Finally, facts about members' health and causes of death provide overall family health history and also may say something about the way individuals are prophesying about their own futures. These prophecies may well have some power of self-fulfillment.

The above demographic data can take us a long way toward understanding the family system. Gathering associations and favorite stories about family members can add to the richness of the portrayal. One can ask, "What word or two or what picture comes to mind when you think about this person?" or, "What stories have been handed down?" These associations tend to tap another level of information about the family as the myths, role assignments, characterizations or caricatures of family members, pop into the reporter's mind.

Finally, certain aspects of the family's communication and/or emotional structure can be indicated. Parts of the family that have been cut off become quite obvious because the reporter generally has very little information about them. Cutoffs can be portrayed by drawing a fence where the cutoff exists, whereas tight emotional bonds can be demonstrated by drawing a line around portions of the family that form close linkages. It helps to keep things clearer if a colored pencil is used to indicate structural linkages and cutoffs so as not to confuse these with the basic genealogical structure.

Analysis of the Genogram

An assessment of the family system over time through an analysis of the genogram develops step by step as the genogram is constructed.[2]

---

[2] This material on analysis of the genogram has been published elsewhere in a slightly different form (Hartman 1979b).

Fact gathering and thinking about the meaning of, and relationships among, the facts are complementary processes. The ongoing construction and study of the genogram continues throughout the contact.

Each family genogram contains so many facts, so much information, it is easy to be overwhelmed and to miss meanings and connections without some guidelines or tentative hypotheses to direct the study. A few suggestions about things to look for in thinking about the facts are presented here.

One key area of investigation centers around the intergenerational identification and transmission processes. Families seem to have a rather universal tendency to identify members of the current generation with members of previous generations. Often these identifications, while exerting considerable influence, are out of the family's awareness. A variety of things can promote these linkages. For example, frequently a child born around the time of the death of an important member of the family becomes a replacement object for that person and goes through life carrying the emotional burdens and the expectations connected with that salient figure. The universality of the replacement phenomenon is rather touchingly demonstrated in the following story. A family's beloved German shepherd was killed by an automobile. Four days later, the family cat gave birth to a litter of kittens. The next day, a friend of the family was talking on the telephone to Billy, the five-year-old son. She inquired after the kittens and asked what they were like. "Well," he replied, "they look sort of like German shepherd puppies."

When a person has identified a family figure with whom he has been strongly linked, an understanding of the impact of this identification on the development of the self can be achieved through finding out as much as possible about that person and the circumstances of his or her life. This process of gathering factual data makes the person more real and understandable and also aids in the process of becoming differentiated from that person, and from the family projections and expectations which have resulted from the linkage. Such identifications seem to be particularly troubling when the family figure is shrouded in vaguely ominous mystery. One young man, around whom there had always been considerable anxiety in the family and expectation of eccentricity or even dysfunction, had always been told, or had assumed, that he was named after his paternal grandfather, as, indeed, he was. But there was another shadowy namesake. On a visit to the family graveyard, usually a rewarding experience in family study, he discovered, next to the graves of his maternal grandparents, a stone marking the grave of an uncle about whom there had been considerable family secrecy. Over the years, it had been communicated to him that this uncle had gone off somewhere, had been "a bad lot," had married out of the faith, and had died when the client was in his late teens or early twenties. In fact, there was so much mystery around his death that the client really wasn't completely sure his uncle was dead. He was amazed, there in the graveyard, to discover that this uncle, also with a name beginning with the same letter, had died two months before the client was born. Although this mystery has yet to be unraveled, it became clear that the client was very much involved with this highly toxic event in the life of the family—an event so toxic that the family for over thirty years had colluded in totally mystifying the figure of the uncle and had unconsciously denied the event to the point that there was even uncertainty communicated about whether the uncle was dead or alive. The importance of the uncle to this client lies in the possibility that in the emotional life of the family he became the uncle's replacement—with far-reaching consequences in terms of family expectations, attributions, and the client's own sense of self. In passing, it is interesting to note that the client was the only other member of the family who married out of the family's faith.

Linkages between current family members and members of the family of origin can develop in other ways. Perhaps the single most powerful factor in this linkage, or identification process, is the place occupied by individuals in the set of siblings. Parents tend to identify their children with others who occupy the same sibling positions in the parent's generations. Family study should attend these connections. Bowen includes sibling position as a major concept and has been very interested in the work of Toman (1961), who developed a series of ten personality profiles which characterize different sibling positions. My own observations have led me to approach this issue in a somewhat different way. Although certain patterns may be widespread, it may be even more useful to discover how each particular family describes those occupying specific sibling positions. It may be that families are rather idiosyncratic, but internally consistent, in making these assignments.

For example, in one family, the second daughter was defined as mother's caretaker. Frequently, throughout the family, this daughter carried her mother's first or middle name. The pattern appeared to be quite consistent over four generations, a period of one hundred years, and repeated horizontally across cousins and second cousins. In another family, second sons have consistently been alcoholics. A study of almost any family begins to suggest some of these patterns.

Clearly, one way of helping a person to organize and assess the data from the genogram, and to learn more about its personal relevance, is to attempt to discover the sources of family expectations and projections through identifying links with particular members of the family of origin. These links may be forged through replacement, through the occupation of the same position in the family, and sometimes through striking or idiosyncratic physical characteristics. However the linkages have been formed, the student of his or her own family will do well to focus particular attention on these linked figures.

Another way to assess data is to search for family themes. Themes may be represented by behaviors repeated throughout the generations. For example, in one family, the male line for three generations went away to war, met their spouses and married far from their origins, started new lives, and became part of their wives' families while cutting off from their own families. Another family seems to have a concentration of fragile, ailing women who need protection. And yet another family had more than its share of tragic losses, is preoccupied with loss, constantly and anxiously expecting the next blow.

Family themes may also be surfaced through a discussion of family heroes and heroines. Generally such "larger than life" people, around whom family mythology develops, express a personification of the family's explicit or implicit values. Sometimes the communications about these heroes or heroines are double binding as the family shakes their heads over Great Uncle George, who left his family and ran off to the Klondike where he became a millionaire. While the heads are shaking, the family may smile with admiration and pride over his independence and resourcefulness. The telling of tales, frequently a favorite family occupation, transmits values to the young in a powerful and colorful fashion. Antiheroes are used in the same way where "cautionary tales" are told of ancestors who took certain paths which led to no good end.

One highly successful professional woman sought help following the end of her marriage of many years. After her children reached school age, she returned to school to complete her professional degree. The more successful she became, the more ready she felt to leave what had been a suffocating marriage, in which for many years she had allowed herself to be dominated by a rather limited and rigid husband. Now she was free—and miserable! She had not adequately dealt with the loss and the work of mourning had to be completed. Mourning, however, did not appreciably lighten her depression.

Genogram work revealed family themes as she talked about three generations of women in her family. She spontaneously described each woman with superlatives: "brilliant," "creative," "extremely competent." The men in the family were seen as rather narrow and simple. They were frequently controlling and kept their wives' light under a bushel. Only one woman had failed to marry and, although seemingly quite active and fulfilled, was throughout the family an object of pity and scorn. The family myth became clear. "Women in our family have much more talent and creativity and competence than the men they marry, but they must suppress their wishes for self-expression and achievement in order to get and keep a husband. This self-denial, however, is necessary and, indeed, worth it, because there is nothing worse than a woman without a husband!" It became clear that this woman was painfully living out the family theme and in these terms, it was a "no win" situation.

Structural issues may also emerge through the study of the genogram. Particularly evident and of major significance are cutoffs, which become obvious as the client has so little information about the cutoff individual or section of the family. As cutoffs tend to develop in order to isolate and deny unresolved family issues, the identification of them earmarks toxic issues and points to areas for intervention.

Finally, interlocking triangles, as they exist intergenerationally, also begin to emerge. An example is the family situation described above, in which the second-born daughter in each generation was strongly identified with and attached to the mother. It also emerged that the first daughter had a special connection with the father. Hence, two interlocking triangles emerge, with the second-born daughter and the mother in the outside position of a triangle which includes older sister and father in a comfortable closeness, and the first-born daughter and father in the outside position in relation to her mother and younger sister's close position. Furthermore, the mother, who was a second daughter, reexperiences in her husband and oldest's closeness the exclusion she felt in the triangle of her childhood, when she was in the outside position with her father.

These are but a few ways of assessing the family genogram. As we continue to study the intergenerational patterns of families, we will learn more about the kinds of connections that could be salient; and out of this increased understanding, will develop more hypotheses to be tested.

Objectifying the Family Emotional System

A second level of assessment is focused on the current family emotional system, which may include two or three generations. Again, the effort is to step outside of the system and to bring to awareness the process operating among the interlocking triangles within the family. An excellent way of highlighting family relationships is through the technique of family sculpture (Duhl, Duhl, and Kantor 1973; Simon 1972; Papp, Silverstein, and Carter 1973; and Papp 1976). In this nonverbal simulation, the person who wishes to gain greater understanding of the family emotional system builds a living tableau, selecting people to "stand in" for members of his or her family and placing them within the sculpture in a way that typifies that family member and his or her relationships with the other members. The sculptor not only has the opportunity to step outside and observe his or her family system but also, the actors are asked to describe how they experience the position in which they have been placed. This not only surfaces the structure of the emotional system but also, through experimenting with various alterations in that system, reveals a blueprint for change. While family sculpting may not always be feasible when working with individuals in family-oriented therapy, it has many other uses. In training groups, members can sculpt their own families; in consultation and supervision groups, client family systems can be better understood by simulating the family. I have also found family sculpture an important technique in working with unrelated adults in groups centered around defining selves in families of origin. When family sculpture is not possible, it can be useful to encourage people to diagram their family systems. Again, this aids in the process of objectification, which can enhance understanding and point the way to possible steps toward differentiation.

The final area of assessment is the assessment of the level of differentiation in families and in individuals. This, too, is a shared process between coach and client. Bowen has discouraged the use of his differentiation of self scale as an assessment tool, not only because it becomes reified in this way, but also because level of differentiation can only be assessed by looking at the total course of a person's life and at the ability to maintain differentiation through periods of stress.

Perhaps the concept of differentiation becomes most clear through an understanding of its opposite: fusion. Fogarty, in his interesting analysis of this state, presents a series of ways fusion manifests itself clinically. They include: one person assuming knowledge of what is happening in the other's head, two people each of whose behavior is determined by the other, the assumption of responsibility for one by another, an attempt to change rather than accept the position of another, and many others (Fogarty 1978). Perhaps the most important reason some estimation of the extent of lack of differentiation in a person or a family is needed is that it keeps both coach and client more realistic in their interventive planning, as well as better prepared for the momentous "togetherness" forces which will rise up to challenge a family member's efforts toward defining a self. To be forewarned is to be forearmed and to engage more realistically in planning.

Planning and Intervention

In the work of defining the self in the family of origin, it is the client who carries the responsibility for bringing about change. How could it be otherwise? Should the coach take responsibility for major change strategies with, or in behalf of, the client? The client would be in a dependent and fused position, which is the opposite of the desired outcome of work. The client-coach relationship will be discussed more fully later. In any event, the client plans and executes change strategies, while the coach remains on the sidelines, occasionally sending in plays and helping with analysis and future strategies during half time. As I sometimes say to clients, "I'll hold your coat."

The family study described above becomes a major part of the intervention. Although it is time consuming and at times frustrating, it is the core of the work. First, knowledge about the family system tends to dispel the myths, expose secrets, and give powerful but shadowy figures substance, thus adding to the understanding both of the immediate family and of the self. The objectification of the system is a major part of the differentiation process.

Not only does the information in and of itself bring about change, but the very process of doing the study can have major impact on the family system. This change can occur in a variety of ways. First, as the seeker sets out to gather information about the family, lively and significant communication lines are opened. The opening of communication around important and shared experiences is a major medium for relationship building. This is most dramatically seen when young adults visit aging relatives to gather family information. They may live in different worlds, disagree on many subjects, and have struggled with stilted exchanges for years. The one thing they share is that they belong to the same family, and as the family pictures, letters, and mementos are pulled out of chests and bottom drawers, a genuine exchange begins to develop.

Second, the establishment of contact may serve to alter the basic structure in the relationship system. For example, Harry, a forty-five-year-old man, had never talked alone with his father. His mother had successfully maintained her central position in a father, mother, son triangle since Harry's boyhood and communications between the two men were transmitted through her. Harry knew almost nothing about his father's early life or family. The father, who was in his eighties, had emigrated from Europe as a young man and had been separated from most of his family. Harry planned a visit to his father on an evening when he knew his mother would be out. His evening with his father not only brought forth fascinating and valuable information about his family but also resulted in a kind of closeness and sharing that had never existed between father and son. When Harry left, his father held his hand, and with tears in his eyes, thanked him over and over for coming. Harry was jubilant! This major change, however, was not without repercussions. First, the prohibition against direct communication between father and son was demonstrated by the fact that Harry "forgot" to mention the visit to his mother. He finally did mention it to her in a phone call. Two weeks later, when Harry went to have another talk with his father, his mother managed to provoke an argument between father and son. Father became depressed and went to bed. Harry left, angry and letdown, and several days passed before he realized that the function of the explosion was to reestablish the old unhappy but familiar equilibrium. It is also interesting, in terms of reverberating changes through systems, that the week after he saw his father, Harry sat down and wrote a long and very sharing letter to his eldest son from whom he had been estranged. For Harry, becoming a different kind of son meant that he also began to be a different kind of father.

Not only does the assessment process and the objectification of the family system automatically begin the change process, assessment also points the way for the planning of specific interventions. The discovery of cutoffs suggests that there is a need to build new connections. The surfacing of toxic issues and nodal events points to important areas for discussion. The growing awareness of rigidly patterned roles indicates the need for reversals and other techniques which alter role structure.

Some of the major change strategies follow. To begin, perhaps the major route to differentiation is for the client to form a person-to-person relationship with every member of the family system. Bowen describes a person-to-person relationship as "one in which two people can relate personally to each other about each other, without talking about others (triangulating) and without talking about impersonal "things" (1978:540). Of course, as Bowen adds, no one could live long enough to complete the task but it does give direction to the change effort. The gathering of information, as described above, is a good medium for the beginning of a person-to-person relationship.

The forming of person-to-person relationships will automatically bring about two other changes which have major impact on the system and on the client. First, person-to-person relationships destroy triangles, and detriangulating is an important route toward differentiating the self from the family emotional system. Detriangulating and forming person-to-person relationships require that one ceases to relate to family members as groups or as indivisible pairs. The classic example of this is the way correspondence usually takes place between adult children and their parents. Usually, the adult writes a letter to "Mom and Dad" as if they were one person and receives a letter back signed "Mom and Dad" but written by mom. This communication pattern tends to continue a not atypical family triangle, where the mother is in the center of the parent-child triangle, monitoring and controlling the communication. In the same way, the parental generation often controls the children's communication with and access to the grandparent generation. One client, a young woman, arranged a visit to her grandmother without doing so through her mother. This simple act caused considerable turmoil in the family as mother struggled to regain her control of the relationship between her mother and her daughter.

Further, establishing person-to-person relationships automatically breaks through cutoffs and opens the system. This process frequently becomes contagious throughout the family with important results. For example, one young man sought out an elder half-brother in a distant state, who had been alienated from him and from their father for many years. He started with a letter or two—then some phone calls. Before long, it was arranged that almost as an emissary back into the family system, the brother's teenage son come to visit not only his newfound uncle but his grandfather. Before long, the half-brother followed his son, visiting the younger half-brother and finally, after years of separation, spending several days with his father. This is one of many illustrations of the principle that if a person maintains contact with people on each side of a cutoff, eventually that cutoff will be bridged.

A major step in defining a self in the family of origin (and in any closed system) is for a person to become able to control emotional responsiveness within that emotional system. This means that the client becomes "unhooked" in the system and when family members embark on a characteristic pattern of emotional moves and countermoves, the client does not get caught playing his or her old part, as the following vignette illustrates. A young man and his father had always had a close alliance, the father dependent on the son, together manipulating and controlling the mother, who was cast in the role of the incompetent. On a visit home, the young man found his parents locked in a struggle about a major life decision in which the mother was taking a somewhat unrealistic stand. The usual pattern would be for the young man to take his father's seemingly more sensible side, thereby totally overwhelming the mother. The son, however, working on differentiating from the central family triangle, stayed out of the fray, experiencing, however, intense emotional pain during the entire visit. He cut his stay short, as he was able to maintain his nonreactive position only briefly. During subsequent visits, however, he increased his ability to refrain from emotional reactiveness, thus detriangulating.

Continued study and observation of the family can support the effort to remain unreactive. The more the emotional processes are understood and can be observed and objectified by the person attempting to differentiate, the less power they exert. The use of planned brief trips back into the system can be helpful in establishing more genuine relationships and limiting reactivity. These visits should be carefully gauged not to exceed the client's ability to remain unreactive. If the client can enter the system, establish emotional contact, and leave without being drawn into the old patterns, the next visit tends to be easier. The client can take a position different from, or even opposite from, that usually held in the family system. This tends to break up rigid role assignments and enhances more genuine interpersonal relating. For example, one client was the competent older sister who had been, and who continued to be, caretaker of a younger and somewhat dysfunctional brother. Considerable hostility and alienation existed in the relationship, enhanced by the parents continually calling to exhort, "You've got to do something about your brother." The strategy which coach and client worked out together was designed to begin a role reversal. It was planned that the client ask the brother for help.

There has been considerable discussion about whether such techniques are manipulative or even slightly dishonest. Friedman's article "The Birthday Party" brings forth particularly strong reactions (1971). I am not so concerned about "manipulation," which in a sense is a negatively connoted word for change. The honesty issue, however, is vital, since no person-to-person relationship can be built on sham. In devising techniques such as reversals, it is essential that they be genuine. For example, in the above illustration, the older sister must find a genuine need, a real area in which she requires help. In this situation, she used her problematic car, about which she had little knowledge, turning to her brother in his area of expertise.

A final strategy, closely connected with all of the others, is easy to prescribe but difficult to enact. The strategy is to take an "I position." I ask clients to think about how rarely they make declaratory statements beginning with the word *I*, statements starting with "I think," "I believe," "I prefer," "I am." Closely related to this is the difficulty in using the word *no*. People who must negotiate so much of the self in the relationship system are fearful of "I statements" and of "No," fearful that they will lose the love and approval of their fellows. They bury the "I," say "Yes" instead of "No" and feel angry and used. Practicing making such statements in key emotional systems without anger or hostility, and discovering that the sky does not fall in, is a useful strategy toward differentiation.

It should be emphasized that the basic motivation underpinning strategies for change must be the wish to define or differentiate the self. Too often, people embark on this kind of work with the hope of changing the behavior of some other family member. This is particularly true of some members of the helping professions, who have probably been cast in the role of family therapist and now have learned some new ways of going about it.

Carter and Orfanidis (1976) have written a particularly useful article, describing and exemplifying the steps in the differentiation process and listing out of their experience some very helpful dos and don'ts. Among other things, they remind all who would undertake this course to avoid sharing their plans with family members, not to underestimate how powerfully the family will react with "change back" maneuvers, to have a plan, and to expand the context of the work. The last suggestion is particularly important. Too often, overenthusiastic clients and overambitious coaches plan to zero in on the central triangle in the family, usually the one including the client and his or her parents. Such a move is very likely to fail and to end in frustration and disappointment. I tend to ask people, "Who in your extended family would it be the easiest to contact and talk with?" I suggest they start there.

Finally, not only is it important to recognize the family's resistance to change but we must also be aware of the powerful forces within each individual that also oppose change. The individual is, after all, a part of the family system and is subject to the family's powerful prohibitions and proscriptions. Perhaps one's own personal experience can teach this lesson best. I had not seen my father's sister since childhood and decided, believing one should practice what one preaches, to contact her. She would certainly appear to be a harmless little old lady of seventy-nine and one that I had remembered with warmth. I was attending meetings in the city where she lived and managed not to call for three days. In the airport, ten minutes before plane time, I called, standing in the phone booth, my heart pounding, short of breath, and overwhelmingly grateful when there was no answer. It took another year before I was able to write to her! This kind of experience enhances a coach's understanding of a client's reluctance to embark on the simplest of tasks. Powerful prohibitions against opening up family systems and gathering family information are also expressed in the rapidity with which this information is forgotten. Time and again, clients have visited relatives, gotten information, and promptly forgotten it. A recording device, or at least note taking during or immediately after a visit, will outwit this defensive maneuver.

These general principles and suggestions give guidance to the pursuit of differentiation. However, at this early point in the development of the art, perhaps the best way to capture the essence of the work is to read the individual case studies describing efforts at differentiation, including of course, Bowen's own report (1978:486–529; Colon 1973; and two anonymous articles appearing in volume 2 of the Georgetown Family Symposia, "A Family Therapist's Own Family" and "Taking a Giant Step: First Moves Back Into my Family," published by the Family Center of Georgetown University).

Coaching and the Coach

In working with a client whose goal is to define a self in the family of origin, the coach performs several tasks. First, adopting a teacher role, or the role of expert in family systems, the coach helps the client learn about family systems and the major principles of their operation. Obviously, this teaching does not come in the form of a didactic lecture but is woven into the study of the client's own family as general principles are exemplified. Second, the coach adopts with the client the role of fellow explorer or researcher, gathering data, devising means of recovering missing information, and drawing maps of the family as it emerges. Third, the coach, again with the client, adopts the role of strategist, helping with the selection of possible entry points and interventions. This process includes detailed and specific planning to give the client an objective structure which helps to protect the client from being drawn into the system. Careful planning can and often does include a day-by-day and even hour-by-hour outline of a visit home, including planned opportunities to take time away from the family, questions to be asked, particular people to talk with, and subjects to be broached. Actually formulating and rehearsing the planned comments, and practicing asking the questions, are also helpful in preparation. A member of a group working together in this model planned a visit to his family in Europe after a two-year absence. General preparation had taken place throughout this two-year period but, as the visit approached, almost every aspect was planned and conversations around major issues were role played with the group and coach. The extensive planning was particularly important in that, due to the distance, the visit was to be a month, rather than an optimum visit of a day or two. This is a long time to maintain a differentiated stance in relation to a highly intense family emotional system.

A fourth role that the coach sometimes adopts is the role of supporter or "cheerleader." However, this role must be assumed with caution. The coach must not too heavily invest in the client's task, as then client and coach are moving toward fusion and the danger is that the client will begin to do the work for the coach's approval, not for the self. I take three primary stances. First, from the initial contact on, I communicate my conviction about the importance of families. As people discuss current conflicts and problems, I tend to comment that this may have something to do with family issues. In the first interview, as family information comes up, I put it into a beginning genogram on a large piece of paper. This tends to pique the client's curiosity and I comment that one day we may want to complete the family map. This lays the groundwork for turning to family work when the pressure around here-and-now issues has been alleviated.

The second message I communicate to clients, which in my case is not hard, is that I think families are absolutely fascinating. The primary affective stance I take is one of enthusiatic interest in all families. This avoids a judgmental stance on "good" or "bad" families and also tends to stimulate whatever propensity the client may have to begin to become a student of his or her family.

Third, I attempt to occupy a realistic position in terms of the difficulty of the tasks and the possibility of change. People tend to become both enthusiastic and overly ambitious and my role is often one of saying "go slow." On the other hand, when people feel hopeless about the possibility of any movement, I take the position that although it may only be possible to make very minute changes in differentiation, these tiny changes may make considerable difference in daily life.

The coach-client relationship may be described as egalitarian and between colleagues and is focused on the client's autonomy and responsibility for the work. The coach has knowledge about family systems and experience in the coaching process but no magic and no special authority.

This brings us to the issue of transference, an issue which has been vigorously discussed. A major principle in Bowen Family Systems work is that transference should be avoided. The aim is to keep the intense relationships between the family members, and to help the client come to terms with those relationships, not via a relationship with the professional, but in vivo, with the real family figures. The ever present focus on the real figures and on the tasks of working directly with these important people tends to help keep the coach less triangled into the intense family system and thus out of the transference. As Bowen points out, the effort is to reduce the assigned and assumed importance of the therapist. "The more the relationship is endowed with high emotionality, messianic qualities, exaggerated promises, and evangelism, the more change can be sudden and magical, and the less likely it is to be long term. The lower the emotionality and the more the relationship deals in reality, the more likely the change is to come slowly and to be solid and long lasting" (Bowen 1978: 345). It would certainly seem incongruent, when the goal and direction of the work is toward increased differentiation and autonomy, to consider a highly emotional, fused, and dependent relationship with the therapist as the route to such growth.

This position requires quite a shift in thinking for most practitioners as it moves the relationship from center stage where it was considered the major instrument of change to a rather minor part in the wings. Finally, the fact that the main change efforts are occuring outside the office means that the amount of time spent with the coach can often be reduced. Once the tasks of learning, assessing, and planning have been well launched, it is often possible to see people on a biweekly or monthly basis.

When, Why, and with Whom

It is much too soon to specify when and with whom this model of help is most useful. Further, it is uncertain whether it is most effective used alone or in combination with other approaches. Different practitioners are taking different routes. I have used it as the exclusive approach and in combination with other marital and family group therapy approaches. I have used it with individuals, with marital pairs, separately and together, with total families, and in groups of unrelated adults. The groups have been particularly interesting and useful. Each member plans his or her family work in the group, using the members as coach, executes their interventions, and reports back for feedback, evaluation, and planning of next steps. The commonality implicit in the fact that members share similar family issues forms a strongly cohesive and effective group. However, the fact that the focus and effort are directed to major figures outside the group means that the relationship system within the group, although supportive and enabling for the most part, remains relatively unintense.

I have also used the model with people of different ages, dealing with different developmental and life tasks. My experience has been that it seems to come into use most spontaneously with young adults dealing with identity and intimacy issues, with dysfunctional marital pairs as they struggle in the grip of transmitted family patterns, and with older adults dealing with mid-life reevaluation and the aging and loss of their parents. Finally, I have used the model with people who were enmeshed in their family systems, more frequently with people cut off from family, and often with people who have lost most of their family through death. The latter situation requires considerable creativity in that the client and coach must devise ways of gathering information about, and becoming reconnected with, an important figure who has been dead for many years. Letters, pictures, and the reminiscences of contemporary friends and relatives can make the lost person more real and help the client come to terms with, and ultimately resolve, the long buried and influential attachment.

There is an urgent need for the monitoring and exchange of methods and of results by people who are making use of defining the self in the family of origin as a primary or major approach. Thus far, reports have been limited to practitioners' rather subjective evaluations of their own cases and reports of professionals' own excursions into their family systems.

Bowen Family Systems Theory and Social Work Practice

We have spelled out in some detail a model of practice, developed out of Bowen Theory, which can be used by social work practitioners in a wide variety of family counseling and mental health agencies. There are, however, other ways in which Bowen Family Systems Theory can inform and shape social work practice in a range of settings and in the performance of a variety of professional tasks. When one adopts the view of the family as a powerful intergenerational system and integrates the understanding of fusion and differentiation, triangles, and cutoffs, practice develops in a different way.

To illustrate, a thorough understanding of the concept of the "cutoff," its impact on identity formation and its power in controlling and directing a person's life, can dramatically alter child welfare practice, which has been in the past, and at times continues to be, rather cavalier about children's ties to kin.

The adoption search movement gives dramatic evidence of the importance of those ties, of the impact of cutoffs, and the restorative effect of finding and dealing with the biological parents (Fisher 1973; Lifton 1975; Trisiliotis 1973; Sorasky, Baran, and Pannor 1978). Family oriented practitioners are turning with concern to examine child welfare practice. Fernando Colon, who was trained at Georgetown, grew up in foster care and reports in a moving article his search for his biological family and his eventual reunion with them (1973). He translates his own experience, training, and convictions into a plea for altered policies in providing care to children—policies which protect and sustain those vital family ties (Colon 1978). Joan Laird, starting from an ecologically oriented family systems approach, spells out the concrete changes to be made in child welfare practice to keep it family centered, suggesting specific interventive strategies which can serve to preserve the continuity of children's important relationships (1979).

In workshop and consultations with child welfare agencies across the country and through PROJECT CRAFT [Curriculum Resources in Adoption and Foster Care Training], the author has taught hundreds of child welfare workers to use the genogram in gathering family information on children coming into care and to insure that this information will always be available to children cut off from their roots. "Life Books" are being used extensively to capture and preserve a sense of continuity and connectedness for children in foster care or heading for adoption. (For a presentation of the use of the "Life Book," a film is available through Image Associates, producers, Santa Barbara, California.) The genogram and other tools and techniques inspired by Bowen Family Systems Theory have been used as bases for involving potential adoptive families in a shared assessment process (Hartman 1979a). Open adoption—open in that it does not close the door on the biological family—is becoming a reality in some places. All of these practice and program developments attest to the importance of the intergenerational family system and the damage done to children where the family is cut off, as we come to realize that unresolved family relationships and issues continue to have powerful impact on the life of the child.

In work with the aging, planning for supportive care can be accompanied by work directed at enhancing a person-to-person relationship between the middle-aged son or daughter and aged parents. This common family transition may be considered not a threat, but an opportunity for change and increased differentiation. At least two institutions for the aging have initiated groups of the children of their aged residents to teach them how to do genograms with their parents (Ingersall and Silverman 1978). There is a high degree of complementarity in the shared discussion of the genogram between the son or daughter and aging parent. For the offspring, it is an opportunity to gain an increased understanding of the family. For the aged person, the discussion and construction of the genogram is an opportunity for life review, for seeing not only one's roots in the past generations, but one's stake in immortality through the future generations. Further, the orderly arrangement of the genogram organizes and clarifies reminiscences. As family ties and family history and culture are valued, so are aged members of the family valued as important links and repositories of vital and cherished information. The reminiscence of the aged has been their effort to pass on information so that it would not die with them, thereby insuring a kind of immortality. Too often, the younger generations, defending themselves against the painful feelings of loss and anxiety about mortality engendered by interactions with the loved old person, are impatient and disinterested. This lack of interest and emotional cutoff is experienced by the aging person as a real invalidation, which in a sense it is. Attention to family ties brings the young closer to the old. Particularly moving have been the many warm and productive visits made by my students and young clients to their grandparents—visits that have radically altered the relationship, validated the aged person, and helped the young person to a greater understanding of the family system.

Bowen theory and practice also has considerable relevance for social workers in health care settings. One of their major tasks is to function productively in a complex work system with professionals of many disciplines. Bowen's work on triangles and his application of that understanding to issues of differentiation in the workplace (1978:461–66; Kerr 1978) are very relevant to those who work in interdisciplinary teams and in hospitals or schools. Work relationships in these situations tend to develop into a series of interlocking triangles, which may serve to reduce tension but which are often obstacles to task achievement. Understanding the dynamics of the work system, and detriangulating within that system, enable a worker to be more effective and more truly autonomous.

In direct work with patients and their families in health care settings, Bowen Family Systems Theory has many applications. Illness, death, and loss are often major toxic issues within intergenerational family sagas. In understanding—and in helping a family deal with—the illness of one of its members, it is important to understand the meaning of illness to that family and to understand the family's history in dealing with health issues. Doing a careful genogram with patient and family, particularly geared to the gathering of health information, may surface some salient intergenerational issues that are implicated in the family's and patient's response to the current situation, and that relate to the ability to make realistic use of health care. Further, strong convictions about the importance of the family, and of direct person-to-person relatedness between family members, will lead a social worker to avoid taking on family functions or becoming triangled between family members. The social worker's role is to help family members help each other by dealing with the issues without emotionally or physically cutting off from each other. Serious illness and potential or actual loss stimulate tension and anxiety in family systems, leading family members to utilize cutoffs and triangulating to deal with that stress. A worker can be used by the family as a part of this process. However, if the worker can help family members to stay in emotional contact, and to detriangulate in handling these tension-filled times, not only will the family be more able to resolve the crisis, but family members may make use of the crisis period to take a step toward greater differentiation. (Bowen 1978: 321–36).

Implications for Education and Training

R. D. Laing has said "Till one can see the 'Family' in oneself, one can see neither oneself or any family clearly" (1961:15). The return to the family of origin as a means for enhancing differentiation began as a part of the training experience at the Georgetown Family Center, following Bowen's report of the work he did in relation to his own family (1978:486–518). The study of—and work in relation to—the trainee's own family of origin continues to be a part of training in family therapy at Georgetown and in other training programs influenced by the Bowen model. Reports of such efforts have appeared in the family literature (Colon 1973; Carter and Orfanidis 1976; Georgetown Family Symposia, Volumes 2 and 3; "Management of Loss" 1979). My own experience, both personally and through the work of students, has been that there is no better way to gain a real understanding of the power of the intergenerational family system than through coming face to face with the power of one's own family. Further, there is no better way to appreciate both the difficulty and the liberating effect of working on differentiating within the family of origin than through struggling with one's own family issues. Finally, it would seem artificial and somehow false to act as a coach and a guide with clients as they embark upon journeys which we ourselves have not even attempted.

In my own work in teaching, training, and consultation, I encourage all those who would be family-centered practitioners to begin work on their family genograms. The work itself entails a beginning opening of the family system as the trainee crosses cutoffs and engages in person-to-person discussions in the course of doing family research. For some, the search is perfunctory and leads nowhere, as the prohibitions against knowing and changing are too overwhelming. For many, however, this family study begins a process that becomes a vital ongoing part of the searcher's professional and personal life. In my advanced family class, I offer an optional final assignment in which students begin a genogram of their families of origin, make an analysis of the genogram, and plan, execute, and evaluate one very small interventive step. Although I discourage students from taking this option, because it is so demanding, many elect to do this assignment and almost universally report that it has been the most important professional and personal learning experience in their graduate education (Hartman and Laird 1977).

Summary and Conclusions

Bowen Family Systems Theory and practice has much to offer the social worker, particularly one who would replace the medical model in conceptualizing practice with an ecological orientation in thinking about assessment, intervention, growth, and change (Germain 1973, 1979; Auerswald 1971). Bowen theory and practice view people as complex bio-psychosocial beings who can only be understood and helped within the context of the social and emotional environment. A salient aspect of that environment is the family system as it extends in space and through time. The focus of study and the focus of intervention is that family system and the individual's transactions with that system.

Particularly congruent with ecological perspectives is Bowen's view of change. Differentiation is seen as a natural growth process which begins at birth and continues, if unobstructed, throughout life. Problems and difficulties are seen as a result of interrupted growth and development, and as adaptive strategies, rather than as disease processes. Therapeutic intervention is aimed at removing obstacles to growth, at helping the individual to enhance differentiation through his own efforts with the family system. Life experience is the primary instrument for change. The clients work through troublesome relationships with major figures in vivo, rather than in the office with the worker through the medium of the transference. Coach and client work as partners in this enterprise, with the client carrying major responsibility for the actual change effort.

The Bowen approach is highly congruent with social work's traditional interest in the family and emphasis on the importance of history. The skills demanded in this work, skills in historical investigation, in support and enabling, in the development of a reality-based egalitarian relationship, are all a part of social work's heritage and repertoire. Finally, the reliance on the client as the primary architect and builder of the change effort gives real substance to the value the social work profession places on the individual's right to work out his or her own destiny.

References

Auerswald, Edgar. 1971. "Families, Change, and the Ecological Perspective." *Family Process* 10(2):202–15.

Bowen, Murray. 1978. *Family Therapy in Clinical Practice*. New York: Aronson.

Carter, Elizabeth and Monica Orfanidis. 1976. "Family Therapy with One Person and the Family Therapist's Own Family." In P. J. Guerin, ed. *Family Therapy*. New York: Gardner Press.

Colon, Fernando. 1973. "In Search of One's Past: An Identity Trip." *Family Process* 12(4):429–38.

——1978. "Family Ties and Child Placement." *Family Process* (17(3):289–312.

Dawkins, Richard. 1976. *The Selfish Gene*. New York: Oxford University Press.

Duhl, F., B. Duhl, and D. Kantor. 1973. "Learning, Space, and Action in Family Therapy: A Primer of Sculpture." In D. Bloch, ed., *Techniques of Family Psychotherapy*. New York, Grune and Stratton.

"A Family Therapist's Own Family." 1977. In J. B. Lorio and Louise McClenathan, eds., *Georgetown Family Symposia* 2, 1973–74. Washington, D.C.: Georgetown University Family Center.

Fisher, F. 1973. *The Search for Anna Fisher*. New York: Arthur Field.

Fogarty, Thomas F. 1979. "Fusion." In *The Best of the Family*, 1973–1978. Washington, D.C.: The Center for Family Learning and Georgetown University Family Center.

——1979. "Triangles." In *The Best of the Family*, 1973–1978. Washington, D.C.: The Center for Family Learning and Georgetown University Family Center.

Friedman, Edwin. 1971. "The Birthday Party, An Experiment in Obtaining Change in One's Own Family." *Family Process* 10(3):345–60.

Germain, Carel B. 1973. "An Ecological Perspective in Casework Practice." *Social Casework* 54(6):323–31.

———1979. *Social Work Practice: People and Environment*. New York: Columbia University Press.

Goodall, Jane VanLawick, 1971 *In the Shadow of Man*. Boston: Houghton Mifflin.

Guerin, Philip J., Jr. and Katherine Buckley Guerin. 1976. "Theoretical Aspects and Clinical Relevance of the Multigenerational Model of Family Therapy." In P. J. Guerin, ed., *Family Therapy*. New York: Gardner Press.

Guerin, P. J. and Eileen G. Pendagast. 1976. "Evaluation of Family System and Genogram" In P. J. Guerin, ed., *Family Therapy*. New York: Gardner Press.

Hartman, Ann. 1978. "Diagramatic Assessment of Family Relationships." *Social Casework* 59(8):465–76.

———1979a. "The Extended Family as a Resource for Change." In Carel B. Germain, ed., *Social Work Practice: People and Environments*, New York: Columbia University Press.

———1979b. *Finding Families*. Beverly Hills, Calif.: Sage Publications.

Hartman, Ann and Joan Laird. 1977. "The Use of the Self in Learning and Teaching Family Practice." Presented at Annual Program Meeting, Council on Social Work Education. Mimeographed. (Available from the authors.)

Ingersall, Berit and Alida Silverman. 1978. "Comparative Group Psychotherapy for the Aging." *The Gerontologist* 18(2):210–6.

Jackson, Don D. 1957. "The Question of Family Homeostasis." *Psychiatry, Quarterly Supplement* 31:79–90.

Kerr, Michael, 1977. "Application of Family Systems Theory to a Work System." In J. B. Lorio and Louise McClenathan, eds. *Georgetown Family Symposia* 2, 1973–1974. Washington, D.C.: Georgetown University Family Center.

Laing, R. D., *Self and Others*. 1961. London: Tavistock Publications.

Laird, Joan. 1979. "An Ecological Approach to Child Welfare: Issues of Family Identity and Continuity." In Carel B. Germain, ed., *Social Work Practice: People and Environments*. New York: Columbia University Press.

Lidz, Theodore, Alice R. Cornelison, Stephen Fleck, and Dorothy Terry. 1957. "The Intrafamilial Environment of Schizophrenic Patients." *American Journal of Psychiatry* 64(9):241–48.

Lifton, B. J. 1975. *Twice Born*. New York: McGraw-Hill.

"The Management of Loss in the Therapist's Own Family." 1979. In *The Best of the Family*. Center for Family Learning, New Rochelle. Washington, D.C.: Georgetown University Family Center. 1979.

Papp, Peggy, 1976. "Family Choreography." In P. J. Guerin, ed., *Family Therapy*. New York: Gardner Press.

Papp, Peggy, O. Silverstein, and E. Carter. 1973. "Family Sculpting in Preventive Work with Well Families." *Family Process* 12(2):197–212.

Simon, R. 1972. "Sculpting the Family." *Family Process* 2(1):42–57.

Sorosky, A. P., A. Baran, and R. Pannor. 1978. *The Adoption Triangle*. Garden City, N.Y.: Anchor/Doubleday.

"Taking a Giant Step: First Moves Back into My Family." 1977. In J. B. Lorio and Louise McClenathan, eds., *Georgetown Family Symposia* 2, 1973–74. Washington, D.C.: Georgetown University Family Center.

Toman, W. 1961. *Family Constellation*. New York: Springer.

Trisiliotis, J. 1973. *In Search of Origins, The Experience of Adopted People*. London: Routledge and Kegin Paul.

Wilson, Edward O. 1975. *Sociobiology, The New Synthesis*. Cambridge, Mass.: Bellmap Press.

Wynne, L. C., I. M. Ryckoff, and S. I. Hersch. 1958. "Pseudomutuality in the Family Relations of Schizophrenics." *Psychiatry* 21(5):205–20.

8

Focused Problem Resolution
[Brief Therapy]

LYNN SEGAL

If you cannot—in the long run—tell everyone what you have been doing,
your doing has been worthless.

Erwin Schrodinger

With the growth in demand for therapeutic and counseling services,
there is an increasing need for competent, skilled practitioners. Limitations of time and money require that most therapists take a greater
responsibility for their own education by studying what others have
written about human problems and their treatment.

This is usually a frustrating experience and oftentimes reputed to be
nonproductive, for written materials are notoriously laden with theoretical concepts and lacking in any concrete advice on how to translate
theory into practice, i.e., what you say and do to help someone solve
a problem. Also, no matter what the theory, it is quite evident to
clinical practitioners that there is always a gap between conceptual
abstraction and the process of dealing with actual people in treatment
sessions.

This introductory article on Focused Problem Resolution (FPR) represents one small step in describing what goes on between the therapist
and patient. I have endeavored to present and clarify fundamental
practice principles, using a modicum of theory while touching briefly
on the major variables necessary to apply it.

Although this article describes the work of the Brief Therapy Center, Mental Research
Institute, Palo Alto, California, the author is solely responsible for its presentation.

The author gratefully acknowledges the helpful suggestions and criticisms provided
by Dr. George Greenberg and Renee Sabourin.

History

The seminal ideas underlying FPR were originally introduced into psychiatric thinking by Ruesch and Bateson (1951). Together, they began sketching the outline of a new epistemology based on the theories of cybernetics, communication, and systems research.

In 1956, the Bateson group—including John Weakland, Jay Haley, and Don Jackson—published the well-known article "Toward a Theory of Schizophrenia" (Bateson et al. 1956). Although this publication is primarily known for the "double bind" theory of schizophrenia, it also stands as a landmark for viewing psychiatric problems as communicative behavior, maintained and structured by social interaction, rather than disease entities which reside inside a person.

The Mental Research Institute was formed by Don Jackson in 1959 for the purpose of exploring how these new interactional insights might be applied to psychiatric treatment. Joined by Haley, Weakland, and other notables in the family therapy movement, including Paul Watzlawick and Virginia Satir, the California Family Therapy Movement got its formal start. Although there were many differences between institute members, they all agreed on a number of basic assumptions: (1) while one family member exhibited pathology—the identified patient—the problem underlying these symptoms resided in the way the family functioned as a group; (2) this group behavior was understood as a rule-governed system, exhibiting homeostasis, feedback, redundancy, and other cybernetic principles; and (3) treating the family meant changing their interactive behavior, i.e., changing their patterns of communication.

Definition

Focused Problem Resolution, more popularly known as Brief Therapy, is a radical new way of conceptualizing and treating human problems. Although FPR gained popularity as a family treatment approach, the model is basically generic in application and has been used successfully with individuals, couples, and larger organizations.

FPR formally began when a small group of family therapists based at the Mental Research Institute, Palo Alto, California, formed the Brief Therapy Project. Initially, we were interested in seeing what could be done to resolve presenting complaints by treating patients for a maximum of ten, one-hour sessions. Additionally, we hoped to demonstrate that treatment was a craft or skill which could be more easily conveyed to others.

The original research design incorporated a number of features which are still in operation today. Patients are not screened prior to treatment, and each case is seen for no more than ten, one-hour sessions. Three and twelve months after the last treatment hour, a follow-up interview is conducted to assess the outcome of treatment. We work as a team. One member does the interviewing, while the rest of us look on from an observation room, equipped with a one-way mirror, sound system, and an audio tape recorder. A telephone connecting the two rooms permits the observers to give the identified therapist feedback, corrections, and suggestions while the interview is in progress. Following each hour of treatment, we discuss the pros and cons of the interview and the best way to proceed during the next session. Follow-up questions are formulated immediately upon completion of treatment.

Before I move on to how FPR is applied in treatment, some additional comments probably should be made concerning where it fits into a typology of family therapies. Most often, family treatment is defined by who attends the interviews and the general goals of treatment. For example, the editors of this volume have used a working definition of family treatment offered by Wells and Dezen: "A therapist engages in family therapy when he sees the natural units as parents and children, spouses, or members of the extended family, together as a group over most of the duration of treatment with the goal of improving their functioning as a unit" (1978:252).

While this is certainly one useful definition, widely accepted by many professionals, there are viable alternatives. In our view, family treatment is defined by the way the therapist conceptualizes problems and conducts treatment interviews. In this sense, an interactional or systemic perspective becomes the key element by which classification is made, not who is in the room or the goal of treatment. It is possible to do individual therapy while interviewing a family, or to do family treatment when only interviewing one family member. What becomes critical is the type of data collected, how it is processed, and the types of interventions made. For example, when a therapist is working with one family member, are his questions focused on the patient's internal dynamics or on his interactions with other family members; does the therapist compute his data according to personality theory, character traits, etc., or along the lines of systemic interaction; and are the therapist's interventions directed at insight into self or at changing patterns of interaction between the client and important others?

From this perspective, who attends the session is not a prime determinant of the type of therapy being conducted. Rather, this reflects a strategic decision by the therapist. Various family members may be asked to attend sessions, depending on who in the family asked for treatment, who is the identified patient, and who in the family is most motivated for change.

Although our ideas grew out of work with families, they are not limited to this natural grouping. The basic theory and its therapeutic techniques can be applied to *any* interpersonal grouping: friendships, work-related problems, patient-professional relationships, and larger organizations. Similarly, in the case of working with a single adult, the therapist still has the choice of viewing the relationship between himself and the patient as the treatment unit.

If one uses goals to define the treatment modalities, the issue of classification becomes even more complex. For instance, some therapists claim that any positive change in the functioning of one family member may improve the general functioning of the family unit. (This is especially likely if one does *not* conceptualize the symptom or presenting complaint of the identified patient as a ''cover-up'' for a more fundamental problem in the family's organization.) Others will argue that goal setting not only reflects theoretical beliefs, but also a general philosophical orientation about the nature of reality, what can be known about it, and, specifically, what is normal or a healthy functioning family. Finally, goals also reflect therapist expectations and beliefs about what can be accomplished with existing therapeutic technologies. We have taken the position that small, concrete, specific goals of treatment maximize the chances for achieving useful change in the patient's presenting complaint and reducing the emotional pain that accompanied this complaint and brought him into treatment. When this is accomplished with one family member, the family as a unit may function better, even though this was not our specific goal of treatment.

Some New Ideas about Solving Problems

Let us begin by considering a series of examples in which problems were solved in an unorthodox manner. In the first two examples, solutions were generated quite spontaneously, while in the third, the problem was solved as a result of careful study and deliberate action.

A Belgian police officer was summoned, late one night, to an apartment house where an elderly woman was creating a ruckus by pounding the floor with a hammer. The tenants complained that she would not stop and that she was "deranged" and in obvious need of hospitalization. The officer, unsophisticated in handling such matters, gained entrance to her home and asked what appeared to be a naive question: "Why are you banging the floor with that hammer?" "To fend off invaders from outer space," she replied. "Oh no, don't use that kind of a hammer," he said. "It only attracts them. You need a soft hammer." The woman became less agitated and allowed him to fashion such a device out of some old clothing. The noise stopped, the tenants went back to sleep, and the difficulty appeared to be resolved. However, the next day, the same woman sought out the officer at his station house and quite sanely asked for help, explaining that her husband's recent death had left her overwhelmed with new responsibilities. She was referred to an appropriate agency and went willingly.

A young woman, living in Berkeley, California, got off a bus on a dark and deserted street. Immediately after the bus departed, a man jumped from behind the bushes, pulling her to the ground. For some reason, she dealt with this in a very unusual way. Instead of resisting, she demanded of her assailant, "For God's sake, if we're going to do this, let's go to my apartment." The attacker became confused, and the next thing she knew, he was running from her as fast as his feet could carry him.

A famous zoo acquired a pair of rare species of bird, attempting to breed them in captivity. The fledglings were born and everything seemed to be going well. Then disaster struck. The mother bird had thrown her young from the nest, along with bits of old straw and dirt, and the fall killed them. The staff was alarmed and immediately set about seeing what could be done to rectify the situation. Everyone pondered the problem, seeking an explanation for such bizarre behavior. Speculation ran high as to why the mother might commit such an act. Unfortunately, this type of thinking was not productive. Seeking pathological causes in the mind of a mother bird, even if she had such a thing, was little help. No one knew of an animal psychiatrist who treated deranged birds who committed infanticide.

Finally the group returned to the field for further study, resulting in a fascinating discovery. When a female returned to her nest with food, the fledglings were actively awaiting her return, and whatever food she brought back didn't satisfy their hunger. In fact, the fledglings were continuously hungry. Mother also tended to her nest-keeping, throwing out pieces of dirt and straw, but not her babies. Somehow the activity of the young birds, stimulated by their hunger, allowed the mother to discriminate between her young and pieces of refuse. In captivity, abundant food left the young birds spending most of their time sleeping. The solution was now simple: cut the food supply and keep the fledglings active. Once this was done, the breeding was successful.

The preceding examples, drawn from nontherapeutic contexts, illustrate a number of key points we have learned about the process of problem-solving: (A) A simple solution can solve what appears to be a big problem. (B) Many times these solutions are the antithesis of the ways people normally go about handling such difficulties. For instance, one would have predicted that the methods used by the police officer and intended rape victim would have made matters worse, but they had the opposite effect. (C) Understanding how a system of interaction works—*not why it works*—provides sufficient information to make useful interventions when problems do arise. (D) Finally, these interventions will consist largely of changing the communicative behavior of one or more members of that system.

Fundamental to our theoretical viewpoint is the belief that behavior—whether "normal" or problematic—is primarily maintained and structured by interaction between people, especially family members. This would also include other social systems—fellow workers, peers, and the doctor-patient relationship.

Human problems arise out of the mishandling of normal life difficulties which are inherent in day-to-day living. Such difficulties include illness, accidents, loss of work, and the natural transitions in the life of a family which always make for some readjustment: courtship to marriage; birth of the first child; children reaching school age; becoming teenagers; when all the children have left home; and loss of spouse through death or divorce.

Mishandling of these difficulties may range from ignoring or denying that anything is wrong and not taking corrective action, to attempting the resolution of difficulties that need not or cannot be solved. Within this wide range, people usually do take action, but the wrong kind. It is assumed that difficulties are not mishandled on purpose, or for some unconscious reason. Rather, they are dealt with in ways which are consistent with the patients' frame of reference—their view of reality and the right way to behave. When the attempted solution does not work, this is usually interpreted as proof of the problem's severity, and is followed by more of the same basic solution.

This vicious cycle of interaction between the problem and the attempted solution is a self-perpetuating system. A patient with a persisting problem is like a man caught in quicksand. The more he struggles, the more he sinks, The more he sinks, the more he struggles (Watzlawick et al. 1974).

All of these theoretical notions can be summarized into two basic assumptions:

> regardless of their basic origins and etiology—if, indeed, that can ever be reliably determined—the kinds of problems people bring to psychotherapists PERSIST only if they are maintained by ongoing current behavior of the patient and others with whom he interacts. Correspondingly, if such problem-maintaining behavior is appropriately changed or eliminated, the problem will be resolved or vanish, regardless of its nature, origin, or duration. (Weakland et al. 1974:144–45)

Application

Given our theoretical assumptions, the primary objective of treatment is changing the behavior which maintains the problem, i.e., the attempted solution. Therefore, therapy will proceed along a path of fairly definite steps or tasks: (1) collecting the necessary information about the problem and its attempted solution; (2) formulating a plan for changing the attempted solution; (3) putting the plan into action, pursuing or modifying it as necessary; and (4) terminating treatment. Each of these steps and the case managerial skills necessary to carry them out will now be considered in some detail.

Pretreatment Considerations

There is an old maxim: "To begin well is to end well." Beginning this approach well necessitates some acquaintance with the following concepts: strategy and its application in treatment; therapist maneuverability; timing and pacing; selecting which member(s) of the system with whom you will work; and the handling of pretreatment contacts.[1]

---

[1] Dr. Richard Fisch, our Project Director, receives major credit for the formulation of ideas in this section on pretreatment.

STRATEGY

In game theory, a branch of mathematics, strategy is defined as taking action based upon how you predict your opponent will respond. This is in contrast to games of chance where you play against the dice, or games of skill which simply test your ability. In competition, strategy is used to beat out the opponent, but this is not its only application. Diplomacy and international relations rely on strategy so that both sides can win through compromise. In the therapy game, the patient wins when the therapist wins, victory being measured by useful and desirable change. The strategic therapist plans what he says and does, when and with whom, depending upon how he predicts such behavior will influence the patient. Thus, strategic therapy of any kind entails planned, purposeful action. To do this requires recognizing the uniqueness of the client, and accepting and utilizing it in the service of change. As the social work adage says, "start where the client is." We agree with this, but we would add, *stay* where the client is! Instead of teaching the client our model or jargon, we speak the language of the client.

MANEUVERABILITY

To work strategically, the therapist must have room to maneuver—the freedom to ask questions, see different family members, choose interventions, and apply the necessary leverage to get them carried out. Patients unwittingly limit the therapist's maneuverability in a variety of ways: being vague, refusing to answer questions, attempting to determine the nature of treatment, or forbidding the therapist to see other family members. These limitations are sometimes easier to see in another context. A patient could limit the surgeon's ability to work by making any of the following demands: the surgeon must operate with only one hand, leave his glasses at home, dim the lights during the operation, or forbid secondary personnel from entering the operating room. In this context, such limitations seem absurd, but for some unknown reason, the same types of limitations placed on the therapist usually go unnoticed.

There are a number of procedures for maximizing therapist maneuverability which, of necessity, limit the maneuverability of the client. Obtaining clear, specific, and concrete data about the problem, and the behavior maintaining it, is a step in the right direction. Freedom to maneuver is further enhanced if during initial sessions the therapist doesn't take a definite stand or strong position. By "playing one's cards close to the vest," so to speak, he buys time to learn about the client, his problem, and belief system. In this way, when we are ready to take a stand or ask the patient to do something between sessions, data is available for framing our remarks. Therefore, during the initial interviews, the therapist appears to be a contradictory blend of two basic therapeutic styles. Since our primary aim is gaining information, the therapist is quite active, asking questions and clarifying patient statements. We take charge of the interview, directing it in a particular direction. Simultaneously, our position or demeanor is not unlike that of the psychodynamic practitioner. We don't argue with patients, but accept what they say and attempt to clarify it when necessary. But even here, clarification is done from a "one-down" position. Questions are framed to imply that the therapist is limited in some way, that the patient could be helpful by giving additional information. Therapist: "Please bear with me, I don't quite follow you. Unfortunately, I have one of those minds that needs to get a picture of things before I grasp what you are saying." Or, "I'm a little slow today, would you please go over that again?" Like our analytic colleagues, neither hope nor optimistic prognoses are given. Conversely, therapist maneuverability is also increased if he does *not* allow the patient to pin him down. Therapist: "I would like to be more definite, but I know so little about you that I can't really say more." There are times when a definite stand will be taken, but only after there is some evidence that such a position will be useful.

Finally, the initial task of data collection is more easily accomplished if the patient is relaxed. It's suggested that first names be used, and we have eliminated some of the rituals of traditional treatment, such as the pregnant pause. So, the interview approximates the sound and tempo of most normal conversations. And since we don't believe that people's problems are primarily emotional, patients are not continuously asked how they feel. Their affect is simply observed and noted.

TIMING AND PACING

The course of treatment is a goal-directed activity, consisting of a number of steps. How far along this path, and how fast, movement proceeds should be based upon the therapist's assessment of key issues: is there sufficient intake data to plan treatment; has a plan been formulated; and is the client ready for therapist directives, or might some preparatory work be needed first? Sometimes it's suggested that clients think about a new way of handling a problem, but they are forbidden to put their new ideas into action. Depending upon their report in the next interview, the plan will be carried a step further, modified, or abandoned.

Many times clients, responding to their emotional distress, will pressure the therapist to "do something right now." There are a variety of countermeasures available to the therapist for dealing with this. However, what may be more important is the therapist's own clarity of purpose: recognizing the pressure, acknowledging the client's distress, but not falling into the trap of acting prematurely.

For example, if a client phones the therapist demanding advice on the spot, an additional appointment would be offered, gaining the time to do a more adequate job with less pressure. The client might protest that the extra session is time consuming or expensive, but we would maintain the position that a good job can't be done over the phone.

PRETREATMENT CONTACT: SELECTING A CUSTOMER

Many new schools of treatment, attempting to get away from the medical model, have replaced the term "patient" with other labels more fitting to their theoretical orientation. We have selected the term "customer" to indicate that person in the system with whom we will work. Like "client," the term "customer" denotes someone who is seeking professional advice, not necessarily someone who is ill or suffering from psychopathology. Furthermore, it denotes someone who wants to change and is willing to get down to the business of problem-solving.

Since our model is basically interpersonal, therapist influence is maximized by working with the member of the system who most fits our criteria for a customer. Although there is no formal definition of such an entity, there are three general criteria used in making this assessment. That is, a person would need to say or imply three things: 1) I have a problem; 2) I have tried to solve it and have been unsuccessful; and 3) I am asking for your help.

It has been our experience that in many families the customer is not necessarily the identified patient. Parent-child problems, delinquency, and marital conflict are just a few examples where frequently the caller for the first appointment is not the identified patient. If this is picked up during the initial phone contact, an effort is made to see the caller first, assuming that he might be the customer. He is asked to come in for one visit to give us his view of what is going on. Who will be seen next is decided during or after this initial interview. In the case example presented later in this article, it is clearly the parents who are the customers, and they are asked to attend all the subsequent sessions.

Frequently, the caller is the identified patient, but this does not mean that he is the customer. Patients have a variety of motivations for seeking treatment, not all of them conducive to therapuetic change. Sometimes couples seek marital counseling because it is court ordered, or the alcoholic may come because his wife has made it a precondition for his returning home. In such cases, an effort is made to help the person become a customer by taking up their predicament in a fashion coherent with our general approach. Rather than working on the presenting complaint, questions will be focused on the person's immediate problem. With the alcoholic sent by his wife, his present situation would be taken up, rather than his drinking. If that also fails, we might ask permission to invite the wife to the next session and go from there.

There is another class of patients who, while not under duress, are not ready to get down to business. They are merely window shoppers. In such cases, the therapist might take a position of doubting the need for treatment, or being obtuse as to why they are seeking help. Our intention is either to get down to business or to agree that treatment is not needed at this time.

Finally, from our perspective, family therapy means conceptualizing problems as the outcome of interaction between people rather than something inside them. Given this definition, we are always doing family work, even though we choose to influence the interactional system via a particular customer or customers.

Basic Information

There are three fundamental pieces of information upon which we base our treatment plan: what is the problem; what is being done to solve it; and what is the client's goal of treatment. This information comprises the bulk of our intake data.

PROBLEM

Treatment begins by simply asking, "What brings you here today?" In order to get a fairly complete picture, subsidiary questions will be aimed at learning (1) the details of the particular problem; (2) how it affects the client's daily life—what it stops him from doing or makes him do; (3) why he called for treatment now; and (4) how he came to choose this particular therapist for treatment. For example, an ideal client might say, "My problem is insomnia. I'm only getting two or three hours of sleep a night for about the last three months. It has affected my job performance so badly that my supervisor called me in to talk about my work. When he learned of my difficulty, he suggested that I give you a call."

SOLUTION

"What have you been doing to handle or solve this problem?" The objective here is to learn what the client says and does about the problem. Some clients don't think in terms of solutions. Asking how they cope or handle the problem, or what they tell themselves about it, may reveal the answers. For example, a client, when becoming anxious, might think about relaxing, remember what the last therapist suggested, or attempt to explain the anxiety as hypoglycemia.

When working with the person who has the problem, the same questioning is then directed to how others react to the problem and what they say and do to help. This would include family members, friends, other professionals, and anyone else who might be part of the interactive loop.

GOALS

Probably the hardest objective to reach is learning the client's goal of treatment. This is really a two-stage process: defining the goal, and whittling it down to a workable size. When working rapidly, one seeks to learn the minimum concrete change that would indicate to the client that a small but significant dent has been made in the problem as a result of treatment. Often answers to this question are usually vague: "I want to be happy"; "We want to learn to communicate or have a better relationship." The therapist then sets about concretizing this statement. It's best to have a positive goal rather than a negative one that just indicates that something has stopped. If a couple's goal is to stop fighting, we would push them to indicate what new behavior of a positive nature would result if their fighting diminished.

PATIENT POSITIONS

Clients, like therapists, hold views about the nature of human problems and what is needed to solve them. These views also reflect a wider orientation about reality and personal values. Such views, called "positions," tell the therapist how to speak the client's language—how to explain things in such a way that it makes sense and fits the client's existential view of the world. (Underlying this principle is our belief that there are many different views of reality, but no *correct* view with a capital R.) For instance, some clients are quite sophisticated about psychology and psychodynamics, while others may lean toward learning theory or plain common sense. These views also imply some expectations about the way treatment should proceed.

The therapist learns about positions indirectly from the answers received about the basic questions mentioned earlier. Further data is collected, quite directly, by simply asking the client what he thinks is the cause of the problem, or what he had in mind in trying to solve it in the ways he tried prior to treatment. A similar question is, "How did you think I was going to help with this; what did you expect me to say or do?"

Many therapists get into trouble early in the game by taking a strong position before getting a fix on positions. Announcing to a family that they have a problem, and that all members will have to be in treatment to help Johnny's school phobia may result in the family's quitting treatment. We are quite willing to have Johnny be the identified patient and to work with those family members necessary to solve things without labeling the process "family therapy." Other family members are implied cotherapists, coming in to help Johnny.

The use of positions might be more easily seen with the following hypothetical example. Let us say there are two families, both having similar problems: school phobia in the oldest child. Furthermore, both sets of parents are mishandling the problem in identical ways, and the necessary interventions for both families are identical. However, in one family, the parents see the child as misbehaving, while in the other family, the child is believed to be suffering from emotional difficulties. When the intervention is presented to the first family, we might say, "After talking things over with you and pondering it for awhile, I'm inclined to agree with you. As you say, I think the kid just needs a kick in his backside to be set straight. But, I think he needs a very special kind of kick—one that will do him some real good, and one that only you are in a position to deliver." This framing recognizes the parents' viewpoint and anger, while allowing the therapist to make the necessary intervention.

In the second family, the therapist might say, preparing to give the exact same intervention, "I don't know how serious Johnny's problems really are, but after talking to all of you (the child is not present in either presentation) I do think some help is needed. There is a small step that might be taken to relieve some of your son's underlying anxiety which, in turn, might reduce his acting out. Would you be willing to help him relieve some of this internal pressure?'' If the answer is yes, the therapist then proceeds with the same example.

While some readers might be concerned that the therapist's remarks to the second family would only entrench their belief in the child's emotional problems, our experience indicates that once the stimulus for such a belief—the presenting complaints—disappears, the assumption of causes, such as emotional problems, dissolves spontaneously.

Case Planning

After the basic data and subsidiary information have been collected, the therapist decides upon a plan of action. In this sense, we are similar to a lawyer who collects the facts about the case, then formulates the best way to defend his client. While all therapists plan to some extent, the Brief Therapist communicates deliberately from the first pretreatment contact to termination of the case. Of course, solving human problems, especially the kind brought to therapists and counselors, is not an exact science. The therapist acknowledges this fact by being willing to modify his plan or to totally reconstruct it, depending upon how things progress.

Making a plan means answering a number of questions: (1) what is the basic solution or thrust underlying all of the customer's different solutions; (2) what new behavior should the customer carry out to resolve things; (3) what is the best explanation or rationale for getting the customer to do this; and (4) what criteria would indicate, at the very earliest, that treatment can be terminated?

FORMULATING THE BASIC SOLUTION

Although people try a variety of specific things to solve a problem, usually there is a basic logic or rule which the person seems to be following. It is not that the customer explicitly and consciously follows this rule; rather, the term "rule" is a metaphor for describing the general pattern which can account for the specific cases. Usually the therapist will be looking for commonalities in *what* the customer is trying to accomplish—the objective—and how they go about *doing* this.

For example, the obese patient may try various diets, limit what foods are brought into the house, take diet pills, eat substances to fill himself up, or weigh himself every time he wants a snack. While each of these is somewhat different, they all share a common denominator: trying to limit intake of food or control the appetite. At the most general level, one might consider appetite for food a spontaneous behavior and, therefore, the solution is trying to be spontaneous deliberately. Other common problems falling into this category would be trying to force sleep, sexual responses, and emotional responses. When the depressive tries to make himself happy, he is also attempting to be spontaneous deliberately.

Another typical pattern is trying to achieve certainty where some risk is inevitable: the salesman who is seeking the surefire pitch; the single adult who fails to approach other singles for lack of the perfect opening gambit. One also finds this pattern when people are making major decisions about their jobs, their marriages, or buying a home.

While these general patterns are useful to convey the thinking behind this principle, they are not sufficient for planning for each specific case. For instance, one young man we saw was seeking certainty when approaching women, but he did this mainly by avoiding the whole business of ever talking to them. He was so busy thinking about what to say and failing to come up with the right words that he rarely approached anyone. Another patient with the same general pattern could make the first step of speaking to a young woman, but he tried so hard to impress her with the right words that he turned her off. His basic solution was coming on stilted by trying to make a perfect impression.

As the last two examples illustrate, each case must be individualized, and there are no simple formulae to do this other than to simply study the data. Furthermore, once a hypothesis is generated, it is tested out in practice slowly and carefully.

FINDING THE NEW BEHAVIOR

Planning a new way for the customer to deal with the problem is guided by two objectives. First, the new behavior should be different from the basic solution rather than another variation of it. Second, if possible, the new behavior should exclude the use of the solutions the customer has been trying. For example, we convinced a patient wrestling with the problem of insomnia to purposely keep himself awake for one week. Trying to accomplish this, the patient stopped all those techniques used for inducing sleep and, in attempting to stay awake, engaged in a "new" solution.

One of the easiest ways of finding the new behavior is by asking oneself, "What would be a 180 degree shift from the basic solution?" For instance, our Project Director quickly cured a patient's premature ejaculation by sending the couple home with a stopwatch, instructing the wife, in front of her husband, to time the speed of her husband's ejaculation. Carrying out this assignment fulfilled the two objectives, and the problem was solved. Similarly, we have had good luck treating shy singles by having them approach someone of the opposite sex and say, "I would really like to talk with you, but I'm very shy and don't know what to say." Rather than hiding their problem, which is what they usually did, they advertised it.

SELLING THE INTERVENTION

At this stage of treatment, the therapist already has a number of impressions about the customer: his sensibilities, attitudes, and, more specifically, his views and expectations about the problem and treatment. This information is then used to "sell" the intervention. Some customers are quite willing to try something new. In fact, they expect to be given advice, and that is why they sought out a directive therapist. Others can be influenced to follow a directive if the explanation makes sense to them. For the scientifically oriented customer, assignments may be framed as trial experiments or as ways of collecting base-line data. This was the rationale used in the case of the premature ejaculator mentioned earlier. The angry parent might be more inclined to follow a directive if it is presented as a way to teach his child a useful lesson, even though it will be somewhat unpleasant. We instructed a woman to make a wrong turn with her car every time her adopted daughter cursed her for driving slowly. Every time the mother did this, she would apologize to the daughter, stating that she didn't know what was wrong with her. This lesson needed to be implicit, breaking with the usual solution of asking or demanding that the daughter show respect. Finally, the psychologically oriented patient might be asked to carry out an assignment to gain new insights that could only be brought about by taking action.

Of course, there are times when such an approach fails, even after making a u-turn and trying a new tack. And with some patients, the therapist has already learned that they have been given new methods of dealing with the problem by former therapists or friends, but for various reasons have not taken the advice. In such cases, the therapist has an alternative approach for change: blocking the basic solution.

Blocking tactics *utilize* the patient's resistance rather than analyzing or fighting it. If it's clear that the patient will resist the therapist's directives, injunctions can be given in various forms which, in effect, say "don't change." This approach can be amplified by defining such seemingly illogical advice as protective. In this case, the therapist takes a strong stand which is calculated to increase the patient's resistance, for the patient is being protected from things he finds distasteful.

For example, a teenager who is getting into trouble may be told she is making a magnificent sacrifice by ruining her life to protect her parents' marriage. The more she gets into trouble, the more her parents' attentions are focused on her rather than on their own problems. This can work quite well if she is angry at her parents. When a patient receives financial compensation for his problem, the therapist may point out that any resolution in the problem means a loss of income, and that the client would have to face a tough job market with little or no skills. This was a commonly used ploy when working with V.A. patients who were receiving over five-hundred dollars a month, tax free, because their problems were service-connected.

PLANNING TERMINATION

Treatment is usually more effective and significantly shorter if the therapist has a clear idea of what minimal change would be sufficient to terminate the case. Many therapists and patients get into trouble by assuming that if a little change is good, a lot of change is better. We don't agree with this philosophy and, in fact, for a variety of reasons, believe that continuing treatment can undo what positive change has been accomplished and may possibly make the problem worse.

When the therapist is gathering basic information, the patient is asked to state what minimal, concrete change would indicate that a small but significant dent had been made in the problem. With some cases, this may be a sufficient target. In other cases, the very nature of the complaint makes this impossible. For example, one might be working with parents whose minimal goal is for their son to achieve C's instead of D's in two of his school courses. However, report cards don't come out for three more months, and the therapist will not wish to extend treatment because of this. In such a case, there may be another objective which would indicate that things are on the right

track, such as having the boy do his homework. If this has been accomplished, treatment might be terminated prior to report card time.

Along with the positive change, the therapist must also get patient
recognition that improvement has taken place. Basically, we are looking for three criteria in the patient's statements: (1) beneficial change
has taken place; (2) it is not temporary; (3) I can now handle things
on my own or can easily accept the idea of termination.

Interventions

Theoretically, everything the therapist says and does can potentially
influence the patient. However, there are a number of specific interventions which have repeatedly proved useful. A few of these will be
presented to round out the picture of our work.

REFRAMING

To reframe is to change the conceptual and emotional meaning of
a situation or set of facts. Reframing is not something new, and it has
probably been part of social intercourse since men began to live in
groups. As Shakespeare said, "There is nothing either good or bad,
but thinking makes it so." Or, a well-known newscaster reported that
during a large outdoor religious gathering, the minister looked up at
the sky full of rain clouds and said, "God loves us." The crowd came
to its feet, applauding the idea that God was holding back the rain.
During the middle of the program the rain did begin to fall, quite hard.
The minister returned to the microphone, looked up and said, "God
works in mysterious ways." He had reframed his original statement
and the crowd loved it.

All therapists reframe every time they attempt to interpret the meaning of the facts or hard data in the case. Explaining to a parent that
a child's problem is due to a form of emotional difficulty rather than
"badness" is a reframing used by most therapists from time to time.

The ways by which one can reframe are too numerous even to begin
listing, for this can be accomplished by the therapist's statements,
demeanor, special assignments, or nonverbal experiences. For instance, Dr. Milton Erickson convinced a patient who would not talk
to anyone to do it in the public library. While this seems to be a small
and meaningless change, it does shift, however slightly, the meaning
of the patient's behavior. To be quiet in the library is appropriate

behavior. It also creates a better chance of the patient's starting a relationship with someone, which is what happened in this specific case.

One final example comes from our own work in the Brief Therapy Center. We treated a salesman who stuttered and wanted to rid himself of his speech impediment so he would make a better impression on people. The therapist was able to reframe his stuttering as an asset, distinguishing him from the usual high-pressured salesmen who people immediately turned off. Once he accepted this reframing, he viewed his impediment in a radical new way—as an advantage. In doing so, he no longer tried to stop himself from stuttering, and the problem all but disappeared.

TAKING A ONE-DOWN POSITION

Therapists will have an easier time collecting information and getting patients to try out new ways of dealing with their problems if they do not present themselves as all-knowing figures who have no problems of their own. Taking a one-down position simply means conveying directly or implicitly that the therapist is a modest person who has frailties of his own. He can be confused, frightened, unsure, and fallible. (Examples of this intervention have already been presented under the section entitled "Pretreatment Considerations.")

PESSIMISM

Many patients feel hopeless about their situation, but in a large number of cases this feeling is implicit. These patients will usually elicit support and encouragement from friends or other professionals, which only further entrenches the problem. In such cases, it's more useful to be more pessimistic than the patient. This has the dual effect of making the pessimism explicit so that it can be examined, and results in the patient's challenging the therapist's opinion. Patient: "Do you think you can help me, Doctor? I just can't take it anymore." Therapist: "Well, it's certainly understandable that you're feeling bad, but I don't want to give you any false hope. I haven't worked with anyone as depressed as you in a long time." Patient: "You're supposed to give me some hope." Therapist: "God knows, I wish I could, but I don't want to make promises I can't keep." Patient: "Well, the last time I was feeling this way, I came out of it." Therapist: "Yes, but that was the last time; your problems are so overwhelming, I'm not sure where to start!'' From here, the patient might be led into telling the therapist what might be of some help.

DANGERS OF IMPROVEMENT

There are times in treatment when the patient is sitting back, letting the therapist do all the work. This is reversed by taking up the question, "What new problems might arise if you did get over your problem?" It can be presented as an interpretation. Either way, it provides a means by which the therapist can hint or suggest that the patient has the best of all possible worlds. For example, a couple who fights constantly can be told that their problem is the only thing holding the marriage together, and that the therapist is reluctant to make further efforts at helping them stop their battles. Of course, this is presented with the intention of having the couple resist such an interpretation. The therapist then implies that the proof of their denial lies in their cooperating in treatment, i.e., getting down to work.

GOING SLOW

Many times treatment goes better when the patient is not under undue pressure to solve the problem immediately or under some real or imagined deadline. Just as dangers of improvement are used to increase the pressure on the patient, "going slow" is used for the opposite purpose. There are numerous ways for the therapist to take this position: formulating a small, concrete goal for treatment; framing statements as not being very important but possibly useful; asking a client to think about an assignment for a week prior to carrying it out; and even directly admonishing the client not to change too fast. Typically, when patients come in happily explaining how well things went during the past week, we acknowledge this but then warn them to slow down. Therapist: "I'm really pleased to hear how well things went for you, but I'm starting to get nervous about your enthusiasm. I think you're setting yourself up for a disappointment. This week sounds more like an exception to me. Even if things continue to improve, there will be some slipping back. So please, take it slowly."

SYMPTOM PRESCRIPTION

A large number of problems brought to psychotherapists fall into the category of attempting to be spontaneous deliberately—forcing sleep, sexual responses, wanting to feel a certain way. With such cases, one of the most effective interventions is prescribing the symptom. As one of my colleagues explains, these problems are the result of being caught in a "be spontaneous" paradox, and the way out is a counter-paradox that solves the problem. There are many reasons or ways of framing that can be used to justify why the patient should try to bring on the problem: making it happen makes it predictable; bring it on so you can study how you do it; make yourself extremely depressed for fifteen minutes a day and get it over with; bring it on during the interview so that the therapist can observe it directly.

In this regard, there is an interesting story about an agoraphobic who finally ended up in the closet of his home as his last solution. Unable to stand the state of his existence, he decided to commit suicide by leaving the house and driving north from San Francisco toward the Oregon border. He was sure that once he was a few miles from his home, he would be consumed by a fit of anxiety, resulting in a fatal heart attack. After an hour of driving, some sixty miles from his house, he started to realize he could not bring on his symptoms, and at that point knew he'd found the solution to his problem.

Case Example

Mrs. X arrived for the first session accompanied by her husband and two sons, thirteen and fifteen years old. She provided extensive documentation of her sons' misbehavior, which included not doing chores, oppositional behavior, and school infractions. Her attempted solutions to these problems included persistent nagging, threats with which she did not follow through, and ever increasing restrictions on their movements. Furthermore, she had enlisted neighbors, teachers, and friends to monitor the boys' behavior and to report the slightest infractions. In the course of her monologue, which extended over several sessions, Mrs. X revealed that her informants were really not necessary because her special sense allowed her to predict precisely when her boys would act out, and that she had used ESP to regulate the medication of one boy. On the basis of her special sense, she often restricted both boys to their home in order to prevent mischief. She felt strongly that her intuitions were always correct. When she grounded the boys, either misbehavior was averted or they broke the restrictions, which she took to validate that they should have been grounded in the first place. Often after breaking restrictions, they went on to further misdeeds.

The therapist treating the X family felt that the mother's attempted solutions were in fact creating a problem out of the normal difficulties that a family encounters when two teenage boys test out their autonomy and start down the road to independence. In keeping with this hypothesis, the therapist's goal was to have the mother decrease her restrictions and empty verbal threats.

The therapist decided to utilize Mrs. X's belief in ESP as a framework for instructing her to change her method of problem-solving. He told Mrs. X that since she had obviously been blessed with a special gift which allowed her to tune into the thoughts of her sons, i.e., receive, perhaps she could also transmit her thoughts to them. The therapist reinforced this idea by various references to ongoing work in parapsychology. Of course, for the mother to test her powers of thought transmission would necessitate reducing restrictions and verbal admonitions. She was led to bring this up herself when the intervention was being suggested, reducing the possibility of resistance that might have occurred if the therapist asked her to back off directly. The mother gave our suggestion a trial test. As her behavior changed, the boys had fewer reasons to rebel and their misbehavior decreased. As the boys' behavior improved, mother had less need to handle things in her old way, nor did she need to use her power of ESP.

Three months later, a follow-up revealed that as the mother became less controlling, the father took a more active role in parenting. Fewer difficulties with the boys allowed the parents to relax their vigilance and to do more things as a couple. The parents expressed great satisfaction with treatment.

Brief Therapy with the Impoverished

Brief Therapy can be extremely useful with "multi-problem" families. Since the model does not necessitate seeing the whole family for each interview, the therapist is free to choose with whom he will work. Who is the most motivated for treatment? Who is in the best position vis-à-vis the family to bring about beneficial change? Rather than trying to work with a large group—which is chaotic and distracting—the therapist can maximize his impact by strategic selection of family members for each interview. Additionally, the Brief Therapist will be focusing on presenting complaints, speaking the client's language, and offering advice in the form of directives. These are all factors that tend to meet the expectations of this population and that should serve to enhance a positive relationship and an atmosphere of cooperation.

One persistent problem among this population is the lack of concrete resources—money, employment, and housing. Many therapists take the view that these problems result from either inadequacy of the client(s) or the inequality of the social system—discrimination, unnecessary bureaucracy, poverty, etc. While there is an obvious measure of truth in this viewpoint, from a practical standpoint it holds little advantage when problem-solving. A physician cannot treat a specific case of tuberculosis with epidemiological procedures.

The interactional view offers another perspective which leads to specific and immediate possibilities for treatment. Namely, how does the client go about solving the problem of resource deficiency? What pattern of action or nonaction has been taken to solve or cope with this problem? What small, concrete, specific action could the client take that might lead to a different outcome—a positive outcome—and what is the best way to influence the client to try out this new course of action? These are the kinds of questions which the Brief Therapy model generates, offering up some fresh ideas for therapeutic intervention.

Research Findings

After working one afternoon a week for approximately six years, we had treated 97 families comprised of 236 individuals. Our sample included people from all socioeconomic classes; blacks, whites, and Orientals; exhibiting a wide range of psychiatric symptoms covering the full spectrum of psychiatric problems.

Each case is followed up by an interviewer who took no part in the treatment. After specific questions have been asked to assess what changes have occurred in the presenting complaint, we also inquire if any new problems have arisen, whether any old problems were resolved spontaneously, and whether there has been any further treatment. Cases are rated as follows: 2 = success; 1 = significantly improved; and 0 = failure. To qualify for a rating of 1 or 2, there must be a significant change in the presenting complaint, no new problems, and no further treatment. If any of our follow-up interviews reveal further treatment, the case is rated 0.

Given the above conditions, our results for the 97 cases, averaging 7.0 sessions, were as follows: Success = 39 cases (40 percent); Significantly Improved = 31 cases (32 percent); and Failure = 27 cases (28 percent).

Summary and Concluding Remarks

Focused Problem Resolution presents a system for understanding how human problems persist and a body of techniques for solving them. The task of the therapist is to correctly assess the problem-solution loop, and to devise individualized tasks or interventions to shift the vicious cycle of interaction, thereby resolving the problem. Given this formulation, it is easy to see that such a method is generic in its understanding and treatment of a wide variety of human problems which present themselves to mental health workers and to other helping professionals, such as ministers, medical personnel, lawyers, and educators.

Given the interactional nature of our work, the therapist is always working with an eye to what is taking place in the family. But unlike many family approaches which label their work explicitly as "family therapy" and insist on seeing the entire family unit for each treatment hour, we choose to work with those family members who offer the best chance of changing the system, defining treatment to meet the patient's expectations.

While many approaches have difficulty orienting their clientele to treatment procedures, expectations, and language, our work accommodates to the specific client. This makes the approach quite useful for patients and their families who come from a lower socioeconomic class. Economically disadvantaged people usually want to talk about what is hurting them and expect some advice for making things better. Focused Problem Resolution easily meets their expectations, and does it in the language spoken by the client.

References

Barten, H. H., ed. 1971. *Brief Therapies* (especially ch. 24, 26). New York: Behavioral Publications.
Bateson, G., D. Jackson, J. Haley, and J. Weakland. 1956. "Toward a Theory of Schizophrenia." *Behavioral Science* 1:251–64.
Haley, J. 1963. *Strategies of Psychotherapy*. New York: Grune and Stratton.
Haley, J., ed. 1967. *Advanced Techniques of Hypnosis and Therapy: Selected Papers of Milton H. Erickson, M.D.* New York: Grune and Stratton.
Ruesch, J. and G. Bateson. 1951. *Communication: The Social Matrix of Psychiatry*. New York: Norton.
Watzlawick, P., Janet H. Beavin, and Don D. Jackson. 1967. *Pragmatics of*

Human Communication (especially ch. 7, "Paradox in Psychotherapy").
New York: Norton.
Watzlawick, P., J. H. Weakland, and R. Fisch. 1974. *Change: Principles of
Problem Formation and Resolution.* New York: Norton.
Weakland, J. H., R. Fisch, P. Watzlawick, and A. Bodin. 1974. "Brief Ther-
apy: Focused Problem Resolution." *Family Process* 13:141–68.
Wells, R. A. and A. E. Dezen. 1978. "The Results of Family Therapy Revis-
ited: The Nonbehavioral Methods." *Family Process* 17(3):251–74.

9

The Focus and Activity of Family Therapists
A Transcript of a Round Table Discussion

RAE MELTZER

The nine participants who were invited to the Charlotte Towle Memorial Conference on Family Treatment met for two days to exchange ideas about various aspects of family treatment. The entire proceedings were videotaped. The author of this paper reviewed and selected portions from the videotape for transcription, so that readers of this volume would have the opportunity to "listen in" as well as read the ideas presented at the conference. The discussions selected for the transcript have been carefully edited to preserve the spontaneous and lively interchange among participants, without sacrificing coherence and continuity of ideas.

The transcript reflects three major themes addressed by the participants. Part 1 focuses on the assessment process in family therapy. In part 2, the discussion centers on the contributions of the therapist to the family treatment process. In the last segment, part 3, specific treatment strategies and intervention are proposed by the participants after they view a videotape of one part of a family session. Not all of the participants were present for the entire last session because of prior commitments.

Part 1

> *Meltzer:* What specific data and information has the highest priority for you in the assessment process? Do you rely more on self-report or on direct observation for gathering data?

Bell: My position is rather an extreme one; I'm assessing all the time. It is never a single process; it is something that goes on through the whole therapy, itself.

Meltzer: Do you think you do something different in that first session than you do subsequently?

Bell: Of course! As far as assessment is concerned, I'm more preoccupied with their availability to communicate; with who participates and who does not participate. And the glimpses I get of what their relationship with me might be.

Meltzer: So, it is very much observing what's going on in front of you, rather than centering on what they are telling you about what has happened.

Bell: The content at that stage is not my main focus.

Segal: I want to know what is the complaint; what have they been doing to attempt to deal with it; and what it would look like when something changed in a positive way. I'm trying to get a fix on how it is a problem in somebody's life or what they would like to stop doing. Do we have a customer here? We will be assessing this by the way the interview is going, particularly how they see the problem and how do they see treatment. When they come in, let's say, for a kid, do they see the kid as "mad" or "bad"; do they feel responsible or angry? Are they hoping for a family interview or are they hoping that we are going to take the kid, retread him like a tire or something and give him back to them, fresh? We want to pick up all that information so that we can then try to work within that, and move the least amount necessary to do what we have to do to bring about change.

Walters: If one is working on the basis of causality and etiology, one is looking for certain things. If one is working on the basis of behavior within the hour which would give the therapist clues as to a way of working which changes the system, that is something else. You either have a frame of reference in one direction and operate in that or in another. It's just that one of the things I think is hardest for all of us to do is to declare where we stand, and say, "This is what I believe and because I believe these things, this is specifically how I work." And what we are forever doing is kind of saying everything is of the same order. There are different orders of change and different orders of work in relation to what we believe creates change. My highest priority is data based on what goes on in front of me—direct observation—because that is what is important to create change.

Bell: I think you are addressing yourself to the issue of therapist's behavior more than to the issue of family behavior, and the literature is just jammed full with stuff about families and very little, actually, about what therapists do—what is going on inside themselves and what their actions are. And we have tremendous lacunae of information of the whole aspect of therapist's behavior and therapist's thought.

Gambrill: One of the characteristics of a behavioral perspective is to go after multiple sources of assessment information. Emphasis is upon direct observations. The presenting problem offers hardly any specific information. Let's take a drinking problem for example. When the client says, "I have a drinking problem," all we know is that drinking is a problem for someone. It doesn't really say what is consumed, when it's consumed, if it is in the normative boundaries of anyone's drinking pattern, whatever their culture. So there would be a strong emphasis to identify, in observable terms, the particular concerns of the client and to identify the surrounding circumstances related to those concerns. How are significant others in the environment involved in the problem? To what extent could significant others take part in an intervention program? Does a mother, for example, know what to say to her child to support the behavior she would like to see more of? What can you utilize to encourage her, prompt her, reinforce her, reward her for offering such incentives? I would like to point out too, that with a behavioral approach self-monitoring is another assessment procedure which is often used; not only self-report, direct observation, but also self-monitoring by the client. While this is not always possible, often the client can gather information about specific behavior and surrounding conditions. If a family seems to have difficulty solving problems, you could ask them to sit down in the office and identify a problem and ask them to discuss that and record their interaction for further, very careful, review to identify specific behaviors that would be helpful to increase and/or decrease in relation to problem-solving skills.

Wells: Let me comment for a moment on another concern rather than on the exploratory data-gathering techniques themselves, as I think it is easy enough, from almost any conceptual framework, to develop a series of areas that should be responsibly and carefully assessed. My concern, however, is with the many potential clients who drop out of treatment at these early stages. I become worried about how much time we can spend on the careful assessment that we believe is needed and, simultaneously, not neglect what we must be doing in order to promote engagement and involvement. The drop-out phenomenon is one of our most neglected clinical problems and these rates run very high in many agencies—up to 80 percent of our potential clients never continue past the fourth or fifth interview, a period of contact which coincides with the assessment phase recommended in a number of approaches. In order to deal with the issues of engagement I think that more experienced therapists become more selective in what they explore and make some sort of clinical judgment about what they will examine. There is no doubt that there is a sometimes monotonous similarity to certain of the problems people describe and we don't always need to examine them in depth. I realize one must be careful not to stereotype, or rush too quickly past an issue of importance but, on the other hand, excessive attention to assessment can neglect engagement and thereby promote client drop-out.

Gambrill: You are really getting into the engagement processes which are indeed an important part and often have been in the past overlooked in the behavioral literature. In the new book by Jacobson and Margolin on marital treatment,[1] they go so far as to say that in their opinion, in the initial session there should be no focusing on identifying the problem, no focusing on getting an overview of the problem; but rather, one should concentrate on being enthusiastic, and building confidence in the creditability of the intervention. They recommend that the focus in the first interview should be on some of the positives in the relationship, and on how the couple got to know each other. Of course, within a behavioral approach, one would try to increase the extent to which the client may see positives in significant others.

Segal: I think a lot of people when they come in, especially if they haven't been trained to be good therapy patients, want to talk about what is bugging them. That is where they are at, what they are willing to do business on, what they want to talk about, what they are invested in. I'm against this idea of starting off in a particular posture, like being enthusiastic

[1] Neil S. Jacobson and Gayla Margolin *Marital Therapy: Strategies Based on Social Learning and Behavior Exchange Principles.* New York: Brunner & Mazel, 1979.

or talking about how the couple got to know each other. In the same way, I'm against giving people rules on how to communicate. Because, I think the nature of interaction between people is complex enough. I know we have seen a lot of clients who do things they have been told is helpful, the right way, by other professionals. That advice and pre-scribed behavior may be the very things that are keeping the problem going. I think one has to be a lot more empirical and maybe go back to assessment. You have to constantly keep your eye on the dance that goes on between you and the client and move accordingly. With some patients, I'm going to come up pessimistic. And the way I'm going to get them to engage is to tell them I don't see why they are even making an effort to change. With other clients, I may be very different, but I do not want to meet someone at the door with a therapeutic posture. Other than, "What are you here for?" Or, "What can I do for you?" Or, "What brings you in?" Or, as Milton Erikson used to say, "What do you want from me?"

(Laughter!)

Hartman: For me, the assessment process is absolutely shared with the client. A lot of the responsibility for making the assess-ment and for gathering the data really belongs to the client. The assessment is not something that goes on in the worker's head. In doing a genogram, the client is the expert and has to give you the material and you're the learner. Then the two of us together are in a joint-sharing process of trying to understand the family system. Then the client him/herself becomes the student of the family, which puts a different slant on assessment. The genogram is one way to objectify this mass of data about the family. I've devised a little map that I call the eco-map which is a similar kind of thing that attempts to objectify the data about the family interaction with other systems.

Bell: I won't speak for you, Ann, but I have a feeling that it is possible to somewhat separate, and meaningfully separate, the interaction with the family and the thinking about that. For instance, I tried to postpone that thinking about the family until after the session is over in order to keep my attention very much centered on my action in reference to the family and the families interaction among themselves. And, if I stop to conceptualize during that process, the family responds to my distancing myself. And, that distancing impedes the progress of the therapy, slows it down, so that insofar as it is possible, my attention is riveted on what is going on right at this very moment not only in one individual, but with all the people who are there. An exercise in observation and attention, which I had to learn because I was so used to thinking about the individual in psychoanalysis, and looking and conceptualizing. I have trained myself, for instance, in my observation skills to keep spanning the whole group constantly and keeping them all, as much as possible in my perspective, not only as individuals but in their interaction with one another.

Meltzer: Do you bring any of that back to the family after you have thought about it?

Bell: No! The focus is entirely on the here and now—and what is going on among them.

Part 2

Meltzer: I would like to ask how each of you directs or influences what goes on in the treatment process. What is your specific role?

Spiegel: We have a name for what we do; we call it being the "culture broker." We go all the way around the transactional field in order to come to some kind of a decision of where to pick things up. But, because we are working with subcultural groups, we usually start at the cultural focus and that is why we talk about being the "culture broker," because we do like to understand the problem in the family . . . from the point of view of conflict of values, to get away from pathology and nosology, to get away from identifying the problem with personality, which is the way it is usually seen by the members of the family, and to relate it to something that they haven't got a cognitive grip on, which is usually the conflict in values. But, when we look at what we do, we probably do all of the things that have been discussed here. We don't have any one method, except we don't use paradoxical, because I don't know how to use it, at least I don't think we do, it could turn out that we do. But, mostly, I understand what we do as cognitive. For instance, we don't try to tell a family how to solve the problem or intervene in such a way as to solve it. We try to help them understand the origin of that problem in terms of values, in terms of a generational thing. We do work with genograms, and then we may say, "Could you come up with some solution?" You know, we don't tell them what that solution is but we do ask them to think about it. Usually they will come up with some kind of a solution so that we don't have to intervene in the sense of prescribing a way of resolving the problem. We work with them on their way of doing it because I think if we tried to do it, it would be *our way* of doing it.

Wells: I can see many similarities between my own approach and the areas that others have emphasized—the nonpathological viewpoint expressed by Ann [Hartman] or the interest in culture to which John Spiegel has referred. . . . At the same time, there is a great deal that the therapist contributes through confidence, enthusiasm, concern, or hope. Also, another area that greatly interests me is what the researchers call "spontaneous recovery." In other words, a lot of the people we see will get better whether we see them or not. This is a phenomenon that I find absolutely intriguing, and at times I wonder whether all our preoccupation with theory and technique is running up the wrong side of the equation. In my own practice I tend to look at what people bring in as representing a crisis, with definite time-limits, and see my function as one of helping to mobilize their available natural resources and networks. This may be one of the most powerful facets of family work—the family itself is one of the most important of these natural systems. If we can do something to reduce its conflict, even in a minor way, the family may well be capable of alleviating other areas of distress without further intervention. On the other hand, I am reluctant to get too involved in figuring out ways to promote spontaneous recovery because then it won't be spontaneous. I'm afraid that if I get myself too involved in this natural process I may interfere with it rather than support it.

Meltzer: I find a tension in the discussion here in the sense that some of you say that the role of the therapist is really to present a new perspective, in a way, to reframe, to present something different to the family. And those of you who are saying, "No, let's let the family direct what is going to happen." If you are going to let the family direct what is going to happen, often their solution is what's continuing the problem. So, if we don't reframe and redirect and re-conceptualize, then how do we effect change?

Segal: If you tell somebody to think about three generations of his family . . .

Meltzer: Is that your way of shifting their focus and in some sense you're reframing it?

Segal: Our basic idea is that when someone comes in with a prob-lem, which we call the presenting complaint, . . . they are distressed about it, they have tried to stop it and they haven't been able to, so they are coming for help. The role of the therapist, therefore, is to intervene to see if he or she can do something about it where the client couldn't. In this sense, I think we are quite close to what John Bell has said, that we think people are fully equipped to solve their prob-lems. We don't operate on a "deficiency model." We think they are simply stuck. We make the naïve assumption that they continue to mishandle things because it seems to be the logical and reasonable thing to do. When they don't succeed, they try harder, but they are a little bit like the man in quicksand, the more they struggle, the more they sink. For instance, just in a very general sense, most people apply opposites to things. If you are cold, you turn on the heat, if you are too hot, you try to cool off. But, there are a lot of things, especially in the nature of emotions and behavior, that we seem to feel don't work that way. If you try to cheer yourself up when you are depressed, we predict in a lot of cases, you may get more depressed. It is fairly observable that in most cases when somebody is depressed, others will be trying to cheer them up, with "come on get with," or "unconditional positive regard." Somewhere along the line the message is—you shouldn't feel this way. The task of therapy, as we see it, is primarily to get them unstuck by taking away the block and our viewpoint is that the block is in the attempted solution, the way the patients try to deal with the problem. What we try to do is that once we get a fix on what people are doing that we think is perpetuating the problem, we try to figure out what we can get them to do differently.

Gambrill: There certainly would be an intent, if we wanted to sum-marize it, to help clients rearrange the contingencies in the natural environment that were related to achieving their desired outcomes. In terms of what the social worker brings to that, hopefully, he would bring a set of competencies in relation to knowledge concerning the relationships between behavior and environmental events, and a set of competencies in how to help the client actually rearrange those contingencies, whether it is antecedents, consequences, or whatever. From a behavioral perspective, it is important to help the client arrange a situation so the treatment plans have a high probability of success. The social worker should consider how positive changes that are made will generalize and be maintained in the natural environment. Now, some aspects of the framework are very much tuned into that from the very beginning: for example, the emphasis on working with significant others in the natural environment, training them, adding to their skills. It is to be hoped that these new skills will not only help the client's family members deal with their particular concerns at present, but with future ones that may arise. In the behavioral approach there is definitely an emphasis on the here-and-now of transactions and interactions of family members.

Meltzer: Do you think that the literature up to this point says anything, either empirically or not, about what is most powerful in the treatment process?

Gambrill: The question that is important is what intervention procedure works best with what client, with what concern. So if you were faced with a child that is a bed wetter, you can easily look in the literature and find out what is the most effective method. Is play therapy any better than, say, behavioral intervention of some sort, and if so, what type of behavioral intervention? Of course, in many areas we don't have information like that, but in some we do.

Meltzer: Are you saying that from a behavioral point of view it is all wide open as to what is most powerful? Would a behaviorist use a psychodynamic approach if the research proved that to be more powerful in a particular case and particular situation?

Gambrill: I would think so. I think the underlying characteristic, the basic characteristic of the behavioral approach, is a commitment to empirical grounding for assessment and intervention processes.

Part 3

In the concluding session of the conference, a fifteen-minute video-tape segment of a family session was shown to the conference participants. After viewing the videotape, the participants were asked how they would intervene in the family situation. The family includes the parents who are in their mid-forties and their son who is seventeen years old. They are an upper-middle-class family. During his summer vacation Jim is working part time on a road construction job and spending the rest of his time at home and acting with a community theatre group.

Summary of Family Session Viewed by Conference Participants

Father tells Jim that it's pretty natural for someone Jim's age to try to avoid working. Jim interrupts to tell his father that he doesn't object to working. Mother chides Jim about his laziness and self-indulgence in sleep and TV. Father quickly comments that he is pleased and satisfied because Jim doesn't give them any real trouble. Nevertheless, he considers it a father's duty to make sure his son gets the right start in life. Father recalls that he started working at fourteen and has been working hard ever since. Jim again insists that he isn't objecting to working this summer. Father urges Jim to save the money he is earning from his part-time job for college expenses. He asks Jim what he wants to do with his life. Jim says that whenever he mentions his interest in acting, his parents tell him that it is not very realistic or practical.

Mother tells Jim to forget the acting business. She complains that when his is home, he doesn't help with any of the chores around the house. She playfully calls him "a spoiled loafer and dreamer." Father chimes in to tell Jim, "You are an okay kid in my book." Jim asks them why they are poles apart about him and so many other things? This remark precipitates an angry reaction from mother who again complains that Jim never does anything he is asked to do. Jim argues with mother about her claim that he doesn't do anything. Jim points out that he and father had agreed that it was all right for him to work part time. Father says he has changed his mind about that—thinks Jim should work full time. Jim objects that this wouldn't leave him any time to participate in the theatre group. Mother tells Jim that she is disgusted with him because he has plenty of time to just sit around and do nothing at all while there is so much to do in the house. Father appeals to Jim to try working full time for a week instead of shirking his responsibilities. Jim insists that he is working hard on his job but wants some free time to find out what he might like to do in the future. Father asks him if he has found out what that is. Jim responds that he knows his father will object to his choice and push him again to study law. Mother says she doesn't care about the future, its what Jim is doing now—just hanging around the house doing nothing, that gets to her. Father replies that he thinks a lot about Jim's future and wants to make sure that they do what is right by him. Mother criticizes Jim for staying up so late at night that he can't get up in the morning. Father offers to reward Jim with something really special if Jim goes ahead to work full time for the next several weeks of his vacation.

> *Reid:* Without putting anybody on the spot by asking, I'd like to get from those participants who want to react to this, their ideas about how they might view this family situation. Marianne, good, I'm glad you volunteered.

> *Walters:* Well, as a therapist, of course, I would have probably come up with a hypothesis and a way I would go. I think what I would have done would have been to ask the mother to help the father not to work so hard in behalf of his son and every time the father intervened and said, "Why don't you do this," I would have suggested that the mother move in to the father, in some close proximity, and interrupt his interaction with his son. Now this is based on an idea that the son's behavior has something to do with conflict between the parents. Jim tells his parents to get together and make a joint decision. I see the son's behavior as a conflict detour: the parents seem to be enjoying having that as the problem rather than looking at what goes on between them—at their conflict. My effort would have been to put mother in charge of interrupting father's transactions with Jim because he seemed to be saving the boy. At every moment that mother would complain, father would come in and instead of allowing the interaction to go between mother and boy, the father would come in and say, well, why don't you do

so and so, and have a lot of suggestions, and then the boy could go and argue the suggestion. That seemed the sort of pattern of transaction that was going on. My first probe would have been to challenge the pattern of transaction and interrupt it at some point. I can see that people would have interrupted it at a number of different points. You can choose a different point to interrupt the patterns of transactions that you see in the hour. The initial challenge to the family can come at any point in the circle. I think I might have asked the father to do something different with the mother, perhaps in terms of interrupting her patterns. But, it depends where you want to go and, being interested these days in issues of women's roles and families, I guess I would have gone the way I described it.

Bell: I can do that kind of analysis too. And I would say that for me, that is not very relevant. If this were the first session and their communication was going on in front of me, in such a lively way, I would wait because I don't have enough assurance of their response to me to move in any other direction than simply waiting. This is a period of building up a relationship. I'm a stranger. If they did this in the first session, it would indicate a considerable confidence, and yet, there are a lot of parameters of that relationship that they haven't had a chance to test, and so I would not get into any kind of interpretation. If this were the third session in the series, I would allow this lively interaction to go on because I didn't see anybody really withdrawing from it. They were all, you know, participating. Sure, momentarily, the mother would step aside while others were communicating with one another or the boy would drop his head and sort of semi-withdraw, never really withdrawing. My function, then, is by my silence, by my intent watching and observing everything that's going on, to facilitate the continuation of this kind of communication. But, there would come a pause. It might not be in this session, if they go on dealing with this issue, but there is going to come a deadlock at some point. And, at that point, I would come in to break the deadlock.

Let's say, that it's the young fellow who blocks himself

out. My intervention would be like this. I would say, "Now I notice as your mother and your father were talking that you did this" (showing son how he bows his head). Turning my attention to him, I would turn away from the parents as a deliberate way of bringing him back into the situation. My primary goal, all the way through, is to keep this family group interacting in such a way with one another that it will bring them toward *their* goal. My goal is to be the best possible facilitator of that kind of interaction and movement that I possibly can be. My role is as an intermediary in accomplishing this task. Their goal is to solve their problems according to the goals that they have and the kinds of mechanisms that they can use in order to attain their goal.

Wells: I would want to try to do some kind of tentative ne- gotiating, perhaps around the matter of getting Jim back to work or around how they might become more effective as parents or a more harmonious family. In any case, I would definitely want to do some negoti- ating about why I'm there or what I can possibly help them with.

Hartman: I would look at the situation as a differentiation strug- gle on the part of this adolescent boy. We saw one after another indication of the extent to which these parents fused with him—the mother telling him whether his body needs sleep, how many hours it needs, the father telling him what kind of work he ought to be doing, how he ought to be feeling. There were an awful lot of "oughts." So that one of the things that you can think about is that his anger and resistance and fighting his parents on every issue is an essential effort to dif- ferentiate from them. So that would be one way to kind of assess it. The content of the struggle is over occupational choice, which, I think, is a very fasci- nating family issue in terms of what do men in a par- ticular family do. I can think about getting some notion from the genograms about occupational careers and life careers of the men in the family who are the heroes. The father says, "I got broken in when I was twelve." I right away heard that piece which is a beautiful ex- ample of how we hear selectively what fits into "our thing." The father was obviously referring to his relationship with his own father around the issue of work. One would have that hunch and begin to get a look at how he struggled with these issues when he was an adolescent in terms of his father. I'm just demonstrating the way I would look at identity issues, differentiation issues and family history issues in relation to occupational choice in this piece of family interaction.

Segal: One thing, when Marianne [Walters] said we all see it as "the boy and the marriage"—I don't think that necessarily connotes the systems approach. I have some doubts about the assumption that when one member of a family is acting up, it is covering another family problem and that is synonymous with systems. One can assume that they came in because, as they said, they couldn't get their kid to work and stop hanging around. If that's what the parents wanted, the main thing I see is that they are very ineffective in dealing with him. Mom is nagging and dad is kind of whining and reasoning and pleading a little bit. If I had seen the three of them going on like that, either during that session or certainly in the next one, I would just see the parents alone and figure out how to get them off that track and onto a new way of dealing with him. If they continued to deal with him in that way, I would predict he would continue not to work because they are making a bunch of threats that they can't back up. So, I would see that as (*a*) ineffective; and (*b*) what needs to be changed. That's their attempted solution, nagging and reasoning. Find something else for them to do.

Question: How do you know that is what they want from you?

Segal: Well, I would get them to agree, first of all, that the problem is that their son is sitting around on his ass and they don't like it. I'm going to assume that if they say they want to change it, I believe them, and I don't start looking around for unconscious forces. If they say they want to change it, I'm going to take them up on it until they prove differently. The way they'll prove differently is when I start giving them things to do and then they come back and say, "Oh, I forgot," or "I mixed it up"; that's when I'm going to start thinking, not necessarily that there's something else going on, but, I'm going to back off on trying to help them with the issue until they convince me that they want to work on this or something else which is of concern to them.

Sherman: I perceive "data" on a number of levels which vary in degree of certainty or speculation. Manifest behavior—verbal and nonverbal—is the least doubtful; implications or inferences, the most speculative, but it is vital to draw them. Speculatively, father is trying to be the master. Mother has the bite, she bites. She is biting at the son. I have a hunch that father is a paper tiger because he rushes to tell the boy to please his mother. This father says, "I work like a dog, but I like to work." This guy has a real pride in being a self-made man who really worked hard. But, he also wants people to give him a little tit in payment for it. And he is very identified with the boy. Father talks out of both sides of his mouth to the kid. He says, "I know how you feel, you don't want to work," and so on; "Good lad there"; and then "You've gotta go to work, you've gotta find something to do." He is doing both and it is as though he keeps articulating his own ambivalence about himself but externalized. He's working it out on the boy. Now, that's a dangerous situation, because I feel mother is biting the boy, but she may be biting in a surrogate way, the father. These are therapist's hunches, things we look for in the family drama as we go on, or invalidate as further evidence arises. It wouldn't be long before I would be telling father to stop talking out of both sides of his mouth, in a nice way—in the interest, in the context of trying to get him in touch with the fact that he is trying to work out some unfinished business of his own on the boy. Mother and the father are working out some kind of marital conflict on the boy. But, I would like to help the trio replace the displaced conflict between the parents so they would not use the boy as the object for the expression of their conflict.

Tolson: Would you keep the boy in treatment with the parents?

Sherman: Yes, I would.

Segal: I think there is an issue here, of once the parents come in and say, look we want this kid to change and then you start selling them marital therapy I think that's the kind of thing that bothers me.

Sherman: We're not selling any marital therapy. We're trying to get them together as parents in relation to their son.

Segal: Do you get them together as parents and start talking about them acting out their conflict on the kid? I can see that if you move the parents closer to each other and get them off his back, he would probably shape up some.

Sherman: Yes, but look at what you're doing. You're saying if the parents want to make a thing out of this kid and send him to work, I'll try to help the parents fulfill their purpose to treat him as an object since his wishes, felt needs, or doubts are not being considered.

Segal: They don't want their kid to lay around the house, and they want him to do a little work.

Sherman: But he's not a thing, an object, he's a person.

Segal: But what's wrong with him doing a few days work?

Sherman: Because if they are using him as an object . . .

Segal: Wait a minute, wait a minute. That's a big jump between asking him to go to work and their using him.

Sherman: They are asking him to go to work for the wrong reasons, and that's important.

Segal: Well, but where do you derive that from? From your assumptions about psychology and human behavior?

Sherman: No, the assumptions that I made from the evidence that I saw on the videotape. You arrived at a different interpretation of what you saw. We're both drawing different interpretations.

Segal: I think there is a different level here, between saying they do this and he does that and you've got a circle going here versus they're doing it for all these reasons and therefore we have to get into all these other areas, trying to change that.

Sherman: Do you think that the father might be seeing his mirror image in his son and behaving toward his son as though he is like father was as a twelve year old?

Segal: Let me answer that. I think you can talk about that a lot of different ways. As to what it could possibly mean or what is father's motivation, I can also see father is trying to be a nice guy and persuade this kid without being the bad guy, to go out and do something. And it may even be because momma is pushing dad and dad is keeping mom at bay by saying, "Look, I'm trying to do it but at the same time I'm trying to keep son happy," so father is in the middle. But I would want to get those parents together at some point and get them to both agree, explicitly, that they want him to do something and I'd want them to spell out exactly what they want him to do. The way they are going about it, they are not succeeding in getting their son to go to work.

Meltzer: Well, this is one of the places where you can do the same thing for different reasons. Because, you see, when you get the parents together, you are working on the marital structure anyway.

Segal: Yes, but then you start to open up the marriage, and that's where I start to get a little upset about selling people on marital therapy. It's like people who went to analysts because they couldn't have an orgasm or an erection and they start off with twenty years of analysis when there are some behavioral approaches that would take care of the problem quickly.

Meltzer: But I am not selling them marital therapy, I am asking them to work on helping their son, and agree on something for their son.

Segal: Well, that's just it. But, eventually, it gets into let's talk about your relationship.

Hartman: Not necessarily. Do you know what Jay Haley would say? He'd say that if you can get those two parents to agree, you've done it. And you can call it marital therapy or you can just call it helping the family.

Segal: Okay, but how about getting them to agree by getting them to agree what they want from the kid and to give them a common line of action.

Sherman: Oh, that's what we are talking about.

Wells: Let me comment here. I agree with Lynn [Segal], that a possible contract that I might negotiate with them is to help get their son back to work, but this is only one possible contract. I still want to look at other options.

Gambrill: I would go after it from the son's perspective. What changes might he like to see? In other words, I would ask each of the three family members to identify what changes they would like to see in their family interaction. And, after that was out on the board, then I would ask them to indicate which ones have priority. I doubt if this family has the skills to set up a contract. One thing I would have to ask myself, is whether negotiating training is required to increase their skills in discussing these differences they have among themselves, to reach resolutions in a more constructive fashion?

Bell: Perhaps you could specify the kind of negotiation training you would use.

Gambrill: The father had this strange habit of saying something supportive and then undermining it. He would give a positive reinforcement, then follow it with a punishing statement. The mother was really good at dumping— really skilled—and sidetracking, going into other issues. The mother was very sarcastic. I don't know how many sarcastic statements I heard her make. There were positives too, which will be very important from a behavioral point of view. We would go after and identify the positive behaviors. That's the first thing to do. For example, many of them were good at stating their feelings. So, the first thing would be to go after those positives and identify those very specifically, pointing out how they help in making resolutions among themselves and then pointing out some things where they might change their behavior in ways that might help them resolve their differences.

Sherman: This is an important question. Did you feel that father's statement to his boy were truly authentically supportive or were they manipulative in having a supportive content but not really. When he said, kept saying, "I understand how you feel about not working," I felt father's statements were not genuine.

Gambrill: See, I wouldn't conjecture that myself, I would ask the boy.

Sherman: But you would ask him if you suspected that it might be phony, you wouldn't ask unless you suspected . . .

Gambrill: I would ask whether I suspect or don't suspect. Because I may be wrong in either instance, as to how that statement may come over to the other person.

Sherman: Are you implying that you're going to ask him how he feels about it?

Gambrill: I'm going to ask him, does he like that. Would he like to have more of those statements? I'm going to ask: "Would you like to have your father say more things like that to you?"

Segal: Would you assume that if the father was open and honest, and said with all sincerity to his son, "God, I really want you to work," or "Damn, I'm really angry you don't get a job," that would get that kid going?

Sherman: Now you're changing a whole configuration of interaction there. If father was generous and authentic with his son, mother wouldn't be where she is and the boy wouldn't be where he is.

Segal: You consider the father lacking in authenticity, displaying disparity in the levels of communication. Rick Wells and I were saying that we see father as just a poor manipulator, or ineffective influencer. But suppose father is straightforward. I've seen a lot of parents who have been through negotiation training, and they are sitting there earnestly and honestly telling the kid how they feel and the kid is being highly unreasonable and saying, "Well, I don't give a shit, I don't want to go to college." We found, in some of these cases, the solution was to tell the kid: "Well, you don't have to like it, you just have to go."

Sherman: You're talking about a different case now, right?

Segal: There is a parallel. When you raise the issue of how the father is coming across to the kid, that implies that if he would be different in the respect that you mentioned, that kid would be different and he'd get to work.

Sherman: I didn't say that if you changed that single detail, that fragment, everything would fall into place.

Gambrill: I would never assume that all family members would necessarily be linked to a given problem. They may or may not be.

Segal: They can have a rotten marriage and you could teach them to be a little better with the kid and the marriage may still stay rotten. And if they come in saying I want to do something about my kid and they don't say anything about the marriage I think that's their business.

Wells: You can have a lousy marriage and still be reasonably effective as parents.

Sherman: But why are we dealing with hypotheses when we have a lot of evidence right in front of us on the videotape. We either read it one way or we read it another.

Hartman: I'd still like to hear what Lynn [Segal] would do.

Segal: The main thing, as I said, is I usually think about what needs to stop rather than what starts. I'd want to stop the nagging and I'd want to stop the ineffectual pleading of the father. So, in general, I'd want to get him to back off.

Sherman: How would you do it? We would all like that.

Segal: Okay, that would depend on the particular family. I have to know a lot more about how they saw and how they fought and felt about this kid and his problem. I might teach them one thing, although I don't believe there is such a thing as a good intervention. We have found it useful once in a while to say to a kid, "I want you to do this, I can't make you do it but I wish you would," to cut down on the symmetrical struggles that get kicked up between people. And I'd have the parents say it once. Then after that if the kid didn't comply, I'd teach the parents to make life a little miserable for him nonverbally. Because one of the things I heard both of them whining about was, "We give you all these things and you haven't been doing what we ask." I might have the parents arrange to keep their mouths shut. Their son might respond a little more if they just backed off.

Hartman: You refer to this kid's problem. I'd like to bring up the issue of norms for an adolescent boy (I live with one). I think three days of heavy physical labor in the summer is a pretty good contribution for a kid of that age, and if the other four days he wants to crawl out of bed in the morning and stare at the TV box—let him do it. All teenagers are like that. The other thing I want to think about is that some of the kinds of criticism that they were coming up with sounds like plain normal behavior for a teenager. I didn't hear anything very abnormal.

Segal: I call that a normal "rotten kid problem."

Sherman: Ann, the father made it the hard way, now he is in the upper middle class. His kid is asking why do I have to work five days at heavy physical labor in order to get the benefits of our upper-middle-class life? There is a real value problem there.

Comment from audience: I just heard you mention values and it seems like everybody believes that it is a value for a seventeen year old to work. I question that. Why shouldn't he be able to lie around seven days a week. When he gets to be twenty-one, twenty-two, twenty-three, he is going to work for fifty or sixty years, so what the hell is the big deal? Why do we assume that if parents come to us and say, "We want this kid to work; we can't get him to work," that we have to go along with the parent's request? The implication is that the object is to get this kid to work.

Gambrill: Not everyone did assume that. I didn't assume that at all.

Reid: This relates to the question I was going to ask. In this kind of model, where you go with the customer's own problem—which we try to do in some of our work in the Task-Centered Approach—the obvious issue that arises is that it works fine if you are dealing with a single person or two people with the same idea of what the problem is. But if you get differences—like you could here—when you ask them to define the problem, the father and mother might come down on one side and the kid would say, "The problem is really that they are on my back." When you have these differing definitions of the problem, how do you cope with that?

Segal: If I could get them off the kid's back, he might work a little more and things would be a little more positive.

In general, I haven't found too many kids (now that might be a function of my style of therapy) who are dying to be in therapy. In terms of the customers, I would guess that the parents are the customers. I would probably try to work along with the parents and clarify where they stand on goals and means. They are more likely to have similar goals but disagree on the means. Momma wants to reason with the kid and the old man wants to come down hard. So it's very likely they fight over method and lose sight of being together on goals. If this were the case, I would try to get them together on a different way of handling the problem, or get one parent to back off while I tried to help the other one deal with the child in a more effective manner. But I would pretty much go along with the parents on most things unless it just violated what I thought was reasonable.

Sherman: I would talk with the family about what their opinions are of each other, or what they want from each other, etc., beyond the presenting complaint. In this case, do we deal with the presenting complaint, which is to get Jim to work, or would we suspect the possibility that there are some things underneath and the "work" issue may not even be the important question? I would leave room for the fact that the "working" may not even be the important question here with regard to the boy. I want to speculate about a number of possibilities—the important thing is are we open to, do we find a way that opens us to this further data?

Bell: I would stick with the family, in the treatment situation, until what I would call, a family problem is identified. That is a problem that each of the members of the family agrees is the problem that the family should be working on, and they ultimately will come to that kind of decision. Then there is a possibility of using the resources of the whole group, interacting among themselves, to help work toward the solution of the problem. That in my mind is family therapy. I think there are lots of other kinds of therapy which are individual therapy or couple therapy in the setting of a group, and for me, I don't regard that as family therapy. That is just my definition.

Reid: Other reactions from faculty toward any of this?

Comment from
audience: Is that an agreed upon definition?

Reid: No, you can assume that nothing has been agreed
upon. Except that the family is important, whatever
the family is. So that hasn't been agreed upon. But,
that is just one definition of family therapy which was
advanced and received some support, I think, but there
were other definitions offered.

Hartman: You know, you pointed out that there is nothing we
do agree upon in this group except that family therapy
is important. And I think that all you do have to do is
bring in a bunch of individually oriented therapists and
we would see how quickly we all got together. Really,
I mean that is why it has been so much fun to hear our
differences because there is so much mutual respect
for a common concern about families.

Bell: The differences grow so much out of the person of
each one of us because we can't get out of our own
skin. We have to be who we are in relation to the
family and to live out the relationship with them in a
way that is congenial for ourselves. That is going to
vary a great deal from individual to individual and until
we can get through to that point, we are not really able
to control, from our own point of view, the therapy
process. We are simply borrowing techniques from
here, there, and everywhere, and trying them out, and
we have no way, really, and no assurance that these
are going to be effective. We are in a learning process,
and that is very desirable. In my work, the goals are
the family goals, they are not my goals for them. In
the treatment my goals are process goals.

Segal: I don't like the word *symptom*. I'd like to scratch that
and talk about *complaint*. I would say that if you get
a positive change in the complaint that there has been
a systemic change, there has been an interactional
change some place. That may or may not spin off. If
the parents are effective, say, in dealing with the kid
differently, then they may have more time to themselves and not be so engaged with the kid. In our
follow-up we consider it a good sign when the parents
have gone off and done something by themselves and
left the kid at home. We don't shoot for that directly

but we will look for that as confirmation that the change has been positive.

Sherman: Precisely! We have our finger on a real difference, when you prefer to call it the complaint rather than symptom. Those are not the same things at all because symptom is a displaced cue to something being wrong. It isn't necessarily in itself what is wrong. The symptom may be a pathway to what is wrong. A "symptom" is different from a "complaint" that the clinician is going to rectify.

Meltzer: In concluding our discussion, I would like to point out that among us there are some differences in what we see as the goal of family treatment. Some would work toward removal or reduction of discrete, defined behaviors—and therefore specify treatment goals in concrete terms. For others among us, the goal is to teach the family a problem-solving process, and that is both the implicit and explicit goal. With regard to assessment we focus on different dimensions based on the theories of behavior we use. For each of us our assessments dictate our treatment strategies. Some of the strategies and clinical operations we use may not look so different, but our explanations of *why* we do *what* we do may vary.

10

The Empirical Base of Family Therapy: Practice Implications

RICHARD A. WELLS

Clinical practice and empirical research in the helping professions have had an uneasy coexistence through the years. The norms of practice emphasize response and action—the clinician must engage himself with the client (or client system) in an immediate and purposeful way, toward a goal of inducing change. Research, on the other hand, has stressed objectivity and methodological rigor, with the researcher often deliberately isolated from the hurly-burly of practice, or concentrating on only a selected aspect of the helping process, in order to maintain control of a complex situation. With such contrasting approaches it is not at all surprising to find that despite the seemingly common goal of providing effective helping services, clinicians and researchers have seldom engaged in any mutually meaningful dialogue.

Despite this seeming disparity in stance, I believe that a meaningful interchange between research and clinical practice is possible and that such an interchange will be of advantage to both. This essay represents a modest move in that direction. What is sorely needed are clinicians—and educators concerned with clinical practice—who have an understanding of, and a respect for, empirical findings and who can construct a bridge between these two vital areas. Perhaps the pure clinician and the pure researcher will always remain separate and distinct, but an active cluster of practitioners and educators ready to extrapolate the findings of research into clinical guidelines may be able to significantly affect both research and practice. Such an active integration is, I believe, particularly suitable for social work, with its unabashed tradition of borrowing and its major responsibility for such a large proportion of direct therapeutic service (Alexander 1977).

Definitions, Limitations, and Criteria

Defining Family Therapy

Because of the varied forms in which family therapy has been practiced, even within its relatively short history, it is difficult to devise a concise and comprehensive definition. Some reviewers have skirted this problem by not even attempting a definition but simply assuming that everyone knows what is meant by the term. Others, such as Gurman and Kniskern, employ a broad definition that encompasses both marital and family therapy:

> We have chosen to review all available studies in which treatment is explicitly focused on altering the interaction between or among family members, whether in the same-generation (husband-wife, child-child) relationships, cross-generation (parent-child) relationships, or both, regardless of who is the identified patient. (1978:820)

DeWitt, on the other hand, employs a more restrictive definition by limiting her review to studies utilizing a conjoint mode of treatment in which "all relevant members of the family . . . have been treated together as a unit for all or a major portion of the treatment (1978:551)." In previous reviews (Wells and Dezen 1978a; Wells, Dilkes, and Trivelli 1972), I have employed a definition that incorporates an emphasis on both the form of treatment and the theoretical intent of the therapist:

> A therapist engages in family therapy when he sees such natural units as parents and children, spouses, or members of the extended family, together as a group over most of the duration of treatment with the goal of improving their functioning as a unit. (Wells, Dilkes, and Trivelli 1972:191)

This definition will be employed in this article as a guideline in identifying approaches as instances of family therapy. It recognizes the family therapist's theoretical and practical interest in understanding and altering family relationships, yet, at the same time, stresses family therapy's unique contribution to therapeutic intervention through its emphasis on seeing family members together. As DeWitt notes, it was this novel approach to treatment that represented "a clear break with treatment tradition, a break that was initiated by, and is associated with, the family therapy movement (1978:551)." Such a definition has

the possible disadvantage of including certain approaches that have
not been generally considered family therapy but, as long as these
interventions meet the basic criteria of working with the family, or a
unit from the family (both parents or mother-daughter dyads, for example), with the goal of improving the functioning of this unit, there
is no reason that they should not be examined.

Scope of the Review

In major respects this article will be a *review of reviews*, examining
and integrating the findings of the series of critical assessments that
have been made of family therapy research and practice over the past
decade. There will also be an effort to draw upon the psychotherapy
research generally, as I do not believe that family therapy research can
be considered in isolation from this larger body of knowledge, any
more than its clinical practice can be separated from the general practice of therapeutic helping. Particularly in the sections of this article
considering implications for practice, I shall attempt to draw from both
the family therapy research literature per se and from this larger body
of empirical work.

Social work research, as the recent review by Briar and Conte (1978)
demonstrates, has paid little attention to the examination of family
therapy outcome. Psychotherapy outcome research, however, includes
the therapeutic efforts of social work practitioners as well as those of
the other major helping professions. Its findings, I believe, are highly
relevant to social work practice, particularly as these findings relate
to the client populations and target problems that typically confront
the social work clinician.

In light of this viewpoint, no distinction will be made between such
terms as "therapy," "counseling" or "casework," as long as the services described clearly meet the definition of family treatment. Similarly,
there will be no attempt to distinguish between the therapeutic efforts
of the three major helping professions of social work, psychology, and
psychiatry. In consonance with much current thought and research
(Parloff 1979; Strupp 1978) these terms will be regarded as largely
interchangeable and the helping practice of the various disciplines as,
in their most important respects, essentially indistinguishable.

In order to manage the increasing mass of research material that is
becoming available on the outcome of the various approaches to family

treatment, the scope of this review will be limited to family therapy where a child or adolescent is the "identified patient (or client)" or where the focus of intervention is clearly on behalf of such a child or adolescent. Although family therapy has been attempted with many client populations, it has been especially interested in the problems of children. Indeed, at a theoretical level, there is a good deal of plausibility to the notion of helping children and adolescents through direct work with their families.

Again in the interests of clarity, nonbehavioral and behavioral approaches will be separately considered, although, in practice, there is a modest but encouraging trend toward eclecticism (more evident, however, in areas other than family therapy). Studies will be categorized following the definition in my earlier review:

> Generally, a family therapy approach was considered behavioral if the authors specifically labeled their work as such and/or the major technology of the approach utilized interventions commonly considered behavioral. (Wells and Dezen 1978a:252)

It should be noted that this division lumps a great number of technically and theoretically diverse approaches into the nonbehavioral category, and it will be important, where possible, to identify the distinctive features of an approach within this category. Furthermore, the division into behavioral and nonbehavioral is not intended to convey that an intervention in the nonbehavioral category cannot have quite specific and tangible treatment goals.

The Relevance of Outcome Research to Practice

In earlier work I suggested three major reasons why examining the outcome of the various methods of family therapy (or of any therapeutic method, for that matter) is of importance both to practice and to the individual practitioner (Wells and Dezen 1978a:252). These are worth restating and discussing at this point.

1. It was contended that the consumers of therapeutic services have a right not only to effective service but to know the limitations and side effects of these services.

2. Practitioners also need to have access to systematic outcome studies so as to be able to make a rational choice between treatments

and thus to provide their clients with the most effective approach available.

3. Finally it was argued that consumers must be protected from the possible deteriorative or negative effects of psychotherapy, and only careful outcome studies could identify these hazards.

It may be naïve (or just hopelessly idealistic) to suggest that the mental health field as a whole should turn to systematic outcome research as its major guideline for practice. Joel Fischer (1973, 1976, 1979) has been sounding this theme for years now, with little perceptible effect. Furthermore, given the limitations of the substantive conclusions that can be drawn from the data, accepting empirical standards might mean that a goodly proportion of the therapeutic enterprise would have to lurch to a halt.

Yet few professionals would disagree with the position that the consumers of service should be able to enter therapies that are of demonstrated effectiveness and that they should be protected from ineffective or harmful treatments. However, professionals might not agree that this information should be *publicly* available, or that the consumer should exercise *his own* choice. The commonest belief, I suspect, would be that the therapist himself, through his knowledge and value commitment, will quite adequately protect the client from any dangers. Perhaps it is pushing consumerism too far to propose that clients should have this knowledge available to them in order to make their own choices. On the other hand, how knowledgeable is the average therapist about the comparative effects of different methods and techniques and how many would even entertain the notion that there are times when their own therapeutic efforts, administered with the best of intentions, can be downright harmful?

At a later point in this same paper I suggested two further reasons for serious study of the outcome of therapy:

> First, could governmental regulation intervene to control the utilization of untested methods? Second, might the growing trend toward malpractice suits spread, and could practitioners find themselves confronted with legal action for the misuse or misapplication of therapeutic methods? (Wells and Dezen 1978a:267–68)

Both of these points may seem fanciful to some and, admittedly, both are speculations about the future of the mental health professions.

A recent review by Strupp, however, voices a very similar concern about the possibility of governmental regulation.

> Perhaps it is not entirely utopian to envisage the creation of an analogue to the Food and Drug Administration to protect the public from worthless or potentially damaging therapies. The mood of the times certainly points in that direction. (1978:20)

Even more ominously, there are some indications that our credit is actually running out, and that neither the public nor the government is willing to continue an unquestioning faith in the services offered by mental health professionals. Parloff (1979) reviews the material submitted to the recent President's Commission on Mental Health and the sections of this report concerning the effectiveness of psychotherapy are chillingly sparse and pessimistic in conclusion. Family treatment is not even mentioned.

Further, a recent report (White et al.) to the federal government on children's services recommends that no funding be given to "major programs relying on therapy, counseling or therapy-oriented casework" and that there should be a reduced emphasis on "professional credential requirements for those therapy and counseling programs that have not been eliminated" (1973:102). These are bleak words, indeed, to appear in a definitive report to a major funding source. The message may well be that the public, if they are willing, can exercise a free choice in entering a psychotherapy but that public funds will not be expended for methods that can apparently offer little beyond advocate testimony in support of their effects.

Clinical Tradition versus Empirical Standards

Before going any further, it may be useful to discuss some of the issues suggested earlier that can create conflict between the clinician's legitimate emphasis on action and involvement, and the researcher's stress on objectivity and empirical validation. This will help set the stage for the rapprochement that must be achieved if there is to be any workable interchange between these apparent polarities.

Most therapeutic methods are practiced with only the scantiest of attention paid to the question of effectiveness. This extreme statement may seem to imply that practitioners are irresponsible or uncaring about their clients' welfare, yet anyone with even the slightest degree of acquaintance with the human services field is well aware that professionals, by and large, care deeply. However, the same observer could hardly help but notice that practitioners are also greatly inclined to rely upon the testimony of authoritative figures in their field, or on the subjective evidence of their immediate clinical experience, in evaluating therapeutic method.

As Jerome Frank (1979) and others have pointed out, most clinicians—prominent or otherwise—have enough successful cases to provide intermittent reinforcement to their sense of therapeutic potency. Dropouts, unsuccessful efforts, or downright failure cases are simply discounted or forgotten. Further, few clinicians conduct any systematic follow-up of their practice (unless the clients themselves take the initiative to return) so that the durability of change from the worker's preferred method is largely unknown. Family therapy is no stranger to this tradition and, indeed, any number of influential texts in the field have been written without the slightest reference to the findings of outcome research or even a suggestion that systematic examination of effectiveness is needed.

Researchers, on the other hand, are not without fault. They are often distant from, or unknowledgeable about, practice. The predominant research methodology, heavily influenced by agricultural research, may well be unsuited to the study of human subjects (Meehl 1978), much less to the task of probing the subtleties of interaction in intimate encounters. Measures of outcome are frequently weak, or irrelevant to the goals of practice, yet sophisticated statistical analyses are applied to these questionable data. The findings may be significant to the researcher (perhaps in achieving a publication or obtaining another grant) but are, often enough, almost untranslatable into viable guidelines for clinical practice.

The Empirical Status of Psychotherapy

All of this is indicative of a field that, in many respects, continues to struggle within a prescientific stage of development. Reid posed this issue rather succinctly when he asked how one could have confidence in the practitioners of a profession with some of the following characteristics:

1. that can produce no solid evidence that its methods are effective;
2. that puts only a tiny fraction of its resources into conducting research to improve the effectiveness of these methods and whose practitioners ignore what little research has been carried out;
3. whose practice is guided by unverified and conflicting theories, often proclaimed as dogma;
4. whose treatment methods are often addressed to hypothetical underlying disorders whose existence cannot be proved . . . (1974:1)

Reid had the grace to point out that he was merely summarizing the characteristics of nineteenth-century medical practice but he continued by reviewing the alarming parallels between the history of that profession and the current status of the helping professions, particularly social work and psychiatry. There is no doubt that the social work practitioner or educator who aspires to being both clinician and empiricist can become very badly battered by the competing demands of these two viewpoints. As a practitioner, for example, one must maintain hope and faith in the process of helping—the clinician must believe that people can be and, in fact, *are* changed through therapeutic methods. As an empiricist, on the other hand, one looks for direct evidence of this belief and, furthermore, for evidence gained through the accepted methods of science.

This dilemma becomes particularly acute in an attempt, such as this, to review the empirical literature in a given area of therapy. It is well known that research in actual therapeutic settings is extremely difficult. From a methodological perspective, extraneous variables abound and are often completely unknown, much less controllable. Clients are a heterogeneous lot, even those with the same problem or from the same socioeconomic and cultural groups. Therapists vary in similar ways and may also differ greatly in their application of a common method. Administrative and ethical constraints can radically alter a projected research design, the available methods of measuring outcome are often unreliable, indirect, or weak, and so on.

If a reviewer holds to strict methodological standards in reviewing psychotherapy outcome research, then it is a foregone conclusion that few, if any, substantive findings will be found. Researchers and reviewers have been criticized, perhaps justly, for their emphasis on the minutiae of research methodology, engrossing themselves in issues that are often quite beyond the practitioner's purview or concern. The practitioner is looking for *reasonable evidence* of therapeutic efficacy and *meaningful guidelines* for clinical practice, not impeccable quality in research design.

Some Criteria for Evaluating Research

In an effort to bridge this gap, some criteria will be identified that, I believe, can satisfy the clinician's need for reasonable evidence without radically diluting the standards of the empiricist. The following points seem especially important in evaluating the evidence that any therapeutic method offers on its effectiveness.

Specification of method: The therapeutic method investigated should be well enough described, in the study itself or in accompanying material, that the clinician can utilize it or other investigators can replicate the study. This may seem like an obvious requirement yet there are existing studies in the family therapy research literature where the therapeutic method is identified by only a general reference or two to a clinical monograph or, in another instance, without any specification of method beyond stating the name of the clinician administering the treatment.

Client variables: Client characteristics such as major problem, demographic variables, and relative degree of distress should be clearly described. This too may appear obvious, yet in another recent study it is impossible to determine anything of the nature of the families' major problems and many other studies are vague or uninformative about such important characteristics as age, race or socioeconomic status.

Outcome measurement: The measurement of outcome continues to be perhaps the single most difficult problem in psychotherapy research. What are reliable and valid ways of measuring the effect of a treatment? Does one method of measuring unduly favor a particular approach over another? From whose perspective should outcome be assessed—do the client's views of change carry more (or less) weight than the therapist's trained judgment? Or do both client and therapist have such an emotional stake in therapeutic outcome that neither can possibly make an unbiased evaluation? These, and other much more technical questions, continue to be debated, and recent reviews of psychotherapy research (Gottman and Markman 1978; Bergin and Lambert 1978) indicate that they are far from settled.

Strupp et al. (1977) propose a tripartite model for assessing therapeutic outcome and I shall adapt aspects of their proposal in suggesting some reasonable standards in this area. This viewpoint postulates that the perspectives of society, the individual patient, and the mental health professional are each distinct and valid vantage points in evaluating the results of treatment. Each, however, emphasizes different standards. Societal expectations are concerned with the ability of people to carry their assigned roles and to conform to the prevailing cultural norms; the individual patient (or a family member) tends to evaluate progress in terms of highly subjective perceptions of happiness and well-being; the mental health professional, finally, is characteristically concerned with the soundness of the individual's psychological structure or functioning, based on the theoretical or empirical principles of a particular therapeutic framework. From this viewpoint, then, a study should incorporate at least two of these three major perspectives for assessing change—therapist judgment, client evaluation, and social functioning—and should give equal credence to each perspective, as long as there are no obvious biasing factors in the manner in which the assessment is derived.

Research design: There should be no *gross* flaws in the research design, or in its implementation, that would preclude drawing reasonable conclusions about the effect of the therapy. For example, in a number of studies it is evident that an unspecified mixture of interventions was employed, thus making any conclusion about a particular ingredient impossible to reach. In other studies, the sole employment of weak measures of outcome, or such difficulties as high rates of client attrition and obvious biases in samples, obfuscate the interpretation of the data. Researchers are usually quite honest in revealing these difficulties (if one reads the report very carefully) but are not always willing to bite the bullet and clearly state the limitations of their material.

Statistical analysis: Statistical analysis should be utilized, as needed, to determine whether there is a high probability that perceived differences in the data could have arisen through chance alone. It is undoubtedly important to recognize such chance fluctuations but, on the other hand, establishing statistical significance (a reasonably low probability of chance occurrence) says little about the clinical or practical significance of the finding. Similarly, in studies where the mass of data is large, or multiple measures are employed, the analysis may be more easily managed through statistical manipulation. However, statistical analysis can be carried too far and the researcher can become a prisoner of the method, searching for statistical significance as an end in itself. The comments of Bergin and Strupp on this matter are still highly relevant:

> With respect to inquiry in the area of psychotherapy, the kinds of effects we need to demonstrate at this point in time should be significant enough that they are readily observable by inspection. If this cannot be done, no fixation upon statistical and mathematical niceties will generate fruitful insights, which obviously can only come from the researcher's understanding of the subject matter and the data under scrutiny. (1972:440–41)

As I have already noted, such misuse may include confusing statistical with clinical significance—or simply making no effort to determine the latter—but may also involve such practices as reporting group averages but not noting that the mean was affected by a few extreme values, or applying sophisticated statistical analyses to data that do not meet the minimum requirements for such a method. Reviewers have to be particularly wary of these and other practices and prepared to identify and criticize their occurrence.

Follow-up measurement: Follow-up assessments, at least four months after termination and utilizing the same outcome measures, should be conducted in order to determine the durability of change. Longer follow-up periods are highly desirable but the minimal time limits suggested would be helpful in determining whether the changes observed at termination of therapy have some capacity to endure or could be more parsimoniously ascribed to the expectancy and demand characteristics of the therapeutic situation.

Source of study: It should be apparent that the study is emanating from an investigator (clinician, researcher, or academician), or a group of investigators, seriously and systematically engaged in the examination of a particular therapeutic approach. This would tend to discount data from such sources as doctoral dissertations or "one-shot" evaluations of the work of a particular practitioner, or clinic, unless these were related to an overall cluster of studies in the same therapeutic area. Thus, the Minuchin group or Guerney and his colleagues in nonbehavioral family therapy, and Gerald Patterson or Alexander and

Parsons in behavioral family therapy, are all examples of this sort of committed and persistent investigation of therapeutic outcome that, I believe, merits our most serious consideration. Mattarrazo (Bergin and Strupp 1972) emphasized a similar criterion when he suggested that a good rule of thumb for assessing the quality of an investigator's work is to see if he continues to examine the same area in further studies.

The Findings of Psychotherapy Research

Although I shall be considering the effectiveness of family therapy methods, in their various forms, it must be emphasized that such findings cannot be considered in isolation. The outcome of the methods of family therapy must be appraised in relation to the overall findings of psychotherapy outcome research. Recent reviews by Frank (1979), Parloff (1979), and Strupp (1978) place these findings in broad perspective.

1. In very general terms, there is sufficient evidence to support the position that psychotherapy produces *modest* gains over untreated groups.

2. There is very little evidence favoring one theoretical approach or one modality (individual versus group versus family) over another. Where such evidence does exist, it is almost always in favor of a behavioral approach to a specific problem area.

3. On the other hand, where comparative studies have been conducted, it has generally been found that relatively brief treatment (up to 15 sessions) has as much beneficial effect as lengthier interventions.

4. Nonspecific factors such as expectancy, suggestion, ritual, or demand characteristics, or such therapist variables as empathy, warmth, and genuineness, form a significant portion of the active ingredients in all therapeutic approaches. This is not to say that such variables are sufficient for good outcome but there is reason to believe that they are necessary, particularly at early stages of the therapeutic encounter.

Thus, the best argument for providing therapeutic services is that, in general, therapy will produce improvement more rapidly than will the passage of time alone. This may seem to some like an exceedingly modest return from the amount of effort that is expended, particularly in preparing therapists for practice, and in comparison to some of the more extravagant claims that have been made for psychotherapy, it is indeed reduced in scale. Yet when one considers the very genuine and painful difficulties that motivate people to turn to a helping source, significantly accelerating the natural remedial processes is not a trivial service.

Family Therapy Outcome Research

Like almost all therapeutic approaches, family therapy developed within the practice arena and, particularly in its first decade, attracted many clinicians who were disenchanted with the prevalent modes of intervention. Its major attraction, however, was not simply this re-action against orthodoxy but an extremely persuasive theoretical ra-tionale that stressed the interaction and interdependency of the family unit in producing pathology or alleviating dysfunction. In addition, as Gurman and Kniskern (1978) have pointed out, the family therapy movement has also been characterized by an unusual number of highly charismatic proponents and proselytizers who have tirelessly ex-pounded its virtues.

Reviewing Family Therapy Outcome

The effectiveness of family treatment did not appear to be seriously examined until the beginning of this past decade when a cluster of critical reviews appeared. The first of these was David Olson's inte-grative critique of both marital and family therapy, published in 1970. This was followed by Winter's 1971 survey of family therapy research and theory and, in 1972, by reviews by Massie and Beels and by Wells, Dilkes, and Trivelli. Massie and Beels were specifically concerned with the family treatment of schizophrenia while Wells et al. attempted to assess the effectiveness of family therapy across its entire range of applications.

Some common themes run through all these early reviews. First, the scanty empirical support for family therapy is outlined and the paucity of outcome research is deplored. Second, each emphasizes the relative "youth" of the family therapy movement as reason for the lack of research support. Third, although the research methodology of the studies reviewed is criticized—in what has been called "the familiar litany" of biased samples, lack of controls and inadequate outcome measurement—the clinical practice of family therapy is sympathetically, even gently, handled. Finally, each review, directly or indirectly, expresses the hope that the future wil bring more plentiful and more adequate studies.

Later reviews by Pacquin (1977) and Dewitt (1978) continue the same cautious treatment of family therapy. Like the earlier reviews, they deplore its lack of a firm empirical base but suggest that further research will substantiate its presumed effectiveness.

The most comprehensive reviews of family therapy outcome both appeared in late 1978 and, although covering much the same material, present some quite contrasting conclusions about the efficacy of family therapy. Gurman and Kniskern (1978) are relatively enthusiastic about the effectiveness of the nonbehavioral approaches. They are reserved, however, in their evaluation of behavioral family therapy. Wells and Dezen (1978a) review only the nonbehavioral studies and, although surveying almost the same data as Gurman and Kniskern, are highly critical of the quality of the research and the conclusions that can be drawn from it. They suggest that nonbehavioral family therapy has demonstrated only limited effectiveness in relatively few areas of clinicial practice. The reasons for these widely varying conclusions have been examined elsewhere, in detail (Wells and Dezen 1978b; Wells 1979), and will not be discussed here.

Nonbehavioral Approaches to Family Therapy

Most of the practitioners who consider themselves family therapists utilize some form of nonbehavioral family therapy (GAP 1970). Although the influence of the behavioral methods is growing, only a minority of clinicians actually employ these approaches. Thus, the issue of outcome in the nonbehavioral methods is of considerable importance to the field because of their predominance in practice.

The empirical support for the nonbehavioral approaches will be surveyed in relation to three types of research investigation: uncontrolled studies, comparative studies, and controlled designs. The critical question that each type of investigation attempts to answer will be identified and the available data examined in relation to this issue.

Uncontrolled Studies of Nonbehavioral Family Therapy

The largest group of outcome reports of nonbehavioral family therapy are in the form of uncontrolled group studies of some variety of this approach. In such a study, a number of cases treated by family therapy are given pretreatment and termination (or follow-up) evaluations to determine if the intervention has resulted in meaningful change. Uncontrolled group studies attempt to answer the question: *Does a particular therapeutic approach work, i.e. does it achieve results consonant with at least the broad objectives of the helping professions?* In other words, is it ethical, and responsive to client needs, for a practitioner to employ this method as a means of offering help? Thus, it would not be ethical to employ a method that had no empirical data supporting its effectiveness nor would it be responsive to utilize a method in a given area if its validating data were irrelevant to that area. Uncontrolled studies can offer some guidelines to such questions of selection and application of therapeutic method.

Thus, uncontrolled studies may be regarded as a legitimate but weak form of outcome research that, if properly conducted, can offer valuable information on certain facets of practice. The evidential value of an uncontrolled study can be strengthened where careful follow-up with clinically relevant measures is conducted, as will be evident in certain of the nonbehavioral studies, or where a time-series design and precise outcome measurement are employed, as in a number of the behavioral studies reviewed later in this essay.

Unfortunately, many of the studies reported in the literature can hardly be regarded as serious empirical examinations of the outcome of nonbehavioral family therapy. In a number of instances the report is simply an attempt to broadly evaluate the overall quality of service in a particular agency; in other instances it is an effort to bolster a predominantly clinical discussion of theory and technique by including a "Results" section; and, finally, in a few instances, although a planned empirical inquiry, the study is actually focused on questions relating to therapeutic process with outcome of only secondary concern.

I shall not attempt to examine most of the uncontrolled studies in any detail. Gurman and Kniskern (1978:828–29) summarize the available studies in their review and, although there are a number of inaccuracies in their reporting of the data, this will give the reader some notion of the work. In all, they cite twenty such studies in the nonbehavioral area.

Difficulties abound in interpreting the data available from the un-controlled studies of nonbehavioral family therapy. For example, even a cursory reading of the material makes it evident that the interventions described frequently included other interventions such as individual or group therapy or various adjunctive clinical services. This makes it impossible to ascertain the specific contribution of the family treatment. Furthermore, fully sixteen of the twenty uncontrolled studies of nonbehavioral family therapy on behalf of children and adolescents reviewed by Gurman and Kniskern report either therapist- or client-rated gross improvement rates (in no cases both) and, thus, rely upon a single, potentially biased, assessment perspective.

Despite these patent inadequacies in many studies, there are still some reasonably useful data to be found. This is particularly evident in the work of Minuchin and his colleagues (Liebman et al. 1974a; 1974b; Minuchin et al. 1975; Minuchin et al. 1978; Rosman et al. 1976) with psychosomatic disorders, particularly anorexia nervosa. These clinical researchers have published a series of reports describing their work in this area and offer concrete follow-up data on the highly positive outcome of the approach. Given the poor response of these disorders to conventional treatments, the Minuchin work, despite its lack of control groups, is persuasive. It should be noted, however, that family therapy is not the sole ingredient in the *series* of interventions utilized by the Minuchin group, although its effect, at the point where it is predominantly utilized, is quite potent. In order to replicate this method, the practitioner will need to become familiar with the skilled application of not only structural family therapy but the utilization of behavioral and individual interventions at designated points.

Another major research effort, from a community clinic associated with McMaster University in Hamilton, Ontario, describes a large-scale (N = 278) study of mildly to moderately disturbed children and adolescents treated with short-term (9 sessions) systems-oriented family therapy (Santa-Barbara et al. 1977a; 1977b; Woodward et al. 1977). This carefully designed study examines not only outcome but the relationship of a number of pertinent client and therapist variables to the therapeutic process. Therapist and client improvement ratings at termination are quite favorable (79 percent), and independent assessment of Goal Attainment Scaling at six-month follow-up showed reasonable durability of change with 64 percent attaining or exceeding goals. The strength of the approach is not necessarily in the level of improvement attained—mildly to moderately disturbed children and adolescents can be expected to show a good deal of positive change with or without treatment—but in the quite brief intervention utilized.

In summary then, the greater portion of the uncontrolled studies of nonbehavioral family therapy must be viewed as either inadequate or completely inconclusive. Perhaps a very general *legitimizing* effect can be drawn, as I pointed out in an earlier review: that is to say, despite the many flaws of this mass of studies they do "identify a beneficial effect that makes their continued investigation and application both ethical and responsive" (Wells and Dezen, 1978a:255). Such an effect is most evident, of course, in the Minuchin work on psychosomatic disorders and, in relation to its brevity, in the McMaster group's examination of the family treatment of moderately disturbed children and adolescents.

Comparative Studies of Nonbehavioral Family Therapy

As I noted earlier, a major factor in the popularity of family treatment has been the belief that, with many client populations and problems, it attains results that are superior to nonfamily approaches. Family therapy exponents have not been at all reluctant to advance this claim and, indeed, to deprecate other approaches as ineffective, if not harmful. Much of this, of course, is an aspect of the epiphenomena surrounding the emergence of any new theoretical approach—the proselytizer can hardly expect to attract adherents with only modest or unemotional claims.

A number of empirical studies have attempted to examine the comparative outcome of family treatment on behalf of children and adolescents and some other therapeutic approach in order to determine whether family therapy offers any advantage. Comparative studies attempt to answer the question: *Does a particular method offer a more effective or more efficient (faster, safer, less training required, etc.) treatment for a given problem or population in comparison to the alternative methods available?* Two main types of comparison have been made: 1) family therapy has been compared to various *nonfamily* therapies; and 2) comparisons have been conducted between differing forms of nonbehavioral family therapy. Studies in each category will be examined separately.

Comparisons with nonfamily treatments: This has obviously been an important question to nonbehavioral researchers, as most of the comparative studies fall in this category. As later sections of this article will make apparent, this is in marked contrast to the behavioral family therapy research which has been relatively unconcerned with comparisons at this level. This may be due to behavioral family therapy having largely developed in university settings, while the nonbehavioral approaches have been centered in clinics and agencies. In the latter context, the *political* need to provide convincing evidence of the effectiveness of family therapy, relative to the individually oriented approaches predominant in such settings, has probably assumed greater salience.

In order to make a fair comparison between a family therapy approach and an alternative treatment, it should be clear from the report in question that 1) both treatments have been administered by equally competent practitioners; 2) such variables as number of interviews, duration of therapeutic contact, assessment points, and so on are approximately the same; 3) the alternative treatment is clearly a nonfamily treatment, particularly in not utilizing conjoint interviews; and 4) there are no obviously biasing factors evident in the assignment of cases to either treatment approach. Except for the third point, the same criteria apply to comparisons between differing forms of family therapy.[1]

The major rivals to family therapy are, obviously, individual child psychotherapy; the various methods of group treatment with children and adolescents; and, in general, the traditional child guidance model, in which child and parent are seen in concurrent (but separate) interviews. In the comparative studies that will be examined, it is often difficult to determine the type of nonfamily therapy that has been administered, as it is usually not described in any detail. Similarly, it is difficult to estimate the experience or training of the therapists in the individual approaches, or to determine if these therapists were functioning with a conviction and enthusiasm similar to the therapists administering the family intervention. These and other uncertainties tend to cloud the intended comparisons.

---

[1] In earlier reviews (Wells et al. 1972; Wells and Dezen 1978a) the importance of random assignment to treatment conditions was emphasized, resulting in many of the comparative studies being considered inadequate. As it is difficult (though not impossible) to manage random assignment in studies conducted in predominantly clinical settings, it will not be stressed here. However, in any comparative study, it is still necessary to watch for indications that selection procedures have distorted or biased the sample. This can happen relatively easily in the clinical setting as the study by Evans et al. (1971) attests.

A total of eight comparative studies of nonbehavioral family treatment and a nonfamily alternative are available. These comprise studies by Budman and Shapiro (1976), Dezen and Borstein (1974), Evans et al. (1971), Ewing (1976), J. L. Johnson (1975), Love et al. (1972), Trankina (1976) and Wellisch et al. (1976). With the exception of the study by Johnson, (1975), these are all drawn from Gurman and Kniskern (1978) and Wells and Dezen (1978a) and are reviewed in both works.

These eight studies represent the sum of the available studies comparing a form of nonbehavioral family therapy with a nonfamily alternative treatment. Gurman and Kniskern conclude their review of this material with the statement:

> We interpret these results as reasonably acceptable evidence that *when one member of a family system or one dyadic relationship within a family present themselves for treatment with problems involving family living, then marital-family treatment represents a more effective general treatment strategy than does individual therapy.* (1978:844; italics in original)

The question is whether the available studies merit so resounding a conclusion. From their comments on the seven studies they review, it is apparent that Gurman and Kniskern consider five of these studies as showing superiority for nonbehavioral family therapy and the remainder as showing no differences. I believe that the picture is far different, with only *one* study showing superiority for family treatment, five showing equality, and one study being unacceptable because of gross bias in sample. (The additional study by J. L. Johnson [1975], which is not reviewed by Gurman and Kniskern, shows no differences between family and nonfamily treatment.) Some of the studies need to be examined in more detail.

For example, the study by Evans et al. must be rejected outright. In this retrospective comparison of fifty cases of conjoint family therapy and fifty cases of nonfamily treatment, the authors specifically note that the family cases were significantly biased toward the less disturbed and higher socioeconomic and, properly, conclude that no conclusions can be reached about the effect of family therapy (1971:109).

In a well-designed study, Love et al. (1972) compare information feedback (a cognitively oriented treatment, devised by the researchers, involving a moderate amount of family contact) with individual child therapy and standard casework parental counseling. The treatments are compared on measures of school achievement and independent behavioral ratings at pretreatment, termination, and two follow-up points.

The authors report that all treatments significantly increased one of three behavioral measures, but that the school achievement scores of both information feedback and parental counseling were significantly (.05) superior to child therapy at the second follow-up point. This suggests a marginal superiority for the two approaches involving family contact, but the difference may not have much practical significance, as school achievement at the final follow-up point averaged only "C" for the information feedback, and parent counseling groups, as compared to "C-minus" for those receiving individual child therapy.

The remaining studies will be briefly considered. Both Ewing (1976) and Trankina (1976) offer modest evidence that a brief, crisis-oriented family therapy is superior (at least on parental ratings) to a traditional child guidance model involving lengthier contact. The Ewing study is poorly designed, particularly in its entire dependence on retrospective ratings by mothers, but both these studies add somewhat to the cumulative evidence, in family therapy and elsewhere, that short-term approaches are usually equal to lengthier treatments.

The follow-up study by Budman and Shapiro (1976) found no differences between individual and family treatment. These findings cannot be taken very seriously as they are based on client evaluations, obtained in telephone interviews, in response to a single, very general question about present status. This was the query, "How are things going now with your child/you?" asked of parents and the identified patient and tabulated on a better-same-worse continuum. Similarly, Dezen and Borstein's (1974) report on family treatment with delinquent adolescents found only a very few instances of superiority for family therapy (in comparison to regular probation), mainly in the parental ratings of identified patient (IP) symptomatology. Other measures showed no differences and a few displayed negative effects. The overall picture is essentially one of equality between approaches (with little evidence that either approach had much absolute effect).

A study by J. L. Johnson (1975) compared two families receiving family therapy with two families in which the IP-only received individual therapy. A time-series design was utilized and cases were randomly assigned to the treatment conditions. The investigator reported that ratings of interaction variables from observations sessions with the families found only minimal support for the hypothesis that family therapy would have a greater effect on family interaction. The very small sample size qualifies the findings of this study.

Finally, the study by Wellisch et al. (1976) is the only report in which there is clear-cut evidence for the superiority of nonbehavioral family therapy over an alternate treatment. This well-designed effort compared 28 hospitalized adolescents randomly assigned to either family treatment or to individual therapy (both limited to 10 sessions). The same therapists conducted treatment in the two conditions, thus controlling the effect of therapist factors. Results showed the family treatment significantly superior at three-month follow-up on measures of rehospitalization and return to work or school. Outcome on ratings of family interaction were equivocal with no clear superiority for either approach.

In summary, the comparative studies of nonbehavioral family therapy show only one instance where there is a clear superiority for family therapy over the alternative treatment. Two studies offer modest support for a brief crisis-oriented therapy as opposed to conventional child guidance models. The remaining studies show family therapy to be, at best, equal to the alternative therapy but several of these studies contain weaknesses that may well vitiate even this conclusion. From this scanty evidence, it is impossible to support the position taken by Gurman and Kniskern that family treatment is generally more effective than individual therapy in treating problems in family living. Neither, I must hasten to add, does it say anything about the effectiveness of individual therapy with such problems. In the Scottish phrase, the case is "Not proven."

In some instances, however, it may be enough to demonstrate that family therapy achieves results that are equivalent to an alternative therapy in order to build a reasonable case for its employment. This argument has some cogency in relation to the studies which showed a brief family approach to be at least equal to lengthier conventional treatment.[2] However, in other studies (Dezen and Borstein 1974, for example) the family therapy approach involved extensive and lengthy training for its practitioners. If it could only demonstrate equivalence with regular services, such an approach would hardly qualify as a cost-efficient means of upgrading clinical services.

---

[2] As I noted earlier, it must be kept in mind that brief treatment approaches have generally demonstrated equality to lengthier treatment (Butcher and Koss 1978). It may be that in these two studies of brief nonbehavioral family therapy it is the time limits that are the operative factor rather than the family therapy component.

Comparisons between family therapies: A total of four studies make comparisons between varying forms of nonbehavioral family therapy. These will be briefly considered and their findings assessed.

The study by Johnson and Malony (Johnson 1971; Johnson and Malony, 1977) alternately assigned twenty-nine families to a condition involving *only* family interviews or a condition combining individual and conjoint interviews. Treatment was brief (four to six weeks) and apparently focused on the problems of elementary-school age and adolescent children. Family tasks at pretreatment and termination were rated by judges on nine communication and interaction variables. An analysis of covariance (the appropriate statistical method as there were significant pretreatment differences between groups) found three of nine comparisons favoring the family interview condition. This can be seen as a very moderate superiority for this approach.

Jansma's (1972) comparison between multiple family therapy and conjoint family therapy (both from a communication-interactional perspective) found the multiple approach superior to the conjoint method on seven of nine measures of family adjustment and interaction.

Finally, two studies compared psychodynamically oriented family therapy with very brief versions of a family approach. For example, Slipp and Kressel (1978) compared a brief (12 sessions) insight-oriented approach with an even briefer (3 sessions) family approach that stressed active and concrete advice-giving and direction. To the surprise of the researchers, the very brief approach was superior on a majority of client-rated measures of satisfaction, family adjustment, and attitude. Telephone follow-up interviews at approximately six months found almost all families, in both groups, reporting satisfactory improvement in presenting difficulties. Similarly, Sigal et al. (1976) compared an early terminator (1- to 2-session) group of thirty-one families with sixty-two families who had received extended treatment (average of 42.7 sessions) at an approximately four-year follow-up point. Telephone follow-up interviews found little difference between groups in improvement in presenting problems or current family adjustment, although the extended treatment group reported significantly (.01) *more* new problems.

None of these studies are especially informative as almost all are making very gross comparisons between treatment conditions. The findings of the two studies involving psychodynamically oriented family therapy are especially puzzling as the treatment was conducted at highly reputable centers. In conjunction with the very poor findings from such treatment in studies by Alexander and Parsons (1973) and Klein et al. (1977)—which will be reviewed in the following section—there may be reason to doubt the efficacy of such approaches or, at the least, for their proponents to engage in some serious research efforts.

Controlled Studies of Nonbehavioral Family Therapy

During the early years of this decade, a number of studies appeared which attempted to determine whether family therapy, in one of its nonbehavioral forms, was superior to an untreated group. In such studies, families are assigned to either treatment or no-treatment conditions for similar time periods and the outcomes between groups are compared. Controlled comparisons of this type are designed to answer the question: *Does a specific therapy achieve better outcome than nonformal treatment (talking with friends, neighbors and relatives, for example) or simply the passage of time?* This question is critical where a therapy is designed to deal with the problems of children and adolescents, who, it is well known, are liable to make major changes in their behavior and social functioning through development and maturation alone (Barrett et al. 1978; Glidewell 1968; Levitt 1971). As I commented in earlier writing:

> It is difficult for practitioners, who are highly acculturated to believe that their clients need them desperately, to grasp the necessity of such research. Yet there is ample evidence that troubled people change as a result of a wide variety of nontherapeutic experiences. Influences as different as religious conversion, a change of residence, talking with a close friend, growing a year older or two inches taller, can all materially affect a person's feelings, thoughts and behavior. (Wells and Dezen 1978a:254)

Prior to the beginning of the past decade there were no studies of nonbehavioral family therapy in which a legitimate comparison was made with a nontreated group. A number of such studies are now available, and their findings will be examined.

Only the two nonbehavioral therapies examined in Alexander and Parsons (1973) and Klein et al. (1977) will be considered in this section. Both studies involved a comparison between client-centered family therapy (N = 19), an approach described as "eclectic-psychodynamic" family therapy (N = 11), and no-treatment control (N = 10). The recidivism rate among the identified patients was the outcome measure in the first study and the percentage of court contact for siblings was the measure in the second report. Both these measures were determined at lengthy follow-up intervals.

Recidivism was 47 percent for the client-centered group and 73 percent for the eclectic-psychodynamic condition in the Alexander and Parson study. These compare unfavorably with the 50 percent recidivism rate for the no-treatment group. Although the sample sizes are small, precluding statistical comparisons, Alexander and Parsons supply data on a countywide recidivism rate (N = 3800) of 51 percent, which further substantiates the no-treatment base line. Similarly, in the Klein et al. report, sibling court contact was 59 percent for the client-centered condition, 63 percent for the eclectic-psychodynamic group and 40 percent for the no-treatment condition.

Beal and Duckro (1977) conducted another study in a juvenile court setting and compared thirty-four families receiving 10 sessions of a communication-interactional family therapy with fifty-one families receiving no treatment. They found that following treatment only 17 percent of the treated families had to appear in courts or be referred to a community agency versus 35 percent of the untreated group. This difference was significant (.05). It is difficult to interpret this finding as the outcome measure is ambiguous and not comparable to the usual objectives of therapeutic intervention. Whether treated families showed better adjustment or less recidivism, for example, is not clear from the fact that they were less likely to have a court appearance or be referred to another agency.

The series of studies by Guerney and his associates represent probably the most sophisticated research conducted in nonbehavioral family intervention. These studies are extensively discussed in my earlier review (Wells and Dezen 1978:258–61) and will be only briefly summarized here. Several studies (Coufal 1975; Ginsberg 1971; Vogelsong 1976) of the Parent Adolescent Relationship Program found significant superiority for this structured communication training approach in comparison to both nontreated samples and a general discussion group. Similarly, both a single-group (Guerney and Stover, 1971) and a controlled (Stover and Guerney, 1967) study of filial therapy (in which mothers are trained in nondirective play techniques with their own children) produced significant improvement. It must be noted that most of the Guerney group's work has been with recruited populations, largely middle-class, and with children and adolescents showing mild degrees of disturbance. Whether their generally positive findings (Guerney 1977) will replicate with more pronounced disturbance or with lower socioeconomic groups remains to be determined.

The studies by Garrigan and Bambrick (1975, 1977) are both well-designed research projects that attempt to assess the effects of the Zuk (1972) triadic model for family therapy in work with emotionally disturbed adolescents. The earlier study found only one of eleven measures to be significantly different (.05) from no treatment and must be regarded as indicating essentially no differences. The Garrigan and Bambrick (1977) study will be examined at length as it is illustrative of the problems inherent in interpreting complex research data and of the difficulties facing the reviewer (or the practitioner) in evaluating the clinical significance of a report.[3]

This is a well-designed study comparing the effects of 10 sessions of conjoint family therapy with a nontreated group. There were twelve treatment families (with seven male and five female identified patients) and fourteen control families (with nine male and five female identified patients) and assignment to conditions was random. Measures administered at pretreatment and termination included parent and independent judge rating of identified patient (IP) behavior as well as parent and IP ratings of family adjustment, facilitative relationship conditions and state/trait anxiety. Finally, the IP's rated themselves on self-concept.

The findings may be summarized as follows: both parent and IP-rated family adjustment showed no differences; neither parent-rated nor IP-rated state/trait anxiety measures showed differences; for the

---

[3] The researchers themselves compound the difficulties in interpreting these findings by their approach to reporting and analyzing the data. First, they list the analysis of measures in tables in which asterisks indicate whether an F-score is significant. However, this does not reveal whether the difference favored the treated or the untreated group. Only by carefully reading the densely written narrative account of their findings was it possible to determine that several findings were negative effects. Second, they attempt to use a probability level of .10 as indicating significance. This breaks the accepted convention and, particularly where investigators are conducting over a hundred comparisons, is quite unjustifiable. Third, although employing multiple criteria is highly desirable, in such cases the investigators must specify beforehand the proportion of significant findings that will indicate successful outcome. The studies by Eyberg and Johnson (1974) and Johnson et al. (1975) offer exemplary models of this practice. Finally, Garrigan and Bambrick are contradictory in their handling of the negative effects. They accept the positive parental ratings as accurate but ascribe the negative findings to "the ways in which the treatment families interpreted and limited the type and amount of change that occurred as a result of therapy (1977:88)." Obviously, they cannot have it both ways.

facilitative relationship conditions two out of eight measures showed significance (.05); IP ratings of self-concept showed no differences; finally, parent ratings of IP symptomatology found two of fifteen items significantly (.01, .05) favoring treatment and the independent judge rated two (different) items as significantly (.05) favoring treatment, *but* parents also rated two items as showing significant (.05) negative effects and the independent judge rated still another item as showing significant (.01) negative effects (it should be noted that all negative effects were with female patients).

In effect, the data show three measures equal, one measure weakly supporting treatment, and a final measure demonstrating both positive and negative effects. Despite Garrigan and Bambrick's claim of strong superiority for family therapy, the proper conclusion from data such as these (if any conclusion is to be drawn) is that in this study family therapy did a little good, some harm (with girls), but mainly had no greater effect than not receiving it.

Jansma's (1972) study of multiple and conjoint family therapy was described earlier in relation to its comparative findings on the two family therapy methods. In addition, a comparison was made between the two therapies and a notreatment control group. Significant superiority was found for multiple family therapy over the control condition on eight of nine measures of family adjustment and interaction, but on only one of nine measures for the conjoint condition. This supports a clear-cut superiority for the multiple approach but not for the conjoint method. However, the findings must be qualified by the employment of only a client evaluative perspective in the outcome measures.

Finally, a small-scale study by Katz et al. (1975) found one of twenty-nine measures of communication significantly favoring treatment. This miniscule finding must be regarded as essentially reflecting no differences for this otherwise well-designed study.

In summary, the comparisons between nonbehavioral family therapy and no treatment have not been at all encouraging. In over half the studies, the treated subjects would have been as well off in the control group and thereby spared the time and inconvenience of treatment. Only Guerney and his associates have produced any consistently favorable data in this area and their findings must be qualified by the parameters of the populations treated. The Garrigan and Bambrick studies represent the only other systematic work on nonbehavioral family therapy and their efforts have been largely unsuccessful in demonstrating superiority to no treatment. In addition, some disturbing negative effects are apparent. This leaves the studies by Beal and Duckro (1977) and Jansma (1972) and these are difficult to evaluate because of their lack of connection to any coordinated program of research. Jansma's findings for multiple family therapy are clearly positive, the Beal and Duckro data are both less compelling and ambiguous. Both studies may be presently regarded as isolated instances of effective intervention, but the issue of whether a nonbehavioral approach can demonstrate consistently superior outcome over nontreatment with distinctly clinical populations remains essentially unanswered.

Behavioral Approaches to Family Therapy

Behavioral approaches to the *individual* treatment of disturbed children and adolescents have been practiced for some time now and are recently reviewed by Ross (1978). The core of these approaches has been one of altering the reinforcing contingencies within the environment, particularly those provided by the parents, so as to shape and stabilize more desirable behaviors in the child. Similar interventions may be used to directly or indirectly eliminate undesirable behaviors, although, for both empirical and philosophical reasons, behavior therapists have preferred to underplay this aspect of intervention. With adolescents, there has been a frequent trend toward the employment of behavioral contracting methods, in which rewards and penalties are explicitly negotiated, implemented, and monitored. There has also been a burgeoning experimentation with the development of behaviorally oriented parent training programs in child management skills. These have involved teaching parents to employ token reward systems, various shaping and contracting procedures, and other behavior change methods in more effectively coping with their parental responsibilities. Graziano (1977) has reviewed the extensive clinical and experimental literature in this area.

In recent years the behavioral therapists have shown an increasing interest in family treatment and have begun to adapt the aforementioned methods to interventions designed to impact not only upon child behavior but upon the functioning of key units within the family. Thus, a number of current approaches advocate direct work with both parents, in either conjoint interviews or in parent groups, or have utilized key parent-child dyads as the focus of intervention. In such instances this appears to be a type of family therapy, albeit rather different in philosophy, theory, and technology from the nonbehavioral approaches.

In this section, I shall review a series of studies of behavioral family treatment. Behavioral family therapy has largely developed around the work of two major research groups: Gerald Patterson and his colleagues, at the Oregon Research Institute, have concentrated upon the family oriented treatment of children with severe conduct problems, while Alexander and Parsons, at the University of Utah, have developed a programmatic approach to behavioral intervention with delinquent adolescents and their families. A number of other behavioral therapists and researchers have contributed to this growing body of clinical and empirical literature, and I shall review certain other studies, particularly as these augment or qualify the findings of the two major research groups.

Rather than examining groups of uncontrolled, comparative, and controlled studies, as in the preceding sections on the nonbehavioral research, I shall review the behavioral approaches in relation to the findings in these two major problem areas, i.e., conduct disorders and delinquency. This is possible, and necessary, as (in contrast to the nonbehavioral research) the behavioral work has been programmatic in nature with groups of clinical investigators systematically examining a wide range of clinical and empirical issues in a series of coordinated studies. Therefore, within each major problem area, I shall examine the related studies, at various levels of inquiry, and their implications for practice will be considered.

Single-Case and Analogue Designs

The behavioral family therapy approaches draw support from two other levels of data. The first of these are the studies utilizing single-case experimental design. The second are the so-called analogue studies, in which behavioral interventions are applied to families who have been *recruited* for treatment.

The single-case studies (which frequently report data on several cases) are usually well-conducted investigations in which specific measurement of change is made across time (in the ABAB designs) or across both time and target areas (in the multiple-baseline designs). A typical example would be the report by Christophersen et al. (1979), in which the compliance rates of three developmentally delayed preschool children were substantially increased through training the parents in reinforcement and time-out procedures. Another example is the study by Weathers and Liberman (1975) on the negative effect of very brief behavioral contracting with delinquent adolescents and their families. No attempt will be made to review the many single-case studies in this paper.

Single-case experimental design has the advantage of offering a clear demonstration that a specific technique can bring about meaningful change in an important target behavior. However, its very specificity— to subject, therapist, and technique—constitutes an inherent limitation in this class of design. Despite this, Hersen and Barlow (1976) argue, the replication of carefully designed single-case experiments by the same group of investigators (or by different investigators in other settings) can accumulate a reasonable body of evidence for the potency of an identified therapeutic technique with designated problems.

Although nonbehavioral researchers and therapists have shown little interest in single-case design, it would be well to remember that the history of behavior therapy (and its growing success) has been marked by the predominant use of this approach. Group designs have only been employed at a later stage in the investigation of an interventive method. Because single-case experiments can be as readily (and as validly) performed by the practitioner as by the researcher, it has been possible for behavioral therapy to develop a cumulative and, in many respects, self-correcting body of empirically based treatment strategies. The argument that nonbehavioral approaches are not suited to single-case experimentation because of their lack of specificity in technique and goals may only be emphasizing the very reason that these approaches would benefit from the discipline demanded by the single-case experiment.

A number of studies of behavioral family therapy have used volunteer or recruited clients as the recipients of the intervention. Gurman and Kniskern (1978) have designated these as "analogue" studies and criticized their employment in behavioral research. Thus, Guzzetta (1976) obtained volunteers by placing a newspaper advertisement and apparently did no further screening. In yet another study, Martin (1977) sent a form letter to the families of all the primary school children in a public school system offering help with recurring parent-child problems. Approximately 2 percent of the parents responded, and an initial screening interview was utilized to eliminate problems that were insufficiently severe. Hardcastle (1977), on the other hand, had school personnel identify children with social and emotional problems and then obtained parental participation through telephone calls and letters. These last two procedures are not at all unlike the procedures followed in such clinical settings as school social work departments or community-based outreach centers.

The explicit analogue design has the advantage of offering an opportunity to test out the effects of a treatment with a volunteer population prior to its employment in clinical trials. At this level, it is possible to determine whether the intervention has any degree of potency before utilizing it with clients who are in serious need of help. A disadvantage is that the nonclinical volunteers in such an experiment may already be at relatively high levels of functioning so that there will be a "ceiling" effect on the changes that can take place. Additionally, there may be unknown differences between true volunteers for treatment and a client population who are genuinely distressed. The argument is that the volunteers will respond more readily but as plausible a case could be made for the distressed clients being more amenable to intervention.

Studies cannot be relegated to analogue status, and consequently discounted (as Gurman and Kniskern do), simply on the basis that subject participation was recruited or voluntary. As I pointed out earlier, certain of these recruiting procedures are little different from the methods employed in some agencies. Additionally, in some studies there is direct evidence, from standardized tests, that the clients were genuinely distressed and, therefore, equivalent to clinical populations. I will consider each analogue study individually and, where either or both of these conditions are the case, evaluate the data on their merits.

Treatment with the Families of Disturbed Children

A major area of interest for behavioral family treatment has been intervention with conduct-disordered children. These are six- to twelve-year-old children (usually boys) exhibiting mild to severe degrees of social and emotional disturbance, often in both home and school settings, characterized by high rates of aggressive behavior, disobedience, and hyperactivity, and, in some instances, stealing, fire setting, and running away. As Patterson points out (1974a:471), such children are frequently referred for treatment, there is empirical evidence that they do not simply "outgrow" their difficulties, and, finally, he cites Levitt's (1971) review of child psychotherapy to substantiate that traditional treatment methods have demonstrated little effectiveness with this type of child.

The procedures developed by the Patterson group for treating such children and their families are based on the principles briefly outlined earlier in this article and are fully described in Patterson et al. (1975). The most comprehensive account of their findings on outcome are contained in Patterson (1974a), with additional data in Patterson (1974b), Reid and Patterson (1976), and Patterson and Fleischman (1979). Along with this core material, I shall also review several other studies that constitute, in varying degrees, replications of the Patterson work in related or entirely different settings.

The Oregon Research Institute: The clinical researchers at the Oregon Research Institute have undoubtedly contributed some of the most careful and sophisticated research that has been conducted in family therapy. Although the major source of data for the Patterson group itself comes from an uncontrolled single-group study, this work is of such a nature, with repeated measurements at base line, during treatment, and at several follow-up points (up to a year after the conclusion of therapy), that the evidence it offers for the effects of intervention is quite persuasive. In addition, two small-scale controlled studies offer very favorable comparisons between treatment and an attention-placebo group (Walter and Gilmore 1973) and no-treatment (Wiltz and Patterson 1974).

Patterson (1974a, 1974b) reports on the results of treatment with twenty-seven families, utilizing parental ratings of attitude toward child and deviant child behavior, and independent observer ratings of deviant behavior in the home. The data from the latter ratings are presented at base line, termination, and at several follow-up points for every case, so that the findings may be analyzed as a series of single-case experiments (Hersen and Barlow 1976), or in terms of the overall group statistics. The identified problem children in these studies were all boys, and the families were white, skewed toward the lower socioeconomic level, and with the father absent in almost one-third of the cases. Treatment took place over a six-month period and involved about thirty hours of professional time, exclusive of the initial screening interview and behavioral observations.

Parental ratings of problem behaviors (available for fourteen of the families) showed highly significant positive change and, similarly, parental global improvement ratings were highly positive. The observer ratings of child deviant behavior indicated that there was a reduction of at least 30 percent on deviant behavior for sixteen of twenty-seven cases at termination, and follow-up data (for twenty families) at four months supported these positive changes. These changes at termination and follow-up were also statistically significant (.01, .05). In addition, a subsample of fourteen children who were exhibiting serious school difficulties received a specially designed classroom intervention in conjunction with the family approach. Observer ratings of appropriate classroom behaviors found highly significant (.001) improvement in positive functioning at termination. Follow-up data on a portion of this subgroup showed that the gains were maintained.

In addition to the two controlled studies (Walter and Gilmore 1973; Wiltz and Patterson 1974) noted earlier, the Patterson group have also examined the effects of intervention on the observed behaviors of the siblings in their treated families (Arnold et al. 1975). Overall ratings showed a significant (.029) decrease in sibling deviant behavior at termination and maintenance of this effect at one- to six-month follow-ups (for the twenty of twenty-seven families where data was available). However, the magnitude of decrease was less among the siblings than in the identified problem child, suggesting that the effects of behavioral intervention are most specific to the target of change.

The data from these studies clearly substantiate clinically meaningful effects at termination from both parental and observer ratings. Parental ratings at follow-up continue to be highly favorable but observer ratings show some slight decline and, moreover, are somewhat clouded by subject attrition. Both Gurman and Kniskern (1978) and Kent (1976) have criticized aspects of this deficit, and Reid and Patterson (1976) have replied to the latter critique. They reanalyze portions of the data in an effort to demonstrate that the follow-up findings are not unrepresentative.

A good deal of the uncertainty about the follow-up durability of the social learning approach to family intervention is resolved by further findings reported in Patterson and Fleishman (1979). They offer data on the total sample from the ongoing research project, which, by this latest report, comprised eighty-six treated families. Complete observational data, for base line, termination, and twelve-month follow-up, were available on fifty of these families, and a more recently developed measure involving daily parental behavioral reports was available on thirty-three cases. The latter measure has the advantage of including low-frequency behaviors (such as stealing or truancy, etc.) that are usually not incorporated in the observer ratings. For both sets of measures the results at twelve month follow-up were highly significant (.001), with most subjects functioning within the normal criterion range of the measures by this point.

Other studies from the University of Oregon: In a related series of studies, Johnson and his colleagues examine the effects of a behavioral parent-training approach modeled after Patterson's work. They consider not only outcome but such issues as the generalization of change from home to school, the durability of change at follow-up, variations in treatment conditions, the development of unobtrusive measures of child and parent behavior, and the relative cost-effectiveness of differing treatment modalities.

Although modeled after the Patterson group's treatment methods, it should be noted that these studies are not strictly comparable as Johnson and his colleagues tended to work with a less disturbed client population, employed less experienced therapists and limited intervention to twelve sessions. The overall effectiveness of the approach, within these parameters, is reported in Eyberg and Johnson (1974) and Johnson and Christensen (1975). Like most of the studies of behavioral family treatment, ratings of deviant child behavior (by both independent observers and parents) were obtained, as well as measures of parental attitude toward the child and satisfaction with therapy. Results are reported at both termination and follow-up, although subject attrition at this latter point make the findings difficult to interpret.

The parental ratings of attitude change, satisfaction with therapy, and child behavior are all highly positive at termination and at follow-up. Observer ratings of overall deviant behavior change at termination are less positive with only 41 percent of the cases showing the desired (30 percent) reduction and 36 percent of families showing the same reduction at follow-up. Observer ratings of targeted deviant behavior indicated that a slightly higher proportion of families (48 percent) achieved the desired reduction by termination and that this change was maintained at follow-up. Again, it must be remembered that the follow-up ratings involved only fourteen of the twenty-two treated families and, as a group, these families had received somewhat more treatment.

Two further studies (Johnson et al. 1975; Johnson et al. 1976) report outcome on small samples. In the first study (N = 8), parental attitude ratings were highly positive but home observer ratings found only slight change and teacher ratings of classroom behavior were virtually unchanged. In the second study (N = 5), parental attitude and behavioral ratings indicated highly significant gains. Independent judge ratings of child and parent behaviors (using a newly developed unobtrusive procedure) largely confirmed these results. Neither study, however, offered follow-up data.

Finally, Christensen (1976) compared the effects of three modes of implementing the social learning approach. Thirty-six families were randomly assigned to individual family intervention, multiple family groups, or to treatment via self-instructional materials. That is to say, families were seen in conventional family interviews, in sessions involving several families simultaneously, or worked independently on the self-instructional material. Measures included parental attitude and satisfaction questionnaires, and parental and judge-rated behavioral observations. There were no significant differences between the multiple-family and the individual-family conditions on the behavioral ratings but both were superior to the self-instructional mode. All treatment groups reported significant positive change in parental attitude toward the child.

It is apparent that the findings from these studies are less supportive of the efficacy of the social learning approach to family intervention than the data from the Patterson group. Problems are especially evident in the disparities between parental ratings and ratings by observers, as well as the difficulties in demonstrating durability of change at follow-up. There is also a suggestion that the training approach may not be entirely appropriate to families where the identified problem child is *not* exhibiting high rates of deviant behavior.

Unlike studies in other areas of therapy, where follow-up has involved only a telephone contact or a brief questionnaire, the behavioral studies have emphasized elaborate and time-consuming home observations. Consequently, there has been an understandable difficulty in eliciting family cooperation and several studies have suffered from attrition at this point. In addition, some of the question about the durability of change at follow-up has been compounded by the researchers' own emphasis on behavioral observations as the only veridical measure of change. Evaluations from a parental and therapist perspective must also be given credence.

The Family Training Program at the University of Kansas: Christophersen and his colleagues at the University of Kansas have concentrated on the development of a home-based program of behavioral family treatment. Many of the procedures used in their program are identical with the procedures used in the preceding studies and their work may be viewed, in essential respects, as a further independent replication of the model. A unique aspect of the University of Kansas work has been their specification of varying programs of training, depending on the age of the child, and these are outlined in a recent publication (Christophersen et al. 1979).

These researchers have also contributed one of the few long-term comparisons of a behavioral intervention with a conventional approach. The study is described in Christophersen et al. (1979) and involved the random assignment of families (N = 20) to the Family Training Program (FTP) or to what is described as "a more traditional office-based psychological treatment program" (N = 14). Outcome was assessed through parent ratings of problem occurrence and a standardized test, the Walker Problem Behavior Checklist. Data to a three-year follow-up point is reported.

The ratings of problem occurrence indicate a clear superiority (.01) for FTP at termination but, by one-year follow-up, the traditional approach had caught up and both approaches maintained significant gains to the final (three-year) follow-up. Data from the Walker Checklist showed no differences between treatments at any point, although a similar trend is evident, with FTP reducing problems more sharply from base line to termination than the conventional treatment.

Interpretation of the results is clouded by the fact that although the behavioral intervention was implemented over a shorter time period than the conventional treatment (10.3 versus 20.6 weeks), it required more therapist time (36.1 versus 21.5 hours), due to therapist travel time in making home visits. A further study (Sykes 1977), comparing home-based and office-based versions of FTP, found both treatments superior to a no-treatment group, with the office-based treatment showing slightly higher levels of improvement than the home therapy group.

This study illustrates some of the ambiguity in interpreting follow-up results where no control group data are available. It is impossible to know whether the equality of the groups at one-year was due to a delayed effect in the conventional treatment or to developmental and environmental factors independent of therapy. A conservative reading of the results suggests that the behavioral intervention brought about improvement more rapidly than the traditional treatment, although, in time, these gains would have taken place anyway.

The University of Georgia: Several studies from clinical researchers at the University of Georgia add further data on social learning-based interventions on behalf of disturbed children. In preliminary single-case experiments and analogue designs, Forehand and King (1974; 1977) and Forehand et al. (1974) demonstrated that significant changes in both parental and child behaviors could be induced by brief parental training (similar to the Patterson model) and that these changes were maintained at three-month follow-up. Parental perceptions of the child were also positively affected.

Peed et al. (1977) extended these findings beyond the laboratory setting in a controlled study of a brief (Mean = 9.5 sessions) behavioral intervention in which six treated mother/child pairs were compared to six similar pairs in a wait-list control group.[4] The IP children were of preschool or elementary-school age, predominantly boys, and characterized by such behavioral problems as temper tantrums, disobedience, and destructiveness. Measures included parental ratings on two standardized scales and independent observer ratings in both clinic and home settings.

Results indicated highly significant positive changes in the treated group, in comparison to control, on ten of fifteen of the behavioral observations, in both clinic and home settings. Parental ratings, however, were less favorable with only three of eight items showing superiority for the treated group as the control group parents also reported improvement.

The study is noteworthy for its development of an observational schedule which examined not only specific child and parent behaviors but *sequences* of interaction between parent and child. This may be helpful in moving observational data somewhat closer to the systemic effects emphasized by family theorists. The finding of parent-rated improvement in the nontreated group is attributed by Peed et al. (1977:347–48) to the inadequacy of such measures to reflect behavioral change. A similar finding was noted by Walter and Gilmore (1973). However, this gain may as likely have been due to the positive changes observed in many untreated groups over a given period of time. Moreover, the control group, who received an initial interview plus eleven observational sessions during the wait period, might be considered much closer to an attention-placebo group, with the changes in parental

[4] This study was classified as an analogue design by Gurman and Kniskern (1978:867), apparently on the basis that three of twelve subjects were recruited through a newspaper advertisement, but this categorization does not seem justified. Three-quarters of the cases were referred by professionals in the community, and, moreover, pretreatment average scores on a standardized rating scale (Parent's Attitude Test, Cowen et al. 1970), for all subjects, were clearly in the maladjusted range.

perception and attitude stemming from the nonspecific influences common to such groups.

Other research studies: As Patterson and Fleischman (1979) note, not all of the studies of the social learning approach to the treatment of aggressive children have reported positive results. An attempted replication of the Patterson model by Ferber et al. (1974) with seven families found only limited success with three families at termination and only one case maintaining gains at a twelve-month follow-up. The employment of inexperienced B.A. level therapists and an eight-week limit on intervention may have contributed to this negative finding.

Another field trial (Gordon et al. 1979) utilized an approach, modeled after many aspects of the social-learning method, involving short-term (eight- to twelve-week) multiple family groups. Termination data is reported on twelve families, seen in two such groups, and indicates moderately positive change on parental attitude ratings and high degrees of family participation and satisfaction with the groups. As no behavioral ratings or follow-up data are presented. it is difficult to assess these findings as other than mildly positive but inconclusive.

On the other hand, Karoly and Rosenthal (1977), in a well-designed replication of aspects of the Patterson model, compared nine families who attended a 10-session parent-training group with eight families in a wait-list control condition. Results significantly favored the treated group on both parent ratings of problem behavior and on home ratings of deviant behavior by trained observers. The nontreated group, in contrast, showed slight increases on both of these measures. Follow-up data at one month confirmed these findings.

Similarly, an early study by Martin (1967) found significant changes on communication variables and school behavior for two families treated by a brief behavioral approach, as compared to two matched no-treatment families. A recent report by the same investigator (Martin 1977) describes a well-designed study comparing a total of twenty-eight treated families with fourteen families in a wait-list control group. The intervention was again relatively brief (Median = 5 sessions) and designed to emphasize both behavioral child management and communication skills. Families were randomly assigned to conditions and parent-child interaction was assessed through systematically gathered telephone data (later rated by trained judges) at pretreatment, termination, and follow-up points. (Additionally, it should be noted, the treatment group was subdivided into father-included and father-excluded groups, so as to examine the effects of father participation. As the findings from the two subgroups were virtually identical, the comparisons with no-treatment collapsed these data.)

Results indicated a strong superiority for the treated group on three of four measures of problematic interaction, and the treated group showed continued maintenance of its gains at the six-month follow-up point. The findings must be qualified, to some extent, by the fact that the population treated was largely middle-class and relatively well educated, yet the durability of improvement from a brief intervention suggests a promising approach. The finding that father participation made little difference in outcome offers an empirical challenge to the clinical belief to the contrary.

In summary, it is evident that the social learning approaches to family treatment with conduct disorder children have developed a reasonable base of empirical evidence for effectiveness. The seventeen existing studies strongly suggest that clinically significant gains are possible, and the approach appears potentially applicable with low socioeconomic level, as well as more advantaged, families. Although five of the studies included control groups, data from large-scale controlled studies are still lacking. However, the employment of a time-series design and precise outcome measurement (and the replication in varying settings and with different therapists) make the available evidence quite persuasive. There has been some question about the durability of change but accumulating data from the Patterson group indicates that this is satisfactory. However, more work remains to be done on methods of enhancing the maintenance of gain and on eliciting cooperation from client families. These and other clinical implications will be discussed in the succeeding sections of this essay.

Treatment with Delinquent Adolescents and Their Families

Another major area of behavioral research has been the investigation of methods for intervention with delinquent adolescents through family-oriented approaches. Perhaps the most significant work in this area has been conducted by Alexander and Parsons and their associates at the University of Utah, although a group of researchers led by Richard Stuart has carried out a series of related investigations. The findings of both of these consortiums will be discussed and their contribution to intervention in this difficult area evaluated.

The research emanating from the Utah group has involved a programmatic approach to intervention within the family of the delinquent, and the steps in this process are fully described in an article by Alexander and Barton (1976). Briefly, the work has progressed through a series of phases in which 1) dysfunctional processes in delinquent families have been identified; 2) procedures for modifying such processes tested; 3) large-scale field studies implemented to evaluate outcome; and 4) long-range effects determined in both identified patients and other family members.

Two controlled studies report on the effects of treatment on family interaction and communication variables (Parsons and Alexander 1973) and on recidivism in the identified patient (Alexander and Parsons 1973). Significant (.05) changes were found for treatment (N = 20) on three of four communication/interaction variables in the first study, indicating that intervention had positively affected family functioning. Comparisons with data from attention-placebo (N = 19) and no-treatment (N = 10) groups in this same study further strengthened the findings. In the second study, the treated group (N = 46) was found to have a recidivism rate of 26 percent, in comparison to recidivism of 50 percent in the no-treatment controls (N = 10) and 51 percent in a countywide comparison group (N = 2,800). Similarly, a parallel study by Klein et al. (1977) found that only 20 percent of the siblings of the identified patients from the treated families had court contact at 2.5 to 3.5 year follow-up, as compared to 40 percent such contact in the siblings of the no-treatment controls. (These latter studies also included recidivism and sibling court contact rates for families treated by two nonbehavioral approaches. These data were considered in earlier sections of this essay.)

These highly positive findings are further supported by an uncontrolled study (Malouf and Alexander 1974) in which forty-five families were treated by different therapists and the favorable recidivism rate of the earlier study was replicated. The work of the Alexander group is somewhat limited by the fact that its client population were status offenders, from essentially middle-class homes, rather than "hardcore" delinquents. However, in conjunction with Stuart's work in the same area, it is evident that some promising approaches are developing, although further work is needed to fit them to the populations most at risk.

The series of research projects conducted by Stuart and his associates (Jayaratne et al. 1974; Stuart and Tripodi 1973; Stuart et al. 1976) have examined the effects of various forms of behavioral contracting with socially and behaviorally disturbed adolescents and their families. Although the setting of treatment has been the school, many of these youths were considered predelinquent or delinquent. The earliest report (Stuart and Tripodi 1973) compared the effectiveness of three time-limited fifteen-day, forty-five-day and ninety-day) versions of this approach and found little difference in outcome. A second study (Jayaratne et al. 1974) compared shorter (twenty-one-day) and longer (sixty-day) versions of the contracting procedures and again found little difference in outcome.

Although these studies were largely inconclusive, a controlled study by Stuart et al. (1976) compared fifty-one families treated through behavioral contracting (average therapist contact = 21.57 hours) with a nontreated group. Ten outcome measures were utilized, including school grades and attendance; school behavior ratings by referral source, teachers, and parents; and home behavior and parent-child interaction ratings by parents. The study is of particular interest as it included sizable proportions of low-income (38 percent), black (34 percent) and single-parent (46 percent) families.

Although no differences were apparent in school grades and attendance, pretreatment and termination comparisons of school behavior found significant improvement on all four ratings, and, similarly, home adjustment was significantly improved on one of four ratings. This suggests some modest support for the overall effectiveness of behavioral contracting, although the investigators caution against the sole use of this strategy of change. They consider it to be most potent as a part of a total interventive package, as in the Alexander and Parson work considered earlier.

However, it should be noted that additional analyses of the data, which controlled for demographic factors, found that the behavioral contracting approach had its greatest effect with families who were black, had older and less-educated parents, and lower incomes. These are certainly families at high risk for delinquency and school failure and, further, a client population where traditional approaches have shown little substantiated effect.

A study by Gant (1977) examined the effects of a slightly different approach to delinquent adolescents developed at the University of Kansas. In yet another variation of the Family Training Program described in the previous section, families were trained in token economy methods, as well as given skill training in negotiation, communication, and use of leisure time. The study compared ten families referred to a juvenile court and randomly assigned to either FTP or to standard probation services. Outcome measures were administered at termination only and included a family adjustment questionnaire and independent judge ratings of constructive and nonconstructive communication (based on audiotapes of family discussions). Data analysis found both measures significantly favoring FTP but, in common with the studies by Stuart and his colleagues, the findings are weakened by the lack of any follow-up assessment.

Finally, a report by Douds et al. (1977) offers some data from a large-scale field trial of behavioral contracting with delinquent adolescents and their families. The paper describes a fifteen-hour program in which the parents were trained in the principles and procedures of contracting and, in further sessions, implementation was monitored. Global evaluations from parents were highly favorable and, in addition, the authors report a recidivism rate of 10.7 percent in the twelve hundred youths who completed the program, as compared to 42.7 percent recidivism in a control group. Although positive, these results must be viewed with considerable caution, as the report does not clarify whether the treated group excluded dropouts or early terminators nor does it specify the exact composition of the control group. At the least, it suggests that behavioral technology can be successfully implemented by personnel in the agency setting and is acceptable to clients as an interventive mode.

In summary, behavioral interventions with socially disruptive and/or delinquent adolescents show promise. Behavioral contracting is the apparent core of much of this work, although, as Stuart et al. (1976) caution, contracting has limited effects as a *single* technique. Packages of intervention that include a direct focus on communication and negotiation skills, as well as behavioral contracting, seem most effective in reducing recidivism, but further studies must examine a wider range of outcome criteria. Follow-up assessments to ascertain the durability of change remain to be conducted, for, in the existing research, only the Alexander and Parsons group have seriously grappled with this issue. Further, there is an unevenness to the present body of evidence, with some studies largely focused on relatively advantaged populations, while others have found beneficial effects with distinctly disadvantaged groups. Continued work should emphasize this latter population, in order to capitalize on what appears to be a potentially useful approach to families that have shown little response to conventional treatments.

Implications for Practice

Drawing practice implications from research material can be a sobering experience, yet it is a necessary task if there is to be any substance to the interchange between the clinician and the researcher. A number of implications for practice have already been suggested in the preceding sections but summarizing these will be useful. Perhaps the most substantive conclusion that can be drawn is that the family approaches to the treatment of children and adolescents do have at least a modest empirical base. There is reasonable evidence that some varieties of family treatment in this area offer satisfactory results, at least equivalent to the equally general finding from the overall research literature which suggests that psychotherapy accelerates the appearance of improvement that would appear more gradually in the natural course of events.

Specifically, family treatment, following a behavioral model, is particularly useful in the treatment of aggressive children and socially disruptive and delinquent adolescents, while certain forms of nonbehavioral family intervention have shown reasonable effectiveness with specific psychosomatic disorders and the management of family crises. These findings are perhaps more specific and more limited in scope than family therapy proponents would like to believe but this, again, is consonant with the general conclusions of psychotherapy research. That is to say, no single approach or modality has been found to be broadly effective across client populations and problem areas.

Behavior Therapy and Clinical Practice

Another major implication for clinical practice should be quite apparent by now, after this lengthy and detailed consideration of the empirical base of family treatment on behalf of children and adolescents. In a few words, the clinical practitioner must seriously utilize the behavioral methods if his practice is to be grounded in a body of reasonably reliable evidence for effectiveness. The nonbehavioral methods show promise in the area of brief crisis intervention, and in work with certain psychosomatic disorders, but generally speaking, have not been able to demonstrate any convincing degree of efficacy in other areas of work with children and adolescents. The failure of the nonbehavioral approaches (with the exception of the work of the

Guerney group) to demonstrate superiority to no treatment, even over relatively short periods of intervention, is particularly discouraging.

This does not mean that clinical practice with children and adolescents, and their families, should be exclusively behavioral. An empirical stance is essentially an openness and commitment to practice based on evidence and, therefore, rules out any single-minded devotion to one theoretical or technological position. Thus, the empirically oriented practitioner may well choose to employ behavioral treatment with a family with an aggressive, acting-out child and then as comfortably utilize a nonbehavioral approach with a family in crisis. The practitioner's commitment in this sort of pluralistic practice is to be knowledgeable and skilled in a variety of methods and able to select and employ the approach that has the greatest probability, based upon empirical evidence, of benefiting the client.

The findings from the behavioral studies are especially rich in practice implications. It is, however, important to evaluate this mass of data, not simply in terms of "nose counts" of favorable outcome, but in relation to the clues offered toward enhancing our understanding of the process of therapeutic change. The behavioral studies certainly support the clinician's belief that positive changes can be induced in deviant and antisocial child and adolescent behavior with relatively brief periods of intervention. Furthermore, the changes brought about are reasonably durable, particularly where the overall environmental situation is favorable.

Family Treatment and the Disadvantaged

This latter finding identifies a continuing problem for the helping professions, in that work with disadvantaged families continues to be disappointing. This does not necessarily mean that the change strategies available are inappropriate but, because of difficulties in eliciting cooperation from low socioeconomic status families, and problems in managing the impinging effects of other environmental and interpersonal factors, gains are limited.

Only a very few studies offer any data on treatment with low socioeconomic status families. As I have already noted, some of the behavioral work has been with such families and it appears that favorable outcome is possible, although much more difficult to achieve. Some implications for practice are evident in these studies.

For example, the behavioral experimentation with various methods of directly strengthening parental participation and cooperation through systematic therapist reinforcement (Eyberg and Johnson 1974), or through monetary reward, (Fleishman 1979) appears to offer an effective means of enhancing familial involvement. Fleischman, using the social learning treatment model, found that a "parenting salary," contingent on attendance and completion of assignments, markedly improved the participation of lower socioeconomic status families. Not surprisingly, payment made little difference with middle-class clients. Supporting these findings is the work of Stanton and Todd (1976) with adult heroin addicts and their families. These researchers found that the groups receiving payment for participation were superior to non-paid groups not only in attendance but in overall outcome.

Many agencies offer treatment at reduced or no cost to disadvantaged families, but it may run against the grain of middle-class therapists to accept the notion that some people should literally be paid to participate in treatment. However, I do not think the issue is as simple as whether people should be rewarded to engage in an activity that they should value for its own sake or, at the least, for the benefits it can offer. For many lower-class (and consequently low-income) families there are out-of-pocket expenses in attending therapy sessions. These include transportation, parking, and baby-sitter costs, which, in relation to a limited income, may be quite sizable. Thus, the payment that is offered may be a way of making participation *possible*, rather than any matter of explicit gain. Making payment contingent upon attendance and participation emphasizes critical factors that must be present if intervention is to be successful.

In regard to the multiple difficulties presented by some families (and it should be noted that this problem is not limited to the low socioeconomic status group), it is apparent that *packages* of intervention need to be devised. The work of Alexander and Parsons (1973) or Christopherson et al. (1979) is suggestive of the programmatic approaches that are possible within the behavioral framework. The dilemma here is for treatment to retain the potency that a relatively focused approach offers, yet be sufficiently broad to be able to contend with more than a few areas of difficulty.

Skill Training or Attitudinal Change?

Another implication suggested by several of the behavioral studies of family treatment lies in what Arnold et al. have called "the often capricious quality of the deviancy labeling process'' (1975:687). Thus, siblings may show higher rates of deviant behavior than the IP child or, in other instances, children identified by their parents as problematic may be within the normal range of child deviant response.

As Patterson (1974a) points out, some of the difficulty may lie in the fact that the characteristics of concern to parent or community are relatively infrequent behaviors such as stealing or fire-setting, which simply do not show up on the observational schedules utilized in these studies. On the other hand, there are also indications that some parents may label a child as deviant for reasons other than the child's explicit behavior. The therapeutic task, then, is one of changing the parental perception or attitude, rather than the child's behavior.

In order to make this distinction, the clinician needs reliable and objective means of differentiating between children who are behaviorally deviant and those who have been labeled as such. This entails the development of abbreviated versions of the observational rating methods employed in many of the behavioral family studies. The present methods are too complex and expensive for everyday agency use. Further, therapeutic methods for effectively changing parental attitudes are lacking. In the latter case, some of the recent work on cognitive restructuring (e.g., Mahoney and Arnkoff 1978) may offer a viable therapeutic alternative.

Length of Treatment

From a clinical vantage point, Zuk (1978) has suggested that family therapy is best operationalized as a short-term method, on the grounds that most families will only make themselves available for a relatively brief period of time. The research data also support this position from at least two perspectives. First, there have been consistent empirical findings that only a small percentage of clients stay in treatment beyond five or six sessions (see, for example, Beck and Jones 1973; Garfield 1971; Lorion 1978). This finding holds not just with the usually lower socioeconomic status clientele in public agencies and clinics but with middle- and upper-middle-class clients seen by private practitioners. Recent large-scale studies by Langsley (1978) and Koss (1979) have confirmed this latter finding. Second, in specific relation to family therapy, there is direct evidence that short-term interventions have equal, if not better, improvement rates than lengthier treatment. These

Table 10.1
Improvement Rates in Family Therapy in Relation to
Length of Treatment

Length	N	Improved	No Change	Worse
Long	471	339	131	1
	(100%)	(72%)	(28%)	–
Short	646	514	124	8
	(100%)	(80%)	(19%)	(1%)

NOTE: Adapted from Gurman and Kniskern (1978). Long = 21 sessions outpatient or twelve or more weeks inpatient. Short = 1-10 sessions outpatient or less than six weeks inpatient.

findings, drawn from Gurman and Kniskern's (1978) review of family therapy outcome are summarized in table 10.1.

These findings are congruent with the trends evident in other areas of psychotherapy. In a recent review of psychotherapy research and practice, Strupp, by no means a prior advocate of brief therapy, concludes that "short-term therapy should be the treatment of choice for practically all patients" (1978:18). Such a move would necessitate a concerted effort in both practice and research (and in education for practice) to identify and refine the active, direct, and focused methods that are characteristic of most brief therapy. Additionally, it would be important for the metaphilosophy of therapeutic practice to shift toward explicitly valuing short-term interventions.

Premature Termination and Dropout Problems

Perhaps one of the most neglected problems in the helping professions is that of the dropout or premature terminator. As I noted earlier, most surveys of practice have found that only a small proportion of clients stay in therapy beyond about five or six interviews. As few therapies, even the most avowedly short-term, consider this a workable length of contact, it is obvious that many clients are receiving an insufficient amount of therapeutic time to draw any tangible benefits. The question is whether there is anything the therapist can do that will decrease this tendency to foreshorten the length of therapy? This should not be construed, however, as suggesting that intervention should be lengthy, but rather that the average duration of contact should be much closer to eight to twelve sessions.

An apparently little-considered area of the psychotherapy research literature may offer some solution. A number of studies (for example, Frank 1978, or Warren and Rice 1972) have been conducted where clients have been given pretherapy training in which the principles and procedures of the therapeutic process are clearly explicated. This is based on the assumption (Frank 1978) that many clients, particularly from low socioeconomic status populations, have only the vaguest notion of what therapy will be like or have expectations quite counter to what it can offer. From this viewpoint, dropping out or prematurely terminating is a reaction to a process that appears, to the recipient, to have little relevance. The research findings have supported the position that informing the client about therapeutic procedures or, in some instances, training the person in how to be a "good" client, reduces premature termination and tends to enhance outcome. Lorion's (1978) review of psychotherapy with the disadvantaged identifies these approaches as particularly beneficial with low socioeconomic status populations.

No direct studies of pretherapy preparation have been reported in the family therapy research. However, some of the work by Alexander et al. (1976) on therapist structuring is suggestive of a similar process taking place within the therapy interview. Extrapolating from this work, and from the literature generally, it appears that utilizing appropriate forms of pretherapy education, particularly with low socioeconomic status clients, might well make the helping process more comprehensible and, therefore, more attractive to these populations. Clinicians could make such explanation an integral part of their initial interview (Wells 1980) or, alternately, clients could be offered special explanatory sessions as they apply for help. (Parenthetically, it should be noted that explanation and explicit structuring run counter to the family therapy approaches that have emphasized paradoxical directives. Once again the clinician is confronted with a choice between empirical data and anecdotal testimony.)

Therapist Qualities and Clinical Practice

In a recent review of research on training programs and teaching methods in marital and family therapy, Kniskern and Gurman (1979) summarize the empirical findings on the therapist factors that appear to influence family therapy outcome. They comment that at least two of these three major clusters of factors may be taught or learned.

1. High levels of therapist experience have been found to improve outcome or, at the least, reduce dropout.
2. Structuring skills such as "directiveness, clarity, self-confidence" (1979:84), along with the ability to gather information and stimulate interaction, are similarly related to good outcome.
3. Finally, the importance of fostering a positive alliance with the family has received consistent research support. For example, Kniskern and Gurman (1979) note that therapist empathy, warmth, and genuineness—the facilitative qualities investigated by Truax and Carkhuff (1967)—are important in retaining families beyond the first interview.

As Garfield (1973) has pointed out, these identified therapist factors may very well constitute a core of common qualities in the effective helper, irrespective of approach or orientation or, for that matter, professional affiliation. Thus, there is reason to believe that *who* the therapist is—in respect to a cluster of important qualities—may be much more important than many of the niceties of technique, or the knotty issues in theory, or the many other questions that so often absorb our attention. All of this suggests implications in many areas of practice, and in education for practice.

The clinician must be aware that the effective helper is an individual who is able, for example, to respond with explicit and immediate empathy to troubled individuals and families. In other important personal aspects, the skilled helper is able to persuade, suggest, explain, and influence—in a consistent and direct manner—throughout the day-by-day pressures of practice. This places a much greater emphasis on the immediate and personal interaction between therapist and client than many of our practice theories have conveyed and, consequently, a greater burden on the technical and personal skill of the therapist.

Thus, in the training of therapists, the present emphasis on theoretical exposition must be counterbalanced by an at least equal stress upon developing the interpersonal skill level of the trainee. This will involve increased opportunities to learn through modeling, simulations, and guided practice in laboratory and workshop settings, in close conjunction with field practice. The work of such researchers and clinicians as Robert Carkhuff (1969) or Allan Ivey (Ivey and Authier 1978) in psychology, or Sheldon Rose (Rose and Edleson 1978) or Dean Hepworth (Hammond, Hepworth and Smith 1978) in social work, demonstrate that key skills in a number of empirically identified areas can be taught.

Finally, the identification of the personal qualities of the clinician as a critical ingredient in the therapeutic equation also carries implications for the administrator and policymaker. The critical importance of the therapist as a person highlights the necessity of agency practices and policies which conserve and enhance this vital resource.

For example, administrators should frequently examine the management procedures of their agencies in respect to this issue. How is the morale of the clinician maintained? What specific efforts—whether through improved working conditions, personal recognition, relief from undue emotional stress, the resources of consultation and supervision, and so on—can be made to sustain the spirit of the frontline worker? If the therapist, and the qualities that he conveys, are perhaps the most important single factor in effective outcome, these qualities must be administratively nourished.

Skill can be attained, but once attained, the question is whether these qualities—empathy, assertiveness, and technical interviewing and change skills—can be maintained unless the agency atmosphere supports the clinician as a human being. In other words, these qualities cannot be regarded as simply technological skills that, once learned, are self-sustaining. Rather, they must be seen, in many respects, as fragile human qualities and vulnerable to the incursions of lowered morale.

Conclusions and Future Directions

From an empirical perspective, the practice of family treatment on behalf of children and adolescents, *in specific areas and through identified techniques*, can be justified. This is not to say, however, that the benefits from even the best-validated approaches are consistent and substantial. Much remains to be done in developing and refining therapeutic methodology, and this can best be accomplished through a continued interplay between practice and research. Moreover, even with a series of well-substantiated strategies of change available, there will still be much of the therapeutic enterprise that will continue to rest upon the skilled and often artful application of this technology. In other words, therapy will always be human.

Both research and practice must direct effort to the populations and problems that offer real difficulty. The day is past for research or practice to concentrate upon (and endlessly examine) work with mildly to moderately disturbed white, middle-class children and adolescents. The need is for tested interventions that will offer some hope of benefit to the disadvantaged families throughout the country, the children at high risk for delinquency or social failure, the neglectful and abusing parents and other such categories of challenge to the mettle of the professional helper.

References

Alexander, C. A. 1977. "On the record." *NASW News* 22(1):24.

Alexander, J. and C. Barton. 1976. "Behavioral Systems Therapy for Families." In D. H. L. Olson, ed., *Treating Relationships*, pp. 167–87. Lake Mills, Iowa: Graphic Press.

Alexander, J., C. Barton, R. S. Schiavo, and B. Parsons. 1976. "Systems-Behavioral Intervention with Families of Delinquents: Therapist Characteristics, Family Behavior and Outcome." *Journal of Consulting and Clinical Psychology* 44:656–64.

Alexander, J. and B. Parsons. 1973. "Short-Term Behavioral Intervention with Delinquent Families: Impact on Family Process and Recidivism." *Journal of Abnormal Psychology* 81:219–25.

Arnold, J. E., A. G. Levine, and G. R. Patterson. 1975. "Changes in Sibling Behavior Following Family Intervention." *Journal of Consulting and Clinical Psychology* 43:683–88.

Baird, J. P. 1973. "Changes in Patterns of Interpersonal Behavior among Family Members Following Brief Family Therapy." *Dissertation Abstracts International* 34:404B.

Barrett, C. L., E. Hampe, and L. Miller. 1978. "Research on Psychotherapy with Children." In S. L. Garfield and A. E. Bergin, eds., *Handbook of Psychotherapy and Behavior Change.* 2d ed., pp. 411–35. New York: Wiley.

Beal, D. and Duckro, P. 1977. "Family Counseling As an Alternative to Legal Action for the Juvenile Status Offender." *Journal of Marriage and Family Counseling* 3:77–81.

Beck, D. F. and M. A. Jones. 1973. *Progress on Family Problems: A Nationwide Study of Clients' and Counselors' Views of Family Agency Services.* New York: Family Service Association of America.

Bergin, A. E. 1971. "The Evaluation of Therapeutic Outcomes." In A. E. Bergin and S. L. Garfield, eds., *Handbook of Psychotherapy and Behavior Change.* 1st ed., pp. 217–70. New York: Wiley.

Bergin, A. E. and M. J. Lambert. 1978. "The Evaluation of Therapeutic Outcomes." In S. L. Garfield and A. E. Bergin, eds., *Handbook of Psychotherapy and Behavior Change*. 2d ed., pp. 139–89. New York: Wiley.

Bergin, A. E. and Strupp, H. H. 1972. *Changing Frontiers in the Science of Psychotherapy*. Chicago: Aldine-Atherton.

Briar, S. and J. R. Conte. 1978. "Families." In H. S. Maas, ed., *Social Service Research: Reviews of Studies*, pp. 9–38. Washington, D.C.: National Association of Social Workers.

Budman, S. and R. Shapiro. 1976. "Patient's Evaluations of Successful Outcome in Family and Individual Therapy." University of Rochester Medical School. Manuscript.

Butcher, J. N. and M. P. Koss. 1978. "Research on Brief and Crisis-Oriented Psychotherapies." In S. L. Garfield and A. E. Bergin, eds., *Handbook of Psychotherapy and Behavior Change*. 2d ed., pp. 725–67. New York: Wiley.

Carkhuff, R. R. 1969. *Helping and Human Relations*, Vols. 1 & 2. New York: Holt, Rhinehart and Winston.

Christensen, A. 1976. "Cost Effectiveness in Behavioral Family Therapy." *Dissertation Abstracts International* 37:3066B.

Christophersen, E. R., S. R. Barnard, J. D. Barnard, S. Gleeson, and B. W. Sykes. 1979. "Home-Based Treatment of Behavior Disordered and Developmentally Delayed Children." In M. J. Begab, H. C. Haywood, and H. T. Garber, eds., *Prevention of Retarded Development and Psychosocially Disadvantaged Children*, Baltimore, Md.: University Park Press.

Coufal, J. D. 1975. "Preventive-Therapeutic Programs for Mothers and Adolescent Daughters: Skills Training versus Discussion Methods." Ph.D. dissertation, Pennsylvania State University.

Cowen, E. L., J. Huser, D. R. Beach, and J. Rapport. 1970. "Parental Perceptions of Young Children and Their Relationship to Indexes of Adjustment." *Journal of Consulting and Clinical Psychology* 34:97–103.

DeWitt, K. N. 1978. "The Effectiveness of Family Therapy." *Archives of General Psychiatry* 35:549–61.

Dezen, A. E. and I. J. Borstein. 1974. "The Effects of Family Systems Interventions on Juvenile Delinquents and Their Families by Probation Officers." Paper presented at the Annual Meeting of the American Psychological Association, August, 1974.

Douds, A. F., M. Engelsjerd, and T. R. Collingwood. 1977. "Behavioral Contracting with Youthful Offenders and Their Families." *Child Welfare* 56:409–17.

Evans, H., L. Chayoga, and V. Rakoff. 1971. "Decision-making as to the Choice of Family Therapy in an Adolescent In-Patient Setting." *Family Process* 10:97–110.

Ewing, C. P. 1976. "Family Crisis Intervention and Traditional Child Guidance: A Comparison of Outcomes and Factors Related to Success in Treatment." *Dissertation Abstracts International* 36:4686B.

Eyberg, S. M. and S. M. Johnson. 1974. "Multiple Assessment of Behavior Modification with Families: Effects of Contingency Contracting and Order of Treated Problems." *Journal of Consulting and Clinical Psychology* 42:596–606.

Ferber, H., S. Keeley, and K. Shemberg. 1974. "Training Parents in Behavior Modification: Outcome of and Problems Encountered in a Program after Patterson's Work." *Behavior Therapy* 5:415–19.

Fischer, J. 1973. "Is Casework Effective? A Review." *Social Work* 18:15–20.

——1976. *The Effectiveness of Social Casework.* Springfield, Ill.: Thomas.

——1979. "Does Anything Work?" *Journal of Social Service Research* 1:215–43.

Fleischman, M. J. 1979. "Using Parenting Salaries to Control Attrition and Cooperation in Therapy." *Behavior Therapy* 10:111–16.

Forehand, R. and H. E. King. 1974. "Pre-school Children's Non-compliance: Effects of Short-Term Behavior Therapy." *Journal of Community Psychology* 2:42–44.

——1977. "Non-compliant Children: Effects of Parent Training on Behavior and Attitude Change." *Behavior Modification* 1:93–108.

Forehand, R., T. Cheney, and P. Yoder. 1974. "Parent Behavior Training: Effects on the Noncompliance of a Deaf Child." *Journal of Behavior Therapy and Experimental Psychiatry* 5:281–83.

Frank, J. D. 1974. *Persuasion and Healing.* 2d ed. Baltimore, Md.: Johns Hopkins University Press.

——1978. "Expectation and Therapeutic Outcome: The Placebo Effect and the Role Induction Interview." In J. D. Frank, R. Hoehn-Saric, S. D. Imber, B. L. Liberman, and A. R. Stone, eds., *Effective Ingredients of Successful Psychotherapy*, pp. 1–34. New York: Brunner/Mazel.

——1979. "The Present Status of Outcome Studies." *Journal of Consulting and Clinical Psychology* 47:310–16.

Gant, B. 1977. "Assessment and Modification of Delinquent Family Interaction." *Dissertation Abstracts International* 37:3393B.

Garfield, S. L. 1971. "Research on Client Variables in Psychotherapy." In A. E. Bergin and S. L. Garfield, eds., *Handbook of Psychotherapy and Behavior Change*, 1st ed., pp. 271–98. New York: Wiley.

——1973. "Basic Ingredients of Common Factors in Psychotherapy?" *Journal of Consulting and Clinical Psychology* 41:9–12.

Garrigan, J. and A. Bambrick. 1975. "Short-Term Family Therapy with Emotionally Disturbed Children." *Journal of Marriage and Family Counseling* 1:379–85.

——1977. "Family Therapy for Disturbed Children: Some Experimental Results in Special Education." *Journal of Marriage and Family Counseling* 3:83–93.

Ginsberg, B. G. 1971. "Parent-Adolescent Relationship Development: A Therapeutic and Preventative Mental Health Program." Ph.D. dissertation, Pennsylvania State University.

Glidewell, J. C. 1968. "Studies of Mother's Reports of Behavior Symptoms in Their Children." In S. B. Sells, ed., *The Definition and Measurement of Mental Health*, pp. 181–217. Washington D.C.: Public Health Service.

Gordon, S. B., L. L. Lerner, and F. J. Keefe. 1979. "Responsive Parenting: An Approach to Training Parents of Problem Children." *American Journal of Community Psychology* 7:45–56.

Gottman, J. M. and H. J. Markman. 1978. "Experimental Designs in Psychotherapy Research." In S. L. Garfield and A. E. Bergin, eds., *Handbook of Psychotherapy and Behavior Change*. 2d ed., pp. 23–62. New York:

Graziano, A. M. 1977. "Parents As Behavior Therapists." In M. Hersen, R. M. Eisler, and P. M. Miller, eds., *Progress in Behavior Modification*, pp. 251–98. New York: Academic Press.

Group for the Advancement of Psychiatry (GAP). 1970. *Treatment of Families in Conflict*. New York: Science House.

Guerney, B. G., Jr. 1977. *Relationship Enhancement: Skill-Training Programs for Therapy, Prevention, and Enrichment*. San Francisco, Calif.: Jossey-Bass.

Guerney, B. G., Jr. and L. Stover. 1971. "Final Report on Filial Therapy for Grant MH18264-01." Washington, D.C.: National Institute of Mental Health.

Gurman, A. S. and D. P. Kniskern. 1978. "Research on Marital and Family Therapy: Progress, Perspective, and Prospect." In S. L. Garfield and A. E. Bergin, eds., *Handbook of Psychotherapy and Behavior Change*. 2d ed., pp. 817–901. New York: Wiley.

Guzzetta, R. A. 1976. "Acquisition and Transfer of Empathy by the Parents of Early Adolescents through Structured Learning Training." *Journal of Counseling Psychology* 23:449–53.

Hammond, D. C., D. Hepworth, and V. G. Smith. 1978. *Improving Therapeutic Communication*. San Francisco, Calif.: Jossey-Bass.

Hardcastle, D. R. 1977. "A Mother-Child, Multiple Family Counseling Program: Procedures and Results." *Family Process* 16:67–74.

Hersen, M. and D. H. Barlow. 1976. *Single-Case Experimental Designs*. New York: Pergamon.

Ivey, A. E. and J. Authier. 1978. *Microcounseling: Innovations in Interviewing, Counseling, Psychotherapy and Psychoeducation*. 2d ed. Springfield, Ill.: Thomas.

Jansma, T. J. 1972. "Multiple versus Individual Family Therapy: Its Effects on Family concepts." *Dissertation Abstracts International* 33:5796B.

Jayaratne, S., R. B. Stuart and T. Tripodi. 1974. "Methodological Issues and Problems in Evaluating Treatment Outcomes in the Family and School Consultation Project, 1970–1973. In P. O. Davidson, F. W. Clark and L.

A. Hamerlynck, eds. *Evaluation of Behavioral Programs in Community, Residential and School Settings*, pp. 141–74. Champaign, Ill.: Research Press.

Johnson, J. L. 1975. "A Time-series Analysis of the Effects of Therapy on Family Interaction." *Dissertation Abstracts International* 36:5796B.

Johnson, S. M. and A. Christensen. 1975. "Multiple-Criteria Follow-Up of Behavior Modification with Families." *Journal of Abnormal Child Psychology*. 3:135–54.

Johnson, S. M., O. D. Bolstad, and G. K. Lobitz. 1975. "Generalization and Contrast Phenomena in Behavior Modification with Children." In E. J. Nash, M. A. Hamerlynck, and L. C. Handy, eds., *Behavior Modification and Families*, pp. 160–88.

Johnson, S. M., A. Christensen, and T. Bellamy. 1976. "Evaluation of Family Interventions through Unobtrusive Audio Recordings; Experience in Bugging Children." *Journal of Applied Behavior Analysis* 9:213–19.

Johnson, T. M. 1971. "Effects of Family Therapy on Patterns of Verbal Interchange in Disturbed Families." *Dissertation Abstracts International* 33:1288B.

Johnson, T. M. and H. N. Malony. 1977. "Effects of Short-Term Family Therapy on Patterns of Verbal Interchange in Disturbed Families." *Family Therapy* 4:207–15.

Karoly, P. and M. Rosenthal. 1977. "Training Parents in Behavior Modification: Effects on Perceptions of Family Interaction and Deviant Child Behavior." *Behavior Therapy* 8:406–10.

Katz, A., M. Krasinski, E. Philip, and C. Weiser. 1975. "Change in Interactions As a Measure of Effectiveness in Short-term Family Therapy." *Family Therapy* 2:31–56.

Kent, R. N. 1976. "A Methodological Critique of 'Interventions for Boys with Conduct Problems.'" *Journal of Consulting and Clinical Psychology* 44:297–99.

Klein, N., J. Alexander, and B. V. Parsons. 1977. "Impact of Family Systems Intervention on Recidivism and Sibling Delinquency: A Model of Primary Prevention and Program Evaluation. *Journal of Consulting and Clinical Psychology* 45:469–74.

Kniskern, D. P. and A. S. Gurman. 1979. "Research on Training in Marriage and Family Therapy: Status, Issues and Directions." *Journal of Marriage and Family Therapy* 5:83–94.

Koss, M. P. 1979. "Length of Psychotherapy for Clients Seen in Private Practice." *Journal of Consulting and Clinical Psychology* 47:210–12.

Langsley, D. G. 1978. "Comparing Clinic and Private Practice of Psychiatry." *American Journal of Psychiatry* 135:702–06.

Levitt, E. E. 1971. "Research on Psychotherapy with Children." In A. G. Bergin and S. L. Garfield, eds., *Handbook of Psychotherapy and Behavior Change*. 1st ed., pp. 474–94. New York: Wiley.

Liebman, R., S. Minuchin, and L. Baker. 1974a. "An Integrated Treatment Program for Anorexia Nervosa." *American Journal of Psychiatry* 131:432–36.

——1974b. "The Use of Structural Family Therapy in the Treatment of Intractable Asthma." *American Journal of Psychiatry* 131:535–40.

Lorion, R. P. 1978. "Research on Psychotherapy and Behavior Change with the Disadvantaged." In S. L. Garfield and A. E. Bergin, eds., *Handbook of Psychotherapy and Behavior Change*. 2d ed., pp. 903–38. New York: Wiley.

Love, L. R., J. Kaswan, and D. E. Bugenthal. 1972. "Differential Effectiveness of Three Clinical Interventions for Different Socioeconomic Groupings." *Journal of Consulting and Clinical Psychology* 39:347–60.

Mahoney, M. J. and D. Arkoff. 1978. "Cognitive and Self-Control Therapies." In S. L. Garfield and A. E. Bergin, eds., *Handbook of Psychotherapy and Behavior Change*. 2d ed., pp. 689–722. New York: Wiley.

Malouf, R. and J. Alexander. 1974. "Family Crisis Intervention: A Model and Technique of Training." In R. E. Hardy and J. G. Cull, eds., *Therapeutic Needs of the Family*, Springfield, Ill.: Thomas.

Martin, B. 1967. "Family Interaction Associated with Child Disturbance: Assessment and Modification." *Psychotherapy: Theory, Research and Practice* 4:30–35.

——1977. "Brief Family Intervention: Effectiveness and the Importance of Including the Father." *Journal of Consulting and Clinical Psychology* 45:1002–10.

Massie, H. N. and C. C. Beels. 1972. "The Outcome of the Family Treatment of Schizophrenia." *Schizophrenia Bulletin*, issue no. 6:24–36.

Meehl, P. 1978. "Theoretical Risks and Tabular Asterisks: Sir Karl, Sir Ronald, and the Slow Progress of Soft Psychology." *Journal of Consulting and Clinical Psychology* 46:806–34.

Minuchin, S. 1974. *Families and Family Therapy*. Cambridge, Mass.: Harvard University Press.

Minuchin, S., L. Baker, B. Rosman, R. Liebman, L. Milman, and T. Todd. 1975. "A Conceptual Model of Psychosomatic Illness in Children." *Archives of General Psychiatry* 32:1031–38.

Minuchin, S., B. Rosman, and L. Baker. 1978. *Psychosomatic Families: Anorexia Nervosa in Context*. Cambridge, Mass.: Harvard University Press.

Olson, D. H. 1970. "Marital and Family Therapy: Integrative Review and Critique." *Journal of Marriage and the Family* 32:501–38.

Pacquin, M. J. 1977. "The Status of Family and Marital Therapy Outcomes: Methodological and Substantive Considerations." *Canadian Psychological Review* 18:221–32.

Parloff, M. B. 1979. "Can Psychotherapy Research Guide the Policy Maker?" *American Psychologist* 34:296–306.

Parsons, B. V. and J. Alexander. 1973. "Short-Term Family Intervention: A Therapy Outcome Study." *Journal of Consulting and Clinical Psychology* 41:195–201.

Patterson, G. R. 1974a. "Interventions for Boys with Conduct Problems: Multiple Settings, Treatments, and Criteria." *Journal of Consulting and Clinical Psychology* 42:471–81.

——1974b. "Retraining of Aggressive Boys by Their Parents: Review of Recent Literature and Follow-Up Evaluation." *Canadian Psychiatric Association Journal* 19:142–61.

Patterson, G. R. and M. J. Fleischman. 1979. "Maintenance of Treatment Effects: Some Considerations Concerning Family Systems and Follow-Up Data." *Behavior Therapy* 10:168–85.

Patterson, G. R., J. Reid, R. Jones, and R. Conger. 1975. *A Social Learning Approach to Family Intervention. Vol. 1, Families with Aggressive Children.* Eugene, Ore.: Castalia.

Peed, S., M. Roberts, and R. Forehand. 1977. "Evaluation of the Effectiveness of a Standardized Parent Training Program in Altering the Interaction of Mothers and Their Non-compliant Children." *Behavior Modification* 1:323–50.

Reid, W. J. 1974. "Competence in Social Treatment." In D. H. Hepworth, ed., *Assuring Practitioner Competence: Whose Responsibility?* pp. 1–16. Salt Lake City, Utah: Graduate School of Social Work, University of Utah.

Reid, J. and G. R. Patterson. 1976. "Follow-Up Analyses of a Behavioral Treatment Program for Boys with Conduct Problems: A Reply to Kent." *Journal of Consulting and Clinical Psychology* 44:299–302.

Rosman, B., S. Minuchin, R. Liebman, and L. Baker. 1976. "Impact and Outcome of Family Therapy in Anorexia Nervosa." Philadelphia Child Guidance Clinic. Manuscript.

Rose, S. and J. Edleson. 1978. "Interpersonal Skill Training for Social Work Students." Processed. School of Social Work, University of Wisconsin/Madison.

Ross, A. O. 1978. "Behavior Therapy with Children." In S. L. Garfield and A. E. Bergin, eds., *Handbook of Psychotherapy and Behavior Change.* 2d ed., pp. 591–620. New York: Wiley.

Santa-Barbara, J., C. A. Woodward, S. Levin, J. Goodman, D. Streiner, and N. Epstein. 1977a. "The McMaster Family Therapy Outcome Study: I. An Overview of Methods and Results." McMaster University. Manuscript.

——1977b. "The McMaster Family Therapy Outcome Study: II. Interrelationships among Outcome Measures." McMaster University. Manuscript.

Sigal, J., C. Barrs, and A. Doubilet. 1976. "Problems in Measuring the Success of Family Therapy in a Common Clinical Setting: Impasses and Solutions." *Family Process* 15:225–33.

Slipp, S. and K. Kressel. 1978. "Difficulties in Family Therapy Evaluation: A Comparison of Insight versus Problem-Solving Approaches." *Family Process* 17:409–22.

Stanton, M. D. and T. C. Todd. 1976. "Structural Family Therapy with Heroin Addicts: Some Outcome Data." Paper presented at the Society for Psychotherapy Research, San Diego, June, 1976.

Stover, L. and B. G. Guerney. 1967. "The Efficacy of Training Procedures for Mothers in Filial Therapy." *Psychotherapy: Theory, Research and Practice* 4:110–15.

Strupp, H. H. 1978. "Psychotherapy Research and Practice: An Overview." In S. L. Garfield and A. E. Bergin, eds., *Handbook of Psychotherapy and Behavior Change*. 2d ed., pp. 3–22. New York: Wiley.

Strupp, H. H., H. W. Hadley, and B. Gomes-Schwartz. 1977. *Psychotherapy for Better or Worse: An Analysis of the Problem of Negative Effects*. New York: Aronson.

Stuart, R. B. and T. Tripodi. 1973. "Experimental Evaluation of Three Time-Constrained Behavioral Treatments for Predelinquents and Delinquents." In R. Rubin, J. Brady and J. Henderson, eds., *Advances in Behavior Therapy*, pp. 1–12. New York: Academic Press.

Stuart, R. B., T. Tripodi, S. Jayarante, and D. Camburn. 1976. "An Experiment in Social Engineering in Serving the Families of Predelinquents." *Journal of Abnormal Child Psychology*. 4:243–61.

Sykes, B. W. 1977. "An Adaptation of the Family Training Program to an Office Setting." *Dissertation Abstracts International* 37:3375B.

Trankina, F. J. 1976. "Aggressive and Withdrawn Children As Related to Family Perception and Outcome of Different Treatment Methods." *Dissertation Abstracts International* 36:924B.

Truax, C. B. and R. R. Carkhuff. 1967. *Toward Effective Counseling and Psychotherapy*. Chicago: Aldine.

Vogelsong, E. L. 1976. "Preventive-Therapeutic Programs for Mothers and Adolescent Daughters: A Follow-Up of Relationship Enhancement versus Discussion and Booster versus No-Booster Methods." *Dissertation Abstracts International* 36:7677A.

Walter, H. and S. K. Gilmore. 1973. "Placebo versus Social Learning Effects of Parent Training Procedures Designed to Alter the Behavior of Socially Aggressive Boys." *Behavior Research and Therapy* 4:361–77.

Warren, N. C. and L. N. Rice. 1972. "Structuring and Stabilizing of Psychotherapy for Low Prognosis Clients." *Journal of Consulting and Clinical Psychology* 39:173–81.

Weathers, L. and R. Liberman. 1975. "Contingency Contracting with Families of Delinquent Adolescents." *Behavior Therapy* 6:356–66.

Wellisch, D., J. Vincent, and G. Ro-Trock. 1976. "Family Therapy versus Individual Therapy: A Study of Adolescents and Their Parents." In D.

H. L. Olson, ed., *Treating Relationships*, pp. 275–302. Lake Mills, Iowa: Graphic Press.

Wells, R. A. 1979. "Family Therapy Outcome Research: What *Are* the Findings?" School of Social Work, University of Pittsburgh. Manuscript.

——1980. "Engagement Techniques in Family Therapy." *International Journal of Family Therapy*, in press.

Wells, R. A. and A. E. Dezen. 1978a. "The Results of Family Therapy Revisited: The Nonbehavioral Methods." *Family Process* 17:251–74.

——1978b. "Ideologies, Idols (and Graven Images?): Rejoinder to Gurman and Kniskern." *Family Process* 17:283–86.

Wells, R. A., T. C. Dilkes, and N. Trivelli. 1972. "The Results of Family Therapy: A Critical Review of the Literature." *Family Process* 7:189–207.

White, S., M. Day, S. Hantman, and K. Messenger. 1973. *Federal Programs for Young Children: Review and Recommendations*, vol. 2. Washington, D.C.: Government Printing Office.

Wiltz, N. A. and G. R. Patterson. 1974. "An Evaluation of Parent Training Procedures Designed to Alter Inappropriate Aggressive Behavior in Boys." *Behavior Therapy* 5:215–21.

Winter, W. D. 1971. "Family Therapy: Research and Theory." In C. D. Speilberger, ed., *Current Topics in Clinical and Community Psychology*, vol. 3, pp. 95–121. New York: Academic Press.

Woodward, C. A., J. Santa-Barbara, S. Levin, N. Epstein, and D. L. Streiner. 1977. "The McMaster Family Therapy Outcome Study: III. Client and Treatment Characteristics Significantly Contributing to Clinical Outcomes." Paper presented at the 54th Annual Meeting of the American Orthopsychiatric Association.

Zuk, G. 1972. *Family Therapy: A Triadic-Based Approach*. New York: Behavioral Publications.

——1978. "Values and Family Therapy." *Psychotherapy: Theory, Research and Practice* 15:48–55.

11

Family Treatment within a Task-Centered Framework

WILLIAM J. REID

For a number of years Eleanor Tolson and I have worked with Laura Epstein and others in the development of the task-centered model of social work practice (Reid 1978; Tolson 1977; Epstein 1980; Reid and Epstein 1972). In planning the Towle Conference, we had considered preparing a paper ourselves on task-centered family treatment but decided not to for several reasons. First, the task-centered model could not be considered a major family treatment approach on par with the others presented at the conference, even though the model is widely used in social work and has been employed in work with families (Wexler 1977; Ewalt 1977; Wise 1977; Bass 1977; Reid 1977; Tolson 1977; Reid 1978; Butler, Bow, and Gibbons 1979). In particular, the model was not well developed in terms of theory and methods for work with total family systems, and we had accumulated only a modest amount of experience in applying the model with two-parent families. Second, it was hoped that papers presented at the conference would help us enlarge the body of theory and methods relevant to treatment of families. Finally, the task-centered approach was designed to be an eclectic model of practice and has in the course of its development incorporated contributions from diverse points of view. Consequently, we thought it might provide a framework that would be able to encompass at least some of the range of ideas and methods presented in the conference papers. These reasons in combination caused us to defer the preparation of the present article until we had an opportunity

Portions of this paper have been adapted from William J. Reid, *The Task-Centered System*.

to digest the wealth of material presented at the conference. As a concluding contribution, it presents our own approach to family treatment—one that is informed by the variety of approaches that form the backbone of this volume.

In general, the task-centered approach can be described as a short-term, structured, problem-solving practice model. In early interviews, practitioners and clients identify and agree upon specific target problems as focus for work. Treatment strategy is centered around developing, planning, and implementing problem-solving actions or tasks which may be carried out either by the clients or practitioners.

If the task-centered model in general is designed to help people with problems of living, its adaptation for family treatment might be thought of as directed toward helping people with problems of living *together*—that is, with problems of family relations. In the summary to follow, I shall present the major concepts, principles, and methods of task-centered family treatment somewhat in the order that they might be considered and applied during the progress of a case.

Target Problems

The central theme of initial encounters with families is the identification of target problems—specific difficulties that practitioners and clients define and agree to work on. Target problems must be *acknowledged* by clients—that is, the client must say, in effect, "This is troubling me," regardless of what he or she thinks may be responsible for the difficulty.[1]

Although a problem in the family relations necessarily involves interaction among family members, the problem may be expressed at different "interactional levels" (Bernal and Baker 1979). At the individual level, the client presents the difficulty in terms that separate himself from other family members. "I lose my temper too much with my children" or "My wife blows up at the drop of a hat." As the second example illustrates, an acknowledged problem may be centered on the behavior of another who explicitly or implicitly may be blamed for the difficulty. Acknowledging that one has a problem is not the same as accepting responsibility for it. At the transactional or relational levels, to continue with the Bernal and Baker scheme, the problem is

---

[1] In what follows "he" will be used to refer to clients; "she" for the practitioner.

expressed as involving at least two family members who may be separately identified (transactional) or referred to as a unit (relational). An
example of the former would be "My husband blows up all the time
but I probably provoke him"; the latter is illustrated by "We quarrel
excessively," or "Our family is full of conflict."

When asked to state problems, each family member may produce
several; thus one normally begins with a pool of problem statements
from different perspectives. Various patterns of initial agreement or
disagreement are, of course, possible. A family member may agree or
disagree with another's acknowledged problem cast at an individual
level. If a wife complains that her husband seldom displays affection,
her spouse can accept, reject, or qualify the validity of her assertion.
Similarly, a statement of the problem at the relational level may be
agreed to or not agreed to. "We constantly bicker with one another,"
says mother about the family. The daughter agrees; father does not.

In our approach, such problem perceptions provide the raw material
from which focal or target problems are fashioned in collaboration with
the family. While the practitioner may attempt to reconcile conflicting
problem perceptions or to provide input that may alter them, in the
final analysis the problems to be worked on are those acknowledged
by clients.

Practitioners do not attempt to work on "underlying" problems of
personality or family dynamics that have not been explicated with
clients or accepted by them. This position, we think, avoids ethical
problems that might arise when pracitioners pursue hidden agendas for
change of presumed difficulties not shared with clients. It also takes
full advantage of the clients' problem-solving capacities. Clients will
work harder and more effectively on problems they acknowledge and
wish to solve than on difficulties defined largely (and often mysteri-
ously) by the therapist. Thus, in the case discussed by the conference
participants (article 9), a task-centered practitioner would agree with
Segal that the parents presumed marital problems were "their own
business."

Acknowledged problems can be contrasted with *attributed* problems,
those difficulties that do not reflect what the person wants but rather
what others think that he may be afflicted with. Family members
are forever attributing problems to one another, and practitioners, of
course, can contribute their own overlay of such problems to the family. "My husband is a slob," "Mr. and Mrs. A have formed an alliance

against their daughter,'' and so on. The husband in the example above may see himself as simply casual and the couple may not be aware of their supposed alliance. They have problems only in the sense that others say they have them. The distinction helps in analysis of problems for assessment and treatment-planning purposes. Thus, the problem of the husband's sloppiness is the wife's problem, not his. Unless he acknowledges the difficulty, remedial action will have to come from her. Similarly, practitioners cannot count on clients as full collaborators for problems that the practitioner has attributed to them but that they have not acknowledged.

For these reasons, the direct target of intervention is always an acknowledged problem, although attributed problems may be dealt with indirectly. Thus, a wife whose husband is abusive may be helped to do things to make her husband less abusive. The target problem would concern the wife's difficulties in coping with her husband, not her husband's behavior as such.

The model is addressed to target problems that are relatively specific. Our aim is not to rule out problems that are globally stated at the outset but rather to try to break down such problems into reasonably clear, manageable units before beginning intervention.

A problem may be considered specific if it is explicitly defined and delimited. To say simply that a mother and her eighteen-year-old daughter ''have a disturbed relationship'' is to make a global statement of their problem. The statement becomes more specific when some particular issue is defined: for example, ''They quarrel over her daughter's boyfriend.'' Additional specificity is obtained if we observe what the quarrel is about (mother thinks the boyfriend is ''unsuitable'' and daughter feels she has a right to choose her own friends), and if we can obtain data on the frequency and severity of the quarrels.

In work with families, we must recognize, of course, that specific relational problems are often outcroppings of more general difficulties, a point elaborated on below. In the example given, the quarrel over the boyfriend may be only one of several conflicts between mother and daughter—conflicts that may, in turn, be connected to their interactions with other members of the family. It is assumed, nevertheless, that more can be accomplished if a small number of specific problems, usually up to a limit of three or four, are concentrated on than if the practitioner and family attempt to struggle with global issues. The relative success of short-term family treatment approaches in which specific problems are usually the center of attention supports this assumption (Reid and Shyne 1969; Gurman and Kniskern, 1979; Wells, article 10).

While problems in family relations are interconnected, there is little evidence to support the notion that alleviation of one problem will be necessarily undone by the emergence of a substitute. On the contrary, concentration on a small number of focal problems can have a positive impact on family relations in general. In fact, resolution of specific relational problems may not be possible without some give in underlying patterns of interaction, which may need to be addressed as part of the work on these problems.

In order for these assumptions to hold, however, the problem to be worked on needs to fall within an "optimal" range of specificity. If it is defined too globally, the practitioner and clients will find it hard to focus adequate attention on essential particulars. If it is defined too narrowly, there is the danger of dealing with difficulties that are too limited or ephemeral to provide sufficient purchase to bring about meaningful change. Thus "conflict between father and son about son's keeping his room clean" might be too narrow if it is one part of a running series of battles concerning the son's contribution to household chores. Although firm criteria for defining an optimal range of specificty have not been developed, it is hoped that the examples provided here and elsewhere in the essay will convey a sense of this range.

The Dynamics of Family Problems

Our theory of problem dynamics is based on a framework developed by Goldman (1970). According to Goldman, the person is propelled by *wants*, or the awareness of what one desires. Wants result in *action* taken to bring about their satisfaction. Action is guided by one's *beliefs* (cognitions and values) about self and world and by affects generated by beliefs. Beliefs, affects, and actions in turn shape wants. Thus major elements of the paradigm continually interact in the process of living.

In our adaptation of this framework, acknowledged problems arise when wants are unsatisfied. Thus, the wife who complains that her husband does not express affection, presumably wants more expressions of affection from him than she is receiving. Children who complain their parents are running their lives presumably want more freedom and independence. People with such problems normally take action to satisfy the wants that underlie them and often they succeed, at least to a reasonable degree. Clients seen by helping professionals have usually acted to alleviate their problems, but their solutions have not worked.

In our analysis of what is wrong, we focus accordingly on what clients say they want and what is preventing them from getting it. Consideration of what clients want is the first order of business, since these wants form the basis of the target problems that will be worked on. Although whatever wants clients express are taken seriously, we expect that a process of clarification and negotiation will take place with the practitioner in the initial session(s) before agreement on target problems is reached. Difficulties in realizing certain wants may be pointed out; vague wishes may be specified; expectations of significant others outside the family system—such as judges, teachers, and physicians—may be introduced; conflicting wants among family members, particularly conflicts over what they want of one another, may be brought to the surface. As a result of this process, the client's initial wants may undergo some modification and new ones may emerge. Wants reflecting "head on" conflicts between family members (I want her to stop spending money foolishly; I want him to stop criticizing me about how I spend money) are, if possible, reformulated to reflect mutual, and attainable, goals (We both want to argue less about money). In other words, we attempt to proceed on the basis of wants that have been considered in response to the practitioner's contributions.

Problems in family relations should also be understood in terms of two additional dimensions that define their character and explain their existence: family members' beliefs about one another and about family life; the patterns or rules that characterize family interaction. The beliefs (cognitions, images, conceptions, values, and so forth) that family members hold about each other have complex and multiple origins that would include (for adult members) experiences in their own families of origin (articles 5 and 7) and interactions within the present family system. These beliefs determine to a large extent how family members will relate to and feel toward one another, since we assume (in agreement with Beck [1976] and other cognitive theorists) that cognitions guide action and mediate emotional responses.

In relations characterized by conflict, participants are likely to develop distorted conceptions of one another. Anxiety, frustration, and hostility breed unrealistically negative and oversimplified images. A wife who may lose her temper with the children two or three times a week, and only upon considerable provocation, is seen by her husband as "always blowing her top at the kids." The wife regards her husband, whom most would see as merely cautious in money matters, as a "miser." Often one finds that spouses tend to think of one another in terms of pejorative labels, and that they lack balanced, differentiated conceptions of each other. Negative, distorted beliefs are likely to become even more dominant during periods of acute conflict; under emotional stress, the pejorative label may closely reflect the image the partner has of the other. The husband who in anger shouts at his wife that she is an "imbecile" may well see her at that moment as grossly limited in intelligence. In the absence of stress, partners may appraise—or be able to appraise—the attributes of their partners more objectively.

Differences among family members in respect to *values* about family life (which we include as a part of a person's belief system) provide additional dimensions to family conflict. The work of Spiegel (article 6) makes a direct contribution to the model in this respect. As he suggests, the notion of variations in value orientations is useful not only in treatment of ethnic families but also of families within the mainstream of American culture.

In general, one can think of each family member (and practitioner) as having a unique set of value orientations derived from a variety of cultural influences, including those within the American mainstream. A good deal of family conflict, or conflict between practitioners and family members, can be viewed in terms of these value orientations.

For example, in respect to time orientation, Spiegel observes that in the American middle class the dominant orientation is toward the future. But variations in emphasis or in relation to specific contexts can occur. Though the variations may be subtle, they may be a source of conflict among family members, particularly as differences grate upon one another over the years. For example, a future-oriented husband and wife may both subscribe to the importance of saving for their children's college educations or for unanticipated expenses. They may differ, however, in respect to such issues as how much should be saved. The wife may be more "present" oriented, let us say, than her husband. She may think it is time that they use some of their resources to get some "fun out of life" and may propose an expensive trip abroad. The husband might see the wife's plan as frivolous, considering their responsibilities. Although parents may agree that their eighteen-year-old son should be accorded a good deal of independence, they may still disagree in critical ways about degree and kind. The mother, whose value orientation in respect to her son may still be lineal, may insist that the son inform them when he plans to return home when he goes out for the evening. The son, who has adopted an individual orientation regarding his place in the family, may feel that this requirement is unnecessary. His father may agree. A bitter quarrel may result and repeated conflict may occur along this line of difference.

Spiegel comments on tendencies to "pathologize" such differences (p. 132). Depending on their own value orientations, family therapists might view the wife in the first example as "impulsive" and the mother in the second as "overcontrolling." Labeling of this kind glosses over important differences in evaluative beliefs about family life—differences that may need to be examined, clarified, and negotiated.

It is also assumed that most problems of family relations, regardless of the particular form they take, are the expression or outgrowth of *rules* that characterize the interaction. This assumption has its origins in the works of Haley (1963); Jackson (1965); Watzlawick, Beavin, and Jackson (1967), and others who have used the concept of rules to organize thinking about marital and family interaction.

As used here, the term "rule" refers to regularities in interaction, either actual or potential. Actual or *descriptive* rules characterize repetitive patterns of interaction in the past or present. When mother disparages daughter, father comes to the daughter's support and attacks mother. As Haley (1963) has pointed out, such rules may be recognized by family members or carried out without their being aware of the pattern, which can nevertheless be discerned by an outside observer. Or the existence of a rule may be asserted by one member and denied by another.

Rules that purport to describe empirical events can be distinguished from prescriptive rules, which express conceptions of how interaction *ought to* occur, as in, "We should be able to discuss our in-laws without criticizing them." A prescriptive rule may have a close fit to actual interaction, but expresses an evaluation, not a description. The difference can be appreciated in such statements as, "We shouldn't argue in front of the children, even though we do." For families in conflict, descriptive rules generally describe problem aspects, whereas prescriptive rules usually express the kind of relationship that family members would like to have. "We always avoid each other; we should enjoy doing things together."

Rules can be considered to be desirable or undesirable from various points of view. Clients usually evaluate rules according to how they may contribute to their satisfaction with family life. The practitioner's evaluation of rules takes into account disagreements between clients about what rules are desirable or undesirable, and also considers the ramifications of different rules (including those not recognized by the clients) for various aspects of family functioning.

Family members' references to rules that they negatively evaluate are likely to be in terms of complaints about each other's behavior. Thus, a wife may accuse her husband of criticizing her in front of company, and the husband may assert that she needs to be reminded when she is making a fool of herself. Neither is likely to put the rule in objective terms: that certain behaviors of the wife are likely to be followed by certain behaviors of the husband. As Watzlawick, Beavin, and Jackson (1967) have observed, marital partners tend to "punctuate" rules in this manner by attributing causation and blame to the other partner.

The presence of a rule of interaction may at first glance be difficult to discern when one partner's behavior is defined as "the problem." "My husband is an alcoholic," a wife may say as a way of summing up the marital difficulty. Her husband may agree with her formulation of the problem. But some reflection will show that the husband's drinking behavior, no matter how much of a problem in its own right, does not define the marital difficulty. It is more accurate to say that the husband's drinking (or his behavior when drinking) causes the wife to be upset. In other words, we have the combination of a patterned action and response which form the nucleus of a rule of interaction. If the wife is not upset by the husband's drinking or associated behavior, we do not have a marital problem.

Interaction rules may be relatively specific and narrow in scope. In the brief case segment viewed by the conference participants (article 9), an interaction rule, which the conferees commented on in different ways, quickly established itself in the interchanges between father, mother, and son. Father reacted to Jim with a sort of benevolent bossiness, his mother with depreciating sarcasm—a pattern that repeated itself several times in the course of a few minutes. Or rules may constitute an overarching theme in a family. In the case presented by

Spark (article 5), Joe and his wife are described as having a parent-child relationship. Higher-order rules of interaction which Haley (1963) has termed metarules, may influence more specific patterns. Thus the norm of reciprocity (article 4) may be used as a guide for determining a couple's interactions in carrying out domestic tasks. Or the general tendency of one partner to dominate another may help predict characteristics of their interactions in new situations.

While rules focus on regularities in *interaction*, relevant data about cognitive and affective reactions of participants can be added. In this way the dynamics of the rules can be better understood. Thus from interactional data only, we might learn that a husband explodes over "little things," that his wife withdraws; and that these episodes appear to be followed by periods when they communicate little and do not have sex. Investigation of the inner reactions of the participants may reveal that the husband's tantrums over trivia make the wife feel deeply resentful and destroy her appetite for either talk or sex. Her withdrawal, which husband interprets as punitive, causes a buildup of anger which leads to the explosive outbursts. The operation of the rule, particularly its vicious circle quality, is obviously illuminated by the cognitive and affective data.

Most problems in family relations that become targets of intervention are, then, reflections of unsatisfied wants about rules. "My parents are always on my back," is a way of saying that "I want my parents to give me more freedom." Or, "We fight all the time over money," reflects a desire for a pattern of interaction in which financial matters can be discussed without quarreling. As the examples suggest, a problem can be analyzed both in terms of the descriptive rule that is not wanted and the prescriptive rule that family members would like to see replace it.

Target problems must also be related to a larger context which includes the patterns of interactions characteristic of the family as a whole, the personalities and behaviors of family members, the family's socioeconomic position, its ethnicity, and it relation to the community. In the present system, the nature of the data to be collected about such factors is primarily determined by the target problems. From these focal concerns, the practitioner branches out into other areas of the family's functioning and situation. The intent is not, as in some models of practice, to gather and sift a large body of information about these areas to serve as a basis for determining what the client's difficulties are. Rather, the purpose is to secure information that will provide guidance in work with problems whose essential outlines have already been determined, not on the basis of what is "wrong" from a theoretical perspective but on the basis of what is troubling the client.

Treatment Structure: Participants; Contracting; Duration

As Tolson observes in the following essay, the question of who should participate in family treatment is answered quite differently by different schools. In the task-centered approach, the answer to this question depends on the nature of the acknowledged problems. Since our targets are problems in family relations, a given target problem involves at least a dyad, such as a marital couple or a parent and child. Our preference is to see clients involved in the same problem or in an interrelated set of problems together in multiple interviews. Multiple interviews appear to provide the best means of exploring and modifying rules of interaction, an objective central to our approach. The opportunity in multiple interviews to work with live interacting systems is a particular advantage. Moreover, this mode of interviewing provides considerable economy in a short-term treatment approach. A common pattern is to use some mixture of individual and joint interviews. Cases in which only one client is seen throughout tend to be those where other participants in the problem are reluctant to become involved in treatment, where the client seen does not want to bring in other family members, or where the family problem is relatively minor in comparison to other issues.

Consideration of single-client cases brings us back to definitional issues raised in preceding papers: In what sense is work with a single client family treatment? In our approach, such work could be considered family treatment if the target problem involved family relations. In respect to this definitional question, this volume has by now probably made one point quite clear: that "family treatment" is a generic expression that can cover a wide range of approaches to helping familes or individual family members. While useful for some purposes (including titles of books such as ours!), it is not helpful if precise descriptions are called for. For example, within the task-centered framework one can describe treatment much more precisely by specifying the kind of problem that is being worked on, and the types of interviews, or other client contacts, that are used.

While the question of who participates in treatment depends on the problem and the willingness of family members to become involved, other aspects of treatment structure are relatively standard. An oral or written contract is developed after tentative accord has been reached on the target problems. The contract states the problems to be worked on, their desired solutions (goals), and the expected duration and amount of service. Formulation of the initial contract establishes the principle that the purposes and nature of the worker-client relationship will be controlled by explicit agreements rather than by the practitioner's hidden agenda. It is normally the first in a series of contractual arrangements, which may include modifications in the initial contract and agreements on additional problems to be dealt with, on client tasks, and on practitioner responsibilities. In this way, the contracting process continues during the life of the case.

Task-centered intervention is generally limited by plan to a specified number of sessions within a specified time period. In current practice, there is considerable variation in number of interviews and time span, depending on the nature of the problem and on the frequency and duration of the interviews. In work with families, a plan for eight sessions within a two- to three-month period is fairly typical. Extensions of agreed-upon limits are provided primarily in response to requests by clients for additional service.

The relative effectiveness of short-term approaches as compared to long-term modalities in work with families has been well documented by Wells (article 10). Exactly why brief treatment appears to work at least as well as more extended forms of service is still an unsettled question. Possible answers include the tendency for most family problems to restabilize (at least to a point of tolerance) rather quickly, difficulties in maintaining involvement of relevant family members in lengthy periods of treatment, limitations on what practitioners can offer a given family at a given time, and the mobilization of practitioner and client effort that may result from working against prearranged time limits.

The core of our intervention strategy consists in helping the family members plan and execute problem-solving actions or tasks. Sessions with the clients are used to determine what they should do and how and why they should do it; to help them rehearse and practice agreed-upon actions; to analyze obstacles that might prevent them from carrying such actions out, and to review what they have been able to accomplish. Although a good portion of each session may be devoted to additional exploration of the target problems, particularly to specify rules of intervention relating to them, the exploration is directed by a search for the kinds of client actions that may be best able to alleviate the problems. Key activities and related concepts are elaborated here.

Task Planning

Once agreement has been reached on the targets and duration of treatment, tasks are formulated and selected in collaboration with the clients. In the context of family treatment, tasks refer to planned actions family members agree to undertake to alleviate target problems. A task may be cast at different levels of abstraction. A *general* task provides a direction for action but does not specify what is to be done. For example, Mrs. A and Harold (her son) are to work toward greater independence from one another. Mr. B will spend more time with Janice (his daughter). Operational tasks call for specific actions to be undertaken. Mr. and Mrs. C are to go out for dinner during the week. General tasks tend to be emphasized by practitioners, including those with psychodynamic orientations, who rely on classical techniques, such as helping clients develop insight into the dynamics of their relationships. In such applications, tasks serve much the same function as statements of goals, that is, the tasks provide explicit foci and directions for work. Not surprisingly, practitioners who are behaviorally or empirically oriented stress operational tasks. This hierarchy of task levels is, of course, compatible with eclectic practice approaches in which the practitioner may derive operational from general tasks, or use both in other combinations. I shall focus, however, on tasks at the operational level, where our work in recent years has been concentrated.

Tasks addressed to problems of family interaction can also be divided into reciprocal, shared, and individual types. Each type has a different structure and different planning requirements. Reciprocal tasks call for different actions by family members on the basis of a quid pro quo exchange. Such tasks are usually used with dyads, although they may involve more than two family members. Since the actions are paired by the notion of reciprocity (article 4), each participant must value the intended actions of the other and must perceive those actions to be a reasonable exchange for his efforts. The details of the actions must be planned, but with allowance being made for variations that may be indicated by circumstances. Planning must take account of how participants may react if certain contingencies arise. For example, if a husband's task is to call home when he is delayed at work, and his wife's reciprocal task is to respond in a calm, accepting manner when her husband calls, one might consider such contingencies as the husband's not being able to get to a phone and the wife's being out when he calls.

A contingency that should be considered is that one participant will not carry out his part of the bargain. In setting up the tasks, it is desirable to have each make a commitment to do his part even if the other does not. If one is able to complete the task, the other may be stimulated to follow through at a later point, or at least make some positive response. The double commitment also helps avoid interactions in which participants back away from doing the task because each perceives the other to be shirking responsibility.

Shared tasks call for family members to work closely together in a cooperative manner. A single task statement beginning with the names of the task participants is used rather than separate statements, as in the case of reciprocal tasks. Thus, a father and son may agree to spend the weekend working together on a project. I shall briefly discuss three types of commonly used shared tasks: joint problem-solving tasks, conversation tasks, and enjoyable-activity tasks.

In *joint problem-solving tasks*, family members undertake to resolve some specific issue or modify a rule of interaction through face-to-face communication. Participants attempt to clarify the issue or rule, discuss alternative means of resolution or change, and try to formulate a plan of action. If a descriptive rule of interaction is under consideration, the participants, with the practitioner's assistance, may try to develop a prescriptive rule they can agree on. Thus, a mother and son may wish to change their pattern (descriptive rule) of the son's leaving the house in a temper in response to criticism from his mother. The prescriptive rule they work out may call for the mother to overlook certain behaviors of the son that normally provoke her criticism, while he, in exchange, may agree to try to maintain normal interaction when his mother does say something critical.

Tasks to be carried out in their day-to-day interaction can then be devised to implement plans that emanate from this problem-solving process, although often participants will carry out necessary action on their own initiative once they have agreed what is to be done. Joint problem-solving tasks can either be worked on in the session (as will be shown later) or at home.

Conversation tasks may be designed to help family members resolve problems in face-to-face communication. Thus, a couple's task may be to discuss one or more issues without making reference to each other's past misdeeds, to refer only to the actual behavior as opposed to inferred motives or attitudes of the other, to stick to one topic for a certain length of time, or to avoid interrupting one another.

A third common type of shared task calls for family members to engage in some mutually enjoyable activity, such as going out to the movies together. Such *enjoyable-activity tasks* are designed to reduce distance and isolation, and to help family members find ways of deriving pleasure from their relationships. Such tasks are often suggested by the worker. Instigation of enjoyable activities may enable family members to "get out of a rut," to break up existing patterns of mutual withdrawal and isolative behavior that no one particularly wants but that no one can take the initiative to alter. For example, a spouse may be reluctant to propose an activity because of fears of rejection by the other but may welcome the worker's suggesting it. That the activity is cast as part of treatment adds to its legitimacy. Obviously, timing is important; enjoyable-activity tasks will be rejected or may be counterproductive if a relationship is seething with conflict. It is also important that all participants regard the proposed activity as enjoyable.

Unlike reciprocal or shared tasks, individual tasks are carried out independently by family members. Although individual tasks may be guided by the norm of reciprocity, they are not paired in explicit quid pro quo fashion as are reciprocal tasks. For example, a couple may agree on a set of reciprocal and shared tasks but one partner may agree to take on an extra task. Or each partner may carry out a task unrelated to the task of the other and without an understanding that completion of the two tasks represents an exchange.

Individual tasks are used in several ways in family treatment. First, there may be need for one member to work on a problem in which the other is not involved but that is still affecting family relationships. For example, difficulties at work may be affecting the way a wife relates to her husband and children. Second, one participant may be willing and able to do more than others during a given phase of treatment; individual tasks can be used as the means. Finally, use of individual tasks may be indicated when the degree of overt antagonism or mistrustfulness in a relationship is too great for the development or execution of reciprocal or shared tasks. In such situations, the individual tasks may have to be limited to whatever each participant is willing to do in whatever area of the relationship he is willing to do it. For example, in one case—where the husband and wife were quarreling continually in the treatment sessions and at home, over a half dozen or so poorly defined issues—the best that could be done at the beginning was for the husband to make an effort to engage his adolescent son in a conversation about his school problems and for the wife to make a listing of their numerous debts.

The kind of paradoxical tasks advocated by Segal (article 8) can be used within the framework of the model, but they are employed on a more limited and experimental basis than in Segal's approach. We make more optimistic assumptions about the client's "attempted solutions" than Segal apparently does. Often these efforts at solution may be on the right track and can be built upon; if not, other keys to alleviating the problem may be found in straightforward common sense tasks. Another reason for our caution about paradoxical tasks is lack of much systematic evidence concerning their effectiveness—particularly evidence that would suggest when they may or may not work.

Two structures for task formulation can be used. In one, the practitioner may elicit task possibilities from each family member, may suggest tasks to them, and help them arrive at feasible, mutually acceptable tasks. In the second approach, the practitioner uses structured interaction among family members as a vehicle for task formulation. She may ask them in effect to discuss task possibilities between themselves and to come up with tasks each might carry out. The practitioner then takes on the role of facilitator, the kind epitomized in Bell's approach (article 2). She may intervene to keep family members focused on the subject, to help them clarify what they are saying to one another, to encourage each to express alternative actions other members might undertake, and to make agreements firmer.

Often the practitioner is the primary generator of task possibilities. The client may not be able to produce much on his own. Moreover, the practitioner may have special knowledge about kinds of tasks that generally work well for particular problems. It should be kept in mind, however, that the practitioner proposes *ideas* for tasks which are then gone over with the clients. The clients' contributions normally become a part of the task plan. The practitioner does not "assign" tasks to clients. In any event, a final agreement on the task is made at the end of the planning process, after it is determined what the implementation of the task will involve.

Establishing Incentives and Rationale

Incentives and rationales for the tasks to be undertaken need to be established with each participant before the task plan is settled. The incentive for each in reciprocal tasks is usually the anticipated change in the other's behavior. As suggested earlier, parity in the exchange is a crucial consideration. Neither participant should feel that he is carrying an unfair burden. This criterion does not mean that the tasks themselves need to be "equal" in any particular exchange. What counts is each partner's *perception* of fairness, which can be influenced by many factors. Metarules concerning social norms can affect their perception: one participant may be willing to take on a more onerous task because his behavior represents greater deviation than the other's from their conception of the norms of family life. Thus, a husband may agree to come home from work without his customary two-hour layover in a tavern in exchange for a pleasant greeting from his wife. One participant may be willing to undertake an individual task with the expectation of being paid back at a later point or in some other way.

Guided Practice and Simulation

In-session work on joint problem-solving and conversation tasks makes use of guided practice and simulation with participants. That is, clients and practitioners can work on actual tasks in the session (guided practice) or can role play task behavior (simulation).

In guided practice, the practitioner assumes the role of a task "coach." She observes the partner's performance, praises actions that further the task, structures their communication, pinpoints difficulties, and provides feedback to help correct them. She may suggest alterations in joint problem-solving tasks or raise questions about alternatives that the partners suggest. These activities are also used in role play; but, in addition, she may take roles of different family members to model desirable responses. Tape recordings of the participant's communication are used to give partners a vivid picture of what has just occurred between them and enable the practitioner to point out specific aspects of their interaction that may need further work.

Structured training in communication skills provides other variants of simulation and guided practice activities (Thomas 1976; Guzzetta 1976; Kifer et al. 1974; Gambrill article 4). In some cases, elements of existing training programs are used; in others such programs are used adjunctively; in still others they provide the core of intervention.

In problems of family relations, analysis of obstacles to task achievement is primarily addressed to beliefs participants have about one another and about the rules of their interaction. Family members who view one another in negative terms, or who disagree about the rules of their interaction, are not likely to complete conflict-reducing tasks.

The practitioner can help family members acquire more accurate and discriminating pictures of each other in several ways. At a minimal level, she can call attention to negative stereotypes and raise question about their validity. Through further probing, she can try to elicit instances of behavior that would give each partner a better-differentiated picture of the other. She may also try to help each view the other's attributes or behaviors within their motivational and situational contexts. Thus, the husband who thinks of his wife as a pepper pot with the children may be asked how often she loses her temper with them and under what circumstances. He may begin to see that this behavior occurs less often than he thinks and to realize that it may be understandable in view of her day-long child care responsibilities and the children's provocations.

In carrying out this kind of image reconstruction in multiple interviews, the practitioner usually forms a temporary alliance with the partner who is being stereotyped. In the example just cited, the wife should be able to supply evidence that would help break down her husband's negative image. The practitioner would then try to take up one of her stereotypes of him, and then ally, again temporarily, with the other partner. Teaching clients how to respond empathically to one another on the basis of realistic images of each other (Guzzetta 1976), having each depict in writing characteristics of the other, or having them collect data on occurrences of certain behaviors, are other ways of undoing negative stereotypes.

Beliefs about rules of interaction, including value orientations, become obstacles when there is disagreement between family members about what these rules (or metarules) should be. The disputes then concern the prescriptive rules that the partners want to have govern their interaction. Mrs. A believes that the family should do things together Sunday afternoon; Mr. A does not want to be locked in to such a routine.

While such disagreements may emerge as obstacles to tasks already planned and attempted, they frequently enter the picture during task planning or clarification of the problem. In any event, some resolution may be necessary before tasks can be satisfactorily planned.

The practitioner's role in these disagreements resembles that of a negotiator. In this role, she does not attempt to impose her own values but may suggest ways of reformulating the rules. The key to the solution may be found in use of a metarule that family members can accept, such as principles of reciprocity or compromise. Mr. and Mrs. A may agree to devote alternate Sunday afternoons to family activities.

Application to Marital Subsystems

Discussion of applications of the model to family subsystems will be limited to marital pairs, since our efforts here have been more extensive and better studied than applications to other subsystems. The presentation of task-centered treatment of marital problems will also provide an opportunity to elaborate further on some features of the model that can be applied more generally to work with families, as well as to introduce a more fully developed example of task-centered intervention.

In any short-term model of marital treatment, practitioners must struggle from the outset with the issue of how to combine contradictory requirements for rapid intervention, on the one hand, and a depth of understanding on the other. While this issue must be faced in any form of family treatment, it is highlighted by the entangled compexities of marital relationships. Although the important problems dividing a couple become visible rather quickly, the intricate patterns of interaction that define the depths of these difficulties may take time to decipher. This puts the practitioner in a dilemma. If she takes several interviews to understand these patterns, the contracted service period may be half over. Moreover, she may no longer have a couple there to intervene with and, in any case, she has lost the momentum for change that is often generated when a couple decides to seek help. On the other hand, if she starts treatment of specific problems in the first interview, she runs the risk of becoming locked into an intervention strategy that may be based on premature premises.

This issue can be dealt with through a two-track intervention strategy. On one track, the practitioner tries to identify and clarify at least one problem of immediate concern to the couple, and to develop with them tasks they can carry out to alleviate that problem prior to the next meeting. By this means, the practitioner can capitalize on initial motivations for change, and develops with the couple, from the beginning, the very useful orientation that if they are going to resolve their problems, they are going to have to do something about them. Often these initial tasks are carried out and, if so, treatment is off to a good beginning. While still dealing with problems as initially defined, the practitioner begins to move along a second track, which is to try to understand the patterns or rules of interaction that give rise to them.

An effort is made to keep this process of probing and clarifying still connected to agreed-upon target problems but, in the process, these problems may become redefined. In any case, the patterns of interaction in which the problems are embedded should become clearer. While some clients do benefit directly from such insight into the workings of their relationship, the main purpose of clarifying the interaction pattern is to lay the groundwork for tasks designed to change them. These tasks, addressed to aspects of interaction that were initially unclear, resemble the non-paradoxical directives or tasks proposed by Haley (1976).

Frequently, the path to these crucial tasks cannot be discovered or even searched for intelligently until initial tasks based on simpler premises have been tried and have failed. This is not to say that simpler or more straightforward tasks are doomed to failure because often they do succeed. When they do fail, the failure can be quite instructive.

Some of these points, as well as other aspects of work with marital pairs, will be illustrated with an example from a task-centered case—a young working couple who had, among other difficulties, a communication problem of the following description. The wife, Dena, complained that her husband, Harold, an accountant, was frequently uncommunicative and irritable in the evening, apparently upset over problems at work. When she would try to draw him out, he would snap at her churlishly, telling her that he wanted to be left alone, that he didn't want to talk about whatever was bothering him, there was nothing that she could say that would help anyway, and so on. The wife responded by becoming hurt and angry, accusing her husband of being secretive. The result was not a quarrel; it was an evening spent in mutually hostile silence with both depressed. Straightforward tasks, such as requesting the husband to tell his wife what was on his mind and asking the wife, in exchange, to avoid attempts to draw her husband out when he was in these moods, failed to accomplish much. The couple seemed unable to carry them out. The pattern persisted.

Intensive analysis of this pattern over two interviews helped to clarify its dynamics. Harold was not normally an uncommunicative person; in fact, he was quite articulate. But he found talking to his wife about his problems at work when he felt depressed about them to be a frustrating and demeaning experience. He had never told her much about the job. It was a relatively new position and highly technical. Although the problems at work concerned difficulties with his supervisor, the problems were intertwined with the technical aspects of his position. The only time they ever talked about his work was when he was upset about it, and then he was in no mood to explain to her exactly what the difficulties were in a way that she could understand them. He would rather make a few cryptic comments about the job problem—comments that Dena could not fully comprehend. She would then respond, at least initially, in a generally sympathetic way, with expressions like, "Gee, that's too bad," or "Well, maybe you should think about getting another job." Rather than soothing her husband, such generalized expressions of sympathy proved irritating. In his words, they reminded him of his mother telling him that a bruised knee would feel better tomorrow. Expecting some appreciation, at least, for her expressions of concern, Dena found her husband's anger incomprehensible and interpreted it as a personal rejection of her. As we know, a person who likes to give to others, and Dena was such a person, likes to be given something in return.

When this degree of clarity had been achieved, a number of task possibilities became apparent. The strategy followed was to develop a shared task in which the couple would discuss his job when he was *not* depressed about it. In order that she could understand what was going on, he was to explain its technical aspects and how they were interconnected with his relationship to his supervisor. She was not to express sympathy or probe for problems but simply to ask matter-of-fact questions so that she could understand what it was all about. They began this communication task in the interview with the practitioner taking the role of coach. The couple continued to work on the task at home. This was followed by a task in which they were asked to spend some time each day talking about events at work—not necessarily problems but other things that for whatever reason might be of interest to both of them. In this way, they could, and did, begin to ease naturally into discussion of his problems at work, but in a way that enabled them both to discuss them in a natural and adult fashion. These tasks proved helpful in alleviating the problem of poor communication when Harold was upset about his job, and this set in motion other positive changes.

Throughout this extended period of exploration and clarification that preceded these tasks, no attempt was made to delve into the past of either spouse or to investigate personality characteristics as such. Though outcroppings of their past and their personalities were very much in evidence, they were dealt with in the context of understanding their current patterns of communication about Harold's job problems. Nor was it necessary to elucidate "deeper" aspects of the relationship—their unconscious bonds, conflicts, and the like. Their increased awareness of their current patterns of interaction may have proved helpful to them, but more important, I think, it pointed the way to a sequence of tasks and ways of implementing them that would not have occurred to anyone had this clarification not taken place.

What was done can, of course, be put in other terms. Segal (article 8) might refer to what was done as an example of reframing the problem. Gambrill (article 9) might see it as an illustration of a complicated behavioral exchange. Within our framework, it exemplifies a way of searching through the complexities of human interaction as a means of locating novel and effective problem-solving actions.

Research on Task-Centered Practice

The task-centered model was designed with the intent that it should be tested and developed through systematic research. Accordingly, a number of developmental (uncontrolled) studies have been carried out (Reid and Epstein 1972; Reid and Epstein 1977) and several controlled experiments have been conducted (Reid 1978; Reid 1975; Gibbons et al. 1978; Tolson 1977; Larsen and Mitchell 1980; Reid et al. 1980). These investigations have provided considerable data on the operations and outcomes of the model across a range of settings and client populations. Findings from the controlled studies have consistently shown that clients receiving the task-centered approach have outperformed controls on measures of problem change.

Three of these controlled studies involved cases concerned with family problems (Tolson 1977; Gibbons et al. 1978; Reid 1978). Using an across-problem, multiple baseline design, Tolson (1977) found that methods of task planning and implementation effectively reduced specific communication problems of a marital couple. Task-centered treatment of marital and personal relation problems received a more extensive test in a large-scale experiment conducted in Southampton, England (Gibbons et al. 1978). Four hundred patients who had taken drug overdoses in apparent suicide attempts were randomly allocated to experimental (task-centered) and control (routine service) groups. Difficulties in "continuing personal relationships," usually problems with a spouse, were reported in two-thirds of the cases. Research interviews were conducted with the patients four and eighteen months following termination of service. Measures of change in personal relationships favored the experimental group at both follow-ups, with statistically significant differences obtained at the second follow-up. In the third controlled study (Reid 1978), task-centered methods were tested with eighty-seven cases divided between adults from a psychiatric outpatient clinic (n = 38) and children and youth, mostly from a public school system (n = 49). About a third of the problems dealt with involved difficulties in family relations. Results showed that significantly more problem alleviation occurred under treatment than under control conditions. It is noteworthy that the adult cases, in which family relationship problems were more in evidence, were relatively more successful than the children's cases.

Programs consisting largely of task-centered treatment of marital or parent-child dyads have been evaluated through several uncontrolled studies (Ewalt 1977; Bass, 1977; Reid, 1977; Rooney, in press). These studies have suggested that the great majority of family units treated have been able to achieve some degree of problem alleviation, though one cannot be certain how much of the change was due to the intervention. Although the research base of task-centered family treatment is still modest, results to date have been encouraging. The premises on which the model is based receive additional support from the relative effectiveness demonstrated by short-term family treatment in general (see article 10).

Work with Poor Families

Our focus on client and practitioner action is in large part the result of our interest in developing a system of practice well suited to the needs and orientation of lower-class (poor) clients. As Goldstein (1973) has documented, clients at lower socioeconomic levels can better utilize and prefer modes of helping that are structured, directive, and action oriented. While reflective methods can be used to advantage within the task-centered framework to help clients examine beliefs about themselves and their situation, these methods are not essential to the model and, when used, are always a part of a larger action-focused strategy. Although the task structure, as we employ it, emphasizes a collaborative effort with the client rather than a unilateral use of practitioner authority, the task-centered practitioner is expected to make use of direct suggestions about task possibilities and about means of task achievement. In fact there is evidence (Reid 1978; Fortune 1979) that considerably more advice giving occurs in task-centered practice than in conventional social treatment approaches. We have not conducted studies comparing the task-centered model to other approaches with lower-class clients but have had considerable experience in using the task-centered model with such clients, who have in fact vastly outnumbered middle-class clients in our work to date. Evaluations by lower-class consumers of task-centered treatment have been quite positive, particularly in respect to such critical considerations as getting the kind of help they wanted and understanding the nature of service (Reid and Epstein 1972; Reid 1978; Rooney, in press).

References

Bass, Michael. 1977. "Toward a Model of Treatment for Runaway Girls in Detention." In Reid and Epstein, eds., *Task-Centered Practice*, q.v.
Beck, Aaron T. 1976. *Cognitive Therapy and Emotional Disorders*. New York: International Universities Press.
Bernal, Guillermo and Jeffrey Baker. 1979. "Toward a Metacommunicational Framework of Couple Interactions." *Family Process* 18:293–301.
Butler, J., Irene Bow, and Jane Gibbons.1979. "Task-Centered Casework with Marital Problems." *British Journal of Social Work* vol. 8, no. 4.
Epstein, Laura. 1980. *Helping People: The Task-Centered Approach*. St. Louis: Mosby Press.
Ewalt, Patricia L. 1977. "A Psychoanalytically Oriented Child Guidance Setting." In Reid and Epstein, eds., *Task-Centered Practice*, q.v.
Fortune, Anne E. 1979. "Communication in Task-Centered Treatment." *Social Work* 24:5.
Gibbons, J. S., J. Butler, P. Urwin, and J. L. Gibbons. 1978. "Evaluation of a Social Work Service for Self-Poisoning Patients." *British Journal of Psychiatry* 133:111–18.

Goldman, Alvin I. 1970. *A Theory of Human Action*. Englewood Cliffs, N.J.: Prentice-Hall.

Goldstein, Arnold P. 1973. *Structured Learning Therapy*. New York: Academic Press.

Gurman, Alan S. and David P. Kniskern. 1978. "Research on Marital and Family Therapy." In G. L. Garfield and A. E. Bergin, eds., *Handbook of Psychotherapy and Behavior Change*. 2d ed., pp. 817-901. New York: Wiley.

Guzzetta, Roberta A. 1976. "Acquisition and Transfer of Empathy by the Parents of Early Adolescents through Structured Learning Training." *Journal of Counseling Psychology* 23:449–53.

Haley, Jay. 1963. *Strategies of Psychotherapy*. New York: Grune and Stratton.

——1976. *Problem-Solving Therapy*. San Francisco and London: Jossey-Bass.

Jackson, Don D. 1965. "Family Rules: The Marital Quid Pro Quo." *Archives of General Psychiatry* 12:589–94.

Kifer, Robert E., Martha Lewis, Donald R. Green, and Elery L. Phillips. 1974. "Training Predelinquent Youths and Their Parents to Negotiate Conflict Situations." *Journal of Applied Behavioral Analysis* 7:357–64.

Larsen, JoAnn and Craig Mitchell. 1980. "Task-Centered Strength-Oriented Group Work with Delinquents." *Social Casework* 61:154–63.

Perlman, Helen Harris. 1957. *Social Casework: A Problem-Solving Process*. Chicago: University of Chicago Press.

Reid, William J. 1975. "A Test of a Task-Centered Approach." *Social Work* 20:3–9.

——1977. "Process and Outcome in the Treatment of Family Problems" in Reid and Epstein, eds. *Task-Centered Practice*, q.v.

——1978. *The Task-Centered System*. New York: Columbia University Press.

Reid, William J. and Laura Epstein. 1972. *Task-Centered Casework*. New York: Columbia University Press.

Reid, William J. and Laura Epstein, eds. 1977. *Task-Centered Practice*. New York: Columbia University Press.

Reid, William J. and Ann Shyne. 1969. *Brief and Extended Casework*. New York: Columbia University Press.

Reid, William J., Laura Epstein, Lester B. Brown, Eleanor Tolson, and Ronald H. Rooney. 1980. "Task-Centered School Social Work." *Social Work Education* 2:7–24.

Rooney, Ronald H. Forthcoming. "A Task-Centered Reunification Model for Foster Care." In Anthony A. Malluccio and Paula Sinanoglu, eds., *Working with Biological Parents of Children in Foster Care*. New York: Child Welfare League of America.

Thomas, Edwin J. 1976. *Marital Communication and Decision Making: Analysis, Assessment, and Change*. New York: Free Press.

Tolson, Eleanor. 1977. "Alleviating Marital Communication Problems." In Reid and Epstein, eds., *Task-Centered Practice*, q.v.

Wexler, Phyllis. 1977. "A Case from a Medical Setting." In Reid and Epstein, eds., *Task-Centered Practice,* q.v.
Wise, Frances. 1977. "Conjoint Marital Treatment." In Reid and Epstein, eds., *Task-Centered Practice* q.v.
Watzlawick, Paul, Janet Hemlick Beavin, and Don D. Jackson. 1967. *Pragmatics of Human Communication.* New York: Norton.

12

Conclusions: Toward a Metamodel for Eclectic Family Practice

ELEANOR REARDON TOLSON

The metaphor of the blind men and the elephant best depicts the problem of knowing about family treatment circa 1979. It depends on what part of the beast one grabs or, in this case, which of the many approaches one reads. The approaches are internally consistent but great diversity exists among them. The diversity seems to be explained by the different positions of the contributors to two fundamental issues. The first issue concerns the orientation to family treatment. Is it a modality or a theory of behavior? Within this issue is the question of its purpose. Is it to change the interaction of family systems or is it to change the behavior of individuals? The second issue concerns the theory of behavior upon which the approach is based. The behavioral theory indicates where the distress is located, what changes are necessary to alleviate the distress, and, to a lesser extent, how it can be alleviated.

Responses to the central issues, in combination, influence the technical treatment decisions. These decisions concern the goals for treatment, who is included, the kind of relationship required, and treatment strategies. No two of the authors agree about all three fundamental issues, definition, purpose, and theory. Nor does complete disagreement exist. As a result, seven different and intriguing collages are presented which, when implemented, direct practitioners to "do identical things for identical reasons, different things for identical reasons, different things for different reasons, and identical things for different reasons."[1]

[1] I am indebted to Bernece Simon for this clever way of summarizing the state of the art.

The growing number of approaches to treatment are welcome. They do, however increase the burden of deciding what to do and when to do it. Not long ago, social workers had only to decide between the diagnostic and the functional school. Now various modalities, approaches within modalities, and strategies within approaches exist. Consequently, a new problem has evolved: How do we choose? Productive eclectic practice is possible for only reasonably sophisticated practitioners: those who are familiar with the fact that approaches to family treatment are quite different, the nature of the differences, and the nature of the issues from which the differences derive. This book has been planned and constructed to aid and abet such sophistication.

In addition to knowledge about what exists, the eclectic practitioner needs guidelines for choosing. Thus far, the only and the best criterion for eclectism is effectiveness (Fischer 1978). This criterion will not be sufficient, however, until an array of empirically validated interventions sufficient to the needs of the multitude of people-problem combinations encountered are developed. During the interim, other criteria are required.

The purposes of this essay are to contrast the models of family treatment and to develop guidelines for selecting among them. The guidelines, in combination, comprise a metamodel for eclectic practice. The source for most of the comparative material is the discussion among the contributors at the conference, since their papers are available to the reader. Furthermore, the purpose of the comparisons is to identify issues or dimensions rather than to be comprehensive. Some of the fun must be left for the reader! The essay concludes with a discussion of the relevance of the model for social work.

What is Family Treatment?

Family treatment, once viewed as a "technique in search of a theory," (Manus 1966), is now in search of a definition. The working definition of family treatment that was suggested to the contributors was articulated by Wells and Dezen:

> A therapist engages in family therapy when he sees natural units as parents and children, spouses, or members of the extended family, together as a group over most of the duration of treatment with the goal of improving their functioning as a unit. (1978:449)

All the contributors agreed that work which conforms to this definition is family treatment. Disagreement occurred over what other forms of work also merit the family treatment label. One definitional variable that was questioned was the composition of the group. Do all members have to be included for work to be considered family treatment? Another disputed variable was time. Does the family or subgroup of the family have to meet together and "over most of the duration of treatment?" The element of purpose was also questioned. If the purpose is to alter family functioning and this can be achieved by working with an individual, is this not family treatment? Finally, some of the contributors argued that even if work occurs with an individual toward change for the individual only, but the practitioner thinks in family terms, that work is family treatment.

Two important concepts clarify the definitional problem. The concepts are models and theories. Models are guidelines for practice. They tell the practitioner what to do. Theories are explanations of phenomena, in this case behavior. (Following the precedent set by Ford and Urban 1967, theory of behavior will be used synonymously with personality theory.) Theories of behavior explain how individuals come to grief. When intervention principles are developed from these explanations, the result is a theoretically derived practice model.

The size of the group, the purpose of treatment, and the time over which the group meets are elements of a model. Directives regarding them tell the practitioner whom to see, how often, and to what purpose. In contrast, the mind-set of the practitioner is a reflection of theory.

Implicit in each of the papers is a definition of family treatment, and these definitions can be categorized as either modalities or theories of behavior, although some of the contributors prefer to refer to the latter as orientations.

Bell's approach is illustrative of family treatment as a modality: the entire family is seen together for the duration of treatment. Bowen's orientation seems to be that family treatment is a theory of behavior. The theory explains how the individual comes to grief; i.e., through lack of differentiation. Since it is a theory of behavior rather than a modality, it can be used with units of any size and it provides a focus for change efforts, increased differentiation.

The return of leaders in the family treatment movement to work with individuals is surprising, considering the convictions that originally prompted the movement. Among them were the beliefs that symptoms alleviated during stays at in-patient facilities would return when the bearer of them was discharged to his family, and that the brunt of carrying the symptoms could be transferred from one family member to another. Work with individuals does not seem to address these phenomena. What then accounts for this shift of attention?

It appears that the practice of working with families has generated knowledge about human behavior and explanations about the nature of problems. These theoretical developments have, in turn, influenced the way family treatment is practiced and the way it is defined. Theories which explain distress as the result of something that did or did not occur in the client's past, like lack of differentiation, enable the practitioner to work with individuals. The contributors who use this kind of theory tend to define family treatment as an orientation or a theory. Conversely, those who use theories which emphasize process or structural propositions are more like to see the entire family at least once and to define family treatment as a modality. The relationship between theory and definition is not unidirectional. The way family treatment is defined also influences the practitioner's choice of theories employed to explain the client's distress.

Another influence on definition is probably the amalgam of client-agency-practitioner purpose. Contemporary family treatment has largely developed in mental health and child guidance settings—agencies which generally serve clients who are somewhat more motivated and enjoy more resources than those served by large public agencies or by medical and educational facilities, which tend to serve greater cross-sections of the population. Mental health and child guidance agencies, and the practitioners who work within them, usually see their purpose as psychotherapy, and their role as psychotherapists, and they are likely to attract and keep clients whose requests coincide with these purposes. Sherman articulates this viewpoint about purpose: "There is something left unfinished in affirming flat family system goals . . . therapy has as its ultimate goals . . . change in individual persons." Is this necessarily so? Even if the practitioner's ultimate concern is for the individual, strongly held beliefs about the effect of the family upon the individual might lead one to differ with Sherman. Those who believe that the family is the fundamental societal unit would almost certainly affirm family system goals.

Finally, the professional and life experience of the individual probably affect how new understandings are utilized. Bell beautifully describes his journey to family treatment. While his professional history is highly unique in the specifics, the general path is probably not too different from that taken by many family practitioners or, especially, from that traversed by other theorists. Most began working with individuals and used a psychodynamic perspective. Beginning with this orientation, it should not be surprising, although it was not predicted, that many of those who became family practitioners would return with their new insights to work with individuals. It is interesting that Bell is one of the few who continues to insist upon seeing all members of the family together when doing family treatment, and the only one for whom group work was a major part of his experience. Bell's motivation for sharing his history is probably determined by his recognition of its influence on practice: "The differences grow so much out of the person of each one of us and that is a very important consideration, because we can't get out of our own skin. We have to be who we are in relation to the family and to live out the relationship with them in a way that is congenial for ourselves" (Meltzer, article 9).

Productive eclecticism, for our purposes, consists of selecting what appears to be useful from various methods so that the ideas and techniques borrowed are internally consistent and appropriate to the amalgam of client-worker-agency objectives. In order to practice this way, the practitioner must recognize his own definition of family treatment and how it is defined by the approach from which he is borrowing. The impact of incongruencies must be evaluated and eliminated when problematic. The practitioner must borrow in such a way that the objectives of the method from which he is borrowing are consistent with the client-worker-agency objectives. Finally, as he experiments with different approaches, he must be sensitive to his own comfort with them.

What Is Wrong?

There appears to be a dichotomy among the contributors between those who rely on the client's statement about his problem and those who filter this statement through a theorectical lens. For example, it seems that Bowen and Spark employ theory to shape the problem, whereas Gambrill and Segal rely on the client's statement. This difference is clearly illustrated by the reactions of the contributors to the film (article 9). Using identical observations, Segal views the problem as the "son sitting around on his ass and they [the parents] don't like it" while Hartman thinks the situation is "a differentiation struggle on the part of the adolescent boy."

What are the influences which determine whether we focus on the client's problem as presented or translate it into theoretical terms? Probably one of the most powerful is the practitioner's beliefs about the nature of man. Embedded in behavioral theories and the derivative practice models are assumptions about the extent and accuracy of the individual's knowledge about his own needs. The implication is that one view of man is the correct one and that it holds across populations and time. For example, psychoanalytic theory attributes motivation to unconscious processes and, since these processes are outside of the client's awareness, accepting his problem statement is inappropriate. Thus, theory including assumptions about the nature of man is one factor that determines what is wrong.

Social workers do not behave as though they consistently hold one conviction about the individual's capacity to identify his needs, however. The most theoretically oriented are now usually willing to assume that most clients accurately know whether they need a refrigerator or the address of the public assistance office. (Social work went through a period when simple requests for concrete resources were not met without a psychosocial assessment.) Conversely, practitioners who believe that the individual is best able to identify his needs are often forced to use theory to understand mystifying or contradictory requests. Practitioners appear to recognize that some clients know their needs better than others and all clients are clearer about some of their needs than they are about other needs. Busy, experienced caseworkers develop methods for determining when they must listen in theoretical terms. It is probable that they quickly evaluate the clients cognitive capacity, his ability to act once he has obtained his request, and the society's response when he acts. This is similar to the assessment of motivation, capacity, and opportunity (Ripple 1964).

Theory is not the only factor affecting the acceptance or translation of the presenting concern. Another is the client-agency purpose. Some clients will not sit still for reinterpretations of the problem, whereas others seek them. Agency purpose and manpower can dictate or preclude one of these approaches.

The meaning of these observations for the eclectic practitioner can best be summed by a series of questions.

1. Am I using a theoretical lens to reinterpret the problem?
2. If so, is it necessary; i.e., appropriate for this client with this problem in this setting?

3. What is the assumption about the individual's ability to identify his needs within the theory employed?
4. Is this assumption consistent with the planned intervention strategy?

In addition to determining the nature of distress, behavioral theory explains it. Here, we find harmony among the contributors. While they use different theories, they all use some theory to explain the problem and plan treatment. The Bowen approach, for example, relies on a theory about differentiation and, hence, treatment entails helping clients to increase their level of differentiation. The behavioral approaches emphasize environmental contingencies and, hence, treatment is concerned with altering the contingencies.

Finally, behavioral theory directs our observations. It acts like a flashlight in the dark, illuminating some areas, while keeping others in the shadows. This is both an asset and a danger, in that it clarifies our understanding of certain aspects of clients' lives while blinding us to others. The relationship between theory and observation means that the kinds of observations emphasized are as diverse as the theories on which the approaches rest. In the behavioral approach, the important observations concern the behavior to be changed and the contingencies for that behavior. In the structural and group approaches, the important observations concern the interactions of family members.

With Whom Should We Work?

Decisions regarding the technical aspects of family treatment are affected by the interaction of the practitioner's theory and orientation, including purpose. Hence, the responses of the contributors to the issue about whom to include in treatment are as diverse as, but consistent with, their responses to issues about orientation and theory. Bell, who defines family treatment as a modality, automatically includes all members. The inclusion of all members is also consistent with the theories on which he relies, and which emphasize interaction. The important question to be asked of practitioners and theorists in this camp is not whom do they include but when do they use this modality. Bell indicates that it is to be used when the problem is a family one, rather than an individual one, or a problem of the social order. It seems that while Bell does not focus treatment on the presenting complaint, he uses this complaint to decide upon the most appropriate modality for treatment. He also identifies populations for whom family treatment is not appropriate.

At the other end of the spectrum are Hartman and Segal. For them, family treatment is more of an orientation—specifically, a theoretical framework—than a modality. Hence they work with units of various sizes including individuals. Their flexibility with respect to unit size and their definition of family treatment are consistent with their own theories, which emphasize, respectively, lack of differentiation, and dysfunctional problem-solving. The question to be asked is when, if ever, they would include family members. Segal starts with the "customer," that person who requests help, and uses the smallest number of people necessary for problem resolution. The nature of the problem and the customer's ability to alleviate it, alone determine additional participants.

Gambrill, Spark, and Spiegel represent somewhat of a middle ground. They neither assume that they need to see everyone nor that they can conduct family treatment with units of any size. All engage clients in a period of assessment and make decisions about when to include others, and whom to include, based on the assessment. Spiegel tends to start small and increase the number of participants, whereas Gambrill begins with the entire family and eliminates those whose behavior is not related to the behavior to be changed.

To What Purpose?

At the most general level, all of the approaches are directed toward alleviating distress. In order to make appropriate choices, the electic-minded practitioner needs to know what kinds of change can be expected to result from the use of the various approaches. These changes are expressed as goals. The kind of goals established are reflections of the orientation and the theory of the model developers. Segal defines a goal as that which "makes the practitioner happy." He and Walters become happy when the symptom or problem which the client identified is alleviated. Hartman looks for increased differentiation, and Spark, improved reciprocal loyalty exchanges and constructive repayment of indebtedness. Speigel's goals cover the spectrum from targeted problem, inter- and intrapersonal conflict, and cultural conflict. Gambrill works for change in dysfunctional behavior. Bell's goals are the most difficult to describe (and probably to measure) as they are set by the family and evolve. In addition to working toward these goals, Bell attempts to help families experience success in problem-solving and develop new patterns for confronting future problems.

The goals identified might be labeled outcome goals. There are also theoretically-derived goals which, when accomplished, are expected to produce the desired outcome. For example, within the behavioral approaches the outcome goal is changing the specific problem behavior of an individual or individuals, but achieving this change usually requires changing the behavior of others. Hence, changing the contingencies is a theoretically-derived goal which is expected to produce the desired outcome. Similarly, in the structural approach, achieving the desired outcome is dependent upon changing family structure, a theoretically-derived goal.

The distinction between these two kinds of goals is vital to effective practice and knowledge development. Clients and researchers emphasize outcome goals. Most social workers have probably focused upon theoretically derived goals. The difference in emphasis probably accounts for much of the client dropout rate, which is high in many social agencies (Levinger 1960; Meltzoff and Kornreich 1970; Silverman 1970) and the negative findings about the effectiveness of social work (Fischer 1973). Focusing upon theoretically-derived goals is appropriate if 1) they produce the desired outcome; 2) they are necessary to the production of the desired outcome; and 3) they are necessary to the maintenance of the outcome.

Practitioners who focus on theoretically-derived goals must ask themselves whether reaching these goals is a precondition for achieving the outcome goal. If they conclude that they are necessary preconditions, then they must be careful to ascertain that the outcome goal is indeed achieved. Furthermore, they must effectively educate and persuade their clients that working toward theoretically-derived goals will produce the outcome goal which is the important end point for the client.

Time Limits and Contracts

In spite of growing evidence that planned short-term treatment is as effective as treatment of indefinite lengths (Wells, article 10), only Focused Problem Resolution (Segal, article 8) and some of the behavioral approaches utilize it. This is difficult to explain. Since short-term treatment and family treatment have blossomed fairly recently and in roughly the same time period, perhaps there has not been sufficient time for advances in either area to be incorporated by the other.

Contracts are described by several of the contributors. Spiegel uses a contract that is probably unwritten and unarticulated. It consists of aligning with the head of the family, when the family values are lineal or collateral, and treating what the clients believe needs to be treated in the way the clients believe will be effective. Bell makes a contract with the family at the beginning of treatment. It consists of an agreement that all family members will attend all treatment sessions; that a session will be postponed if a member cannot attend; and that a trial period of treatment will occur, so that he and family can decide if this form of treatment is appropriate. Written contracts are often used in behavioral approaches. They usually include descriptions of the objectives; the interventions, including the responsibilities of client and practitioner; criteria for evaluation; time limits; and signatures of the participants.

Although neither time limits not contracts have many advocates among the contributors, the empirical support for them suggests that experimentation might be fruitful. Practitioners might begin to estimate how long it will take to accomplish the objectives and share this information with the client, with the suggestion that an evaluation of their accomplishments will occur at the end of the stipulated time. This practice would not result in short-term treatment but it might mobilize worker and client efforts, and produce knowledge about how long it takes to reach particular ends with particular clients. With respect to contracts, practitioners might consider what information their clients need for ethical reasons and in order to help them participate in treatment. Various formats for sharing this information might be tried.

How Do We Intervene?

Throughout this article differences have been emphasized. This is in keeping with the purpose of enhancing productive eclecticism. While differences in intervention will also be focused upon, it is probably erroneous to assume that the contributors use only those strategies which they describe in their papers. It is likely that there is a great deal of borrowing. When Spiegel addresses intrapsychic conflict, for example, he is no doubt using a number of techniques that other family and individual therapists use at various times. The strategy of "culture broker" is uniquely his own and, hence, that will be referred to here.

Another general observation is in order prior to a discussion of the specific interventions. They exist! When these papers are contrasted with those in *Theories of Social Casework,* the product of the first Charlotte Towle Conference and the model for this conference, the development in middle-phase technology is clear. Most of the papers in the first book emphasized assessment and goals. Each of the contributors to this volume has suggested at least one strategy that goes beyond the concept of relationship. While we still have much to learn we have come a long way.

There are a number of dimensions in which the treatment strategies of the various approaches can be contrasted. These dimensions provide criteria for the practitioner to evaluate when choosing the most appropriate interventions. Hence, they are stated in the form of questions and they are as follows:

1. What is the relationship between the treatment strategy and behavioral theory, assessment, and goals?
2. To what extent do the interventions emphasize behavior change?
3. What resources are necessary to implement them?
4. Are they described so that they can be replicated?
5. To what extent are they congruent with the expectations of the client, setting, and referral source?
6. Do they take generalization and maintenance into account?
7. Are they utilized in a natural environment?
8. Does evidence of effectiveness exist?

These criteria are discussed in the order presented.

The relationship between theory, assessment, goals, and treatment has received more attention in the literature than any of the remaining suggested criteria. It necessitates knowing what is to be changed (the problem) and who is to be changed (an individual or the family). Bowen's approach may not be appropriate for specific behavioral change and Gambrill's would not be sufficient for increasing differentiation. Bell's approach is not intended to be the most efficient for helping an individual solve a specific problem, and Segal's model does not aim to help families discover their own goals and find alternative problem-solving methods.

Related to the first criterion is the question of the extent to which behavioral change is needed. Simplistically categorized, clients come to us with three kinds of complaints: problems of resources; behavioral problems; and problems of intra- or interpersonal discomfort. Behavioral change is usually needed to solve behavioral problems. Sometimes behavioral change is needed to solve other kinds of problems, including those of discomfort. Finally, behavioral change is sometimes required by society as represented by courts and schools. Some of the models are more appropriate than others for changing behavior. These models can be used in conjunction with others when professional judgment indicates that behavioral change, while necessary to keep a child in school for example, is not sufficient to alleviate other discomfort.

Two very pragmatic questions about the appropriateness of a particular strategy concern the availability of necessary resources and our knowledge about the intervention. The second of these is a reflection on how precisely the developers can describe what they do. This is an old and often discussed issue which must be answered individually. Certainly the interventions in some approaches are clearer than those in others. Questions about resources pertain to the practitioner, the setting in which he works, and the client. Manpower limitations might preclude using approaches like the behavioral and ecological ones. The necessary people may not be available to use the intergenerational approach. Sometimes the necessary individuals will not be sufficiently motivated. Judgments about motivation should be tested by offering the opportunity, however, because various investigations have provided evidence that, while most clients rated as unmotivated do not cooperate, some do. It is not possible to know in advance who will prove us wrong.

The expectations of our clients, the setting in which we practice, and sometimes the source of referral, can be powerful determinants for intervention. Lack of congruence between the practitioner and the client is probably an important determinant for the discontinuance of treatment. Segal and Spiegel are particularly sensitive to the need to adapt the intervention to the client's expectations. There are times when the intervention most appropriate and effective for meeting the goals deviates from what the client believes most helpful. This dilemma has no easy solution. Some alternatives are to disguise the intervention by relabeling it in terms acceptable to the client, as suggested by Segal; give the client what he asks for first, as Spiegel advises; or persuade the client gently and over time as implied by Hartman and Spark. The expectations of the agency and referral source are particularly powerful when social work is a secondary service in the setting. They, too, must be considered when interventions are chosen.

Another issue to consider is whether generalization and maintenance are necessary. There is a tendency to react to these concepts as though they are positive values, and hence their importance is automatically assumed. They are probably always significant when the goal is behavior change but not always important for other kinds of change. When they are deemed vital, the theoretically-derived goal must be emphasized as well as the outcome goal. Outcome goals can be made sufficiently desirable to change behavior in isolated settings and on isolated occasions, but the behavior is unlikely to be maintained and generalized unless the environmental contingencies are altered. The importance of generalization and maintenance is not limited to behavioral approaches. The fond hope of many practitioners is that the client, with the professional's help, will not only resolve his problems but learn new problem-solving skills. Spivack et al. (1976), found that it took two years of training to improve the means-end thinking ability of adults. Apparently, hope is not enough, and if the client needs something other than specific problem alleviation, additional treatment strategies have to be chosen and implemented.

Related to generalization and maintenance is the issue of the appropriate environment for the intervention. Should our work take place in the office or in a natural environment like the home or school? Among our contributors, only Spiegel and Gambrill advocate home visits. This is an example of practitioners doing the same thing for different reasons. Spiegel does so because the office is alien to his clients and because he seeks ecological data. Gambrill's purpose is to gather accurate data about the problem behavior and its contingencies, moreover, she chooses the home because the generalization of new behavior from office to home is unlikely to occur. These reasons provide guidelines for the discriminate use of home visits.

Finally, and perhaps most usefully, there is the criterion of effectiveness. What evidence exists about the most effective way to alter the problem in question? There are increasing data about what works best for a number of problems and, furthermore, there are a number of readily available sources for this information (Gurman and Kniskern 1978; Wells, paper 10). It behooves the responsible practitioner to become, and remain, acquainted with it.

Relationship

"Beneath all therapies and modes of benign psychological influence lie the stirring and securing nurture of empathy and the warm acceptance and caring that emanate from a helper who seems secure, genuine, real, and empowered by knowledge or social sanction'' (Perlman 1970:151). Such was the notion of relationship on which many social workers cut their teeth. This loving and powerful succorer (Perlman 1970:151) seems considerably different from contemporary ''coaches,'' ''culture brokers'' and helpers who have ''customers.'' The latter kinds of relationships seem less special and more similar to relationships clients encounter in their everyday attempts to procure goods and services.

Some family practitioners advocate relationships of equality (Hartman) and even relationships where the practitioner assumes the one-down position (Segal). Contributors, in general, are more sensitive to the need to sell interventions and do so by aligning themselves with the values of the family (Spiegel), framing them in terms acceptable to the client (Segel), and demonstrating enthusiasm (Hartman). Some pay ''parenting salaries'' to reduce attrition (behavioral approaches). Do these relationships connote inauthentic, manipulative hustling? Not as employed by the contributors; that is, used to help the client secure his wants. They can, however, be used by practitioners suffering from superego lacunae to legitimate their behavior. Ethical questions may be on the horizon.

The purpose for using hyperbole is to dramatize the fact that new and different kinds of relationships are advocated. The practitioner can make choices about the kind of relationship most appropriate for the client and their mutual purposes.

A discussion of relationship is not complete without what Spiegel referred to during the conference as ''the excommunicated subject of transference.'' The contributors who refer to it seem to think that it is indeed to be avoided and that the intense transactions should occur among the family members.

Are We Effective?

Research is not for researchers. Its purpose is to enhance the quality of practice. Its beneficiaries are practitioners and, ultimately, their clients. Furthermore, the responsibility for research is not solely the obligation of researchers. The practitioners must identify the questions, define the concepts, and provide the data. The current separatism that exists within social work between those who intervene and those who research is to no one's advantage.

Two ambitious reviews of the empirical studies of family treatment now exist. One of them was prepared by Wells for this book. The authors of the earlier one are Gurman and Kniskern (1978). The conclusions of the reviewers differ and the reader will have to decide with whom he agrees. The effectiveness of Focused Problem Resolution, the behavioral approaches, and the structural approach, among the models presented here, have been examined and the contributors share some of the relevant findings.

The deficit of investigations of effectiveness and the disagreement among reviewers are problems. A more serious problem for the practitioner who wants to use effectiveness as a criterion for selecting interventions is the fact that we have not begun to approach the pinnacle of clinical-research questions: What works for what kind of person with what kind of problem? Group studies are not sufficiently sophisticated to control for type of problem and type of client, assuming either can be validly categorized. Single-subject designs do test interventions with particular clients and particular problems, but the methodology limits the extent to which findings can be generalized. Futhermore the multiplicity and kind of differences that exist among the approaches practically preclude comparative studies. There is little agreement about what treatment is and the aims of the approaches differ. Studying their comparative effectiveness at this point in time is probably premature.

Two developments are needed. First, we need some consensus on the definitional question. Second, the developers and practitioners of the various approaches must, as Hartman said during the conference, "do their homework." The confusion about the definition of family treatment seems unnecessary. Those who think it is not a modality use it as a behavioral theory. Behavioral theory is a perfectly good and understandable concept. Confusing the concept of theory with the concept of modality only serves to build stumbling blocks in the advancement of knowledge. Family treatment should be defined as a modality and differentiated from family theory. The definition of family treatment as a modality still requires further specifications. A useful starting place might be to define family treatment as a form of intervention that includes work with at least two related individuals for the purpose of resolving one problem. This definition does not preclude as forms of family treatment work with family members that occurs separately, but it does preclude work with them that occurs separately and around different problems. Hence treating a husband and wife separately for their individual problems would not be family treatment. Involving one spouse to resolve a problem of the other would be family treatment. The rationale for this definition is that it might enable us to begin to identify the kinds of problems that are most effectively alleviated by including a family member in treatment.

Two kinds of homework or research efforts must begin. First, the effectiveness of our practice must be evaluated. Second, we must begin to test the assumptions on which practice is based. This activity is particularly important because many of the contributors emphasize family theory rather than family practice. One approach to testing assumptions is to examine the theoretically-derived goals with respect to their usefulness for securing outcomes, their necessity to secure outcome goals, and their effect on the maintenance of outcome goals.

During the conference, Wells articulated the necessity for examining effectiveness. He noted the increasing attention to the value of consumerism, referring to the client's right to effective and efficient intervention. He found a parallel between the present state of psychotherapy and the early years of medicine in the reliance on methods that might actually be harmful (Reid 1974). Finally, Wells questioned whether we were "running out of credit" with policy and funding sources. There was little disagreement about the necessity for research endeavors and for experimenting with various research models including increased use of single-subject designs and naturalistic studies.

Family Treatment and Social Work

As Sherman observed, social workers have been seeing families since the inception of the profession. The development of family theories and practice models had, however, to await the entrance of psychiatrists, which occurred in the late fifties.[2] As previously observed, the development has largely occurred in mental health and child guidance clinics. Most social workers ply their trade in less hospitable

---

[2] The fact that the modality was not developed durings its ownership by social workers is often attributed to either the lowly status of the profession or the fact that for much of our history, we were not productive as scholars. There is, however, a parallel with obstetrics, which was the domain of women (midwives and witches) for hundreds of years. It was only after men became involved that treatises were written about delivering babies (Rich 1976). The important factor in the development of family treatment may not be the professions but the sex of the practitioners of those professions.

settings: schools, hospitals, correctional facilities, public assistance
and child protection agencies. The clients served in these settings confront much more than inter- or intrapersonal discomfort. The problems
they face include serious illness, criminal prosecution, poverty, and
child abuse. The demands on the social workers from the clients, the
host agency, and society are great. All expect the social worker to
solve enormous problems with few resources. These are the trenches
of social work, and social workers are most needed where the most
severe battles for survival occur. This is the mission of social work
and it is an honorable one.

A personal experience clarified the distinction between the social
worker and psychotherapist for me and eliminated the last remnants
of my desire to be, or teach others to be, the latter. Sharing this
experience in undisguised form is in keeping with the pattern established by the Bowen school. Several years ago my husband suffered
a cerebral hemorrhage which resulted from an arteriovenous malfor-
mation. Brain surgery and rehabilitation followed. I needed social work
service and had ample opportunity to watch social workers in action.
The surgery and first month of hospitalization took place at an acute
care, university-affiliated hospital which serves a high proportion of
poor and minority patients. Families of patients in intensive care gathered in a waiting room during the fifty-five minutes which separated
the allotted five-minute visits with the patient. As might be expected,
a supportive informal group evolved.

The social service department in this hospital prides itself on the
psychodynamic sophistication of its employees. This is what I saw and
heard. First, the social worker for the service entered the waiting room
no more than three times, for visits of less than five minutes, during
the two weeks when I was an almost constant occupant. Second, members of two families who were poor and lived in other states slept in
this waiting room. Nurses assisted them by securing pillows and blan-
kets and finding them places to bathe as well as necessary toilet articles.
Knowing that community housing resources exist, I sent the families
to the social worker. She did nothing to help them and they continued
to live in the waiting room. Third, on one of her quick trips to our
gathering place, the social worker was asked for information about
transportation by a woman who had found temporary housing for herself about ten or twelve blocks from the hospital. She confidently
instructed the woman. After she left, another group member, who was
a permanent resident in the same building, said that she "didn't like

to correct the young girl in front of her" and proceeded to give correct transportation directions. Fourth, the social worker was "unavailable" when a very young woman collapsed upon learning that her husband who was expected to do well suddenly died.

Finally, I needed help to apply for my husband's admission to a rehabilitative facility. The social worker gave the necessary forms to me and the doctor two weeks before discharge. We completed and returned them to her the next day. Having little confidence in the social worker, I learned when the admission committee met, and checked with the social worker on the preceding day to assure that the application was complete. The application had not been sent! When I expressed my outrage to the nurse, she volunteered that the nursing staff was unable to figure out what the social worker did. All she seemed to want to do, in the nurse's opinion, was "gossip" with the nurses and they didn't have time for that.

The social worker at the rehabilitation hospital (also master degree level) provided a much different, and badly needed, experience. She was helpful with the pragmatic concerns and, in addition, she performed some excellent family treatment. There were differences between the staff and myself on one side, and some of my in-laws on the other, with respect to my husband's care. The most pronounced issue was that some of them were visiting around the clock and interfering with his participation in various therapy programs. The social worker asked me to participate in a family session. I refused and explained that I thought I had already erred in the extent to which I had involved them when the ultimate responsibilities were mine. To my surprise and pleasure, she accepted this. She met with them by herself and successfully disengaged them, after which my husband began to make rapid progress.

These experiences have been described in some detail because they illuminate fundamental issues. First and foremost is the subject of mission. Services offered by social workers to people in circumstances similar to mine are invaluable. We must return with our best practitioners and renewed energy to the trenches, and we must reverse our internal status hierarchy, which grants status according to the practitioners' distance from them. The second issue concerns the practice of social workers in difficult settings. The first social worker saw her role as psychotherapist. Her definition of this role precluded doing what was most necessary. In fact, it left her without any role, because while some of the patients and their family members might have benefited from psychotherapy, they were not there for that purpose, and they were preoccupied with pressing concerns. The second worker defined her role in a way that was consistent with the purpose of the institution: facilitating the patient's recovery. She used her knowledge about human behavior to implement client-agency-practitioner goals.

Finally, both social workers were in a position to utilize family treatment.[3] The one who defined her service in a way that was consistent with the goals of the patient and the agency did so. Her approach bore little resemblance to the models presented here, however. This raises two questions. How can practitioners who work in settings where the desperation is less than quiet use these models? How can we learn from those who are developing their own effective family treatment approaches? The first question is partially addressed by the guidelines for eclectic practice suggested in the first part of this paper. Answers to the second question will have to be developed by practitioners and researchers. Practitioners must become empiricists to the extent that they record their observations about the client and the problem, the intervention, and the results of the intervention. These observations must be shared in the appropriate professional journals. Researchers can assist by identifying effective practitioners and helping them collect the necessary information.

Summary

The necessity for modifying family treatment models to fit the kinds of practice in which most social workers are engaged has been de-

[3] One of the patients in the acute care hospital was a man in his twenties suffering from a malignant brain tumor. He had surgery during a previous stay and was in for reevaluation. His behavior consisted of much screaming and loud swearing and he was very demanding. He was upsetting to the other patients and the nurses, who believed that there was no medical reason for his behavior and considered him "obnoxious." His several family members and girl friend were constantly in attendance and responded to his demands to push the wheelchair faster or slower, supply more ice for his drink or take some out, etc., like puppets whose strings had been pulled. When members of his entourage were able to join the waiting room group, they complained of their frustration and fatigue. They implied that they had to respond as they did because he was "terminal." The effect of stress on family members of seriously ill people has been well documented. This family appeared to be experiencing stress in the extreme. Effective social work intervention, probably using some crisis or behavioral techniques, might have made a considerable impact. Unfortunately, it was not offered.

scribed. Some guidelines for eclectic practice have been identified, and
they are here summarized in question form.

A. Definitional Issues
   1. Am I defining family treatment as a modality or a theory?
   2. Which is appropriate in this setting, with this client with this
      problem?
   3. How is it defined by the approach from which I am borrowing?
   4. Are definitional incongruities between A-2 and A-3 problematic?
B. Behavioral Theory
   1. Am I accepting the client's problem statement or translating
      it into theoretical terms?
   2. Which is appropriate for this client with this problem?
   3. Which theory is appropriate to explain the client's distress?
   4. What is the assumption about the individual's ability to identify
      his needs within the theory being borrowed?
   5. Are B-2 and B-4 contradictory?
   6. How is distress explained by the theory being used?
   7. What information is needed to use the theory?
   8. What is the process for acquiring this information?
C. Treatment Group
   1. Who must be seen to gather the necessary information which
      is employed by the theory chosen?
   2. Who must included to use the planned intervention necessary?
   3. Are they available?
D. Purpose
   1. What are the client's goals?
   2. Which approach is most likely to achieve them?
   3. What theoretically-derived goals are necessary to achieve the
      outcome goals?
E. Time Limits and Contracts
   1. How long is it likely to take to achieve the outcome goals?
   2. Should this estimate be shared with the client?
   3. What information does the client need?
   4. How is this information best shared?
F. Intervention
   1. What kind of intervention does the client believe will be
      effective?
   2. What is to be changed?
   3. Who is to be changed?
   4. Is behavioral change needed?
   5. Are the necessary resources for using the intervention available?
   6. Can the intervention be replicated?

7. What kind of interventions are appropriate in this particular setting?
8. Are generalization and maintenance of change important?
9. Where should intervention occur?
10. Is the intervention effective?

G. Relationship
1. What kind of relationship is necessary for this work with this client?
2. What kind of relationship does the client expect or want?

H. Generation of Knowledge
1. How can the work with this client be recorded, evaluated, and shared?

References

Fischer, J. 1973. "Is Casework Effective? A Review" *Social Work* 18(1):5–20.
Fischer, Joel. 1978. *Effective Casework Practice: An Eclectic Approach.* New York: McGraw-Hill.
Ford, Donald H. and Hugh B. Urban. 1967. *Systems of Psychotherapy.* New York: Wiley.
Gurman, Alan S. and David P. Kniskern. 1978. "Research on Marital and Family Therapy: Progress, Perspective, and Prospect." In S. L. Garfield and A. E. Bergin, eds., *Handbook of Psychotherapy and Behavior Change.* 2d ed. pp. 817–901. New York: Wiley.
Levinger, G. 1960. "Continuance in Casework and Other Helping Relationships: A Review of Current Research." *Social Work* 5(8):40–51.
Manus, G. I. 1966. "Marriage Counseling: A Technique in Search of a Theory." *Journal of Marriage and the Family* 28:449–53.
Meltzoff, J., and M. Kornreich. 1970. *Research in Psychotherapy.* New York: Atherton.
Perlman, Helen H. 1970. "The Problem-Solving Model in Social Casework." In R. W. Roberts and R. H. Nee, eds., *Theories of Social Casework*, pp. 131–79. Chicago: University of Chicago Press.
Reid, William J. 1974. "Competence in Social Treatment." In D. H. Hepworth, ed., *Assuring Practitioner Competence: Whose Responsibility?* Salt Lake City, Utah: Graduate School of Social Work, University of Utah.
Rich, Adrienne. 1976. *Of Woman Born: Motherhood as Experience and Institution* New York: Norton.
Ripple, Lillian. 1964. *Motivation, Capacity, and Opportunity.* Chicago: School of Social Service Administration, University of Chicago.

Silverman, P. R. 1970. "A Reexamination of the Intake Procedure." *Social Casework* 51(10):625–34.

Spivak, George, Jerome J. Platt, and Myrna B. Shure. 1976. *The Problem-Solving Approach to Adjustment*. San Francisco, Calif.: Jossey-Bass.

Wells, Richard A. and A. E. Dezen. 1978. "The Results of Family Treatment Revisited: The Nonverbal Methods." *Family Process* 17:251–74.

Author Index

Subject Index